Shimon Peres

"*Shimon Peres wrote many books and books were written about him. None, however, offer the compelling portrait of him that Avi Gil provides in* Shimon Peres. *Though deeply admiring of Peres and his visionary efforts, Gil lets the reader see his faults—including the need for credit. But he also shows Peres's self-awareness, his deeper understanding of trends in the region, his capacity to see what was important and strive to achieve it—and, most of all, his readiness to take risks that are an inherent part of leadership. Because he was rarely the leader, he had to maneuver others to do what he believed was both necessary and right. For anyone who wants to understand both who Shimon Peres was and what is also possible between Israelis and Palestinians,* Shimon Peres *is a must read.*"

Dennis Ross, special Middle East coordinator under President Bill Clinton

"*A captivating behind-the-scenes account of Shimon Peres, a unique leader and a special friend and colleague of mine, who relentlessly strived to change the face of the Middle East. The intricacies of international diplomacy and the secrets of the Israeli political kitchen are candidly exposed, as only an insightful insider can do. Being a player alongside Shimon Peres does not lessen Gil's intellectual honesty and capacity for self-reflection. This essential book excels in analytical wisdom, flowing narrative, smart political insights, good sense of humor, and a deep understanding of the indispensable human factor.*"

Javier Solana, former EU High Representative for Foreign Affairs and Security Policy, Secretary-General of NATO, and Foreign Minister of Spain

"*A major contribution to the study of a major figure in Israeli politics… illuminating and completely gripping. The account of Peres is nuanced, penetrating, and strikingly fair-minded.*"

Avi Shlaim, Emeritus Professor, Oxford University, UK

Shimon Peres

An Insider's Account of the Man and the Struggle for a New Middle East

Avi Gil

Translated from Hebrew by Eylon Levy

I.B. TAURIS
LONDON · NEW YORK · OXFORD · NEW DELHI · SYDNEY

I.B. TAURIS
Bloomsbury Publishing Plc
50 Bedford Square, London, WC1B 3DP, UK
1385 Broadway, New York, NY 10018, USA

BLOOMSBURY, I.B. TAURIS and the I.B. Tauris logo
are trademarks of Bloomsbury Publishing Plc

First published in Great Britain 2021

Originally published in Hebrew in 2018 as *Nuschat Peres* by Kinneret, Zmora-Bitan, Dvir

A catalogue record for this book is available from the British Library.

A catalog record for this book is available from the Library of Congress.

ISBN: HB: 978-0-7556-1701-2
          PB: 978-0-7556-1702-9
          ePDF: 978-0-7556-1703-6
          eBook: 978-0-7556-1704-3

Typeset by Integra Software Services Pvt. Ltd.
Printed and bound in Great Britain

To find out more about our authors and books visit www.bloomsbury.com
and sign up for our newsletters.

Dedicated to my late parents, Eliezer and Aviva, and to Naomi, Yotam, Yael and Babu, may they all have a long life.

Contents

List of Illustrations

1

Call Uri and Give Him the Green Light

"Call Uri and give him the green light." I wanted to be sure that I understood Shimon Peres's instruction correctly. The decision to send the director-general of the Foreign Ministry, Uri Savir—an official representative of the State of Israel—to conduct negotiations with the Palestine Liberation Organization (PLO) in Oslo marked a dramatic shift in Israeli policy. So I persisted.

"You want me to give Uri the green light, even though that's not exactly what Rabin asked for?"

Peres looked at me impatiently and said, "You understood me right."

The "Oslo channel" meetings with PLO officials had developed at the initiative of the deputy foreign minister, Yossi Beilin. The purpose of the talks, which had begun in January 1993, was to draft an unofficial document outlining the principles of a future peace deal between Israel and the Palestinians. The negotiators on the Israeli side were two academics: Yair Hirschfeld and Ron Pundak. Officially, Israel was hiding behind their backs without moving out front. It was reserving the option of denying the talks with PLO officials in the Norwegian capital. But the more promising these contacts in Oslo began to look, the more pressure Foreign Minister Peres started exerting on the prime minister, Yitzhak Rabin. Peres wanted to go to Oslo to meet the Palestinian representatives himself. Rabin rejected that idea but eventually succumbed to the pressure and agreed for a lower-ranking Israeli official—not the foreign minister—to depart for Oslo.[1]

Rabin then stipulated some conditions: the Palestinians had to commit to keeping the contacts secret, to attend the talks being held at the same time in Washington (as part of the negotiations with a Jordanian–Palestinian delegation),[2] and to agree not to discuss Jerusalem. Peres promised to check the Palestinians' commitment to Rabin's conditions and decided to delegate the task to his brilliant protégé, Uri Savir, the director-general of the Foreign Ministry.

My conversation with Peres—when he instructed me to give Uri Savir the green light to depart for Oslo—took place during his trip to India and China as foreign minister in May 1993. On the eve of our departure, May 15, Peres summoned me and Uri to his home. He updated Uri on the progress at the talks in Oslo, presented him his dramatic mission, and told him, "Prepare to leave as soon as the conditions Rabin requested are met." Uri and I drove to the Foreign Ministry after that conversation.

I opened the heavy safe in my room, equipped Uri with the relevant material on the talks, and we had a long conversation about the challenge awaiting him in Oslo.

One serious problem that concerned us that night, however, remained unresolved. Was the authorization that Peres had received from Rabin to send Uri a 100 percent approval or something less? We both had our doubts. "Pack a bag of toiletries and some spare clothes," I joked with Uri, "just in case you're woken up in the middle of the night with a knock on the door and taken away for interrogation."

We agreed that Uri would update me by phone about the Palestinians' answer to Rabin's conditions. And indeed, while we were traveling in Asia, he reported that there was agreement from the Palestinians, and that they intended to abide by Rabin's conditions. I passed this onto Peres, who asked me, "Should I talk with Rabin?"

"Of course," I answered.

Peres thought for a moment and decided, "Let's wait till the morning." He feared that Rabin might torpedo Uri's mission. That he might waver. I was not by his side when he finally spoke to Rabin, but I was quick to ask him for details of their dramatic conversation. "I told him that there was agreement for our conditions," Peres replied. I asked how Rabin had reacted. Peres replied dryly, "Yitzhak said: let's talk about this in Israel."

I could not disguise my disappointment. I knew in my heart that Rabin's answer meant the dam had not yet been breached. Who knew when and whether he would overcome his hesitations? But I had no time to get carried away with my doleful thoughts before Peres surprised me with his instruction to call Uri and give him the green light to fly to Oslo. "I'm not sure Rabin understood from your phone call that Uri was on his way," I pressed again.

But Peres muttered impatiently, "This is a sensitive subject, I can't go into detail on the phone."

For some reason I retorted, "And my conversation with Uri, giving him the order by phone to go, that's not a sensitive subject?" This simple question remained unanswered. Peres did not deign to respond. I called Uri and wished him safe travels.

***

It would be hard to overstate the significance of sending an official Israeli representative to hold political negotiations with the PLO. Ever since the organization's establishment in 1964, Israel had treated it as a loathsome terrorist group whose objective was Israel's annihilation, and whose whole raison d'être was its total opposition to the existence of the Jewish state. Formal negotiations with the PLO were nothing short of a revolution in Israel's foreign policy.

But I had to understand: Peres had decided to put an end to the prime minister's dithering and, in a dramatic move, instructed an official representative of the Israeli government—the director-general of the Foreign Ministry—to hold direct negotiations with the PLO. Rabin would have to reconcile himself to the fait accompli. I asked Peres later whether Rabin had been surprised by Uri's journey to Oslo, having said explicitly that they would discuss the matter back in Israel. Peres gave me a mischievous look but replied bluntly, "I told him that Uri had gone on the basis of our understanding. I know he doesn't have a good memory, so sometimes you have to be daring and exploit it." When I stiffened and said that he had made a decision that most people I knew would have balked at, he replied, "It wasn't the first time, and it's not the last. When it's time to decide, people get cold feet. That's the moment I come in and take a risk."

Over the years, I would discover just how determined Peres was to fight tooth and nail to realize his dreams—even when the odds were stacked against him and unlikely to favor him in the short term, and even when he did not exactly have the necessary authority. Peres was motivated by grand visions. The New Middle East, one of his central dreams, required the realization of another, no less ambitious dream: peace with Israel's Palestinian neighbors. The talks in Oslo were part of that grand vision.

This vision was sweeping, and many dismissed it as delusional and impractical. But in Peres's mind, there was no contradiction between being a man of dreams and of deeds. On the contrary, he was convinced that great actions began with great dreams. In his speeches, he repeatedly spelled out his belief that "the great achievements of humanity were born in dreams." Peres insisted on his right to dream, and would not agree to anyone or anything limiting his dreams or dictating their content. His stubbornness was not restricted to his love of sailing on the wings of imagination. Peres was also immensely stubborn about making his dreams come true, even if the mission looked impossible and even if fulfilling his mission meant violating accepted norms and usurping powers that were not, strictly speaking, his.

The Bed Sheets Do Not Dictate the Dreams

In 1989 I accompanied Peres at a series of diplomatic meetings in Cairo. The Egyptians set us up at Qasr al-Andalus, the guesthouse where they regularly hosted the Palestinian leader and PLO chief Yasser Arafat and his people. The Israeli journalists who joined our trip were quick to discover this titillating detail and insisted on taking photos of the bed in which Peres had spent the night. Back in those pre-Oslo days, Arafat was still strictly taboo. I feared that a picture of the bedroom might reach the newspaper front pages. I could only imagine the juicy headline: "Peres sleeps in Arafat's bed." With the help of our Egyptian hosts I managed to prevent anyone taking a photo of the incriminating evidence, but not the journalists' question of "Mr Peres, how was it to sleep in Arafat's bed?" Peres paused for a moment and then answered decisively, "The bed sheets do not dictate the dreams."

These "dreams" played a major role in what made Peres. During one of our visits to Washington, I suggested that we visit DARPA, the agency that supplies groundbreaking technology to the U.S. military. Peres agreed and listened keenly to the CEO of DARPA describing his organization's achievements: from the internet to GPS and stealth jets.

Peres bombarded the CEO with incisive questions and asked him about DARPA's success rate for the projects it had tried to advance that year.

"We've reached a success rate of fifteen percent," the CEO replied.

Peres tried to console him by saying that it didn't matter that the success rate was low. But he was surprised by the CEO's response: "I'm disappointed because the success rate is too high. It's a sign that we haven't been daring enough. We are paid to dare."

I kept this lesson in mind whenever I watched Peres fail. When dreams are great, failures are more forgivable, and successes should be valued even more highly, even when they come along less frequently.

Peres's path from Dimona[3] to Oslo was astonishing. In Dimona he realized the dream of generations—to provide security to a battered and persecuted people. In Oslo he made a breakthrough toward another great Jewish dream—peace. There is an intense affinity between these two monumental tasks: the guarantee of Israel's existence made it possible to strive toward reconciliation with its enemies. Peres made an indelible mark on the efforts to realize these dreams, but the task of achieving peace is not over yet. Completing this mission, I believe, remains the essence of Peres's legacy and the core of his bequest.

Dreamers are not usually known for being great doers. Their heads are in the clouds and their minds are not focused on day-to-day trifles. Peres embodied a rare combination of both dreaming and knowing how to realize those dreams. His head was in the clouds, but his feet were firmly grounded in reality. Two US presidents—Barack Obama and Bill Clinton—remarked on this unique phenomenon in their eulogies over Peres's coffin. It would be a mistake to view him as naive, they both argued. "He knew exactly what he was doing," said Clinton. "And being overly optimistic, he knew exactly what he was doing with his dreams."

Although I was familiar with the full force of Peres's dreams, both intellectually and in their power to generate political momentum, I was wary of the image that stuck to him of being an "astronaut."[4] I tried to persuade him several times to tone down the enthusiasm with which he rallied support for his dreams, and even to let go of ones that others deemed delusional. Whenever he got carried away with his imagination and became, in my view, unrealistic, I reminded him of the reports of the legendary camel train to Eilat, in which he had participated aged 22 in January 1945.[5] Returning from his voyage, Peres had announced that he could see the Suez Canal from the top of a mountain in the Negev Desert, and that it was a matter of strategic importance. The fact that the canal was 250 kilometers away and was obviously not visible from the peak did not trouble this enthusiastic young man.

The more Peres was enchanted by his grand dreams, the more I tried to temper his enthusiasm. He generally appreciated the thankless task that I assumed of identifying for him the dangers latent in his dreams. He was conscious of the need to hear contrary views questioning the freedom that he gave himself to adopt unconventional ideas and to strive toward goals that looked unachievable. But this was not the case during our first trip to the United States after the murder of Prime Minister Yitzhak Rabin in November 1995.

The Israeli Embassy in Washington had recommended that Peres ask the American administration to let an Israeli astronaut join a space expedition. Peres was enthusiastic, and at a meeting of embassy officials asked whether anybody objected. I was the only one with reservations. "You're the prime minister now," I told him. "The public wants a leader whose feet are rooted to the ground. You need to shed the impression you're an astronaut, not fuel it. I'm worried that people will say: now Israel's got two astronauts." Peres brushed my comments aside and said that paranoia had got the better of me. He was probably somewhat right. He often grumbled that I had little faith and was being overly doubtful whenever I heard him share his dreams.

And indeed, working with Peres for many years, I accompanied a leader who never stopped dreaming and battling whatever obstacles stood in his way. He usually charged at his goals from his position as a supporting actor, in both the political and psychological—if not necessarily official—senses of the term. Both when he worked at Ben-Gurion's side and when he settled into the President's Residence, he remained a supporting actor. The final word was rarely his. It was the prime minister's.

The fact that he was a supporting actor for so much of his political life was obviously not the only factor explaining Peres's conduct—conduct that earned him both praise and scorn. His personality and accumulated experience were also vital components of his nature. Nevertheless, I believe Peres's status as a supporting actor is key to deciphering his nature, modus operandi, and contribution to Israel's politics and history. This was the "Peres Formula."

It was a status that tormented and frustrated him, but it also cleared for him a field of action that suited him and his skills. His feeble powers and grand dreams were separated by a wide gulf, which he bridged by unique and controversial means and with the assistance of an efficient and pugnacious team of advisors, who perfectly suited him and the way he worked. Like him, most of his advisors despised officialdom and the shackles of bureaucracy and were not opposed to engaging in subterfuge.

Peres must have been born to be a supporting actor. It was from this position, frustrating as it was, that he gave maximum expression to his personal advantages and perhaps even achieved goals that would have been unattainable as the leading actor—as the number one. From this standpoint, he was free to dream and to act on a far longer timescale than he could have afforded in a more senior role. In politics, leading actors are busy putting out fires, rallying public support, and managing fractious coalitions—especially in Israel's system of coalition government. They cannot easily invest political capital in sweeping initiatives that exact a painful price in the present and will bear fruit only in the distant future, long after election day. But as a supporting actor, Peres was largely free from these constraints.

To Write or Not to Write?

Peres was aware that I kept a diary. "Why don't you sit and write down your memoirs?" he used to admonish me.

"Don't try to talk me into it," I replied. "You won't come out as well in the book as you might expect. If I write, I'll write the truth."

Peres was not deterred. "Write," he said. "You're allowed to criticise me." He asked for examples of critical comments that appeared in my diary.

"I describe, for example, how you caused major damage by leaking the secret talks with the king of Jordan in November 1993," I replied.

"It's the truth," Peres responded quite openly, to my surprise. "I was wrong. I don't object to you writing the truth." I believed him when he said that he was willing to absorb criticism. But I suspected that he would not be happy to be stripped of the flashy suit he wore and the pose he struck in public. Whether he hated anyone, was envious, or swore—that was all irrelevant gossip to him. In the car, in visits around Israel, he often used to curl up in the corner of the back seat and fall asleep. In his slumber, he looked worn out and scruffy. Neither majestic nor glorious. Sometimes he let out a little snore. A minute before reaching our destination, I used to give him a tap on the thigh and say, "Shimon, we're here." He would wake up, rise like a lion, whip out a small comb, tidy his mane, and leave the car with a stride. He used to speak to those who greeted him with a deep voice full of vigor, radiating alertness and power.

But for me, these stolen moments of sleep in the car were no less "Peres" than what followed, when his voice boomed and he warned people again that while an omelet can be made from an egg, it is impossible to make an egg from an omelet.

The same goes for when he used to return to the car to call Sonia and check how she was doing: "All well, my wife?"

"Luxe," she used to answer. "And what about you?"

"Luxe Deluxe, sweetie," he replied. "Is there anything for lunch? I'm on my way."

Or when he insisted on never returning from a foreign trip without buying Sonia the Bandit perfume that she so loved and a new pair of earrings. "Sonia, with her good heart, gives away the earrings I buy her," he used to tell me later, peeved.

Leaders who bear their inner hearts to their advisors want to be able to count on their loyalty. To trust them not to reveal sensitive and potentially embarrassing details that might harm their image. But besides personal loyalty, advisors must also be loyal to the truth. After all, these details are not gossip about a private individual, but information on an elected public figure responsible for matters of life and death.

In October 2000, at the outbreak of the Second Intifada,[6] I drafted a letter for Leah Rabin (Yitzhak Rabin's widow) to sign, imploring Prime Minister Ehud Barak to let Peres meet Arafat in a bid to stem the bloodshed. I did so because I believed in Peres's ability to find a common language with Arafat, and because it required Barak's permission (of which more, anon). I was later asked in a media interview whether I was the one who had written "Leah's letter." I said the truth: "Yes."

A letter from the public relations consultant Ran Rahav quickly landed on my desk. "I was stunned," he wrote.

The story behind Leah Rabin's letter should never have been told. There's a limit. After all, 99.9 percent of the public was unaware of the bitter truth. You'll be surprised to hear that I, who was closer to her than anyone, didn't know … It's inconceivable the public understood Leah wrote it all herself, and signed a document that was prepared for her in advance. It doesn't suit an analytical person like you.[7]

While writing this book, I went back to Rahav's emotional letter and reflected on it. Was I supposed to bottle up my experiences forever? The truth has a habit of chipping away at myths and undermining the image of heroes. Should I allow myths to freely traverse the pages of history that my grandchildren will learn from, or do my grandchildren have a right to understand the leaders of their nation as they truly were?

The closer I got to the heart of politics, the more clearly I understood that, just like every other participant, I too was only witness to a partial version of events. This book, therefore, does not pretend to be an authoritative history. It presents a select number of events from my own limited vantage point: a restricted view, but one that was often exclusive—of the sort that allows me to delve deep into the secrets of the "Peres Formula." To a great extent, history books are written on the basis of eyewitness accounts. But we should always make space for a nagging doubt that perhaps the most significant eyewitness accounts are missing from the record. Perhaps the key witness was too lazy to write down his account and departed this earth without ever sharing his secrets? I am well aware that my impressions are not the whole picture. They are merely a few more tiles in a larger mosaic that will never be completed.

I felt a need, and even a duty, not to keep my impressions secret, so I have written them down. In so doing, I have based myself on my personal diary and the records I kept in all my years at Peres's side: from my first work with him, in 1988, till the day he died, in 2016. I have added the fruits from several interviews that I recorded with him. I was interested to understand how flesh-and-blood leaders behave in the heat of great events. Leaders who are humans like the rest of us, with their own ups and downs. And chief among them, of course—Peres.

I was particularly intrigued by Peres's protracted battle to realize his dreams from the position of a supporting actor. I was, at the same time, both an observer of and a party to his endeavors, frustrations, ruses, and complicated relationships with the leading actors—the prime ministers under whom he served. I am not an impartial historian, but rather an actor who was involved with and loves the subject of his book. Nevertheless, I have made every effort not to let this fact damage the truth.

Upon our return from Washington after signing the Interim (Oslo) Accords with the Palestinians,[8] we received a wonderful photograph of Rabin and Peres. The official White House photographer had snapped an intimate moment, in which Peres had turned to Rabin while placing a hand on his heart. I told Peres that I would keep the photo, and that I would be happy if he could write something on it for me. Peres, unaccustomed to such requests from me, seemed surprised. "What do you see in this photo?" he asked, his interest piqued.

"When you place your hand on your heart like that and tell Rabin something," I replied with a chuckle, "it's clear that you're bullshitting him."

Peres smiled, held the photo, took out a pen, and wrote: "To Avi—Only you are capable of knowing what we discussed. With friendship and caution, Shimon."

And indeed, I remained cautious for many years despite feeling duty-bound to tell the truth. Peres knew that my book would not skip over the moments and perspectives that he would not have chosen to include in his own memoirs. But still, he urged me to write. He knew that I saw him as the decisive force behind the Oslo Accords and was personally acquainted with his major contribution to the peace treaty with Jordan. He believed that my account would be accepted as reliable. I told him once that my book would be finished only when one of us died, and it looked like the task of publishing

Figure 1 Peres talking to Rabin. Peres signed the photograph: "To Avi—Only you are capable of knowing what we discussed. With friendship and caution Shimon." (Official White House photograph by Callie Shell, September 28, 1995.)

the manuscript would fall on him. We both laughed. But now, after he has passed away, the time has come.

My story about the "Peres Formula" weaves together his great dreams, his modus operandi as a supporting actor in trying to make those dreams come true, and his complicated relationships with the "number ones" he served under, whom he tried to steer toward his own objectives and make—sometimes reluctantly—partners in those dreams. As such, the first part of this book focuses on Peres's working environments: the Foreign Ministry, his advisors, and his basic toolkit, with an emphasis on his complicated relationship with the media. The second part focuses on his great dreams, chiefly the New Middle East and the Oslo Accords. The third part focuses on his relationship, as a supporting actor, with the prime ministers above him.

Peres's inimitable conduct will be clear from each of these sections. The perspective throughout will be my own personal one as a close advisor—sometimes as a fly on the wall, and other times an active and involved co-conspirator.

The final words are Peres's own. We had several conversations in which I asked him to address the key questions in this book, including some that are critical of him.

My work and acquaintance with Peres spanned nearly three decades. There would be no chance, and no point, of trying to cram everything that happened in those years into a single book. I have chosen not to write a history book that records events chronologically, but to focus on two elements that for me sum up the "Peres Formula": on the one hand, the great dream; on the other, the pursuit of that dream from a position of intense frustration. Covering these elements compels me at points to recount, in a single breath, events that took place at different times. In order not to ruin the pace of the storytelling, I have included footnotes wherever necessary to point out the dates of key events.

Dare to Dream

Peres frequently shared his pain with me. "I'm thinking about how everything would look different if I were prime minister," he used to confess to me. Very often I found myself trying to console him. I watched him weave a spectacular dream about a New Middle East, and I helped him in his quest to achieve it. This great dream propelled him toward many other ideas, most of which were rooted in his optimism about the future of humanity in general and the Middle East in particular.

Peres loved talking to young people who wanted to learn from his experiences. "Dare to dream," he used to tell them. And although he was never thrilled to share his pain at being a supporting actor, this frustrating position was an integral part of his legacy.

After all, few people ever reach the top. Most of us, like Peres, are supporting actors, each in our own respective fields. And that makes the lessons we can draw from Peres's journey all the more meaningful: to dare to dream, and dare to fight, even if you're not at the top of the pyramid, and even if the power to call the shots doesn't seem to be in your hands. Be determined, aggressive, and creative. Don't relent, and don't read too much into official titles, because dreams can be made to come true in so many different ways.

Despite the differences in age and status between Peres and me, and although we quarreled quite a bit, we developed special friendship. He became a major force in my life, and I owe him the defining moments of my professional career. His death left an indelible void in my world. Sometimes he appears in my dreams, and I miss him.

By working closely with Peres, I was able to get to know him up close, as a person. Sometimes such intimacy can lead one to focus excessively on petty human foibles at the expense of the bigger picture—one that highlights the great accomplishments and lofty plans. Whenever I felt this was happening to me, and I was focusing too much on the trivia, I liked to go back to a letter from a colleague from the Foreign Ministry cadet course, Shmuel Ben-Shmuel.

Shabash, as we called him for short, was the proud son of members of the Betar movement and pre-state paramilitary Irgun, and a loyal Likud voter. He lost his brother in the Lebanon War in 1982. He wrote to me from his posting in South Africa:

I envy you for two things: for being a partner in changing the course of history, and for having the fortune to be the right-hand of one of the greatest statesmen of our times, who towers head and shoulders above the rest of the short-sighted and narrow-minded Israeli political class. A vicious wind of hatred and cheap demagoguery, which swept through the country over a decade ago and drove hundreds of thousands of people out of their mind (including someone you know well), deprived Peres of the victory he deserved, even then. The cost of this mistake has been too great to bear: a national tragedy in Lebanon, which for many of us has been a difficult and painful personal tragedy too.[9]

I showed Peres the letter and promised myself that even in moments of anger and frustration, I should be grateful that I had the good fortune to work by the side of a rare leader and an exceptional man.

How I Got Caught in Peres's Net

My work by Peres's side began in July 1988. I had returned from diplomatic service at the Israeli Embassy in Ottawa, Canada, and gone straight to the bureau of the foreign minister and into the fever of an election campaign. It was a dream come true for me. But it was not a childhood dream. I may have settled on center-left political views in my youth, but I never saw the point of a career in politics. As a student, I was invited to join the Labour Party Society at the Hebrew University of Jerusalem, and I rejected the invitation without a moment's hesitation. I had not planned on a diplomatic career either, and I reached the Foreign Ministry cadet course by chance. Some of my fellow students, who had decided to apply for the entrance exams, teased me and said that I was refusing to join them because I was afraid of failure. I was young enough to fall straight into the trap of arrogance that they had laid for me.

When I completed the theoretical part of the course, I started my training in the ministry. I kept up my academic work at the same time. I was studying for a master's degree in political science and worked as a teaching assistant. I postponed a decision about the best path forward till graduating. My aspiration to join the "blazers"—the coterie of aides around Shimon Peres, so known for their love of jackets—came only later.

The Lebanon War of 1982 boosted my desire to leave the comfort of the sidelines. I was called up with my reserve unit on the eve of the invasion of Lebanon. I served as a combat medic in a medical unit. At first, we were stationed on the Golan Heights, in case the front expanded to include Syria. We were later relocated to the detention camp in Megiddo, to deliver medical treatment to the thousands of Palestinian detainees transferred there from Lebanon.

The experience of Megiddo was a severe shock. Like everyone, I had been brought up believing in the righteousness of our cause and purity of arms. My late father, Eliezer, symbolized for me these basic principles. In his humility, he never shared stories of his own heroism with me till his dying day. His friends directed me to the books and documents that described how he had been captured by the British in a daring attempt to smuggle weapons for the Haganah, how he was brutally tortured but never opened his mouth, and how he insisted on successfully saving the life of a Lebanese Arab, whom his Haganah friends had considered killing to ease their journey back from a mission to acquire weapons in the north.

At Megiddo, my world was turned upside down. I witnessed a litany of abuses against handcuffed detainees. I saw my own compatriots beating them with wooden sticks and irrigation pipes and kicking them in piques of fury, sometimes smiling and with genuine glee. I was sure that I was watching the implementation of a policy from high up. I complained. After a while I was called in for questioning by the military police. I described what I had seen, but I was mainly asked about a specific detainee who had died. I had been summoned with one of the doctors to treat him in the interrogation wing, but by the time we arrived he was already dead, with visible signs of severe beatings all over his body. The officer at the military police told me that the man must have banged his head against the wall until he died. "It's common among Arabs," he informed me knowledgeably.

As for my other complaints, I was presented with a dozen witness statements that refuted my testimony and denied the existence of any violence whatsoever in the detention camp. The military prosecutors told me that I had to provide the names of the soldiers who had been involved in the abuse. I said that I would not do so, and that the account had to be settled with the more senior ranks that permitted the violence and gave soldiers the impression that abusing handcuffed detainees was a valuable contribution to Israel's security.

I was shocked by the violence and by the fact that everybody but me and a friend in the unit, Yaakov Arazi from Kibbutz Gonen, preferred to ignore it. I felt that, for the men beating and abusing the detainees, it was as if their great hour of vengeance had come: *we're allowed to do this, because we've suffered so much.*

During my first furlough, I rushed to the Foreign Ministry in a fluster to tell people what was happening and found Israel's diplomats hard at work denying malicious stories spread by the Arab propaganda machine. The problem was—some of the stories were familiar to me from the field and were absolutely true. I was astonished to read self-righteous interviews in the press with military police officers, who boasted of the humane treatment afforded to Palestinian detainees and said that they hoped the detainees would tell their compatriots about it after their release from jail.

Inside the unit, I developed a reputation for being an "Arab lover." After a while, we were transferred with the detainees to the Ansar Camp in Lebanon. One morning, when I returned from a weekend break, I entered my tent and was surprised to find a wrinkly, old Lebanese woman asleep in my bed. My fellow soldiers burst into laughter. "The old woman's sick and came for medicine," they said. "Since you're such an Arab lover, we let her rest in your bed."

It was not a "love of Arabs" that shaped my political convictions. I am convinced that it is an Israeli interest to achieve peace and free ourselves from ruling over another people. But besides cold calculations of interests, I must admit that Bible class at school left a mark of its own. I was profoundly influenced by the moral exhortations of our prophets, and I am proud to belong to a nation with such spiritual teachers. The difficult events at Megiddo showed me the extent to which the Occupation[10] really was a corrupting influence. I was convinced that the situation had to be changed before it irreversibly transformed the face of Israeli society. I was increasingly won over by Peres's approach. Increasingly, it became my aspiration to help him.

Opportunity in Ottawa

My opportunity to catch Peres's eye and that of his inner circle came when he visited Ottawa in 1986, toward the end of his term as prime minister. I was the spokesman at the Israeli Embassy in Canada and made great efforts during the trip to impress the group of "blazers," Peres's closest advisors. I leveraged the contacts I had cultivated in the Canadian press to ensure that Peres's visit received the broadest and most positive possible coverage. The effort paid off.

After the visit I was approached by Nimrod Novik, Peres's diplomatic advisor, who asked me to cut short my stay in Ottawa and join Peres's office as his aide. I agreed, but the Foreign Ministry objected to shortening my service and vetoed my return to Israel. Toward the end of my service in Canada, in summer 1988, Uri Savir approached me to ask whether I would serve as his deputy in running the foreign minister's bureau. Again, I agreed. "Excellent," Uri responded dryly. "Don't forget to say your goodbyes nicely to your family."

And indeed, I soon got stuck into my work at the office, which had been completely mobilized for the elections. It was my first experience as a civil servant adrift in the no man's land between public service and politics. It was also my first and obviously not last chance to experience a defeat with Peres. The Likud, headed by Yitzhak Shamir, won the 1988 elections. We were in acute distress. I did not want Peres to quit politics and wrote him some overblown rhymes:

> We took a major hit, Shimon.
> No breakthrough, no victory to report on.
> Just frustration that makes me want to cry.
> So depressed, I can't look my son in the eye.
> We took a major hit, Shimon.

> Now, Shimon, the jackals are howling from inside,
> And others crush that olive branch you tried
> To offer, and now it's time for Shamir to stride,
> Leaving us one last hope to cling on:
> Do not forsake us, Shimon!

Peres welcomed this poetic message with a smile. I later learned that he would enjoy exchanging such rhymes with me on topical issues. But in this case, there was no need for me to beg him in verse. A man like Shimon was not going to give up. Peres and the Labour Party joined the national unity government under Prime Minister Shamir. He became the finance minister and asked me to join him as a media advisor.

It was not long before I was able to check how immune I had become to the agony of defeat. Peres ended his paralyzing partnership with Shamir and concocted the "dirty trick," as Yitzhak Rabin called it: the attempt in 1990 to topple the national unity government and replace it with a new government that he, Peres, would head. Interior Minister Aryeh Deri and his ultra-Orthodox Shas Party were his accomplices.

During these efforts to destabilize the government, I worked to undermine Shamir's position by encouraging internal tensions inside the Likud. I did not ask for Peres's permission. These were simply my operative conclusions from the objective he had set. I developed a technique of leaking "cut and paste"-style tables of information, which appeared in the papers and described Israel's defeatist positions in negotiations with the Palestinians. Ariel Sharon used to turn up to cabinet meetings with these information tables in hand and embarrass the prime minister. I also used to leak horror stories about how the PLO was infiltrating the diplomatic talks. I tipped journalists off about how the Palestinians would arrive at the talks in Cairo in vehicles bearing the PLO flag and hold press conferences at the PLO Embassy in Cairo, and similar stories in the same imaginative vein. The goal was simple: to provoke embarrassment and encourage infighting in the Likud.

Peres was determined to play for the jackpot. "I'm going for maximum brutality," he declared proudly. And to our delight, the government fell and President Chaim Herzog invited Peres to form a new government. Yossi Beilin, Peres's deputy in the Finance Ministry, asked me to serve as coordinator of the Labour Party's coalition negotiating team. I said that it would be inappropriate for me as a civil servant to get so deeply involved in politics, and that even without the position on offer, I had already crossed the line. Beilin, with his dry sense of humor, brought up my birthplace as evidence of my provincial thinking. "These Haifaites are so odd," he quipped. "Peres will be prime minister in two weeks anyway."

A few days before the crucial vote in the Knesset, I joined Peres for lunch in Tel Aviv with the American journalist and television star Barbara Walters. Peres told me that he had decided to give her an interview the next day as if he were already prime minister. She would therefore be the first to have an interview with him, which would be broadcast immediately after his swearing-in. I told him he was making a mistake and should not play make-believe. The Knesset vote would take place in four days, and he should wait till then. But if he still wanted to be interviewed, he should do so without pretending that he was already prime minister.

I put my foot down, and Peres ultimately took my advice. The following morning, a few hours before the interview, he called me to ask whether we could cancel it. I told him that the television crew was already in position in his Tel Aviv office. Peres told me that he had heard from politicians in the ultra-Orthodox Agudat Yisrael Party that one of their members of Knesset—Avraham Verdiger—had backed out of supporting his prospective government. Peres understood that he lacked the numbers for a government, but still he gritted his teeth and gave the interview that was never broadcast. Later in the day, when it was finally clear that the political trick would fail, I saw up-close the tears that welled up in his eyes.

Figure 2 Avi Gil coordinates a stormy press conference with Peres and Rabin during the government crisis, the "dirty trick," which led to the collapse of the unity government, March 11, 1990. (Photo: Hananiya Herman, 1990)

Back to the Foreign Ministry

Being a civil servant, I returned to the dreariness of the Foreign Ministry and received a junior role in the North America department. I quickly discovered, perhaps as a result of my experience in Peres's political academy, that with a little bit of elbow grease I could work in my chosen field. The new foreign minister, David Levy,[11] needed help performing his job in the Shamir government. Before his first visit to the United States, I volunteered to prepare his briefing book. I learned that the diplomatic documents about the peace process were under lock and key in the ministry's legal department. I told a secretary that I needed to photocopy one little piece of paper from the whole bulky folder, but I rushed to photocopy the whole thing and became an authority on the subject.

Together with the ministry's deputy director-general, Eitan Bentzur, I worked on drafting diplomatic initiatives. Our "two-track peace plan" was published when it was leaked in full to the media. I wrote the foreign minister's letters to his American counterpart, Secretary of State James Baker. I helped Levy's people behind the scenes on media relations and his image, and I wrote them a manual on the subject. I was already friendly with Levy's advisor, Aliza Goren, and soon also befriended his right-hand man, Uri Oren. He told me that when he read the minister the speech I had written for him—which Levy believed Uri had written—Levy cut him off and asked, "Did you write this speech, or Shimon Peres?"

I felt comfortable helping Levy and his team, who were taking a more moderate approach than Shamir. It was my way of trying to influence things. I preferred working behind the scenes. When U.S. Secretary of State James Baker came to the ministry for diplomatic talks, I sat in the adjacent room with headphones connected to the translation system. My job was to write the summary that would help the minister brief journalists after the meeting.

The deeper my ties to the foreign minister's bureau grew, the more the minister's staff pressured me to come to work in their office openly. I said that I would prefer to leave things as they were: I was already identified as Peres's man, and letting my connection to Levy become public would create difficulties. I also felt uncomfortable, as if I would be crossing a red line and serving a political rival. But Uri Oren did not relent and explained that Levy put the national interest first and bore no grudges against people who had worked with his political opponents. I was summoned to the ministry's human resources director and told that I was being given an unambiguous order: to turn up for work at the minister's bureau, or else my refusal would be presumed to be for political reasons, which were inadmissible in public service.

I called Peres and Beilin to seek their advice. They both urged me to go for it. "I'm sure you will influence them, not vice versa," Peres said. On the first morning I was supposed to start working in Levy's bureau, the *Maariv* newspaper ran a front-page headline: "Peres's Former Spokesman—to David Levy's Bureau." The report said that senior political officials in Jerusalem had expressed surprise at my appointment because of my closeness to Peres. "They stressed that despite their respect for his [Gil's] skills, the appointment was peculiar. Foreign Ministry Spokesman Yosef Amihoud explained last night that this was a temporary appointment to reinforce the bureau."[12]

As a result of the report, my appointment was scrapped. "The appointment of Avi Gil as an advisor in the foreign minister's bureau," the press explained, "was cancelled owing to the uproar at the top of the Likud."[13] It was said that Levy had received a shower of criticism from his Likud colleagues. Someone even warned him that he would make 3,000 photocopies of the article and send it to every member of the Likud Central Committee. Levy, for his part, claimed that the appointment had been made behind his back and that he had no knowledge of my past. In later days, I joked with Peres that it must trouble his conscience that he was responsible for blocking my path to a glittering career in the Likud by David Levy's side.

The end of my romance with Levy boosted my desire for a change of scenery. The Wexner Foundation invited Israeli public servants to apply for an attractive master's degree scholarship at Harvard University's Kennedy School of Government. I got in. The teaching faculty consisted of genuine stars, who had all made a significant mark in their work for the US government and in academia. The synthesis of theory and practice caught my heart. I started thinking again that perhaps a career in academia might suit me more than in diplomacy, but Peres's appointment as foreign minister in the new Rabin government in 1992 put an end to my indecision. I returned to Israel and joined Peres as the director of his office.

Unconventional Performance

"What do you reckon, is there a chance I'll have a meeting with the king of Jordan in the near future?"

Peres posed this question at a meeting of the Foreign Ministry's senior management. It was the afternoon of November 3, 1993.

He listened to the cautious answers of Israel's most senior diplomats. He was told that Damascus would react harshly and take revenge, fearing that the Jordanian king was collaborating with Israel to isolate Syria and demonstrate that it was possible to make progress toward a regional settlement without it. They raised the hard-line positions of the opposition in Jordan, chiefly the Muslim Brotherhood and extremist Palestinian forces that rejected any compromise with Israel. They argued that the king was a hesitant man who would not take risks for fear that the domestic criticism might spark violent protests.

Peres shot me a furtive glance. His eyes glinted mischievously while listening to this gloomy analysis, but his voice did not betray his secret: folded in the inner pocket of his jacket was a four-page document describing the principles of a future peace treaty between Israel and Jordan, and initialed by Foreign Minister Peres and King Hussein. We had just returned from a secret meeting with the Jordanian king in Amman shortly before this meeting at the Foreign Ministry. I had insisted on holding the staff meeting as planned, to project business as usual and as a precaution to avoid the secret leaking. I had not guessed, of course, that Peres would choose to "consult" with the ministry's management about the possibility of meeting the king of Jordan, with whom he had spent many long hours only yesterday. But Peres could not resist the temptation and entertained himself by tiptoeing on the edge. My impression was that he enjoyed abusing these doubtful diplomats and maybe even making me nervous too. I knew that after the meeting he would crack a few jokes with me at the expense of "the bureaucrats in your ministry."

The meeting in Jordan had taken place shortly after the signing of the Oslo Accords at the White House. Peres was determined to take advantage of the positive diplomatic atmosphere that had produced the breakthrough with the Palestinians by adding Jordan to the circle of peace. "We have to storm Jordan now," he had urged Rabin repeatedly, to get his agreement to travel to meet the king. The mission was not simple. The doubts raised by the Foreign Ministry experts were shared by many other experts.

But Peres was unimpressed. As usual, he waved off such bothersome analysis with a quote from Ben-Gurion: "Experts are always for the past, never for the future." In his own stubborn way, he also overcame the doubts of the Americans and enlisted their support, which was vital for the success of his endeavor. He chose not to bring his most senior official—Deputy Foreign Minister Yossi Beilin—to the meeting in Jordan, because he was angry that "Yossi is insufficiently loyal and takes the credit for himself." In Jordan he put on a stellar diplomatic performance that bore valuable fruit, but on returning to Israel he succumbed to the same temptation that had so often tripped him up in his complicated relations with the media. "Remember November 2," he said inadvertently, causing the fact of his secret trip to Amman to leak and thereby seriously sabotaging his relations with the Jordanian king.

I shall return to this episode later and describe it in more detail. But for now, let's skip ahead and recount the key points because it illustrates a core component of the Peres Formula—Peres's unique and unconventional conduct as a leader who was part of the establishment his whole life but almost always preferred to act an arm's length away from institutions and conventions. Such was the case with his attitude to government bureaucracy, the type of teamwork he encouraged, and the controversial methods that characterized his behavior. In this chapter, I shall try to shed some light on each of these elements. I shall describe his attitude toward bureaucracy through the saga of his relations with the Foreign Ministry; I shall highlight the type of teamwork he preferred with an account of his relationships with his close advisors; and I shall illustrate his methods—a running theme throughout the book—with a focus in this chapter on his troubled relationship with the media.

An Ideal Foreign Minister Who Despises the Foreign Ministry

For many people in Israel and around the world, Peres was the ideal foreign minister. Even some of his opponents admitted that the role fitted him like a glove. And indeed, he proved himself to be a consummate diplomat. He had a dominant presence in every diplomatic engagement. World leaders thirsted for his ideas. He strode across the world stage and assigned roles to the rich and famous as if they were obedient chess pieces on his own private board. In every diplomatic endeavor, he projected cultural wealth, strategic thinking, practical skills, powers of persuasion, and negotiating nous. This was the man the Foreign Ministry should have coveted to lead it.

But this ultimate diplomat had no love for the Foreign Ministry or its staff. He despised them. "Your friends in that ministry have no ideas of their own, can't get anything done, and can't write a basic diplomatic memo," he often teased me. "All they understand is cocktails. Frankly it's an outrage that a group of nobodies managed to land the most enticing jobs in the country." Peres would often search for, and find, evidence for his fatalistic conclusions in the telegrams that landed on his desk. Once he delighted in asking me, "Avi, have you seen the telegram about the corpse's head yet?" Of course I had seen it: I was the one who sorted the mail that reached his inbox. One of our diplomats in Asia was explaining why he had made the right call in deciding, after some hesitation, to attend the funeral of a local official.

"I was welcomed with great respect and invited to sit with the family," the diplomat cabled. "Right behind the head of the corpse." This privileged location, right next to the dead man, had allowed our diligent ambassador to converse with ministers and other dignitaries and enhance Israel's prestige in the region.

"I'm sure the workers' union will give him a promotion now," Peres scoffed.

And indeed, it was not always easy to defend my Foreign Ministry colleagues from the minister's mockery. It was a lost cause when one of our missions in Africa reported that the death of the ambassador's wife had received widespread media coverage, and that the many guests who had come to console the Israeli envoy had received an explanation on the Jewish religious laws of burial and bereavement. This unfortunate loss had turned into a "media and public diplomacy event about Judaism, the Jewish people, and the State of Israel," the embassy staff crowed. Peres asked whether I had forwarded the telegram to our other ambassadors around the world: "Let them learn how they too can improve Israel's public diplomacy."

Instead of granting Peres his wicked wish, I made it up to him by referring him to an academic article that proved that the professional literature did not belittle "funeral diplomacy." The funeral ceremonies of world leaders, it explained, served as a valuable forum for diplomatic hobnobbing. The practice had become an "important institution" and, according to the dry academic text, had been given serious momentum by advances in the technology of embalmment, refrigeration, and transportation.[1]

But, of course, Peres did not need academic approval to pounce on diplomatic funerals as if he had discovered a treasure chest. Any trip with him to a diplomatic funeral turned into such an exhausting marathon of meetings with foreign leaders that I was almost ready to swap places with the deceased, so peacefully lying down in repose. On our way back to the plane after the funeral of Turkish prime minister Turgut Özal, for example, Peres boasted of the number of diplomatic meetings he had conducted in Ankara, including quick handshakes on the way to the bathroom. "In *one* day, I do alone what your ministry doesn't do in a year," he said. "We've earned the right to stop off and buy our wives some Syrian pistachios and Turkish delights."

The Frequent Flyer

During Peres's many trips abroad, he was always welcomed at the airport by diplomats from the local Israeli embassy. When his visits ended and the minister's plane had disappeared over the horizon, many of the diplomatic staff breathed a sigh of relief. During the drive from the airport, Peres used to interrogate the excited ambassadors and take joy in discovering that Israel's most senior representatives did not know the rate of inflation, the latest gossip about the prime minister, issues in local party politics, and other vital details about the countries of their service.

"Look how ignorant your ambassadors are," he used to sneer without a hint of humility. "All they understand is wine. I know more than they do about the country where they're serving." And indeed, Peres was a walking treasure trove of assorted knowledge. He was curious, read a lot, had a good memory, and was capable of absorbing a great deal of material in very little time. He was an avid reader of the jam-packed travel briefs that we prepared ahead of all his foreign trips. Very few ambassadors passed Peres's exams. The others became his punching bag and the butt of his jokes.

The ambassadors most often tripped up when they spoke with great self-importance about their own achievements and the respect that everyone accorded them. Such was the fate of the ambassador who reported, with immense sensitivity to the minutest nuances, on his "historic handshake" with the foreign minister of Namibia, who had held his hand "for a longer time than is conventional, with a broad and genial smile, and was obviously interested in giving maximum publicity to the encounter." The same went for the diplomat who gushed about the praise that the local press had heaped on him as an ambassador who "made history here like no diplomat before him" and would have a bustling boulevard named after him.

Although Peres was not averse to flattery, some diplomats went too far and spoiled their own efforts. Take the diplomat who cabled after the minister's visit:

> The media and especially the press continue to report on and highlight the minister's transcendental visit ... I have even met indigenous inhabitants of the Amazons who knew of and were interested in the minister's visit ... When I asked whether they knew about anyone else visiting the capital—and there were at least six such visits—they answered in the negative ... We emphasise again the importance of the foreign minister's visits overseas, which contribute towards and strengthen ... our public diplomacy apparatus abroad.

In later days, whenever I broached the possibility of another foreign trip, I added to the list of pros the guarantee that the visit would be of "transcendental" value. "Your reasons haven't convinced me till now," Peres used to respond with ridicule, "but if the visit really will be transcendental, then you win, and I'm on the next flight."

Between *Hasbara* and Policy

Although many people admired Peres's prowess in the field of "hasbara," or public diplomacy, the subject was a major source of tension and hostility between the minister and his ministry. Peres arrived at the Foreign Ministry in 1986 as part of a rotation agreement with Yitzhak Shamir.[2] He was already highly accomplished, having eliminated Israel's hyperinflation and won broad admiration for his performance as prime minister. But soon enough, there developed enmity between his bureau and the ministry employees, and Peres did not conceal his disappointment in their abilities. Nor did his aides, the "blazers," hide their own criticism from them, and one advisor was quoted in *Haaretz* as saying:

> Peres is the only Israeli leader in recent years to have managed, single-handedly, to secure sweeping achievements in Israel's foreign relations. When have we ever had such good ties with the United States? When has an Israeli leader ever been welcomed with such warmth in Europe? In just one visit, Shimon Peres achieves

more than 300 diplomats have achieved in two years. It really pains the Foreign Ministry. It pains them that he doesn't follow the bureaucracy's rules. He won't adapt himself to them. On the contrary, they need to work like in the Defence Ministry, till 1 AM.[3]

And indeed, the Defence Ministry was Peres's natural habitat, and he missed it. It was where the power, the budgets, the ability to influence, and the resources all resided. "I knew guys there who could work like demons," he told me longingly. He complained about the laziness of the Foreign Ministry staff in contrast to the can-do attitude of their counterparts in the Defence Ministry and the IDF. "They chase foreign trips and respect. They lack knowledge, they're experts in nothing, and all they're proficient in is restaurants."

Even when he moved into the Prime Minister's Office, Peres enjoyed cracking jokes at the expense of the square, buttoned-up diplomats. One concerned citizen, who had watched the television report on Peres's meeting with the king of Jordan, complained in a letter that it was impolite of the prime minister to have sat with his legs crossed in front of the king. I jokingly suggested to Peres that before answering, we should ask the Foreign Ministry Protocol Department for a professional opinion. Peres, amused, supported my suggestion, and we were treated to the following opinion written in total seriousness: "It is indeed unacceptable to cross one's legs. It is preferable to sit with one's legs straight and pressed together." Peres, of course, took the opportunity to tease me. "Now do you understand what your friends in the Foreign Ministry are good for?" he said.

Foreign Ministry staff used to complain of a rift: that the minister and his advisors were arrogant, closing themselves off in their office and failing to consult the ministry's experts. But Peres neither felt that he needed their services nor was he willing to fall in line with the rules dictated by the bureaucracy. He complained that the bereavement notice the ministry released in his name after the death of former minister Haim Bar-Lev, who was serving as ambassador in Moscow, was too small. He refused to calm down when we explained that these were ministry regulations. Every ambassador who passed away earned a bereavement notice of the same size. Peres saw this as "bureaucratic idiocy." How could Bar-Lev be compared to any old ambassador? When Colombia was hit by an earthquake, Peres pushed to send more humanitarian aid than usual. He was friendly with Noemí Sanín, the exotic foreign minister in Bogotá, and did not want to let her down.

The tension between the minister and his ministry was most palpable on the subject of how Israel's policies should be explained. It was a matter that, in contrast to other issues stripped away from the ministry's purview, was still his responsibility. Peres entered a ministry that for years had been honing and propagating messages around the world that applied to a reality of profound existential conflict: it presented the Arabs as hoping to bring about Israel's annihilation. But Peres and his group thought otherwise. In their opinion, recent changes in the Arab world had presented Israel with a new reality. A coalition of moderate Arab states was now ready to reconcile with Israel's existence. The Arab world was not a monolith: there was someone to talk to on the other side, and peace was within reach.

Whereas the "profound existential conflict" school of thought chose to pin all the blame on the other side and blacken its name, the Peres school of thought believed that Israel's interests were not served by continuing to make the other side look bad. Israel's enemies had become its interlocutors, he believed, and it was important to groom them as partners for a future peace deal and to inspire optimism that they had already changed their spots, or would do so soon.

Foreign Ministry staff were torn between two essentially different schools of hasbara. They were used to the whole universe of arguments they had developed, adapted, and learned to convince others of. They found it difficult to shake off what had been their bread and butter for so long. The Likud had generated extensive hasbara material in its time running the Foreign Ministry. The disciples of Ze'ev Jabotinsky, the founder of Revisionist Zionism and the Betar movement, placed great emphasis on the written and spoken word. Thus when Menachem Begin penned his "Foundations of Hasbara Abroad," he wrote: "Do not mix into the language of the past the linguistic barbarity 'Palestine' ... Why can we not say amongst ourselves and to other nations: 'Arabs of the Land of Israel'? It is certainly a more natural name than what was used before. And in saying this, we immediately create a different moral and political perspective."[4]

Peres came from a political culture that did not believe that merely replacing a word was sufficient to create a new political reality. When Likud lawmaker Yehoshua Matza attacked the use of the term "West Bank" in a Foreign Ministry briefing paper, arguing that it undermined the project to settle the Land of Israel, Peres responded, "I do not accept MK Matza's bombastic interpretation, as if words can change anything."[5]

Peres's right-hand man in the Foreign Ministry, Yossi Beilin, demanded that it scale back its use of negative propaganda and place peace at the center of Israel's hasbara. He also demanded that diplomats stop sending everyone copies of the Palestinian National Charter.[6] When Likud MK Geula Cohen criticized Beilin in the Knesset for doing so, Peres rose to defend him from her anger and replied mockingly, "We have already sent booklets on the Palestinian National Charter from the Fiji islands ... to Paris. Do you know what happens to these booklets we send? In Fiji, people drop everything, and the whole island gathers around to read the booklet they received in the post from the Israeli Foreign Ministry."[7]

Peres and his staff concentrated the bulk of their efforts on diplomatic action. Hasbara was less important and was to be derivative from that diplomatic process, riding on its coattails. "Hasbara is not a replacement for policy," Peres explained. "Without a policy of peace, without a policy of a peace initiative, Israel cannot—in my opinion—conduct an effective policy of hasbara ... The problem is not just what we're explaining, but to what extent we believe our own explanations ... The best way to improve our standing in the media is to improve our position on policy."[8]

The Peres school of thought despised Israel's conventional hasbara booklets and preferred to frame diplomatic initiatives in ways that would be amplified by the media. The core of the message was to be diplomatic action, with hasbara left only to raise its profile and enhance the positive image of its initiators. There was no need for an unwieldy network of ambassadors, spokespeople, and crates full of brochures that nobody read, when millions of people could watch a single appearance by Peres on a prestigious television show. "Peres's appearance on TV, his picture in the newspaper, and his voice on the radio," explained his spokesman, Uri Savir, "are worth more than an op-ed by any of the greatest writers."[9] Peres's few advisors, who had also worked with him when he served as prime minister, were convinced that Israel could cultivate a successful image abroad even without the Foreign Ministry's hasbara system. It would be ten times more efficient to leverage diplomatic action and play on the modern media's hunger for drama and news, they thought, than to rely on the ministry's old-fashioned mode of hasbara. This bulky system was accustomed to the wrong messages, they believed, and change would be painful and would take time. In any case, the whole system was inefficient, and could be dropped and found a rapid replacement—of the sort that understood and accepted the fact that Peres *was* the message.

Power in the Air

But it was not just in hasbara that the Foreign Ministry disappointed Peres. He despaired that it lacked professionalism, creativity, political depth, and functionality. He got by without it on matters of substance too, using its help mostly for logistical support: flight tickets, ground services at airports, hotel bookings, and restaurant reservations.

Peres worked aloof from his own ministry. The force with which he worked was incredible. He jet-setted between world capitals, feeling at home even as he jumped between interlocutors and languages. He promoted his initiatives and pulled strings as if he were the leader of a superpower. He had boundless energy. He could visit three continents in a single trip. In early June 1994 we visited the United States and South America, rounding them off with Morocco. In the United States Peres met with top figures in the administration, including President Bill Clinton. He had a long list of tasks on his agenda. Peres pushed for a regional economic summit in Morocco, made sure money continued to flow to the Palestinian territories, and persuaded UN Secretary General Boutros-Ghali[10] in a meeting to appoint Terje Rød-Larsen, our friend from the Oslo process, to the post of UN Special Coordinator for the Middle East Peace Process. And that was only part of Peres's shopping list.

Peres's hosts rolled out the red carpet and lavished him with respect and honor. The Nobel Prize-winning author Gabriel García Márquez returned to Bogotá especially to attend a lunch hosted by the Colombian president in Peres's honor. The president also put his plane at Peres's disposal to fly him to his next destination—Santiago de Chile. We landed in Buenos Aires for a few hours, where President Carlos Menem left his holiday to meet Peres. They fell into each other's arms. I alerted Peres during the meeting that we were going to miss our connecting flight. Menem shot me a withering look. "No plane will take off in Argentina without my friend Peres," he said, waving his hand dismissively. He ordered the pilots of his private helicopter to land us at the bottom of the stairs to the plane. We landed in Madrid, where the private plane of the king of Morocco awaited to whisk us off to Rabat.[11] Peres persuaded King Hassan II to host the first regional economic summit. Our host also agreed to open an Israeli liaison office in his country.

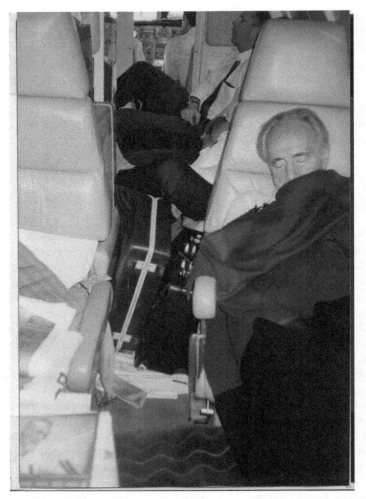

Figure 3 Not exactly a pleasure flight … Peres catches up with a few hours' sleep ahead of landing at the next destination. (Photo: Avi Gil.)

The report that I filed on the trip listed forty diplomatic meetings, twenty speeches and public appearances, eight meetings and audiences with Jewish communities, and twenty-one media interviews, including eight press conferences. All in all, eighty-nine different events. One can understand why on his return to Israel, Peres mocked the day-to-day problems of the Foreign Ministry. "Has your workers' union managed to reduce the price of schnitzel in the canteen?" he asked me disparagingly. The ministry's staff seemed to him to be living in a bygone era. He was conducting negotiations with the PLO while Israel's ambassadors were fighting against it.

While secret talks were taking place in Oslo, for example, one of our ambassadors in South America reported that Suha Arafat, the wife of the Palestinian leader, had been invited to take part in a local conference and that a meeting was planned between her and the first lady. The diligent ambassador cabled us that he had spoken by phone with the interior minister and told him that a meeting between the first lady and Mrs. Arafat was tantamount to recognizing the PLO and had to be stopped at any price. "No doubt, your ambassadors are risking their lives to save us," Peres hissed.

The Root Problems of the Foreign Ministry

The bad chemistry between Peres and the ministry was not merely the by-product of an unsuccessful partnership. It grew out of the severe root problems that characterize the foreign service. The ministry's status and purview have been whittled down ever since Israel was founded. The physical threat to Israel's existence had given the defense establishment dominance and seniority while encouraging it to encroach onto the Foreign Ministry's territory. One painful indication of the ministry's status is the way in which it defines its role on its website. While the other government ministries list what they do, the Foreign Ministry says on its Hebrew site what it would like to do: "The Foreign Ministry is responsible for formulating, implementing and presenting the foreign policy of the Government of Israel."

In reality, the Foreign Ministry's weight in designing Israel's foreign policy is generally minimal. It is the victim of a debilitating pincer movement: the defense establishment and the IDF gnaw at it aggressively from one direction, and from the other, the prime minister jealously guards the crown jewels of Israel's foreign policy for himself—relations with the United States and peace with the Arab world.

The meetings of the Political-Security Cabinet—the Israeli government's inner cabinet—were clear reflection of this reality: during my time as director-general of the Foreign Ministry, the person who was responsible for convening the cabinet, setting its agenda, and summarizing its deliberations was the prime minister's military secretary. Most of the cabinet's advisers were men in uniform or representatives of other security services—the Mossad or Shin Bet. There was no permanent seat at the table for the director-general of the Foreign Ministry, the head of the ministry's Centre for Political Research, or the ministry's experts. The men in uniform were responsible for explaining the political behavior of the main actors in the regional arena. They were also the ones responsible for gathering, analyzing, and assessing most of the political intelligence. Valuable political information never reached many of its natural civilian addressees, including Israel's most senior diplomats. In many cases the prime minister himself preferred to rely on military organizations in political matters: they had a wealth of resources, were high-quality and disciplined, and bestowed legitimacy on any leader's decisions because of the Israeli public's high esteem for the IDF.

I have never understood how exactly a military career qualifies soldiers to perform important political functions. Nevertheless, many of the cabinet's political decisions were given a familiar, if somewhat irrelevant, preface: "Further to the recommendations of the security forces and the IDF, it has been decided ..."

The top echelon of the IDF got carried away with dealing with various matters of diplomacy and making Israel's case abroad. The IDF's Planning Directorate, for example, coordinated Israel's response to the 2003 Road Map for Peace,[12] which was aimed at producing Israeli–Palestinian peace; the head of the IDF Military Intelligence Directorate Research Department and his colleagues were dispatched to world capitals to explain Israel's position to political figures; and the top brass of the IDF publicly voiced its own positions on matters that were not strictly military (for example, opposing the evacuation of the Israeli settlement of Netzarim during 2005 Gaza Disengagement).[13]

In the course of Operation Defensive Shield in 2002,[14] the IDF amassed its forces extremely close to Arafat's headquarters in Ramallah. The US government condemned Israel. Prime Minister Ariel Sharon, who was highly sensitive to criticism from Washington, ordered the troops to retreat, and the next day he chaired deliberations in which IDF Chief of Staff Moshe Yaalon openly confessed, "I did not accurately predict the reaction of the United States."

"Why do you think it's your job as IDF chief of staff to predict the reaction of the United States?" I asked him. My question went unanswered, of course. Paradoxically, the drive to train officers to think beyond their individual fields of responsibility had become a dangerous syndrome in its own right. Officers were parking their tanks all too eagerly on turf that was not their own. But can anyone succeed in persuading them of the merits of confining themselves to their original jobs?

Peres gave Israeli diplomats a low score but the truth is that the Foreign Ministry was blessed with very high-quality personnel. The recruitment process through the cadet course allowed it to choose and train the finest. The challenge in managing the ministry was to translate its quality manpower into tangible results in its fields of responsibility. This mission required tackling a number of obstacles buried deep in the ministry's organizational heritage: low morale, born of a sense of inability to influence core issues in Israel's foreign policy; the difficulty of accumulating expertise in specific fields, given a career path in which there was generally no reason for expertise (diplomats know a little about a lot, and not a lot about a little); a problematic geographic gulf between the headquarters and the field operations; never-ending tension and a feeling of instability, with employees spending long periods of time competing for their next post; difficulty-laden family relocations abroad and back to Israel; the impossibility of firing employees who had reached their peaks well before retirement age; and the system of promotions that valued seniority and put employees in positions of management and leadership at a relatively late age, which made it difficult to cultivate leadership, entrepreneurship, and management.

As someone who grew up in the Foreign Ministry, I was desperate to help rehabilitate its status. As director-general, I initiated an organizational project at the dawn of the new millennium—Foreign Ministry 2010—that sought to identify future trends of change that were relevant to the functioning of the Foreign Ministry, and that recommended changes and operational adjustments in the activities and organization of the ministry.

These included a more rational deployment of missions abroad; updating the profile of the model Israeli diplomat, as well our methods for recruiting and training them; changing the ministry's working practices; adjusting the ministry's internal organization, and so forth. The reform was designed to enhance the ministry's ability to generate top-notch, operational results, which would leave no doubt as to the ministry's professionalism and precedence over competing actors. At the same time, it was clear that we had to fight over status and fields of responsibility by making an unceasing effort to correct the distortions that had become institutionalized over the years. Accomplishing this mission required the enlistment of the foreign minister and the support of the prime minister. We started implementing our recommendations, but the fact that the average tenure of a ministerial director-general in Israel was only a year and a half at that time made this an uphill climb.

Peres did not obstruct my efforts and gave me a free hand in running the ministry, but he did not personally have high hopes for attempts to reform the foreign service. As far as he was concerned, the ministry was a lost cause: it was a shame to invest in the chaff at the expense of the wheat. "I have no intention of investing energy in this ministry," he told me. He got on perfectly well without it.

The crowning glory of his activities—the Oslo Accords—was the clearest expression of this attitude: the secret signing of the agreement on August 19, 1993, took place only after the ministry staff accompanying the minister on his seemingly innocent trip to Scandinavia had already gone to bed. The foreign minister made history on the floor above them while they were sound asleep. Director-General Uri Savir did indeed involve his ministry in the supplementary negotiations over the implementation of the Declaration of Principles signed with the PLO on September 13, 1993, but this was a purely temporary revival for it.

Better Poems than Cables

I was not discouraged by Peres's disparaging attitudes toward my diplomatic colleagues and I made repeated efforts in my various roles alongside him at the Foreign Ministry, and especially as the director of his office and later director-general, to enlist him in the cause of rehabilitating the ministry's status. I enjoyed questionable success. He was an excellent foreign minister, who disliked his own ministry. He preferred to devote his free time in his office to reading and writing. He admired writers and poets and aspired to be included in their ranks. Urgent and secret reports from senior diplomats never excited him as much as the package he was once sent by the poet Dahlia Ravikovitch with an anthology of her new poems. He caressed the dedication she wrote him with his eyes: "To Foreign Minister Shimon Peres, with ever-growing appreciation, asking again that you invite [the Palestinian national poet] Mahmoud Darwish to visit in Israel. From Dahlia." Whenever I protested to him over his tendency to belittle diplomatic cables, he replied, "Most of what your ambassadors write, I have already read in the newspaper. Tell them to write me poems."

Peres loved quoting a poem by Nizar Qabbani, which said that if birds needed a government permit, they would never fly. His admiration for the Syrian poet was not at all diminished when I read him a few lines from the poem "The Hasteners," which Qabbani penned after the signing of the Oslo II Agreements in Taba, Egypt. Qabbani furiously claims that the agreement is no less than an act of rape comparing the Palestinians' achievements to a "can of sardines" (Gaza) and to a "dried bone" (Jericho).[15]

Peres was a prolific author. One of his books—*Reading Diary*—was an anthology of letters he had written to various authors, in which he lavished them with unctuous praise. His language in these letters was flowery, sophisticated, and sycophantic. In my opinion, it was grandstanding but hardly literature. Consider what he wrote about Nissim Aloni's book:

> In the last few days I have performed a double journey: one on the planes that draw us and the PLO together and apart, and one in reading your book … Your book flutters like a giant butterfly in a breathtaking array of colours, whose massive wings take it from flower to flower to gather the juices of times and contradictions. It is a pleasure to fly with you on such a rich and unique stylistic route.[16]

Peres offered indiscriminate admiration and praise. Even a book of poems by one of the ministry's staff earned outsized praise from Peres, printed on the dust jacket. The poetic consul might not have known that he was "the poet of pain and hope," but that was the title that Peres awarded him.

I tried to convince Peres to use less bombastic language, and I told him how, earlier in my career, I had cabled the ministry from the Canada mission: "I need a video machine for work purposes as a matter of necessity."

"If it isn't a question of life and death, perhaps drop the claim about 'necessity'?" the ambassador had warned me privately.

Peres pulled a face and said, "All your ambassadors are schmucks."

I completely identified with the harsh comments of the journalist Gideon Samet, who wrote of Peres's letters to the authors:

> In none of your letters have you said a single bad word about any book or had any biting criticism for any writer. They bear the constant echo of your craving to be liked by this creative community and even, quite touchingly, to belong to them … There is a certain eagerness and even forcefulness in your evident passion in the "Diary" to penetrate the creative world that so enchants you, to embrace it, and to grade it. It must give you a sense of fulfilment and value beyond the pinnacles of your own most fulfilling political career.[17]

Peres asked me whether I thought Samet's criticism was justified. "Yes, it's very much justified," I said. Peres shrank a little. It was clear that I had hurt him.

"What makes you think that?" he asked. I replied that the book was supposed to be a work of literary criticism but contained not the slightest tone of criticism, only compliments, praise, and wordplay. "That's also allowed," he replied. He sent Samet a quotation from the works of a Romanian poet: "When I no longer have the strength to love another person, I shall die."[18]

Although he knew that I would not spare him criticism, he asked me to read drafts of his books and to share my observations. I thought that the autobiography he wrote with the journalist David Landau was a missed opportunity.[19] "The reader has to get through 400 pages before you admit you made a mistake somewhere," I told him.

"What can I do if I didn't make mistakes?" he replied grudgingly.

Peres's literary world and rich language were also expressed in his political statements, which set him apart from others. When Yitzhak Shamir stayed in Bulgaria in the official guesthouse where Arafat had been hosted earlier, he was asked by journalists in the morning, "So how was it to sleep in the same bed as Arafat?"

Shamir answered dryly, "I hope they changed the sheets."

As I already mentioned at the beginning of the book, when Peres had a similar experience and was asked the same question at the official guesthouse in Cairo, he replied: "The bed sheets do not dictate the dreams."

The Advisors by His Side

As an employee of the Foreign Ministry, I was torn between my role as the minister's confidant and my role as a professional. I tried as much as I could to bridge these two worlds, of the professional advisor and the political leader, but I realized that this bridge would forever remain wobbly. These two roles come from worlds that operate by different rules. Professionals learn to set objective tests for their conduct. Politicians, meanwhile, inhabit a world based on shady deals, inglorious compromises, and endless rounds of negotiations, in which agreements are a matter of patchwork and never fully live up to politicians' original promises.

All this, of course, takes place under the watchful eye of an attentive media and a fickle and ungrateful public, which will determine the politicians' future in the next elections. As such, politicians also have a different concept of time. Advisors are free to pick the best option, while political leaders are unenthused by options that will bear fruit only after elections. In order to be able to influence a political leader, it is insufficient to be merely a professional. One must learn the rules of the political game inside out and gain a deep understanding of one's client. There was one way to persuade Shimon Peres, and another to persuade Ariel Sharon.

After the signing of the Oslo II Accords in September 1995, which granted the Palestinians self-rule in the towns of the West Bank and Gaza Strip and in a further 450 villages, Peres prepared himself for a public battle and a difficult debate in the Knesset over the deal's ratification. I stayed up overnight reading the agreement and preparing a detailed list of topics that would likely provoke a crisis if the Palestinians violated the deal or failed to honor their obligations—from not taking meaningful counterterrorism action to not amending the Palestinian National Charter.[20]

Figure 4 Peres and Gil consulting before the ceremony in which President Obama awarded President Peres the Medal of Freedom. Blair House, Washington, DC, June 13, 2012. (Photo: Yosef Avi Yair Engel, President's Office.)

In the morning, I told Peres that I had prepared him a brief on the accord. "Did you write down all of its good points?" replied Peres. "Good job, it'll help me in the Knesset."

"No," I answered. "I made a list of expected problems. The list will help you prepare for attacks from critics, and maybe even address the problems before they become crises."

"I have no need for that right now," replied Peres, disappointed.

I learned that if I wanted to make a difference and have any influence, I had to be attentive to the minister's needs and to make him see me as someone who could be useful to him at the right moments. I would have been more successful had I presented him a two-part document: the first part equipping him with arguments to help him in the political battle; and the second, recommending ways to deal with problems that might arise later. Advisors become ineffective if they merely list problems without adding ways to solve them.

My studies at the Harvard Kennedy School had helped me understand more clearly the code of conduct for advisors who want their hard work to influence political leaders and not merely gather dust on the shelf. But not everything can be learned at prestigious universities—especially not the techniques of statecraft that I learned from Peres himself and his closest advisors.

Sometimes Peres and I discussed the nature of the connection between advisors and political leaders. "Perhaps you don't know it, Shimon," I would generally begin jokingly,

> but you're living a lie. You think we're your advisors, your subordinates. But the truth is that you serve us. We have no interest in wasting time chasing the public for votes. We leave that drudgework to you. You ingratiate yourself with voters, go to weddings, hug babies, and reach a position of influence—and then we use you as a tool to achieve our own objectives.

Peres smiled and replied humorously, "That's my fate. I can't reach the peaks that my advisors can. I humbly accept my bitter fate as a tool in your service, and I feel satisfaction from the little that I can contribute to helping you accomplish your vital missions."

Despite the lighthearted tone, these conversations were a testament to Peres's power as a leader. Peres chose to work with opinionated people who were motivated by an aspirational agenda. He preferred to surround himself with people of an independent, creative, and entrepreneurial character, not those whose primary quality was obedience and routine. He knew that this choice would at times entail a heavy cost, and he was willing to pay that price with his eyes wide open.

I was taught a seminal lesson in political entrepreneurship at the start of my career in Peres's office, from his diplomatic advisor Nimrod Novik. In early September 1989 he showed me a nine-point document about future elections in the Palestinian territories ahead of negotiations for a comprehensive settlement based on the principle of land for peace. I said that a document with ten points would be better than one with nine: "It plays better in the media." Novik wanted to know what tenth point I recommended adding. I said that in my opinion, as a confidence-building measure and in order to contribute to a better campaign atmosphere, Israel should refrain from building in the settlements during the Palestinian elections. Novik accepted my suggestion and revealed to my astonishment that he had decided to prepare this paper for Egyptian president Hosni Mubarak in order to advance the peace process. I suspected that Novik was teasing me or merely fantasizing, but a few days later Mubarak published the ten-point document as his own diplomatic plan. Peres welcomed the document, despite being unaware of its provenance. I had been given a crash course in daring, diplomacy, and political creativity. I took note of this lesson, although you won't find it in the syllabus of any respectable school of government.

Leaders who give their advisors free rein are likely to let them forget that the power they wield is not their private domain. This can lead to hubris, a sin of which I have been personally guilty. On the eve of Pope Francis's visit in Israel in May 2014, I drove to Jericho for a meeting with the chief Palestinian negotiator, Saeb Erekat. On my way, I received a number of messages saying that the Pope was aware of our meeting and expected us to agree that during his visit, President Peres and President Abbas would join him for a joint prayer for peace.

I knew that Mahmoud Abbas was vigorously opposed to this suggestion, and Erekat proposed in our meeting that we offer the Pope to invite both presidents for a joint prayer service at the Vatican instead. I liked the idea. But then I received a text message saying that the Pope wanted to speak to Erekat himself. I knew that the Pope's only chance of changing Abbas's mind was to speak directly to Abbas, not through Erekat. So I ignored the message. Later I explained that I had been unreachable by phone: "After all, I was at the lowest point on earth." It was an unjustified decision. Never ignore a request from the Pope. I was carried away by arrogance.

The Iron Law of Mrs. G

In all my work at Peres's side, I operated according to the "Iron Law of Mrs G." It's a personal law that I devised to remind me at low points of my place at the leader's side, especially if I want to influence him. The law states: "The credit for your actions belongs to the boss. You remain in his shadow." The more relaxed the boss, and the less worried about a new competitor stealing his limelight, credit, and public recognition, the more open he becomes to receiving advice and then claiming it as his own. It's a good rule even if the boss is a decent and worthy person.

I received an introductory lesson on this during my maiden diplomatic posting in Kathmandu, Nepal. I persuaded Anne-Marie Lambert Finkler, the director of the department where I had worked as a cadet, to accept the post of ambassador there. This brave woman had fought fiercely against the Nazi occupiers as part of the French Resistance, and I admired her greatly. After moving to Israel, she founded and headed the Foreign Ministry's human rights department. When I returned to the ministry during the 1982 Lebanon War, rocked by my experiences there, she lent me an attentive ear and invited me to work in her department. She convinced me that it was not enough to let off steam about my difficult experiences, when I could devote myself to the task, however modest, of setting things straight.

Despite our friendship and the respect we had for each other, Anne-Marie was the boss and I had to know my place if I wanted to have any influence over her. And indeed, whenever I pitched her a new idea, she responded in an almost Pavlovian manner: "Interesting … So you think just like me." I never felt a need to safeguard any sort of credit so replied, "Yes, I think just like you."

Advisors must be able to forgo the credit on small things as much as big ones. They must take comfort in achievements that only they and their bosses are aware of. Thus, when I wrote Peres's speech for the Rabin remembrance rally on November 1, 2014, he told me with a mischievous grin that he had passed my text off as his own when he asked his friend the author Amos Oz for an opinion. He even gave me a copy of the speech with Oz's handwritten notes as a keepsake: "Dear Shimon, an emotional and hard-hitting speech. You speak for me too. I have made a few mostly stylistic suggestions, two or three minor deletions, and two or three small additions. Love you, Amos." I joked with Peres that I could quit on a high now. "What more can I possibly dream of, now the best writer in Israel, Amos Oz, has reviewed my own text and given me a passing grade!"

For an advisor, the strict protection of intellectual property rights is inconsistent with an ability to influence the boss. Indeed, the "Iron Law of Mrs G" is based on a noble act of ultimate sacrifice, in which the advisor gives his everything in secret, and the boss reaps the rewards alone. Consider an example. I accompanied Peres to an international lakeside conference in Europe. After our return, a video cassette was delivered to the office with a letter addressed to Peres. The writer of the letter—a woman called Gabriella[21]—said that she had seen on TV that Peres was at a lake. She was sending him a short video of the lake as a memento. I wrote her a thank-you letter, and for some reason went overboard in describing my longing for the sight of that magical lake. How at sunset the gentle ripples on the water gracefully plucked my heartstrings and gave me peace of mind. I signed the letter, of course, as "Shimon Peres."

A week later we received an emotional letter from Gabriella, telling Peres she had pored over his letter a hundred times and could not get enough of it. She was overwhelmed by an emotion that could not be put into words. She knew that her soul would be forever tied to Shimon's. She was in love. From that point on, Gabriella continued sending Peres love letters and videotapes in which she professed her feelings for the foreign minister. I used to tell Peres that Gabriella symbolized the essence of the relationship between an advisor and a leader. My heart conjured the words that caught her heart and set it aflame with undying, burning love. But I remained faceless, my personality erased, so that I could devote myself entirely to serving him alone. She was in love with Peres through the power of my words.

Peres took great pleasure in the stories that I shared with him about Gabriella. I think he suspected (and was perhaps a little jealous) that I had met her in secret on one of our visits to Europe. I swore to him that his claim was groundless. "She's all yours, just yours. I won't cheat on you!" I promised. To console me over my plight, Peres jotted down a poem about the fair maiden and gave me the handwritten version for safekeeping:

From a distance, Gabriella is so lovely.
Gabriella, Gabriella, answer me:
Who is like you and will ever be?

The corner of her still-warm dress
She sent signed to Avi to his address,
And won his heart, he must confess.

From deep inside the distant lake, you see,
She made his heart rate rise by sorcery,
Released from innocence, she set him free.

And Avi, like the finest song,
Beamed and frowned at her along,
As feelings in his heart did throng.

Gabriella, Gabriella, feel his plight,
His heart brimming to speak or write,
When like the burning bush, his heart's alight.

I did not feel that I was sacrificing much by operating behind the scenes. I had no great interest in the media spotlight. For an advisor, leaving the stage to the leader maximizes his own powers of influence; and his benefit is sometimes in successfully steering the leader away from pitfalls, although nobody gets credit for mistakes that were not made.

It can also bring a smile to one's face sometimes to operate behind the scenes. That happened, for example, when I was asked to obtain greeting messages from Shimon Peres and Mahmoud Abbas to be read out at a ceremony attended by Secretary of State Hillary Clinton at a prestigious institute in Washington. I drafted both messages and asked each leader to sign his respective version. Both did so without changing a word. After the letters were read out to the excited audience, I wondered whether I should also accept the request to help draft the thank-you letters—and I was amused to think about the diligent historians who pick apart such documents and analyze their style to reach scholarly conclusions about their authors.

Between Loyalty and Creativity

Peres used to call advisors and aides who could be reliably trusted "loyal dogs." But he also hinted that loyalty and creativity did not go hand in hand. He was slightly confused when I asked him whether I met his definition of a "loyal dog," and whether in order to be more creative, I was supposed to betray him occasionally.

The truth was more complicated. Peres let different types of advisors flourish around him. He loved working in a chaotic environment and gave his advisors free rein. He was both angry and proud when they exercised independence and aggressively initiated unconventional moves. They reminded him of himself when he was younger, and he was proud to have raised them, even if some of them grew wings of their own and flew out of his nest.

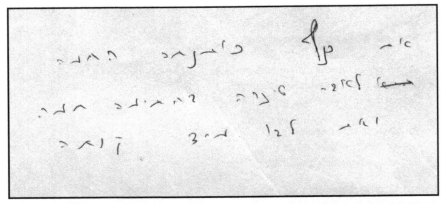

Figure 5 Extract from a handwritten poem that Peres penned for Avi Gil. (Photo: Avi Gil.)

When he was debating whether to make Uri Savir director-general of the Foreign Ministry, he told me: "Our guys are running ahead too quickly. Before they're ready. It's a shame we're losing Professor Shlomo Ben-Ami, who's interested in the job. If we'd appointed him, we'd have had broad public support. He's a very serious force, and the ministry is full of nobodies. All I have is Yossi [Beilin], Uri [Savir], and you."

Peres loved quoting with a smile Syrian president Hafez al-Assad, who used to ask his critics: "I don't understand why people accuse me of surrounding myself with yes-men. When I say 'no', all my advisors say 'no' too."

Peres and I had many conversations about the complicated relationship between leaders and their advisors. Peres believed that leaders must not tie their advisors' hands. "When you choose quality people," he said, "let them work, let them feel independent. It takes me longer to monitor them than to pick their brains."

I asked him whether, in the case of Yossi Beilin, whose disloyalty he used to complain to me about, he was aware of the inherent cost of advisor's hopes for political independence. "Yossi Beilin has cost me dearly, but I thought he was worth it," Peres answered keenly.

I thought that if you want people of value—well then, my friend, they come at a price … I saw talent in him, he flourished, and he was excellent. As my advisor and my deputy, he was excellent. I knew that I could not trust him personally. That man knows no personal loyalty … He wants to be a leader, right … but I knew one thing: if I imposed discipline on him, he'd do the job. He'd hide things from me, that's for sure, and he'd surprise me, that also true. But if I told him to do something, he'd do it, he wouldn't double cross me, in terms of his actions. So I knew I was paying a price. You remember what grief they gave us when we appointed two directors at the Foreign Ministry,[22] it was endless. I fought with everyone. Why? Because if you want someone of value, you need to fight for them. Pay the price.

Peres knew well that there was little to gain from advisors who exalted and glorified their bosses. But he still expected to receive support and encouragement from them. "I work hard enough, I deserve a little comfort at least from my aides," he said. He felt offended that his dedicated media advisor, Behira Bardugo, criticized him so much. "Isn't it insulting? She criticises me from morning to night and never has a good word to say."

After every speech and meeting, Peres asked, "How did it go?" I learned that in order for my critical remarks to be effective, I had to preface them by telling him what he had done right. When the Labour Party walked out of the Sharon government in 2002 and he parted from the staff of the Foreign Ministry, he affectionately called me the "no-man" at his side. I made an effort to tell him the truth as I saw it. Sometimes we quarreled and I caused him anguish. But I felt it was always to my credit—in Peres's eyes—that I didn't look for media exposure or for a political career for myself.

Easy to Advise, Difficult to Implement

Advisors and commentators tend to ignore the difference between the ease of giving advice and the difficulty of carrying it out. My experience has taught me that this simple truth must always be at the forefront of any advisor's mind. In 2004, I tried to persuade my friend Ami Ayalon[23] to enter politics. I had met him when we studied together at Harvard, and I thought that Israel would benefit if people like him joined the national leadership. After Rabin's assassination and the resignation of Shin Bet director Carmi Gillon, I had advised Peres to appoint Ami to this demanding role. Ami had displayed exemplary leadership in the Shin Bet and military service. But since he was hesitant to dive into the political swamp, I decided to try to persuade him in a supportive environment. I asked him to join me paddleboarding. Far away from the Tel Aviv shore, we put down our paddles and I listed the reasons why he had to throw his hat in the ring.

When I finished, Ami replied that he thought I was exaggerating somewhat in describing his personal strengths. "There's something uncontrollable in me," he said.

When I'm offered a role, I always feel I need to decide on my mission for the day after the welcoming ceremonies and the first day on the job. I won't hide it, sometimes I think about running for prime minister. But then I think about the most important mission facing the prime minister of Israel. And my answer is that his first duty is to safeguard Israel's character as a Jewish and democratic state. That's why we must reach an agreement with the Palestinians and evict tens of thousands of settlers from their homes. I've been the director of the Shin Bet, so I know perhaps better than anyone how difficult and terrible this mission is, and even bloodshed it could cause.

"You received the Medal of Valor," I said, "the highest honour in the IDF. Do you think you lack the courage for this mission?"

"For a mission like this, it's not enough to be brave," Ami replied with resolve. "You also need to be a megalomaniac."

This insight came back to me whenever I found myself advising a political leader: *it's easy to give advice, hard to carry it out.* It is easy to explain why Israel must cut back its sovereignty in Jerusalem, for example. It is the way to bolster the size of the Jewish majority in Israel's capital city. But for a prime minister, the decision would involve other, heartbreaking considerations that are not his advisors' concern. It is he—not his advisors—who would be forever recorded in the history books as the one under whose watch Jewish sovereignty was eroded in the holy city.

30,000 Feet in the Air

The more time I spent with Peres, but especially the more flight hours we clocked up together, the more deeply I got to know him. We flew together to the four corners of the earth, and our endless hours in the air and at airport lounges let me to talk to him about issues that were not necessarily connected to work. Whenever our plane took off from the tarmac, Peres managed to unwind and leave the political turmoil that preoccupied him on the ground. He became calmer, more open, and gave free rein to his humor and inner sense of mischief.

He always packed the two or three books that he was reading simultaneously. His curiosity was insatiable. He urged me to read the same books so that he could share his thoughts about them with me.

Whenever Uri Savir flew or dined with us, Peres made him choose the wine. Peres himself was something of a culinary connoisseur. Once we flew with a Korean airliner, and he did not forgo the shark's tail soup and caviar, washing it down with Armagnac and reveling in the smells and flavors. Our conversations focused on a variety of topics—politics, gossip, literature, and even well-worn questions about the influence of individuals on history. Peres's position on this was, of course, unsurprising. "History is certainly influenced by the deeds of individuals," he said. "Just look—the Dimona reactor, the Israel Aerospace Industries, Entebbe, Oslo."

Peres had no difficulties jumping in seconds from debating philosophy to giving a stand-up comedy routine. He had a mischievous streak and loved taking part in bizarre conversations, which often repeated themselves in a kind of ritual that would have been unintelligible to onlookers. I used to start locker-room banter saying, "Did you notice the pretty shiksa [non-Jewish woman] who took us to the plane?"

Peres jumped into this role-play, asking, "Tell me, Avi, have you done it with a shiksa before?"

My role was to play it dumb. "But Shimon, what's the difference? All women are created with the same anatomy."

Peres looked at me like I was a complete idiot and explained, "Jewish girls are always doing you a favour. It's like they're suffering from the whole business. There's always something hurting or bothering them. But the shiksas—they enjoy every moment, they have no complexes, they love to pamper you, and they put their whole hearts into the job."

He was always ready, of course, for my inevitable follow-up question: "Where would *you* know about these differences from?"

His modest answer: "That's what friends tell me."

Sometimes these shiksas clouded his senses. Peres attended a reception hosted by Argentine president Carlos Menem at one of the World Economic Forum summits in Davos. The flamboyant president of Argentina was invited to dance by a tango dancer, and he instructed her companion to invite his friend Shimon Peres to the dance floor. "I couldn't say no," Peres later said in his own defense. "The president would have been offended, and who knows what could have happened to our relations with Argentina."

We were sent a video of the event, which showed a dancer wrapping a long leg like a boa constrictor around Peres's leg as the pair spun in a dizzying tango. When I played him the video, he ordered me in a worried voice, "Destroy the tape."

"It's no use," I told him. "The Argentinians are sending out these tapes as a memento to everyone who attended. But have no fear, that dance with the long-legged shiksa was forced onto you in diplomatic circumstances." Peres agreed and proceeded to watch the dancers' moves on the screen.

We had our fair share of strange conversations. More than once I asked him to analyze the advantages and disadvantages of two options for putting on shoes: sock, shoe and again sock, shoe—or sock, sock and then shoe, shoe. Peres used to play along. Sometimes I posed him hypothetical questions. "Imagine, Shimon," I asked him once,

> that there's a perfect, enchanting woman you've dreamt your whole life of spending a night with, and she calls you and says it's your lucky night. You won't get another chance. You're feeling passionate and getting ready, all excited for your date, and then the phone rings. Arafat's on the line. He wants you to come urgently to meet him in Gaza. You have to choose: the woman of your dreams or Arafat?

Peres replied without a moment's hesitation: "Obviously I'd go to Gaza. A man must control his emotions and know what really matters."

The Inner Circle

In our internal deliberations, I was generally the least gentle when voicing positions that clashed with Peres's. Yossi Beilin and Uri Savir did not hold back from speaking their minds, but they phrased themselves in ways that would be less hurtful.

Peres often got angry during these consultations when his analysis was rejected, but he quickly calmed down. Sometimes he accused us of being too ready to compromise. Our negotiators, he once told me, were going out of their way to understand the Palestinian side, and their desire to reach an agreement was leading them to be too flexible. The remark was directed at Uri, but it was expressive of a passing flash of anger, not Peres's real feelings toward him. Peres was enthralled by Uri's sparkle, the breadth of his horizons, the richness of his writing, his command of languages, and his experiences in the big, wide world. He loved Uri's wonderful sense of humor and appreciated his sophistication and his natural negotiating nous.

The man who most intensely infuriated Peres was one he valued enormously: Yossi Beilin. I liked Yossi because as a politician, he was completely different from everyone else. He was not built to chase the public's affection, nor has he ever tried to do so. He is clever, learned, funny, and never raises his voice; he is also unconventional, daring, and aggressive in pursuing his political initiatives. Rabin called Yossi "Peres's poodle" in 1990. The nickname hurt him. "Rabin inflicts some serious damage with his nicknames," he once said, in an uncharacteristic tone of pain. "High-school kids in Tiberias called me a poodle. They basically called me a dog." But Yossi is the opposite of a poodle. He is a Doberman hound in a poodle's fur. Do not be mistaken by his gentle exterior. He is tough and knows how to bite and not let go.

When I first started working with this group, I was asked to inform Peres of a family tragedy. His nephew had been killed in a plane crash in Nepal. I called Yossi, who had experience, and asked his advice: Would Peres take the news badly? Perhaps there should be a doctor nearby? Yossi sounded surprised and answered dryly, "You Haifaite, is that what you really think? Call him and tell him. He's used to hearing bad news."

Yossi's dedication to advancing Arab–Israeli reconciliation did not sprout out of some lofty vision of human brotherhood. During one meeting in 1989, I heard Ariel Sharon, the then-minister of industry and trade, warning anxiously, "Are you aware that 400 Arabs have bought apartments in Beersheba and are demanding Arab kindergartens in the city?" I was appalled by Sharon's derisive attitude toward the country's Arab minority and passed Yossi a note saying so. He wrote in response: "Believe me, I'm with him on this one. We didn't become doves out of love for them."[24]

Peres disapproved of Yossi's excessive leftism and was worried it would contaminate his own image as well. "He's going to trip me up big time one of these days," he told me. Yossi knew that his political attitudes raised suspicions that he was unpatriotic and would likely undercut his effectiveness as a politician. Sophisticated as he was, he adopted the recurring practice of occasionally fueling up his left-wing engine with supplements of patriotic petrol. With fairly consistent regularity, he chose an issue that was on the agenda and took a hard-line, hawkish position on it. That was what happened when the National Alliance, an Italian party accused of fascism, joined Silvio Berlusconi's coalition. To Peres's dismay and without coordinating with him, Yossi furiously attacked the Italian government and tried to dictate an extremely belligerent stance against Rome.

Yossi served Peres for many long years, recruiting and managing some talented people. Peres was not strong on management. Yossi did that for him. But Yossi also wanted his own political career. Coolly and wisely, he worked to build up his own political identity, one that gradually distinguished itself from Peres—and this drive for independence hurt Peres terribly. Peres was furious about Yossi's independent maneuvers as deputy foreign minister: hardening Israel's line against the Apartheid government in South Africa; floating the idea that Israel might renounce American aid; and his harsh remarks against Turkey over the Armenian Genocide just when Peres was working to strengthen strategic ties with Ankara. Yossi went further and embarrassed Peres with his instructions to Foreign Ministry staff. Consider his instruction, for example, not to require dignitaries to visit Yad Vashem, Masada, or the Golan Heights, which had been compulsory stops on every itinerary drawn up by the Foreign Ministry.

When the possibility arose that Peres might be able to appoint another minister from his own camp to the Rabin government, I told him to appoint Beilin. "My party colleagues are telling me not to pick Yossi," Peres replied. "They're suggesting I choose someone else, maybe less clever but more loyal. He has another thing coming if he thinks I don't hear the rumours that he said Rabin and Peres are two muddled old men whose time is up."

Peres believed that Yossi was making intensive efforts to build up the impression that *he* was the true architect of Oslo, and that he had only let Peres into the secret relatively late.

I fought for him to be director-general, then deputy foreign minister. No one's ever fought as hard for an aide as I have. And he, together with Hirschfeld and Pundak, took Oslo from me. They're depicting me as an ungrateful miser. Did I receive any thanks from Ben-Gurion? I created Israel's power of deterrence, if there is such a thing: Dimona. I did France. And the Sinai.[25] Ben-Gurion didn't believe any of this would succeed, but he got the credit. Only when there were problems, *then* the responsibility was thrown at me. I never complained. I don't need to be pampered, but I must be surrounded by loyalty and discretion. If Yossi feels trapped, he should decide: is he in or out?

Peres was keen to keep Yossi away from the heart of the diplomatic action and replaced him with Uri. He neither sent Yossi to Oslo, nor involved him in the talks in Paris about recognizing the PLO, nor made him part of the dialogue with Jordan. Yossi and Peres had no interest in publicizing the tension and hostility between them. They kept their dirty laundry at home. Yossi never challenged Peres head-on, but he did ramp up his own independent activity despite being Peres's deputy. As far as Peres was concerned, the pinnacle of his humiliation was discovering that his deputy had— without his knowledge—drafted a memorandum of understanding with Mahmoud Abbas on a final-status accord.[26] The document said, among other things, that the Temple Mount would be under extraterritorial Palestinian sovereignty.[27] The Likud was headlining its election propaganda at the time with the slogan "Peres will divide Jerusalem." Peres feared that if the document leaked, it would validate the Likud's arguments and spoil his chances of victory. But beyond his concerns for the election results, he was most profoundly appalled to discover that his deputy and disciple had dared to make such a sensitive move behind his back.

Shortly after Peres learned of this document's existence, we received a copy of a letter sent by Palestinian leader Nabil Shaath[28] to a friend in Paris: John Whitbeck, an international lawyer who was advising the Palestinian negotiating team. Shaath invited Whitbeck to his wedding and added, "I must add that your ideas on Jerusalem 'sharing' have now become our gospel, they were the centrepiece of the very 'secret' negotiations on permanent status with Yossi Beilin."

I stormed into Yossi's office angrily and told him there was no reason to think the letter would not leak. "You've just ruined Peres's chances of winning the elections with your own bare hands," I said. Yossi, ever composed, dismissed my concerns.

I spoke to Peres often about his painful partnership with his beloved protégé. I also spoke to Yossi, to explain why Peres was so offended. Yossi was smart enough and had spent long enough with Peres to know what hurt him even without my explaining. But he had decided to be independent, come what may. By picking fights with Peres, Yossi distinguished himself from his mentor and built his own political personality. I asked Peres on countless occasions to invite Yossi for an honest heart-to-heart and tell him what was on his mind. "You have so much in common," I said. "One heart-to-heart and everything will go back to the way it was."

"I don't like the kind of heart-to-heart you're proposing," Peres replied grudgingly. "There's no benefit, and I'm not even convinced we need to wind the clocks back. I'm not sure it's possible. Yossi has his own agenda."

Despite these harsh remarks, Yossi continued coming to our regular weekly meetings for years. Peres valued Yossi's wisdom and loved him like a son. He craved hearing Yossi's analysis and devoured it. He always directed his first question to Yossi, and once when Yossi was abroad and missed a meeting, Peres could not hide that something was amiss and he asked anxiously, "Does anyone know what happened to Yossi?"

Raucous Inside Jokes

The atmosphere in Peres's inner circle of advisors was generally amicable. Peres himself contributed to that, in both the independence he gave his staff and his tolerance of their mistakes, and in his ability to quickly regain his composure when he got angry, accepting and even adapting to criticism. We dissipated the tension, and sometimes Peres's fury, with raucous inside jokes. We staged enactments of imaginary conversations between Peres and Arafat: Uri Savir did an excellent imitation of the Palestinian leader while I put on Peres. The topics of our conversations veered wildly away from hot-button political issues, often touching on sensitive and intimate subjects.

Peres knew that we used to mimic him. Sometimes when I was tired, I spoke to him on the phone and answered in his voice. Once Peres even believed that the line was faulty and he was hearing himself speak. In his own moments of mischief, he asked me to speak to some party members in his voice: "That way you'll spare me the torture." There was also an incident in which he made some quite hateful remarks in a bitter phone call with a reporter. If published, they would likely have caused a political crisis. The reporter was initially shocked by Peres's remarks but ultimately concluded that he did not have a story because "it was Avi having a laugh and imitating Peres." Or consider the naughty notes we passed each other around the negotiating table. Sometimes we scribbled lewd rhymes, which I found the courage to show Peres only years later. I have kept the embarrassing verses I scrawled in one of the duller discussions with the Palestinians while Peres went off on one of his rambling, visionary monologues about a "comprehensive peace, dilution of hostile forces, and a transnational regional economy":

> One magical night, when passions were high,
> The girl dropped her clothes and to Shimon did sigh:
> "Come here, I'm so hot for you, my big guy."
>
> Shimon was staring, his eyes at full thrust,
> And he quickly extracted his baton of lust.
> "Grab my dilution and peace by the spade,
> Take comprehensive bilateral trade!"
>
> The girl gave a gasp, and here's what she said:
> "His vision is great, but he's lousy in bed."

The Palestinians could not understand why Peres's advisors kept cracking up while their boss was serenading Arafat with his vision of transforming Gaza into the Palestinian Singapore.

I Tried Fishing Once, the Boredom Drove Me Mad

Peres used to unwind mainly by working. One thing he liked doing for relaxation was to take to the waves. Whenever the opportunity arose, he asked to sail on a luxury yacht and dine to his heart's content on forbidden seafood. Before one visit to Athens, I asked our ambassador to reach out to a yacht owner we knew to see whether he would let us sail with him. One previous time on his yacht, he had amazed us by frying tiny sardines, which Peres gobbled down from head to tail with the help of a bottle of local Ouzo. But the ambassador returned with bad news: this time, the yacht owner was inviting us to his house. He was hosting an event with the Greek songwriter Mikis Theodorakis and wanted to ask Peres to recommend to the Nobel Committee to award him a Nobel Prize. I asked the ambassador to explain to our host that the appropriate forum for such a request was not his home but the deck of his yacht. And so we set sail with Theodorakis, but not before I warned Peres that on absolutely no condition could he commit to sending a letter of recommendation. "If you do so, you'll be accused of corruption: a letter of recommendation to the Nobel Committee for sardines and a yacht." I was relieved to learn that Peres was not blown away by Theodorakis anyway.

But even a pleasure cruise should not last too long: it would be a pity to waste valuable work days. Peres never understood why his staff longed to go on holiday. "I'm not interested in a vacation," he once said firmly. "I tried fishing once and the boredom drove me mad." I described to him the stress that our work was causing our wives and children. "It's women's nature to always keep us men apologising and explaining ourselves," Peres replied. "Nothing will help. Nothing you do can change this. Children don't need parents. Let them grow up by themselves and trust everything will work itself out. You don't need to keep explaining to your children that they can't cope in the world without endless parental attention."

Figure 6 Relaxing on a boat on Lake Como, September 9, 2009. (Photo: Ido Sharir, 2009)

Indeed, Peres was astonished when I told him that Uri Savir had gone on holiday with his family to the United States. I explained that Uri's family had hardly seen him for months. "Families are not a normal thing," Peres replied. "Look at Bedouin children. Nobody watches them, running around the tent without much supervision. They never cry and they always look happy."

Complicated Relations with the Media

It was no coincidence that the people who were closest to Peres began their careers with him as his spokespeople. Just like Yossi Beilin, Uri Savir, and me. I got the feeling that I had passed the test as early as my first trip abroad with him. Peres had given a speech in Italy and spoke in favor of elections in the West Bank and Gaza Strip. "Let the Palestinians turn from bullets to ballots," he had said. The next morning Peres read in the Hebrew press that he had said in Italy that the Palestinians should choose the rule of the majority [*shilton ha-rov*] over the rule of the gun [*shilton ha-roveh*]. He asked whether I had translated his remarks, and when I admitted that I had, he said, "Pretty good, actually."

The media serves to mediate between the public and its elected officials. Politicians use the media to learn what their voters want and to try to win their affections. Public support is the oxygen of political life. As such, the media constitutes a vital tool in any politician's arsenal, and any political or diplomatic strategy has to take them into account. If you place a secret intelligence briefing, the morning paper, and a fresh public opinion poll on a minister's desk, he will read them in reverse order.

Peres's romance with the media was the tale of a miserable partnership. Peres needed recognition, love, attention. Who among does not? But Peres's needs were insatiable. I used to tell him in jest that in my opinion, as his spokesman, the press stopped performing its democratic function every morning it failed to cover him, forgot to publish his thoughts, or declined to print his picture. Peres used to reply with a smile, but he still believed that the media was short-changing him and did not understand the profundity of his ideas—because they were ignorant.

In Peres's opinion, reporters were covering unimportant matters and had been charmed by his political rivals' brutishness and military résumés. Peres never skipped a single article. Whenever he read a piece he liked, he lavished the writer with superlatives—"brilliant," "intelligent," "brave." But whenever he was dissatisfied with an article, he was not averse to slamming it in the harshest terms—"sold out to the right," "narcissistic," "megalomaniac." Peres complained that the Israeli press was self-obsessed, got carried away with sensationalism, and had no respect for the country's leadership. He had a good reason for remaining loyal to the gossip columnist Mira Avrech, and he loved her method of journalism—of always speaking kindly about him. Peres loved watching his own interviews on TV. He looked straight into the screen, roared angrily at anyone who dared to disturb him, and nodded at himself in agreement, egging himself on. He was happy to hear compliments about his own gripping performances. Sometimes, when I wanted to pry him away from the screen, I told him, "Shimon, did you know people say you look clearer on TV than in real life?"

Peres's relationship with the media involved a complicated symbiosis. They both needed each other, that's for sure, but Peres's need for the media went far beyond the practical requirement of a public figure for a line of communication with the public. The press was not just a mediator or another tool in his toolbox. It was his partner. A partner that disobeyed him and cheated on him, but whose allure increased the more it spurned him. Peres chased it with devotion but would never admit it. He once declared, "The press is not important to me, I'm not interested in headlines," and in the same breath asked me whether I had seen what was written at the bottom of page 19 of the low-circulation paper *Al Hamishmar*.

The press was not indifferent to Peres and reacted to his attempts at courtship. It served as a mirror for him, and he was captivated. Every newspaper edition and news broadcast offered a new chance for excitement. Peres knew how to satisfy the media's insatiable appetite for new stories, drama, and scandal. Reporters either loved or hated him, almost always with an intensity that exceeded what was expected from professional and impartial journalists. It follows, therefore, that Peres's media advisor was also his couples counsellor. I learned that Peres had difficulty controlling his emotions when he came face-to-face with his wayward media partner. It was hard to keep him disciplined. Journalists knew that Peres was his best when he was angry. The wiser ones, of course, knew how to deliberately wind him up.

But Peres did not need such provocations to get himself into trouble. He was well aware that the modern media needed short and sharp sound bites, the powerful slogans that strongly affect the sensitivities of viewers and listeners. So he did not restrict himself to meek and cautious statements and tended to get carried away with his own rhetoric. When he was invited as Israel's foreign minister to a ceremony in 1994 marking 40 years since the installation of the Japanese Peace Bell at the United Nations, it was clear to us all that this would be a difficult story to sell to the press. But Peres, given the honor of ringing the bell, caused a media firestorm. He declared that there had been two holocausts in the Second World War: the Jewish Holocaust, and a Japanese holocaust in Hiroshima and Nagasaki. Peres propelled a low-key ceremony into the media's agenda. He was bitterly attacked for comparing the Holocaust to the dropping of two atomic bombs on Japan. The saving grace of media screw-ups, however, is that the newspapers will always print a new edition in the morning, and no story has a long shelf life. Not even the ones you would rather forget.

The Audience at Home

Like most politicians, Peres did not credit his voters with terribly much intelligence. Image and strategy consultants also rely on working assumptions that are hardly complimentary toward the quality of voters' judgment. If you want to look like a real man in a photo, smoke Marlboro cigarettes. And if a popular football player like Eyal Berkovic is voting for you as prime minister, get a photo with him, pronto. In politics, like marketing, marketers would like to believe that Berkovic's fans are sufficiently dim-witted to believe that being able to perform deft double-pass on the way to the goal also makes one an authority on politics.

I discovered that it was no easy task in Israel to find football players who supported the Labour Party. Several such attempts were made in the 1996 elections. I spoke by phone with Haim Revivo. The football star surprised me, saying that he would vote for Peres for prime minister—but was unfortunately unavailable for a joint photograph. He was in a rush to join a team training session in Spain. Eyal Berkovic, however, agreed to come to Jerusalem for a photo op. This made me happy for two reasons. My heavy workload had been keeping me away from home, and now I had the chance for a gesture of fatherly love. My youngest son, Eliav, was a big fan of Berkovic's team, Maccabi Haifa. I arranged for my son to come to the prime minister's office to see his idol up close, and eight-year-old Eliav ran into position wearing his team's kit. He was extremely excited to be given a double embrace—Berkovic on his right, Peres on his left. The cameras snapped away, and I brought him a large framed photo the next day memorializing that exciting hug.

I always liked presenting this photograph in the opening lessons of the courses I taught on the nexus between politics and media. Next to it I showed another photo— of President Clinton standing in front of Yitzhak Rabin's grave, holding the hand of Rabin's widow, Leah. I promised my students that whoever spotted what the two pictures had in common would get a pass from attending future lessons. Nobody was

Figure 7 My youngest son, Eliav, asked for Peres to step out of the shot (1996). (Photo: Avi Ohayon, GPO, 1996)

able to guess that in both cases, I was presented with the same demand: to remove Peres from the picture.

For his part, Eliav asked nicely. "Daddy," he inquired hesitantly when I gave him the photo, "would you be offended if I asked you to get the photographer to crop Peres out of the photo?" The demand from Mort Engelberg, meanwhile, was tougher and unequivocal: "Nobody but Clinton and Leah Rabin will enter my frame." Engelberg was heading the American advance team that was in Israel to prepare Clinton's visit in March 1996. As the director of the Prime Minister's Office, I was his opposite number.

The wave of deadly terror attacks at the start of 1996 had eroded Peres's lead over his rival, Benjamin Netanyahu. We were looking for ways to boost Peres's stock ahead of the upcoming elections, and Yossi Beilin and I came to one meeting with the exact same idea: an international counterterrorism conference. We would stage a huge media event with world leaders presenting a united front against terrorism, mandating a joint plan to fight it, and, most importantly, showing Israelis that they were not alone in their fight. That the world stood with them and with Shimon Peres.

Peres gave the idea his approval. He spoke with Jordan's Crown Prince Hassan and secured his support. He then called President Clinton, graciously relinquished the credit, and told him that Prince Hassan had suggested holding a regional counterterrorism conference. "I think it's an excellent idea," Peres said. "Could you come, even for a few hours, and chair the conference? The message will be: stop terrorism and continue with peace." Peres suggested that the event be held on an US Navy vessel. "It would be a dramatic gathering. We should bring as many Arabs as we can. Even Saudi Arabia's Prince Bandar could come if it's on an American ship." The idea of having the conference aboard an American ship was dropped and replaced with Sharm el-Sheikh.[29] We settled with President Clinton's staff that at the end of the event, Peres would board Air Force One and they would fly to Israel together. Clinton's visit was also, as far as we were concerned, part of the effort to save Peres's campaign and raise Israeli morale.

I learned that the right idea at the right time can lead to an impressive media event. The media is thirsty for drama, and once there is momentum toward a certain event, world leaders find it difficult not get swept up in it. The production of such events is always laden with difficulties and unexpected hiccups. Consider, for example, President Ezer Weizman's request to join our flight to Sharm el-Sheikh—a request that we had to reject. Protocol requires that the president be given precedence in any meeting, but the whole point of the event was to place Peres center-stage.

A furious Weizman exacted revenge. He refused to welcome his American counterpart on the runway at Ben-Gurion Airport, insisting on having the welcoming ceremony in the Rose Park in Jerusalem. But we arranged for an honor guard on the runway regardless. I was told that the minister Moshe Shahal, who had remained in Israel as acting prime minister in Peres's absence, would likely demand to act out his role till the last second, and stride together with Peres and Clinton in front of the rows of soldiers standing to attention. I demanded that the protocol department insist, "He must not be allowed to walk with them. Settle with him on a handshake when the dignitaries get off the plane."

At that moment, hungry for ceremonies and parades, I remembered the fierce battles I waged at school against the commemoration of Memorial Day with a quasi-military parade by Gadna—the army's pre-military training program for high-school students. I refused to take part in the ceremony because I thought it looked fascist. "The sight of students in khaki uniforms marching left-right left-right is a sign of an anti-democratic education," I told Yitzhak Shapira, the stunned headmaster. "You're turning individuals into obedient sheep, responding like house-trained animals to stupid orders: stand at ease, stand at attention!" Years later, as a media advisor, I quite wanted more "at ease, at attention" ceremonies.

A Tear Down His Cheek

I soon discovered that Mort Engelberg, the head of the American advance team, was a Hollywood movie producer. Having directed films with Burt Reynolds and Steve McQueen, he was now directing a production with President Clinton. He was determined to script a presidential visit that would include a series of media events, each staged in such a way that viewers in the United States would discover more and more exciting layers of Clinton's personality and leadership. As for the existence of Shimon Peres, he almost completely failed to take that into account.

I lost my temper at one point and told Mr. Engelberg in undiplomatic language that I thought he had completely failed to understand the purpose of his president's visit to the Middle East: to help Peres win the upcoming elections. I complained directly to the White House, and I was promised that Engelberg would be asked to be more understanding of my requests. The producer did indeed tone down his demands, but he remained absolutely unwilling to compromise on his conditions for the president's visit to Rabin's grave.

It was one of the toughest negotiations I had ever conducted. Every item on the president's itinerary was the subject of an argument. Engelberg fought tooth-and-nail, and he had the upper hand in the battle over the composition of the photograph at Rabin's grave. For him, every element of the visit had to be dramatized in a way that would convey a sharp and clear message to American viewers. The angle of the shot and the components in the picture could not be left to chance. The photo of Clinton holding Leah Rabin's hand in front of the grave had to convey a message about a compassionate and sensitive president. A tear down his cheek would be an added bonus, but what use would it be if other figures were tacked onto the message? Peres, Rabin's children, Jerusalem mayor Ehud Olmert—they were all background noise that would have made it difficult for viewers to simply absorb the message that Engelberg had crafted for Clinton.

I was profoundly impressed by this American's uncompromising professionalism. I remembered how it had been almost impossible at the Foreign Ministry to get a picture of Peres with any of the high-profile guests who visited him without having the grinning face of a ministry driver poke into the shot.

It was no use explaining that Peres was the prime minister of Israel, Rabin's partner, or suchlike. Engelberg's expertise as a Hollywood professional was in transmitting simple messages. In fact, this was also what my son Eliav understood instinctively without being a professional. He wanted to impress his friends with a picture with Berkovic. Peres's presence in the photo complicated the message, drew attention to itself, and required explanations. It would have been better without him.

Viewers at home, of course, see the final product. They are generally not privy to the considerations and manipulations behind the scenes. But such considerations always exist. For example, I insisted to Engelberg that Clinton not address the Knesset; I wanted him to appear in front of high school students in Tel Aviv instead. Why? The reason, of course, was far from noble. If Clinton had given a speech in the Knesset, custom dictated that the head of the opposition be permitted to give his own remarks. Why give the stage to Netanyahu?

Media vs. Health Considerations

My career with Peres could have been very short. My dedication to my job as his media advisor nearly led me to gamble with life. After the 1988 elections, Peres found himself finance minister in a national unity government led by Yitzhak Shamir. Peres loaned me from the Foreign Ministry to serve as his spokesman.

In October 1989, I accompanied Peres on a tour of the Galilee; in the afternoon, during a meeting with local Arabs, I noticed that his coffee was shaking in his hand. His face turned white and he started speaking slowly. I begged him to wrap up. He dismissed me and said everything was fine. I refused to accept his stubborn insistence not to acknowledge pain or illness. I asked the security guards to prepare for an evacuation to the nearest hospital. I knew that the situation was serious when Peres finally gave in to my supplications and agreed to cut the visit short. We rushed to the hospital in Afula. Peres sat on the edge of his car seat, shrunken and shuddering. To my surprise he told me, "I feel unwell, touch my forehead, see if I've got a temperature." I put my hand on his burning forehead to gauge his temperature and perhaps also to give him some encouragement. It was an intimate and unusual moment in our fresh relationship.

Peres was diagnosed at the hospital with an acute internal inflammation. Tucked up in a hospital bed and connected to a drip and a catheter, Peres had suddenly lost his aura of leadership, transformed into a normal human being. I took up residence in the hospital and took care of his wellbeing, but I also repeated to myself over and over: *don't forget, you're his media advisor. The public must not find out that Peres had succumbed to illness—he is immune to such forces of nature.* But still I felt I had to take advantage of his pitiful state to earn some public affection. Even the nastiest journalist would steer clear of bad-mouthing a sick man. The dead tend to receive positive coverage from the press, and the seriously ill are only one rung below. If you want to write about them, you have certain obligations—like writing the first draft of an obituary.

I learned that shortly after President Ronald Reagan was shot by a would-be assassin, his image consultants debated how best to exploit the event to boost his popularity. I had great respect for the professionalism of American media advisors and had eagerly read about how they maneuvered to control the media agenda. I learned how they designed an impressive itinerary for the president by carefully planning the desired headlines and accompanying pictures; how they staged dramatic media events to play with the public's emotions and keep them glued to the screen.

What worked in Washington should also have worked in Afula, I thought. I briefed reporters on how Peres was coping bravely with his illness and responding with humor, and I described the sheer numbers of people who had got in touch from all around the country and the world. They had all wished Peres a speedy recovery and were concerned for his wellbeing—from the most powerful people in the world to ordinary citizens. I spun them yarns about a whole bounty of voodoo remedies that concerned citizens had left at Peres's door—even a "concoction of crushed snake scales." The reporters scribbled everything down eagerly and the papers printed it.

The press photographers who crowded the corridor of the urology department kept on pressing for a chance to take a picture of Peres. I was adamant to stop that happening. Peres looked really bad in his hospital gown. The tubes sticking in and out of him hardly added to his beauty. I made the hospital directors swear that they would not let any reporters or photographers enter Peres's room without my approval. It was not every day that a hospital in Afula welcomed a celebrity like Peres. I received their full cooperation and I was happy to learn that the doctors were quick to digest the media significance of treating such a special patient.

But Peres's fever remained high. He did not seem to be responding to the medication. I updated him about the death from cancer of the artist and author Dahn Ben-Amotz.[30] The two had studied together at the agricultural school in Ben Shemen. I drafted a letter of condolence in Peres's name: "In the difficult months when he was fighting for his life, we all prayed for his wellbeing, we couldn't resist his sense of humour, and now we stop breathing and shed a heavy tear over this heartbreaking end, from which there was no escape." Peres first read the condolence letter that I had penned when it was published in the paper. That was how we did things in the minister's office. Whenever Peres was told that someone had died, he instructed, "So send my congratulations." And whenever there was a wedding or bar mitzvah, he requested, "So send my condolences." This time he read the lofty words published in his name with satisfaction. He was so feverish that he was certain he had written them himself, and he even brought the article to my attention with evident pride: "Have you seen yet what I wrote about Dahn Ben-Amotz?"

The Peres family's number one concern was his wellbeing, and in the absence of an improvement in his condition, they asked that he be transferred to Tel Hashomer Hospital near Tel Aviv. That way he could be treated in a more reputable medical institution and closer to home. I asked Peres to hold back on giving an answer. His family left and I stayed with him. "Shimon," I said firmly,

you must not be transferred to Tel Hashomer. People will say you're in critical condition, and even worse, they'll say the hospital in Afula is good enough for residents of the Jezreel Valley and the Galilee but not good enough for Shimon Peres. The public's affection for you is growing thanks to your illness. We mustn't ruin this achievement with a gross public relations mistake.

Peres thought for a moment and accepted my advice.

It was a Friday. I decided to get some fresh air at my mother's home in Haifa. During our Friday night meal the hospital called me and one of the doctors told me in an anxious voice, "Avi, Peres's condition has deteriorated in the last few hours. We know how sensitive you are to the media implications of every development and we wanted to talk to you before we move him to the emergency care ward."

I felt I was about to need emergency care myself. "Have you lost your minds? Give him whatever medical care he needs. Don't start thinking about public relations!" I was racing back to Afula within seconds, unable to shake off the disturbing thought that doctors at Tel Hashomer would have already resuscitated Peres, and I might have just sacrificed his life to promote his image.

Fortunately, Peres recovered. His fever slowly dropped. It was time to let the public see that he had overcome his illness. I called Hananiya Herman, our traveling photographer, and told him that I hoped his camera would be able to show the public Peres looking energetic and refreshed. We seated Peres on a chair next to his wife Sonia, making sure to conceal the catheter that he was still connected to with a blanket, as he had expressly demanded. "Just don't let them take a picture of that bloody tube," he said angrily. Suddenly a family friend, the singer Nisim Garame, entered the room and joined the photo. I tried to intervene and a commotion broke out. A few photographers managed to barge into the room. The cameras snapped away.

I could not fall asleep that night. I kept replaying nightmare scenarios in my mind, in which the catheter could be seen in the newspaper. The picture appeared in its full glory in the Friday supplement of *Yediot Aharonot*. To my horror, it was not the photo we had staged, but one taken amid the commotion. And yes, you could indeed make out that infernal catheter. How could I look Peres in the face? But he didn't say a word, and neither did anyone else. Out of hundreds of thousands of readers, I must have been the only one who noticed that loathsome tube. I was saved.

The "Ironing Maid" Document

Working with the press can give you a feeling of immense power, which is intoxicating. A short conversation with a reporter can produce a headline, which in turn often produces a public and political stir. If working in diplomacy trains you to exercise discretion and consider every word, then working with the press requires you to act quickly. Events develop at a dizzying speed, deadlines are short, and if you tarry too long, the moment is lost. It is easy to make mistakes and hard to repair the damage.

I had personal experience of this contradiction between diplomacy and press relations when I was invited for questioning as part of the process leading to my appointment as Foreign Ministry director-general. It was made clear to me that I would be asked whether I had ever transferred secret material to people who were not authorized to hold it. "Of course I have," I answered the stunned interviewer. "That's my job as a spokesman. When I join the foreign minister in a meeting with the president of the United States, I brief reporters from the same document that I cable simultaneously to the prime minister with a top-secret classification." I was asked whether the foreign minister approves which sections I may release to the media from the same telegram. "The foreign minister doesn't have time for that and he trusts me," I replied. Luckily for me, the interviewers regained their composure, developed an understanding for my position, and chose not to waste their time with questions that were relevant for diplomats but not spokespeople who are in constant touch with journalists.

I learned about the power of media storms, and the damage they can do, as soon as I started working with Peres. Following the 1988 elections, Peres was appointed finance minister. *Haaretz* was leaked Peres's "list of demands" in preparation for his new role. Among them: "an ironing maid."

In reality, the paper had obtained a copy of an administrative document from Peres's time at the Foreign Ministry, which listed the minister's requirements for his official residence. The title "ironing maid," given to one of his housemaids, did not match the housemaid's actual work. It seems to have more accurately reflected the lifestyle of Foreign Ministry employees used to serving in Asia and Africa, where it was normal to employ staff as chefs, washerwomen, ironing maids, and so forth. Peres and Sonia lived modestly. But the "ironing maid" document had a powerful effect in the media. Peres was depicted as the lord of a manor who employed an ironing maid, and it caused tangible damage to his reputation.

The lesson of the "ironing maid" remained seared in my mind like a third-degree burn. In later years, I fought against anything that might have given rise to another "ironing maid document." I was so concerned that when Peres became prime minister, I refused to allow a satellite phone to be installed on his plane. I thought the price looked too high and I feared public criticism. It was a baseless decision, but it illustrates how traumatic media scandals can be.

Journalists love stories about the profligacy of public officials. As a graduate of the "ironing maid" affair, I exploited this fact to exact revenge on Peres's political enemies. When Economy Minister Shimon Shetreet, in a moment of hyperactivity, organized a delegation of businesspeople to Kazakhstan and so rudely encroached on the Foreign Ministry's turf, he had to be deterred. Peres made this demand in a difficult conversation with Rabin,[31] and I threw in a malicious leak to the press from an administrative cable in which Minister Shetreet's aide innocently asked one of our embassies to book the minister a comfortable suite. No minister likes to see a report revealing that he "insists on sleeping in a luxury suite."

Sometimes I resisted the temptation and held back. One Friday night, during a conference in a European country, a friend invited me to spend the evening in a local nightclub. Taking turns to perform on the small stage were magicians, jugglers, and strippers. An Israeli minister was hugely enjoying himself dining at the table closest to the stage. It was Shabbat, the place was not kosher, and naked ladies were exposing their breasts right in front of an Israeli minister's eyes—what a juicy story! But I decided to forgive him. To exercise some gentlemanly solidarity and keep his secret safe.

Hiding Things from the Media

Sometimes an advisor's task is to keep the media away from the political action. The exposure of a delicate development can provoke opposition and create enemies who might try to torpedo it. Foreign Minister Abba Eban once argued that between the public's right to know everything immediately and its right to enjoy the fruits of a peace agreement that requires clandestine contacts, the latter right triumphs.[32] When an agreement is reached, the achievements and concessions can be presented in a single package for the voters to judge. It would not be fair to put an agreement on trial and judge it when only a single part of it has been leaked.

This argument sounds reasonable, but reality makes the moral dilemma even more acute. When Ehud Barak put Israel's willingness to divide Jerusalem on the negotiating table at Camp David, and when Rabin gave Clinton the "deposit" indicating Israel's willingness to withdraw from the Golan Heights, they sealed the fate of Jerusalem and the Golan Heights to a certain extent. While no agreements were reached, and nothing was brought for the approval of the public or the Knesset, failed negotiations have residual consequences of their own for the content of talks when they are renewed in future. That said, there is also no ignoring that for a government to submit its red lines for the public's prior approval would eliminate its bargaining power and would likely produce a less convenient agreement.

This ethical dilemma, therefore, will always remain, and governments will continue concealing the substance and sometimes even the existence of negotiations. Take the negotiations in Oslo. The secret partners on both sides proceeded from a clear assumption: an early leak would kill off the talks. So what helped to keep the talks secret? I can speak mostly for the Israeli side, but I was told by Norwegian Foreign Minister Johan Jørgen Holst that Arafat had prided himself on his cunning in concealing these contacts from the reporters who were sniffing around for scoops.

Although it was clear from the beginning that we were dealing with a process of historic importance, the Oslo negotiators subordinated their urge to take credit for the endeavor to their sense of historic responsibility, which required them to preserve a spirit of teamwork and to work in harmony. No juicy stories about infighting or intrigue surrounding the foreign minister appeared in the press at the time. There was great care not to drop hints that would lead inquisitive journalists to rummage around on the matter. We refrained from using the Foreign Ministry's communications system and its telegrams, because we knew from personal experience that a top-secret classification is no guarantee that the contents will not be leaked. In fact, Peres used to joke that if we labeled a document "unclassified," we would minimize the temptation to leak it. True to this backward logic, we used regular telephones and unprotected fax systems and employed code names. I used to personally photocopy and print documents concerning the developments. Very few people were in on the secret, fewer than a dozen on the Israeli side. This extreme compartmentalization reduced the chances that the secret might leak but it came at a price: fewer minds were in on the process, so it was never going to be of the optimal quality.

Rabin did not let his own people in on the secret, did not keep an organized archive of the talks (as far as I know), and generally preferred giving Peres back his drafts and reports. They were the only two present in their most fateful discussions, which took place shrouded in mystery. I used to prepare Peres a list of talking points ahead of these meetings and wrote down his reports of the conversations when he returned. The "Rabin-Peres Talks" file was kept in a heavy safe in my office, and I did not share the code with anyone. We maintained strict discipline regarding Rabin for the sake of industrial peace. We refrained from publicizing the disagreements between Peres and Rabin, and we did not fan media attention with stories of the friction between them. They discussed their clashes in their joint meetings. Sometimes Giora Eini, the director of the Tel Aviv Literature and Art Foundation, helped to smooth things out. Eini, with his suit and long hair, who always avoided the glare of the media, had earned the trust of most of the leaders of the Labour Party. Whenever disputes arose, he mediated well between the various sides, including between Peres and Rabin.

Peres understood that he had to grit his teeth and hold back from retaliating against the blows he sustained. At times of tension between him and Rabin, we in the office took extra care in preparing his public appearances and interviews. We wrote down the expected questions and recommended answers in advance in order to save him from any outward expressions of anger at Rabin.

The iron discipline we enforced for the sake of industrial peace strengthened the perception that Peres had been pushed aside as the "minister for cocktails." The media depicted him as having a role limited to discussions with neighboring countries (the multilateral negotiations), while having no involvement in the truly meaningful talks with the Jordanian–Palestinian delegation (the bilateral negotiations). Peres found it difficult to exercise self-restraint and hold himself back. And indeed, when he was asked on the radio about his estrangement from the peace process, he could not contain his frustration and replied, "When the accounts are added up in future, there will be a different assessment of the contribution made by the Foreign Ministry."[33] His team maintained ironclad tactical discipline in not alerting the media to their failure to pick up on this slip of the tongue.

Reporters concluded that there were no scoops to be picked up around Peres. They believed that he was uninvolved in the truly important matters. Little wonder that they chose not to join his trips abroad. That enabled us to travel to Oslo and initial the accord without a traveling press pack and with total freedom from the media.

The journalist Akiva Eldar explained in *Haaretz* why there was nothing to look for around Peres. "The negotiations are taking place at the table," he wrote, "and there is no room for clandestine contacts underneath the table, where Peres found fertile ground for his problematic activities in the past."[34] His colleague Gideon Samet slammed Peres: "The foreign minister has been chickening out for months. How long does he intend to remain silent, and when will he initiate something? ... What is he waiting for?"[35] The journalists fell asleep on the job and we, of course, helped to tuck them into bed. Not only did they presume that Rabin would not allow his foreign minister to handle sensitive briefs, they also instinctively viewed direct talks with the PLO as a taboo and not a practical diplomatic option.

The task of keeping Oslo a secret confronted me with classic questions of professional ethics. Was I allowed to lead journalists astray if they posed me a straight question? A conventional way out is to adopt a standard answer when faced with questions about existent or non-existent secret contacts. We say: "As a matter of principle, we do not respond to questions about secret political contacts." But in the dialogue between the government and the press, especially in Israel, such an answer immediately elicits journalists' suspicions that something is going on. Some will even see such an answer as confirming a rumor's veracity. If a government spokesperson were asked whether Israel has secret contacts with Hamas or Iran and replied, "We don't answer such questions," that response would likely provoke widespread surprise and perhaps even complications with the United States.

On the day of the secret signing in Oslo, I received a call from the journalist Shimon Shiffer. He said he had information that on our previous stop in Sweden we had met PLO officials. "That is completely unfounded," I replied. And indeed, we had not met any PLO officials in Sweden. Instead we had spent the whole night on the line with them in Tunis, with Norwegian mediation. This was a weak argument that hardly justified my response to the reporter, and certainly did not completely satisfy the public's right to know.

Between these two evils—failing to tell the truth to a reporter versus jeopardizing the agreement that was about to be signed with the PLO—I obviously preferred not to jeopardize the agreement. But the dilemma kept on cropping up, and it is not easy to lie to everyone with a straight face. For some cool-headed politicians, the media is just another tool in their available toolbox, and their relationships with journalists are instrumental; but others have a more complicated approach and find the tension between their principles and the political-media reality to be more fraught. A week before the secret signing in Oslo, for example, Rabin was asked on TV[36] about the possibility of a future meeting between him and PLO leaders and maybe even Arafat himself. "Forget about it," he answered the interviewer, Ya'akov Ahimeir. "Certainly not in the foreseeable future."

Ahimeir doubled down: "Sorry, could it happen in the three years you've got left in office?"

Rabin: "I hope not."

Those who were listening closely could sense that Rabin had not completely ruled out this option. Experienced journalists can sometimes trip up politicians who find it difficult to betray the truth.

Media Manipulations

In order to keep the Oslo channel clandestine, we also took more sophisticated steps to send the media on a wild goose chase and keep their eyes off the prize. For a good example, consider a headline that appeared in the *Hadashot* newspaper:[37] "The Secret Mediator between Israel and the PLO: A Canadian Jew." The journalist Amnon Barzilai reported that Peres had persuaded Rabin to use the services of a Canadian Jew called Steve Cohen. Peres denied the report, but according to Barzilai, that denial caused some embarrassment among Peres's own staff. "Some of Peres's people laughed and suggested not to take the denial seriously." In other words, Peres's people had advised the reporter to ignore Peres's own denial. Why? In my assessment, this was a leak that was intended to draw fire away from its real target in Oslo and to dispatch the press to less dangerous hunting grounds. I told the newspaper's editor, Yoel Esteron, that the report was untrue. "We were given the story by a source who's higher up than you," he replied with total confidence. "There are probably things you don't know either." Eventually, someone from the *Hadashot* paper told me who the source was, indeed higher up than me. I deduced that the same cunning source had sent the newspaper looking for news far from where it was actually happening.

Two and a half months before the signing of the agreement in Oslo, Pinhas Inbari, the Middle East correspondent at *Al Hamishmar*, reported:[38]

> Foreign Ministry officials have had unofficial contacts with the Abu Mazen [Mahmoud Abbas] group in the PLO … Sources downplayed the significance of these meetings, noting that Prime Minister Yitzhak Rabin is aware of them but continues to give top priority to the negotiations in Washington. The head of the Palestinian delegation [in Washington], Haidar Abdel-Shafi, confirmed yesterday that there had been contacts between Israel and PLO officials in Vienna and Washington, but stressed that they were not an alternative channel to the talks in Washington but rather a Palestinian attempt to better understand Israel's positions.

The scoop, which should have been explosive, failed to make a tangible impact or receive the coverage it deserved. Perhaps because it was published in a paper that the media elite considered unimportant.

There is an enormous temptation to plant lies and half-truths in the press, which cannot always be excused on the grounds of "defending the public's right to enjoy a peace accord." Politicians and government officials make things up to promote themselves and the prestige of their organizations. They make things up to damage their competitors and to be able to maneuver more freely in negotiations. There are endless reasons why. It can be difficult sometimes to guess where a lie was born. Such was the case when the big news broke that we intended to appoint television analyst Ehud Yaari as our ambassador in Cairo.

I'll admit it, I was behind that story—but why? Because I wanted to protect Ruth Yaron, who had been in my class in the Foreign Ministry cadet course and was the spokeswoman at our embassy in Washington at the time. When the media reported that the new ambassador in Washington, Zalman Shoval, was trying to tempt Ehud Yaari to come to replace her, I decided to try to torpedo his idea. I leaked the story that Yaari was going to be appointed to the role of ambassador in Egypt because I both thought it was not a bad idea and assumed that anyone who read in the paper that he was a candidate for ambassador in Cairo would not settle for the relatively junior role of spokesman in Washington.

Gossip columns are also an excellent forum for creative mistruths. As long as you don't offend anyone who is alive or set your opponents up against you, you can concoct the most fanciful stories your imagination allows. It is enough for there to be a small kernel of truth, and sometimes even that is unnecessary. A story needs to project your boss's most wonderful qualities: hard-working, good-humored, sporty, admired around the world, clever, and able to bring his country respect. Thus, for example, one paper published a figment of my imagination: that Peres had informed the organizers of a conference in Italy that he had to cut short his stay to return to Israel for the Rosh Hashanah prayers. The organizers had hastened to assure him that they would make sure a local rabbi came, but Peres explained that he needed a *minyan* (a group of ten Jewish men) to pray. After a brief stay, the organizers had returned with a list of ten Jews who could take part in the prayers. Peres had inspected the list and noticed that it ended with none other than Gaddafi's son, Saif al-Islam. The story was intended, of course, to convey a message about Peres's loyalty to the Jewish tradition and faith. I discovered that, in many cases, the temptation that journalists face to publish titillating stories trumps their obligation to check their veracity.

Media exposure is the lifeblood of any politician. Without it, they cannot enjoy recognition or public support. It is easy to become addicted to the media's charms and the power it puts in one's hands. Politicians who become obsessive about their image find that their behavior is increasingly driven by their quest for instant ratings. Long-term policy considerations become irrelevant. Peres had one big thing to his credit in this respect. He needed the media, worshipped it, and waited impatiently for the publication of the next article about him. But he still remained completely focused on his long-term goals, some of which he could not see being achieved in his own lifetime and would not be covered in tomorrow's paper. He knew that he would not reap the media credit, and yet he still remained faithful to his great and distant dream—the New Middle East.

3

The Big Dream: The New Middle East

One evening in April 1995, Peres hosted Palestinian Authority official Nabil Shaath at his official residence in Jerusalem. He had just had a meeting with the Israeli Hollywood producer Arnon Milchan. Peres took advantage of the opportunity to introduce the two, and Nabil Shaath could not hide his excitement the moment he understood that he was standing in front of the producer of *Pretty Woman*, the blockbuster starring Julia Roberts and Richard Gere. "I have watched your movie at least 20 times," Nabil confessed.

> I was going through a difficult time, my wife had just died. I was in the grips of depression, but your movie gave me hope. I watched it again and again and it renewed my faith in the future, in the possibility of finding love again, of finding a partner. That's the truth, and I have to thank you for it.

I knew Shaath, with his gleaming bald head and silver tongue, as a cunning negotiator, a skilled propagandist, and a man with a healthy sense of humor. In one of our meetings with Arafat, the Palestinian leader complained that the donor countries were demanding transparency about how their money was being used. Shaath explained his master's complaints with a broad grin: "We believe in transparency—but only from belly dancers."

Yet here we were, and I was surprised to see Shaath waxing lyrical and pouring his heart out as if we were in a couples therapy session. Milchan was also startled, and the pair practically fell into each other's arms. Peres looked at his guests with astonishment and particularly at Shaath, who was trying to tease out of Milchan whether the romance between Roberts and Gere had or hadn't spilled over from the screen into real life. His thoughts were clearly somewhere else. In another movie.

"Tell me, Arnon," said Peres, "was it difficult to make *Free Willy*, the one about the whale?"

Milchan, who had to cut off this gushing conversation with Shaath, answered honestly: "The production of the film was relatively cheap. All around the world, young people love stories about animals and identify strongly with them. It's a proven formula."

Peres looked like he had struck gold. "Look, Arnon," he said purposefully,

I want you to help us make a film that will promote the idea of the New Middle East to the youth of our region. Instead of Willy the whale, make it about a camel. That's more suitable for our region. We'll write a script about a camel who's walking to Mecca, gets into dangerous situations, has a really tough time, but eventually reaches his destination—and peace. Such a film would present an alternative to fundamentalism and give a push to democracy and peace, speaking in a language that the youth understand.

Milchan was evidently surprised by the responsibility placed on his shoulders and perhaps also by the ease with which Peres had jumped from Willy to the camel and from there straight to the New Middle East.

The Arabs Are People Like Everyone Else

For Peres, it was no great wonder that a Hollywood film pulled at the heartstrings of a Palestinian like Nabil Shaath just as it had excited cinemagoers in America and Europe. "I don't consider myself an expert in Arabs," he used to say, "but I understand people, and the Arabs are people like everyone else."

A flustered Milchan asked to have a word with me in private. He was in no rush to open auditions for Peres's camel. I did not try to encourage him. My years in academia had damaged my ability to get carried away with the excitement and apply myself to turning Peres's dreams into a reality at the pace required of someone working at his side. I told Milchan that Peres's working assumptions about the power of Hollywood to transform the Middle East required careful examination. Why had the *Rambo* series, screened throughout the Middle East, not brought democracy and human rights to the region yet? Was screening a combination of ostentatious Western wealth and sexual license helping to bequeath progress or to embolden conservative forces? Was exposing Arabs to Western values cultivating a resistance to fundamentalism or triggering feelings of jealousy and rejection? Milchan was grateful for the doubts I raised, quietly dropped Peres's camel, and went on to produce *Free Willy 2*.

Peres believed that no culture could ignore the power of the modern economy, globalization, groundbreaking media, and the internet. Unbound by any tradition of political correctness, he repeatedly told anyone who would listen that just like women all over the world, Arab village girls also wanted to look svelte in stylish jeans and were open to dieting. "These are different times," said Peres. "Young Arab men don't want to be *effendi* when they grow up, and young Arab women have no interest in looking fat and frumpy like their mothers. They want to look like skinny stars from Hollywood." Even a stubborn and violent Middle East would surely succumb to these forces. It was only a matter of time, and leaders like Peres could shorten how long it took. His mission was to present a coherent doctrine for the New Middle East, formulate a comprehensive agenda, and devote himself to getting people mentally prepared and kick-starting the necessary developments.

You could argue with Peres when it came to ideas, but there was no denying his power to generate momentum. After a meeting with the heads of several major technology companies, in which Peres tried to bring them on board for his plan to digitize the Middle East, I told him, "I think you're becoming increasingly dangerous. Your power to promote your ideas and recruit the whole world to back them—that's all down to you, not the ideas themselves. Today it's computerisation and tomorrow you might decide the order of the day is to open a computerised brothel in Caracas."

"It's a shame I don't have long to live," said Peres with a hearty laugh. "I'd have a few other tricks up my sleeve."[1]

Writing and Doing

With his signature diligence, Peres worked to put his worldview into words in his book *The New Middle East*. In January 1993, Peres informed Rabin that he intended to write the book with the assistance of the historian Professor Shlomo Ben-Ami. He told me that he had convinced Rabin to write the preface, on the grounds that doing so would squash any gossip about whether Rabin was comfortable with Peres's ideas. But Rabin did not deliver, and it soon became clear that Ben-Ami too was backing out. Peres's team assumed that Ben-Ami had been offended by Peres's decision to pass over him for the role of Foreign Ministry director-general, in favor of Uri Savir. Uri told me that he intended to advise Peres that *I should* help him with the writing; and with a great deal of insistence, I forced him to give me his word that he would not do so. I was not born with Peres's optimism and I was mortified by his willingness to skip the necessary research before declaring with such conviction where the region was heading.

I showed Peres Samuel Huntington's book *The Third Wave* (1991), which explores paths of democratization around the world.[2] I marked out for him Huntington's prophecies of doom concerning the prospects of democracy in the Islamic world. How difficult it was to separate religion from state in Muslim countries, how serious the contradictions were between Islam and democratic theory, and how weak the cultural and economic foundations were for a successful democratic experiment in the Arab world. Peres responded derisively and disdainfully brushed away any evidence that risked undermining his rosy view. I pointed out the internal contradiction in his approach. He wanted to harness the world media to breathe winds of change and democracy into the Arab world while at the same time striving to reach peace agreements with the region's tyrants. "You want to reach a peace agreement with Arab tyrants and also to destabilise their rule. Why should they cooperate with you?" In later years, I showed him an article in the *Economist*, which argued that without dictatorships in Egypt and Jordan, these countries would have faced serious difficulties in reaching peace agreements with Israel. In neither country did a majority of the public support the agreements. The article asked, correctly: If Jordan and Egypt were democracies and acted as the majority saw fit, could these peace agreements survive?

I slowly learned that Peres was not afraid of contradictions. His thinking was dialectical. He found it natural to flit between extremes and opposites. He pushed to bring his ideas into contact with reality, and his brain kept whirring in an effort to reach the truth. Whenever he was deep in thought, he remained faithful to the idea of the moment and preached it out of a deep internal conviction, totally devoted to seeing it through. But when he drew his own conclusions and switched to the next subject, which often contradicted the one before it, he channeled his powers of prophecy and worked with the same awe-inspiring dedication. Peres found it difficult to understand why some people struggled to keep up with him on these slalom slopes. I learned that his ability to act naturally in a reality full of contradictions was a source of strength for him—but also provoked resistance from parts of the public.

In the end, Peres tapped Arye Naor, formerly Menachem Begin's cabinet secretary, to help him write his book. And this feverishly concocted treatise became Peres's ideological calling card, the doctrinal text that brought together the logic behind his activities: the pursuit of bilateral peace agreements with our Arab neighbors, based on a solution to the Israeli–Palestinian conflict; the creation of frameworks for regional cooperation; and the promotion of forces of modernization, which would change the face of the Middle East while integrating Israel into it as an integral member of its family of nations. Peres believed that the Middle East stood at a historic crossroads. "One path leads to modernization, individual rights, separation of church and state, democracy, prosperity," he wrote. "The other leads to messianism, extremism, servitude, totalitarianism, irrationality, poverty. Which path will the region's nations choose?"[3]

If they took the path that Peres fantasized about, their final destination might be the emergence of a "regional community policy, with development of official institutions ... Western Europe is a shining example."[4]

Multilateral Negotiations

Peres's focus on the New Middle East became all the more important in light of his complicated relationship with Rabin. From the outset of his second time as prime minister in 1992, Rabin kept the bilateral negotiations with Israel's neighbors to himself and left Peres responsible for the multilateral track. This was the framework for the negotiations launched after the 1991 Madrid Conference,[5] which was supposed to deal with issues of regional significance: security, economy, refugees, water and the environment. These topics, and the planning for tangible regional projects, were discussed in working groups and occasional meetings of the respective steering committees. From Israel's perspective, the logic of pursuing a multilateral peace process had to do with its desire to gain recognition, normalization, and integration into the Middle East in return for the territorial price that it would be expected to pay in the bilateral tracks.

Rabin insisted that the security working group be led by the Ministry of Defence. "Everyone messes around with this subject, but only the guys at the Ministry of Defence know what they're talking about," he told Peres. But even so, the launch of the multilateral track created an opening wide enough for this supporting actor to crawl through and strengthen his grip on the peace process.

In November 1992, we used indirect channels to send the US administration a position paper that I had written with a colleague in the minister's office, Jeremy Issacharoff, which aimed to alert the administration to the centrality of the talks that Peres was involved in. The regional talks were supposed to lead to the establishment of a Middle Eastern common market, a regional defense system, a new desalination and water distribution network, a solution for the Palestinian refugee problem, and so forth. These plans were meant to provide solutions for regional problems, or seize opportunities facing the Middle East, that could be addressed only through regional cooperation.

We argued in the paper that since the Arab–Israeli bilateral agreements would require Israel to make tangible concessions, the framework of the regional talks would have to balance them. Israeli citizens had to be convinced that their country was being accepted as a legitimate member of the Middle East, and that the painful concessions demanded of them would indeed lead to security and stability. We also believed that as the regional talks bore fruit, Arab populations would recognize the importance of peace and their interest in preserving that peace would be strengthened. Moreover, Arab governments would be able to make the necessary decisions to promote reconciliation with Israel while confronting the forces of fundamentalism. The paper emphasized, of course, that Washington's assistance in this task was indispensable.

In talks in the United States and Europe, Peres tried to push for the establishment of a regional bank and a Middle East development fund. He did his calculations and found that if the petroleum industry, which was concerned for regional stability, put aside one dollar per barrel for this regional fund, it would accrue $8 billion a year. If at the same time an equivalent sum were obtained in credit, the fund could grow to $160 billion in ten years. "Imagine going to Mubarak with an offer to give him $40 billion," Peres used to say in conversations, trying to illustrate his proposal. His audiences struggled to understand why any oil exporter would voluntarily transfer money to Peres's fund. Peres explained that the fund was needed to excite the Arab world about the possibility of a New Middle East. The fund's members would commit to conditions of creating free market economies and building pluralistic institutions.

Peres decided that the region needed democratization "as much as a human needs oxygen." "Democracy is not only a process that guarantees personal and civil freedom," he wrote, "but also is a watchdog for peace, working to dispel the factors that underlie fundamentalist agitation."[6] In the face of a frustrating regional reality, Peres the dreamer agreed that he had to make a tactical concession to Peres the politician. Making democratization a condition would have likely been problematic for Arab despots, so he decided to make do with a coded reference to the "establishment of pluralistic institutions."

Peres never tired of explaining to Arabs just how much good would come to them from his plans. He showed Jordan's Prince Hassan his plan to establish a genetics research center on the Israeli–Jordanian border in the Arava Desert. Peres claimed to have brought on board Professor Daniel Cohen, an internationally renowned genetics expert from France, "who personally discovered the code of 25 genes and is guaranteed a Nobel Prize." The center would employ 100 researchers, with one gate into Israel and the other into Jordan. The project required $5 million for construction and $10 million in annual running costs, and Professor Cohen would raise the entire sum.

It was easy for Peres to fly high with Prince Hassan, who was also a man of letters and visions, and was willing to launch into long conversations with him about innovations in biotechnology and their fascinating implications. Peres waxed lyrical about remarkable developments involving featherless and almost boneless chickens and fish engineered to fit the size of a plate. The Bedouin-ruled kingdom of Jordan, with a gross national product similar in size to the assets of a handful of Peres's friends, would leap in an instant into an age of hypermodernity. I pestered Peres with irritating questions, including whether he had checked how many geneticists Jordan even had and why he possibly thought they might want to relocate to the middle of the desert.

But Peres stuck to his destination even when he changed paths, and he started pushing for the construction of an Israeli–Jordanian cancer hospital at the Naharayim site on the Jordan River. He convinced the Memorial Sloan Kettering Cancer Center to provide for free its hugely expensive diagnostics computer software. The head of this prestigious American research institute, even agreed to lead an international committee to promote his project. But the Jordanians dragged their feet and the plans remained only on paper, leaving Peres frustrated with the Arabs' failure to embrace his plan and their refusal to recognize and be thankful for the "superhuman effort I am investing for these ungrateful people."

End of the Hunting Season in Human History

When pursuing a goal, Peres employed all available means and explored every possible avenue. He was unconcerned by internal contradictions and problems of coordination. He gladly gave the exact same task to different actors. By accumulating bargaining chips, he improved his chances of winning the political roulette. He smiled mischievously when I told him that he was like the conductor of a chamber orchestra, whose musicians played off different scores. Peres liked complicated situations. Where others lost their direction, he believed he could find his way. He despised routine and he was ready to try tools and techniques that were not necessarily part of the conventional diplomatic toolkit.

Peres met occasionally with Tal Ronen and Shmuel Merhav, of the Coaching business consulting firm. They were critical of the coterie of Blazers around him. They believed that his staff were insufficiently enthusiastic to help him drive his idea of the New Middle East, and they advised him to host a seminar. They decided to invite some thirty key figures to a four-day strategic course, run by two experts from the Center for Management Design, who used new and pioneering strategic design technology to create a strategic plan with the course participants in order to translate Peres's vision into reality. The participants, the thinking went, would spread Peres's gospel. The possibility of forming a group that would promote him and his ideas seized Peres's imagination. "I'm encouraged to learn that like everyone else, you too need a support group and empathy," I said trying to wind him up, when I realized that it would be impossible to steer him away from the idea of a seminar.

The experts landed, and the seminar took place in a hotel on the shore of the Dead Sea in November 1994. Ed Gurevitz, the American chairman, explained to the participants that they were going to do something unprecedented. "From here, we will change the Middle East, and then the whole world."

Peres in turn hailed confidently, "The hunting season in human history is over." The most valuable assets in the modern world could not be captured or seized. Human intelligence, the true asset of the new age, could not be conquered. There was nothing more to learn from history because it was a history of wars. It would be a pity to waste time ploughing the killing fields trodden by Napoleon and his contemporaries. It was time to seize the future.

I was horrified by the pretentiousness and superficiality of this production. I snuck away to the hotel swimming pool and found other runaways who were sick of the discussions: Terje Rød-Larsen, Jacques Attali, Avishai Braverman, and Nimrod Novik. There was no critical discussion about the soundness of the idea of the New Middle East, nor did it generate any long-term commitment from a core of supporters. Gurevitz returned to the United States and wrote Peres back that the "mindset" of those closest to him would not permit change.

Peres did not despair. In his speech at the Nobel Prize ceremony in Oslo in December 1994, he excitedly sketched the picture of the New Middle East again: no wars, no enemies, no rockets, and no nuclear bombs. A Middle East in which there would be free movement of people and goods, without customs or import licenses, a place of religious freedom, cultural pluralism, universal education, an advanced quality of life, and running water: "A Middle East which will serve as a spiritual and cultural focal point for the entire world."

The Ability to Lead Change

True leadership, in Peres's eyes, was measured by the ability to lead change. His loathing for Yitzhak Shamir was based on Shamir's devotion to preserving the status quo and his obstruction of anything that might undermine it. Peres felt offended by the fact that the Israeli Right put Shamir up against him in the elections. He felt that he deserved a better-quality rival. Peres had his eyes on the future and lived in that future long before many others. He wanted to change history. And if you want to change history, he thought, then nostalgia and a focus on the lessons of history will only put a spoke in your wheels. Learning about old habits will only stifle new ones. And so Peres believed that people needed to know how to ignore history. I read him "Anticipation," a short poem by Rainer Maria Rilke, from a book I liked and had kept since high school:[7]

I am like a flag surrounded by distances.
I sense the winds coming, and must live them,
while things down are not stirring yet:
the doors are still closing gently, and there is silence in the chimneys;
the windows are not yet shaking, and the dust is still heavy.
I already know the storms and I am as excited as the sea.
And spread myself out and fall into me
and throw me off and I'm all alone
in the big storm.

Peres listened, enchanted. He nodded, concentrating, as if looking at himself through a mirror—at his hopes for the future, his loneliness beholding that future, and the fate that was sealed for him, to inhabit a reality that did not yet exist. Peres's heart led him to the future, and he naturally expected the march forward to be accompanied by much hue and cry. Peres lived big and never minced words in describing his journey. In the dedication that he penned for me in his book The New Middle East in late 1993, he wrote: "To Avi, who brings joy through his serious deeds, may we march up a great path together."

Science Will Design Our Tomorrow

The future that Peres envisaged was built on his characteristic optimism and reflected his breathless pursuit of technological innovations. He was spellbound by the revolutionary implications of scientific breakthroughs for what our lives will look like in the future. When I started working in his office in late 1988, I jealously inspected the rich collection of books on his shelves. I was no less jealous for the Macintosh computer on his desk, but I soon discovered that it was not even connected. It was just for show, but it definitely fit the set.

Peres could go on forever about the consequences of the digital revolution. He spent ages reading up on it and meeting technology experts. I tried to teach him a few times to use a computer, without success. But although he could not find the "enter" key, he fully understood the significance of this technology. He was enchanted by what it meant for the future, and enthusiastically found a place for himself in the new possibilities for action that it opened up.

Peres was particularly captivated by search engines and social networks. He was thrilled to meet Google founder Sergey Brin, Facebook founder Mark Zuckerberg, and many of their colleagues. It seemed completely natural to him to have his own social media pages. As soon as I started working with him I learned about Raj Reddy, an American professor of Indian descent who had achieved recognition for his work on artificial intelligence. Peres used to fantasize with him about completely computerizing a kibbutz in the Arava, to serve as an example for the whole region. We used to crack jokes behind his back, and sometimes to his face, about the chickens on Shimon's computerized kibbutz that would get addicted to Tetris, or the cows that would approach the sheep to borrow the software to plan the safe days when they would not get pregnant. But Peres was not deterred. He explained in his lectures in Israel and around the world that Israel had completely computerized its children's education, and now it was the turn of the children of the broader Middle East. He carried on doing so even after I told him that my children had never received more than two hours a week of computer studies at their school in Jerusalem.[8]

Peres took advantage of his stay at the World Economic Forum in Davos, Switzerland, to establish an international task force to familiarize children of the Middle East with the world of computers. He also suggested holding a conference to debate ways to propel the Middle East into the digital new millennium. That would shorten the path to the inevitable future, facilitate a comprehensive educational effort, and introduce the youth to the modern world and the challenges it posed. I asked Peres how his plan would work in areas that did not yet have an electricity grid. "We'll provide them battery-powered computers," he said, brushing me off as if I were a fly bothering him with my irrelevant buzzing. He rebuffed Piet Bukman, the Dutch minister for development and international cooperation, the same way in 1989 when Bukman politely explained that he thought it was better for deprived areas to develop in small steps, taking into account their cultural and social implications, and based first and foremost on the technological reality that characterized the local area.

I tried to reinforce what the Dutchman was saying and showed Peres *Small Is Beautiful*, by the development economist E. F. Schumacher.[9] The book, which opposes megalomaniacal Third World development schemes, failed to impress him. He thought that the Middle East needed to march toward free markets and political pluralism in large leaps, not hesitant sputters. He explained to audiences that a military response was not enough to address the growing threat of rockets and weapons of mass destruction. The answer had to be a combined political, military, and economic effort. In the new world, there was no more point to wars, and therefore it was not a world of enemies but of dangers like AIDS, environmental pollution, and international terrorism. Dangers of a regional character that respected neither nations nor states. A response to these dangers, therefore, required regional organizations. It was vital to change the face of the Middle East in order to make it stable, prosperous, and peace-loving. He invoked the experiences of Europe as proof: "In fifty years, it was transformed from an arena of terrible internal wars into a continent united around the interest in the economy, development, stability, and peace." Peres was adamant that Middle Easterners were not made of different genetic material from Europeans.

Learn from Our History

Peres's assumption that people everywhere are alike in their essential characteristics and desires also came across in the analogies he liked to draw. In talks with the Palestinians, he encouraged them by comparing the process of Israel's own establishment to the one the Palestinians found themselves in now. His comments elicited an instinctive resistance from me. How could he compare our nation to Arafat's? Nevertheless, I felt tremendous respect for how liberated Peres was in his thinking. He was never a slave to the axioms of the Israeli national ethos and never fell victim, like so many others, to our own propaganda.

In March 1994, in a conversation with the Palestinian leader Faisal Husseini,[10] Peres articulated an argument that compared Mufti Haj Amin al-Husseini to Ze'ev Jabotinsky. Both leaders had insisted on all or nothing. Faisal was the son of the leader of the Arab rioters Abd al-Qadir al-Husayni, who was killed in the battle of Castel in 1948. Peres told him, "The mufti led the Palestinians for many years and he was popular, but he brought disaster on his own people by rejecting the partition plan that would have given the Palestinians an independent state. Arafat, in contrast, has turned towards a path of pragmatism, a path that isn't paved with acclaim but promises concrete achievements: land, an economy, and rights." Peres did not say so explicitly, but it was clear from his words that he thought that Arafat was not walking in the footsteps of the mufti or Jabotinsky—but in those of Ben-Gurion.

Peres also offered his Palestinian counterparts some practical advice from the experience of the establishment of Israel. In January 1993, when he secretly hosted Husseini and the Palestinian politician Hanan Ashrawi[11] at his home, he instructed them in the virtues of a gradual approach to nation-building. "You must learn from our experience," he said in a tone that combined empathy with condescension. "Everything the Zionist movement accomplished was accomplished gradually. Another dunam, another goat. You receive many guests from abroad. You give them a kebab and a shishlik, and they go back exactly as they came. You must demand meaningful economic assistance." Ashrawi explained that the fact that the Palestinians lacked a state made this task difficult. Peres was quick to reply, "We were not a state either when we started off, and we still took meaningful steps and made achievements."

As a man who was able to peacefully hold two contradictory positions in mind, Peres sometimes slipped into expressions that were unflattering toward his Arab interlocutors and might have indicated that even a peaceful person like him still had his prejudices. He was not aware that he came across as patronizing. This behavior sometimes sent Amr Moussa, the sharp-tongued and proud foreign minister of Egypt, into a frenzy. Their relationship deteriorated.

Whenever they spoke, Peres emphasized his egalitarian outlook: "I don't look down at you when I talk." As a host, he made an effort to give his Arab guests a sense of worth and equality. He served them their food himself and urged them to down the drinks he poured them. But in the same breath he also told them, "Israel has no interest in remaining a lone island of prosperity and progress in a regional ocean of backwardness and poverty." As for allegations that his plans for a New Middle East were designed to impose Israeli hegemony on the region, he replied, "If somebody today were to offer Bangladesh to the Queen of England, she would tell them to get lost. What does she need Bangladesh's deprivation for? Why does Israel need your poverty? You have no economy worth seizing, you have grinding poverty, and to what end does Israel require your poverty?" Peres's Arab interlocutors were normally left speechless given his logic but resented him for his condescending tone. For his part, he usually failed to understand that his remarks had been offensive.

In one meeting at the World Economic Forum in Davos, Switzerland, Peres and Amr Moussa appeared before a crowd of businessmen. Peres repeated his catchphrase that Israel had no interest in remaining "an island of prosperity in a sea of poverty," but in his enthusiasm, and thanks to his penchant for poetics, he gave into the temptation and added: "Nor is Israel interested in being an island of cleanliness ... " I noticed he suddenly stopped speaking mid-sentence. He realized that he had stepped into a minefield, but his literary bug got the better of him and he completed his soundbite with aplomb: "Nor is Israel interested in being an island of cleanliness in an ocean of dirt."

A fuming Moussa demanded the floor and vigorously attacked Peres's arrogance, declaring, "With such an attitude from Israel, there will never be genuine peace in our region." The hostility between them intensified. Peres was convinced that Moussa was jealous of his popularity, which was clear whenever the two shared an international stage. Peres used to recount with joy how Moussa suffered every time he was forced to watch the crowds at Davos rise to their feet and cheer Peres—a gesture that was not afforded to the Egyptian foreign minister. Although Moussa had made a tangible contribution to the Oslo process at its outset, Peres dubbed him a "hostile Nasserist" who was working to enhance his status in Egypt as Mubarak's successor by embracing anti-Israel populism.

Moussa revealed his cards in a difficult conversation with Peres in January 1995. "You thought you could advance your ties with states in the region while ignoring Egypt. You'll discover this is a big mistake." He threatened to call off the multilateral talks unless there was progress in the security working group on clearing the Middle East of weapons of mass destruction. The Egyptian foreign minister was not satisfied with the position paper we presented him, which said that Israel was ready to enter negotiations for a Middle East Weapons of Mass Destruction Free Zone, which would also encompass delivery systems, two years after achieving peace agreements with all members of the Arab League and with Iran. He dubbed the document an "*Inshallah* [God willing] paper"—all vision and no purpose.

Moussa demanded the addition of a clause on the nuclear issue in the security working group's agenda, and Israel demurred for fear of a slippery slope that would expose it to unnecessary pressures. Peres warned Moussa that his eagerness to trip Israel up would probably gravely impair the peace process: "In Camp David we agreed on the principle of land for peace, not a principle of land and Dimona for peace," he angrily berated him. At a certain stage of the talks between the two, I sensed that Peres was veering off the messages agreed with the defense establishment. In a private word, joined by Yossi and Uri, I expressed my fear that he would be publicly depicted as making concessions on the nuclear issue. "But I built the Dimona reactor," Peres retorted, dismissing my concerns.

"You built the reactor," I said with a laugh, "and therefore you have the full right to close it." Peres couldn't see the funny side.

Peres's anger toward his Egyptian counterpart was not particularly intense until in the heat of one argument, and mainly to score a verbal victory over him, he almost shouted that he would scrap his vision of the New Middle East. "If the Arab side is not interested in economic cooperation," he snapped at Moussa in a tense meeting in Cairo in May 1995, "that's fine by Israel. We have a strong economy and our market can continue prospering even without cooperation with you. If the Arabs don't want normalisation, so be it. We won't impose. What do I need Oman and Qatar for? We have lived a hundred years without them, and that's how we'll live for a hundred years more."

The Regional Economic Summit

Peres belonged to a rare breed of leaders who had the power to set the agenda for his country and region. His ideas about the New Middle East, and the breakthroughs in Oslo and later with Jordan, inspired hope in the hearts of many Israelis. Others believed that Peres was deluding himself about the region's future. The image he cultivated for himself was of not having his feet on the ground in the brutal soil of the Middle East, and many Israelis feared that he was allowing their enemies to lead him astray. In the elections of 1996, he paid a heavy price.

Despite the flaws in Peres's vision, he presented the states of the Middle East with a serious challenge. He received mixed reactions: worries about Israeli domination, a fear of change and of the subversion of regime stability, reservations about an invasion of Western culture, and suspicions that this was an Israeli ruse to achieve recognition and normal relations with Arab states without paying the price—a Palestinian state on the 1967 borders with a capital in East Jerusalem, and an agreement with Syria based on a withdrawal from the territories occupied in the Six-Day War. But at the same time, Arab rulers faced the tempting option of promoting their own countries' prosperity and a chance to help douse the Palestinian fire that had always threatened to foment unrest at home and jeopardize regional stability.

This ambivalent attitude toward Peres's ideas was clear at the regional summits, another massive project that Peres devised and pursued. When Peres informed Prime Minister Rabin in October 1993 that he intended to stage an economic summit in Amman or Rabat, Rabin said that it should take place after peace and Arab recognition of Israel. The supporting actor decided not to pick a fight with Rabin, his superior and man of little faith. Instead, he reassured him and promised this was indeed what he meant. He believed that he had managed to persuade Rabin as early as February 1993 that Israel had to secure a bigger payback for any concessions. That payback was to be the New Middle East.

But a doubtful Rabin was not totally on board. He feared that such a summit was an Israeli concession, while Peres thought it was an Israeli interest. He was determined to let nobody, not even Rabin, knock him off course. Ultimately, Rabin showed up at the summit to take some of the credit.

Peres proselytized to American and European leaders about his idea for a summit; in November 1993 he presented the plan to Jordan's King Hussein at a secret meeting in Amman and tried to convince him to host the first summit. As the organizing force, Peres had already enlisted the support of the World Economic Forum at Davos and the US-based Council on Foreign Relations. In so doing, he had formed a European–American axis to support his vision and give it an umbrella of legitimacy and prestige. He did not despair when Jordan proved hesitant about hosting, and in early June 1994 he met with King Hassan II in Morocco and secured his promise that Morocco would play host.

The Arab leaders and their economic delegations arrived in Morocco. President Clinton and many other leaders chose to join in the action. The air traffic controllers struggled to cope with the unusually heavy air traffic as planes made their way from every corner of the earth. It was an extraordinary show, which provided an initial taste of the possibility for regional change borne on the wings of peace. For me, it was also a magnificent display of the force of Peres's leadership and personality. One man from a small country had shaken up the whole world with his ideas, writing his own screenplay and dishing out roles to VIPs and world leaders, who played along with him, got swept away with his vision, and dutifully played the roles he cast them. I felt blessed to have had the chance to work alongside a leader whose many disappointments and failures had scarred him, and who like anyone else had his weaknesses, but who was still a unique, miraculous giant.

We returned from Morocco with a sense of accomplishment intermingled with the feeling of a missed opportunity. The large Israeli delegation had caused quite a loud stir and made an arrogant impression, which provoked misgivings and criticism. Peres was pained to hear that President Weizman had explained to visitors at the President's Residence that the Casablanca summit was not to the liking of Mubarak and Assad. They were not ready for Israel to impose on the Middle East a modern economy, a digital education system, and other ideas that Peres's mind was cooking up. Weizman said that he had learned a lesson in Arab pride when he suggested to the Egyptian general Mohamed Gamasy that his sick wife be treated by an Israeli specialist doctor. The general had declined the offer and explained that Egypt had doctors who were just as good as Israel's. Weizman believed that Israel had to avoid "pushing or getting pushed" in the Middle East's business.

The Arab Side's Sensitivities

Peres, as is clear by now, was not always aware of the other side's sensitivities. Sometimes he slipped into a tone of derision. He was never averse to giving a tongue-lashing to Arabs who aroused his anger. Egypt's foreign minister Moussa was a regular victim, but Peres also called Palestinian official Yasser Abed Rabbo[12] "that schmuck" to Moussa's face. Sometimes it looked like Peres was having fun deliberately messing around with the Arabs' sensitivities. In 1995, he bumped into the secretary-general of the Arab League, Asmat Abdel Meguid,[13] in the corridor at the United Nations in New York. Peres told him jokingly that it would not be long till Israel submitted a request to join the Arab League.

This story made the press and exposed the Arabs' humorlessness. Jokes about Arab unity, it seems, were too risqué. The agitated responses started pouring in. People claimed that Israel was threatening the Arab character of the Middle East, and that this threat was part of the New Middle East that Peres was plotting. Peres was in no rush to clarify that he had been joking. Partly because he was starting to be won over by the idea—politicians take silly ideas more seriously once they see them in print—but mostly because he was amused by the consternation he had provoked from his future partners around the Middle East.

The Swiss resort town of Davos became an important landmark in Peres's efforts to engineer change in the Middle East. Every year, the World Economic Forum brings together world leaders and the super-rich there. Peres's vision was welcomed with enthusiasm in Davos and his speeches won plaudits. His effort to harness the forum's operational abilities for the task of organizing the regional summits had proven itself. The forum deepened regional cooperation with Israel and cultivated meetings between Israeli businesspeople and their Arab counterparts. It also came to be a site for negotiations with the Palestinians.

In one meeting, in January 1994, Arafat delivered Peres a flowery speech about his vision of a Middle Eastern Benelux:[14] a common economic structure for Jordan, Lebanon, Egypt, Syria, Israel, and Palestine. "There is no alternative but to live together in partnership, good neighbourliness, and open borders," Arafat argued. "I have read your book about the New Middle East," he added proudly, "and I admire your ideas." I guessed that Arafat's wily advisor, Saeb Erekat, had put these words in his mouth and that his flattery would soon be followed by complaints and demands.

Davos is up in the Alps, and Peres soared at such altitudes. But Davos was also where Peres absorbed some painful punches that made him crash-land on the rock-hard ground of reality. He got dragged into bitter clashes with Egypt's Foreign Minister Amr Moussa and later Turkey's President Erdogan in 2009. He also gave Netanyahu's 1996 election campaign a priceless gift—a photo of him embracing Arafat. Most painfully, he shared a stage with Arafat in an embarrassing episode in which Arafat—in breach of their agreement—stunned his Nobel co-laureate by cursing and vilifying Israel, leaving Peres profoundly offended and sparking a desire for revenge, which intensified with time.

But Peres did not relent and continued prophesying about the New Middle East, which was slow to appear. Having joined him in conversations with Arab leaders and at the regional summits, and despite my sustained skepticism, I cannot help but feel that Peres gave us a glimpse at a Middle East that was ready to accept Israel's existence and to cooperate with it. Our Arab interlocutors were desperate to get the tragedy of their Palestinian brethren off their conscience. Maybe then, many believed, the main obstacle to Israel's acceptance in the region could finally be lifted.

The Arab leaders' sensitivity to the plight of the Palestinian people was intertwined with many other sometimes contradictory sensitivities and interests. Thus, for example, King Hassan II anxiously asked Peres in Morocco whether Israel intended to transfer the Temple Mount (or what Muslims call the Haram al-Sharif) to Arafat's control. Peres said no, and asked the king why he was concerned. The king, who headed the Organisation of Islamic Conference's committee on Jerusalem, explained agitatedly: "Arafat's hands are completely blood-soaked. This man is not fit to control the mosques that are so sacred to Islam."

The Arab Spring Marks a New Middle East

Peres took the Arab Spring of 2010 as validation of his vision for a New Middle East. In a speech thanking US President Barack Obama for awarding him the Medal of Freedom[15] in June 2012, he said, "Just imagine what could be. Now, a young Arab generation has opened its eyes and stood up against oppression, poverty and corruption. They seek freedom. They need freedom. They understand that freedom begins at home. I pray for their success."[16] The dramatic fashion in which political Islamism had proven its resilience in the Arab world, the military coup in Egypt, and the side-lining of the liberal forces of progress had failed to shatter Peres's belief that we were indeed on the path to his New Middle East. Difficulties were to be expected, the road would be long, but the trajectory was clear.

My natural inclination, of course, was somewhat less optimistic. I put the argument to Peres that the Arabs of the Middle East still had a long way to go before embracing pluralism and democracy, permitting religious freedom, granting equality to women, and respecting human rights. I reminded him how we had learned this lesson in Oman back in 1996. We had departed for a lightning visit to Oman and Qatar. The visit had been planned with a keen eye on the upcoming elections in May. We wanted to present Peres as the man with the power to bring peace—an opportunity to prove that despite the terrorism, there really was a way for Peres to strive toward a different Middle East. The Israeli reporters who joined us on the flight were used to these photo ops. One of them told me the night before the flight, "It's going to be tough for you to excite us with pictures of more Arabs in galabeyas, even if their galabeyas are embroidered with gold." I knew that this was the bitter truth and I instructed the advance team, which had already landed, to insist on a military honor guard and the playing of Hatikvah when Peres stepped off the plane. "Warn our hosts: if they don't play the national anthem, the visit's off." Our hosts acquiesced. I decided to hide that fact to maintain the element of surprise.

I also kept the secret from Peres. Experience had taught me that at an altitude of 30,000 feet and with the help of a glass of whiskey, his tongue became loose. I asked General Danny Yatom, his military secretary, to prepare his uniform: he was going to accompany Peres on a historic walk down the sultanate's red carpet. The spectacle was indeed emotional—even our cynical reporters admitted as much. We were led to the sultan's summer palace in the town of Salalah. The meeting with Sultan Qaboos bin Said took place in a magnificent hall that looked like something out of *Arabian Nights*. Thickset carpets, crystal chandeliers, shiny marble tables, wooden furniture with intricate embellishments, and all around us bustling galabeya-clad servants with curved swords stowed into their sashes. We sank into the couches for a conversation that was intermittently interrupted when tall, dark-skinned, big-bellied, barefoot servants served us local delicacies out of enormous gold bowls.

"We are in a period of transition from the old Middle East to the new one," Peres told the sultan. "My visit to Oman is a clear testament to this basic truth." The sultan concurred and said that he was encouraging his people to deepen their dialogue and commercial ties with Israel. He even told us that he had stressed to his ministers that allegations that Israel was trying to take over the region were bunkum. At the sumptuous dinner hosted in our honor, we were treated to background music played on wind instruments. We wondered aloud to our host whether we were listening to a recording. The sultan, somewhat shocked by our offensive question, immediately pulled a curtain aside to reveal a live, shiny brass band. The sultan proudly explained that he had been trained at Britain's Royal Military Academy, where he developed his love of brass bands; on returning home, he had ordered the establishment of one in Oman as well.

Only Aliza Goren, Peres's media advisor, was unable to take part in this exciting event. Our hosts had strenuously insisted that the dinner be a male-only affair. We gave in. A small price to pay on the road to a New Middle East.

4

Oslo: The Supporting Actor's Triumph

The 1993 Oslo Accords triggered firestorm in Israel. As difficulties piled up on the path to fulfilling the hope that Oslo represented, and as Palestinian terrorism became more deadly, the agreement became more controversial. The deal's supporters were soon outnumbered. My three young children looked at me with alarm whenever we saw the sign "Oslo criminals to justice!" in the streets. I told them that the personal price that I would pay would be relatively small: "I was very young at the time, so I'll be tried in a juvenile court." My children were not much comforted by my wisecracks. In 2002, a Palestinian faction published a list of names of Israelis who were marked down for attack.[1] My name appeared on this list of dignitaries, and my children, who had since grown up, were afraid. "Dad, even the Palestinians hate you because of Oslo," they said sarcastically when this news made the front pages. "Now you can choose who gets to kill you—a Jew or an Arab."

Despite the criticism and the lingering questions, Peres saw Oslo as a mighty historic achievement because it had produced mutual recognition between the Israeli and Palestinian peoples. In my opinion, his assessment was correct. Although the path to a permanent peace would be long, blood-soaked, and full of potholes, in Oslo, the die was cast. The land would be divided between the two nations. Peres believed that this was the only way to preserve Israel's Jewish and democratic character, to bolster its existence in the region, to facilitate reconciliation with the Arab world, and to lay a key milestone on the long road to the New Middle East.

Peres saw Oslo as a natural waystation on a direct track from Dimona. The route that passed between these two stations was the story of the realization of his lifelong dreams. Dimona, as a symbol of the foundations he installed for Israel's security, and Oslo—as a historic breakthrough that would transform Israel from a state forced to live by the sword to a state living in peace with its neighbors. Peres was proud of Oslo and felt aggrieved whenever he sensed that the credit was being taken away from him.

Working alongside Peres, I was privy to decisions that would fascinate future historians. And the closer I was to the eye of the storm, the more clearly I understood how restricted my field of vision was. I make no pretense of showing the full picture—only the parts that I witnessed. And with this restricted view, my attention was seized by what many might consider peripheral, not just central. I was fascinated by the great developments of history, but no less by the people who led them. Even facing the most fateful decisions, people are still people, with their own strengths and weaknesses. Like all of us.

Indeed, not long after the Oslo process started, the Israeli participants understood that they were involved in a development of historic significance, which future historians would pore over in detail. The battle for the credit, like the battle for peace, was sometimes highly sophisticated and at other times gave rein to human follies. To the credit of those who fought for the plaudits, I must say they did not allow their personal ambitions to sabotage their common cause. Despite the temptation, they were careful not to leak anything about what was going on; and despite interpersonal tensions, they were able to preserve their team spirit, faithful to their higher purpose.

The question of credit provided fertile ground for some bawdy inside humor. In a moment of mischief, Uri Savir—the chief negotiator in Oslo—said with the humor with which he was so abundantly blessed, "One day they'll make a film about Oslo and I'll obviously be played by Tom Cruise."

To temper his enthusiasm and influence the producers of this future blockbuster, I gave Uri an additional code name in our secret correspondence: "Danny DeVito." I eventually revealed this secret to that short and well-rounded actor, who took the joke well.

So, Who Deserves the Credit for Oslo?

So, who deserves the credit for Oslo? The easy answer is "everyone." The academics— Ron Pundak and Yair Hirschfeld—who opened the channel with Ahmed Qurei[2] and first presented us a draft declaration of principles. Yossi Beilin, at whose initiative and on whose instructions they went to Oslo in the first place. Uri Savir, the head of the Israeli negotiating team. Joel Singer, who turned the understandings into a legal document. Shimon Peres, who headed the Oslo team and suffused it with the spirit of his vision. Yitzhak Rabin, without whose decision to sign the agreement any effort would have remained barren. And of course—the Palestinians and the Norwegians. They were also partners, after all.

Each one of these actors played an important part but from my vantage point, only one person—on the Israeli side—had the decisive role: to drag Prime Minister Yitzhak Rabin into the process, hold on to him tightly and to not let go despite his misgivings, protestations, hesitations, and distaste for the people leading the effort. This central, decisive role was played by the supporting actor Shimon Peres. In seeing this mission through, he demonstrated immense political skill, an ability to synchronize complex developments and problematic actors, the stubbornness of an Amstaff terrier sinking its teeth into its prey, and a proclivity for controversial and risky tricks. Yossi Beilin put it this way: "Rabin was a hero against his will … The whole story of Oslo is the story of a man who got there against his will … He didn't want it. He wasn't interested. He basically gave his agreement the whole way under duress, almost just not to rupture his relationship with Shimon Peres, in my opinion."[3]

It is easy to be tempted into depicting Oslo as the result of precise planning, sophisticated skills in diplomatic architecture, and the artful orchestration of complex steps. But things looked different in reality. Four different streams merged to form the mighty river that made the Oslo process possible. No architect matched them up, and sometimes chance was responsible for channeling them at the right times.

The first stream nurtured the necessary geopolitical foundations, which forced the PLO to make concessions and made the whole process possible: The end of the Cold War and Arafat's disastrous bet in backing Saddam Hussein in the Gulf War had weakened the PLO. Nobody from the Oslo team claimed credit for these developments.

The second stream brought the ideas at the heart of the agreement to maturity: "Gaza first" (an idea that Peres touted as early as 1980), Arafat's return to Gaza, rehabilitation schemes, economic cooperation, etc.

The third stream strengthened a reliable channel of communication (with Norwegian assistance), from the first meeting in London between Yair Hirschfeld and Ahmed Qurei to the secret signing of the declaration of principles in Oslo.

The fourth stream ripened the political will in Israel to accept this development: the impact of the First Intifada on the Israeli public, the Likud's defeat in the 1992 elections and the formation of a Labour-led government, but, above all else, Rabin's agreement to join the process.

Nobody arranged for these streams in advance. What we had was a series of events happening in close proximity, which appeared to be orchestrated by a political architect of tremendous energies—but no such architect existed.

On November 16, 1992, Peres traveled to Cairo and tried, through the Egyptians, to plant the idea of "Gaza first" in the Palestinians' minds, which went on to be a central foundation of the Oslo Accords. It was a familiar trick in Peres's diplomatic repertoire. If the Palestinians had known that the idea had come from Israel, they would have rejected it. They had to be made to propose the idea themselves as if it were their own.

In December 1992, Yossi Beilin led the first reading of a bill in the Knesset to amend a law that prohibited meetings with the PLO.[4] On December 4, 1992, Yair Hirschfeld met Ahmed Qurei in London on the sidelines of a meeting of the steering committee of the multilateral talks. On January 8, 1993, Peres met Rabin and presented him with an audacious diplomatic plan.[5] "I told Rabin that we must take a big step towards the PLO," he told me on his return. "So long as Arafat remains in Tunis, he will represent the [Palestinian] diaspora and will hinder the negotiations. We must offer Arafat and his friends to move to Gaza, where they will have the right to vote and be elected."

"You're out of your political mind!" I told Peres, alarmed. "Nobody will accept Arafat's return to Gaza. Such a short distance from Ashkelon and Tel Aviv? How did Rabin react?"

Peres smiled, his eyes gleaming craftily: "I told Rabin, consider the proposal. Don't give an answer straight away."

Mission Creep

These events were closely connected to the weaving of the Oslo process, but at the time, none of the actors were aware of what the others were doing. Nobody pre-arranged these events as a comprehensive, coordinated policy. It was not even clear at the outset whether the track with the PLO was a substitute for the talks in Washington or a clandestine channel to support them, without Israeli recognition of the PLO. Peres even rejected Hirschfeld and Pundak's basic proposal in their initial documents for a trusteeship in Gaza, and the idea fell off the agenda. Although the media likes to call Beilin the "architect of the Oslo accords," he has admitted that there was no execution of an organized plan but "mission creep": "Just like military operations experience mission creep, these were negotiations that crept towards peace, more than once against the inclinations of those who were later called its architects. I was not an architect of Oslo either, although I admit I was extremely flattered to be given this title."[6]

In March 1998, a small gathering took place at the Peres Centre for Peace at my initiative, in which the people behind Oslo were asked to explain the path that led to the talks with the PLO and the accords. Yair Hirschfeld described an orderly process of immaculate internal logic, in which he and Yossi had played a central role. In his account, the process started in early 1989, in an Israeli–Palestinian meeting at the Notre Dame Hotel in Jerusalem. "It was the beginning of an intensive dialogue that produced the substance of Oslo ... the formulas that went on to become the success formulas of Oslo."[7] In his understanding, Oslo was a product of the "Track-Two Diplomacy" techniques that he had developed over the years, the fruits of his expertise in informal Track-Two Diplomacy.

Peres did not put much stock by the formulas and techniques that were so critical in Hirschfeld's eyes. "I was suspicious of these two gentlemen," he said. "I thought that Yair and Ron were too keen." Ron Pundak stressed that at the heart of Oslo stood the pair's success in changing the logic of the negotiations. In Washington, the talks had a zero-sum logic: one side gains, the other loses. But in Oslo, the logic was win-win: both sides gain. Peres had little patience for theoretical formulas. He had not come to diplomacy as a graduate of the school of Mother Teresa. "Win-schwin," he said dismissively,

> my problem was to see whether there was a partner, not a plan ... What was really proven to us was that this group, the Palestinians, were serious. That is, they knew how to tempt Arafat ... The sharpest, most central figure was Abu Ala [Ahmed Qurei]. With Abu Mazen [Mahmoud Abbas], I'd go out for a party. With Abu Ala, I'd go out plotting. These are two different things.[8]

Peres checked how serious the Palestinian delegation was at Oslo. Through Yair and Ron, he requested that Qurei ensure that no member of the Palestinian National Council—which as far as Israel was concerned belonged to the PLO—be included in the Palestinian delegation to the multilateral talks, as had happened earlier. "To my surprise, that's exactly what happened," he said, closing down the debate. "At that moment, I deduced that this was a channel that was worth working with. Nothing else mattered."[9]

Academic discussions with PLO officials were not uncommon, but this time Peres was convinced that there was a real partner. Nevertheless, he was in no rush to cross that frontier and talk to the PLO. There was no emotional barrier stopping him: rather, he was afraid of losing public support. He also feared that talking to the PLO would commit Israel to solving the problems of all the Palestinians, while to his mind, it could only provide a solution to those living in the territories. As early as 1975, he had suggested treating the PLO as a leopard that might one day change its spots and turn into a pussycat. "In theory, a leopard can also be a cat, and if that happens, we'll start stroking it as if it were a cat."[10] Peres's circle developed an approach of dictating conditions to the PLO in the spirit of the 1974 Yariv–Shemtov formula: recognition of Israel and an end to terrorism. If the PLO met these conditions, then it would be fit for dialogue. This approach was of course different from the Right's, which said that a leopard could not change its spots and that even if it made a rhetorical commitment to certain conditions, that would just be a sneaky ruse led by the logic of the "Phased Plan": the Palestinian' strategy to induce Israel's collapse, step by step.

As early as 1985, Peres had secured Yitzhak Shamir's approval for contacts with the PLO, on the pretext that they might shed light on the fate of our missing soldiers, but that secret effort did not produce a diplomatic breakthrough. Peres later dithered and hesitated about publicly dictating conditions to the PLO. He preferred the "Jordanian option" and only migrated to the "Palestinian option"—regretfully and for want of a better choice—after Shamir had torpedoed the agreement he had reached with King Hussein in London in April 1987, and after the Jordanian king announced that he was relinquishing his claims to the West Bank and leaving responsibility for its fate to the Palestinians themselves.

In the first days of the Rabin government, Peres made an intensive effort to promote an agreement with the inhabitants of the territories. He was in no rush to talk to the PLO. In November 1992, when Egypt's Amr Moussa told Peres that he would bring his ideas to the attention of the leaders of the PLO, Peres replied with a broad grin: "I didn't catch what you just said." He also declared, "We're prepared to be pragmatic, but if we're asked to talk to the PLO—that's not going to happen." We held a series of secret meetings with high-ranking Palestinians living in the West Bank: Faisal Husseini, Hanan Ashrawi, and Ziad Abuzayyad.[11] "We recommend you prepare for elections," Peres told Faisal.

> We'll try to find a way for anyone who wants peace to be able to take part. You must have noticed that we are not denying the connection between you and Tunis ... The situation would change if the leadership in Tunis declared that it was stopping terrorism. We support the idea of a two-stage solution. We are aware of your concerns that a temporary agreement will take root as a permanent solution ... [But] the two stages would be interlocked, there would be a timetable ... We're suggesting that any territories where Palestinians live should be administered by Palestinians. Similarly, the areas where Jews live will be administered by them. Empty spaces will be jointly administered. That, by the way, should be your guarantee that no more settlements will be built.[12]

Peres pushed for elections in the territories on the assumption that this would produce a legitimate local authority, independent of the PLO leadership in Tunis, which could reach binding agreements with Israel. He had despaired of the talks in Washington with the joint Jordanian–Palestinian delegation. It was clear that the PLO was operating behind the curtain, instructing the Palestinian negotiators and effectively frustrating any progress. In a moment of mischief, I blacked out the dates from the cables reporting about the talks in Washington and offered Peres, Yossi, and Uri to try their hand at arranging the reports in chronological order, based on the developments in the talks. We all knew that this was a hopeless task because the discussions had been circular and were going nowhere.

Peres's persistent efforts to cultivate a local Palestinian partner failed. Husseini and his friends had made it clear to Peres that they could not oblige—and we had to conduct direct talks with the PLO. Husseini even stressed that his secret meetings with Peres were happening with Arafat's permission and at his instruction, and that their contents were being reported back to Tunis. In one meeting, he conveyed a message directly from Arafat:

> Our commitment to the peace process is very strong but we have concerns. We have found ourselves in a difficult position after the expulsion incident.[13] We hope that you will now be more attentive to our needs. We view with favour the Knesset's decision on the law about meetings with the PLO. We didn't understand why you reacted so strongly to Yael Dayan's visit to Tunis.[14] What are we meant to understand from this? Is the PLO still taboo? You can only push the negotiations forward and erase suspicions through direct talks with the PLO.

Husseini added his own explanation for Arafat's remarks: "Every nation has its own disaster, its own holocaust. Everyone thinks his own holocaust is the worst of them all. For us—it's the expulsion [in 1948]." I was personally outraged by the comparison. Husseini added on a personal note: "I want to share with you, Mr Peres, a picture that I keep in my memory: the night my father was killed. I could hear my mother crying in the next room: she didn't want to cry in front of us, the kids. I heard her saying: this was the day we lost." It was the first time that I was so intimately exposed to the Palestinian side's grief.

The expulsion episode, which Husseini raised on Arafat's behalf, was indeed a milestone and helped to expedite Peres's personal conviction—already slowly maturing—that the only actor with whom a deal could be reached was the PLO. In mid-December, Peres visited Japan. The distance from Israel allowed him to leave his troubles behind. Besides our official meetings, Deputy Foreign Minister Hisashi Owada took us to enjoy a prestigious geisha house. Peres struggled to pronounce the Japanese man's name and Hebraized it to "Ovadia." We were joined by the then-governor of the Bank of Israel, Jacob Frenkel, who immediately became the geishas' favorite and even taught them some words in Hebrew. The geishas insisted on singing and playing us ancient Japanese music and we were forced to listen politely.

It was while we were still in Japan that over 400 Hamas members were expelled to Lebanon. Rabin had decided on the move following the kidnapping and murder of the border policeman Nissim Toledano. He did not consult Peres, which infuriated him. I knew that Peres's self-imposed discipline tended to unravel in such circumstances. I drafted him a press statement:

> Recent events have made clear that there are two camps on the Palestinian side. One we can talk to about peace and another that wants to kill any chance of peace.

This dividing line cuts through the territories as well as through the PLO. I propose that alongside our uncompromising fight against those who oppose peace, we must perform a serious reassessment of our policy on dialogue with the parts that are willing to talk.

Peres slipped the statement into his pocket. I sensed that he was ready to publicly express positions on the PLO that diverged from his past statements. His fury toward Rabin had contributed to this. Without explicitly asking him, I encouraged *Yediot Aharonot*'s diplomatic correspondent Shimon Shiffer to call Peres at home and ask him about his position on negotiations with the PLO. And indeed, the next day's headline announced: "Foreign Minister Shimon Peres hints in interview to *Yediot Aharonot*: If the PLO wants a peace deal with us—we need to talk." Shiffer called this a "dramatic change in Israel's position."[15]

Moving the Tunis Leadership to the Gaza Strip

Once Peres had made up his mind, he was determined to persuade Rabin. On February 9, 1993, I wrote down his report of their conversation in his own words:

We moved onto a "where are we going?" conversation. I told him that the Palestinian delegation was not strong enough. It did not have the authority of an elected delegation, because there were no elections. It was subordinate to the PLO and we were ignoring this relationship. It was ostensibly acting in tandem with Jordan but in reality was a separate entity. We had to choose: elections, recognition of the PLO, or Jordanian hegemony. We had missed the boat for Jordanian hegemony. I was in favour of elections. Rabin expressed concern that the subject of elections would bring up the question of Jerusalem, and that that's what the Palestinians were hoping for. The debate about elections would likely stop the peace process ... I told him that my opposition to the participation of the PLO was based on its being an organisation that represented the Palestinian diaspora. We had no solution to offer other than for the Palestinians in the territories. So long as the PLO and Arafat remain in Tunis, they reflect and support the diaspora. The delegation in Washington is subordinate to Tunis, and we had contacts with the subordinates, not the decision-makers ...

I propose relocating the Tunis leadership to the Gaza Strip. We have received a proposal through Hirschfeld and Pundak from Abu Ala [Ahmed Qurei], who says he is speaking on Arafat's behalf, about 'Gaza first': Israel should announce the evacuation of Gaza within two to three years and the activation of a small Marshall Plan for Gaza; it would be said that this would not prejudice negotiations for the West Bank; and an economic cooperation plan between Gaza and Israel would be implemented: the construction of desalination plants, a seaport, tourism, a water carrier. The plan could not be revealed to the local Palestinians. Rabin said that he was not ruling out the idea of 'Gaza first'. But we had to wait for the upcoming visit of [US] Secretary of State [Warren] Christopher. I told him that I would follow up on the issue. That there was a broad consensus on Gaza. Rabin asked: What about the 4,000 settlers there? I replied: If possible—let them stay and we won't have to evacuate them.

Rabin was full of doubts, torn between two options: "Gaza first" or "Syria first." He wanted to wait, therefore, for the visit of the US secretary of state. He had told Peres more than once that he could not lift both weights at the same time. "I believe that we must focus our attention and energies on both the Syrian and Palestinian tracks," he told President Clinton, "but give priority to achieving an agreement with Syria first."[16]

I'll Be Like a Predatory Beast

The more Peres grew convinced that the Oslo track could bear fruit, the more he tried to dissuade Rabin from the Syrian effort. "Without a withdrawal to the border line ten metres from the Sea of Galilee, there won't be peace with Syria, and that's a serious problem," he explained to Rabin. "Assad is not pressed for time, while we promised progress on the peace process in the election campaign. If this year passes without progress, we'll be in a difficult situation—we haven't solved the unemployment problem, and we haven't solved the aliyah[17] problem either."[18]

Rabin could not wriggle out of his election promise to reach an agreement on the territories within nine months. Peres occasionally unsheathed his ultimate weapon against Rabin:

There's one thing you have to understand about the relationship between me and Rabin. He's always suspicious, of course, that I'll run [against him] again. It weighed on him ... and I told him: listen, I can strike a gentlemen's agreement with you. If you take the path of peace—you have nothing to worry about from me, you'll find I'll be the most loyal friend you've ever had. But if you veer off that path—you won't recognise me. I'll be like a predatory beast.[19]

And indeed, this threat remained in the air the whole time and was a major component of Peres's toolkit for obtaining Rabin's consent for his initiatives.[20] Beilin summed up this truth as follows: "Peres played an irreplaceable role in the Oslo process ... He was the only one who could have persuaded Rabin to give a green light."[21]

In conversations with foreign dignitaries, Peres repeatedly attacked the thesis of "Syria first." He argued that Israel had to make progress wherever it could, "even facing a knife or a missile." He knew in his heart that it was not possible to make simultaneous progress against both the Palestinian knife and the Syrian missile. He did not want the focus on Syria to foil the opportunity created in Oslo. Syria played a schizophrenic role in Peres's rhetoric: to Rabin, Peres described the difficulties of reaching an agreement with Damascus in alarming tones; but speaking to the Palestinians, Peres warned that an agreement with Syria was within reach, and that if they did not hurry up and moderate their positions, we would sign a deal with Assad and leave them in the lurch. The Palestinians were indeed afraid of such a scenario, and on the eve of a decisive round of talks in Oslo, in order to make it easier for them to soften their positions, I drip-fed information to the English-language press that an agreement with Damascus was just around the corner.

Peres kept on raising the topic of "Gaza first" with Rabin, who replied that he rejected the idea because the Palestinians would not honor it. "What will we have gained if the agreement includes Gazans working in Israel? The knife attacks would continue. If anything, it's better to leave Gaza unilaterally and close it off." Peres replied that this would be as explosive as a barrel of dynamite. Better to allow the residents of Gaza work in Israel and let Arafat come to Gaza. Rabin replied that Arafat was afraid to return. Peres said that he could talk to the Americans about a small Marshall Plan for Gaza. Rabin was against it.[22]

Peres bleakly dictated Rabin's paralyzing reactions to me. Rabin had even bluntly and discourteously asked that while he was out of the country, Peres should keep a low profile. It was not easy for Peres to swallow the humiliations that Rabin and his people heaped on him. In difficult times like these, I used to remind him of this mantra: "In order to make progress on the secret channel, we must not respond to provocations. A public spat between you and Rabin would destroy Oslo." And to those in the office who were not in on the secret of the contacts with the PLO, I repeatedly explained that industrial peace with the Prime Minister's Office was a necessary condition for Peres to build up his political influence. Sometimes even painful blows had to be met with gritted teeth and self-restraint.

I was not a Rabinologist, but I could spot a pattern in Rabin's responses. He often used to get caught up in technical, less substantive details and spot faults in them. If a solution was found for a particular fault, the matter could be taken to the next stage. He neglected the broader, more substantive questions because he was too busy dealing with the small print. In order to clarify my thoughts and cheer Peres up a bit, I described to him an imaginary conversation between him and Rabin:

Peres: "Let's bomb the White House with two sorties of F-15 jets, each dropping a two-ton explosive. The trajectory of the attack will be from north to south."

Rabin: "Have you gone mad, Shimon? Only an F-16 could perform such a mission, a one-ton bomb will be enough, and the flight path must be from east to west, because that's the direction to fly back to the Hatzerim base."

Peres looked at me with a forgiving smile, not exactly amused. He knew Rabin and apparently had no need for my imaginary illustrations.

No Intelligence

Peres did not relent from applying pressure on Rabin. Hirschfeld and Pundak continued sending us reports of their conversations with Ahmed Qurei. Peres wanted to pick up the pace. I was worried that the secret would leak and Rabin would instruct us to end the talks and shut the channel down. In late April 1993, the official talks in Washington radiated a certain optimism. I advised Peres to go easy on Oslo until the

Washington channel hit a crisis. That would reduce the risk of Rabin terminating the sensitive Oslo track. Peres agreed and even asked Hirschfeld to refrain from discussing these contacts on the phone. He was afraid of a leak but also of the inquisitive ears of intelligence agencies, and chiefly of Israeli intelligence.

Peres had a complicated attitude toward intelligence. He took a dim view of the abilities of intelligence agencies to get to the bottom of complicated political matters. He believed that their approach was unoriginal and that they failed to consider the power of individual leaders to bring about historic changes of the sort that would make a laughing stock of conservative predictions. He preferred to act without the help of the intelligence services, which may have been monitoring the Arabs but which Peres believed were also snooping on him.

Peres was convinced that Qurei was not telling Arafat the whole truth in his conversations with Tunis. "I'm sure he's exaggerating his achievements, downplaying the importance of his own concessions, and making manoeuvres against his leader to squeeze him for more rope to continue the talks." Peres believed that intelligence agencies took every joke seriously, turning every rhetorical exaggeration into a matter of strategic concern. He liked to summarize this conception with a devastating quip: "One Arab lies to another Arab. One Israeli soldier listens in on the conversation and a second Israeli soldier turns it into a national intelligence brief."

I was in an argumentative mood for some reason and said, "The most important thing, Shimon, is that you trust the credibility of the reports you receive from your own people."

Peres smiled and said, "Come on, Avi, I wasn't born yesterday."

As soon as it became clear that the optimism in Washington was indeed premature, Peres urged Rabin to renew the talks in Oslo. Rabin, characteristically, was in no rush to give a green light. Peres insisted: we had been pushed into a corner with the Palestinians on Jerusalem. Another round in Washington would only aggravate the situation. Negotiations managed by bureaucrats could not produce serious results. He reminded Rabin again that the government's time was running out because it was not fulfilling its promises and achieving results. Rabin protested the Palestinians' demand to add Jericho to Gaza, and Peres tried to assuage his concerns with a rather lame argument: turning Jericho into the heart of the Palestinians' autonomy would likely weaken their demand for Jerusalem as their capital.

Who Would Travel to Oslo?

Peres kept arguing that there was no chance of progress on the Syrian track: Assad had slowed things down. American involvement had revealed itself to be ineffective. Rabin agreed that "our" issue was not the center of attention in the United States and that "[Warren] Christopher is no [James] Baker." Peres went even further in his displeasure at the Clinton administration's secretary of state. He called him "the dry cucumber." Rabin feared that entering the negotiations in Oslo would cause the Palestinians to snub the talks in Washington. Peres kept up the pressure. He wanted to go to Oslo and meet the Palestinians himself. Rabin rejected this idea but Peres finally achieved a breakthrough. Rabin agreed that a low-level official could go to the talks in Oslo on the condition that the Palestinians commit to keeping the contacts secret, continue attending the parallel talks in Washington, and agree that there would be no discussion of Jerusalem.[23]

"If Rabin agrees for me to go to Oslo, should I take Yossi with me?" Peres asked me before putting this suggestion to Rabin.

"Of course," I replied. Peres did not respond, but after it became clear that Rabin had ruled out such a trip, I discovered that Peres had other plans.

"What do you think about sending Uri?" he asked me. "I don't want to leave Yossi exposed. Better for it to be a civil servant." I didn't buy his excuse. My assessment was that Peres feared that by sending Beilin to Oslo, he would likely lose control of events. I said that I was strongly in favor of sending Uri.

In all our work together, Uri revealed himself to be one of the most sophisticated people I knew. He had a sharp mind and great powers of persuasion, and, on top of that, personal charm and bountiful humor. He was driven by an indomitable impulse to always assess the reality that faced him strategically, as a comprehensive whole. After Peres appointed him director-general of the Foreign Ministry, following much hesitation and a nerve-racking battle, I found Uri immersed in a mild state of melancholy. "What's the matter, Uri? You're allowed to smile," I scolded him.

"I'm used to always planning a few steps ahead," Uri confessed, "and it worries me that I have no idea what I'll be doing after I finish as director-general." "Your problem," I told him, "is you're incapable of going to the toilet at the end of the corridor without planning alternatives and exit routes in advance, in case it's occupied. Sometimes you can just go and pee." Uri smiled but was clearly unconvinced.

And here we were: Peres had chosen Uri for the mission of a lifetime, to fly to Oslo. As I described at the start of the book, Peres instructed me to give Uri the green light by phone during our travels in Asia. An official representative of the Israeli government, the director-general of the Foreign Ministry, was on his way to conduct direct political negotiations with the PLO. Rabin would have to make his peace with this fait accompli.

Rabin Demands to End the Talks

Rabin remained hesitant for the whole course of the Oslo talks. On June 7, 1993, two and a half months before the agreement was signed in Oslo, he sent Peres a formal letter demanding that we halt the talks. The harsh and measured language in the letter shows the difficulty of Peres's task, to continue holding onto Rabin, pushing and pulling him without dropping him along the path to a deal.

Subject: The Oslo contacts

Further to our conversation on this matter on Sunday 6 June 1993, I wish to repeat the main points that I made.

In the present situation, the contacts known as the "Oslo contacts" constitute a threat to the continuation of peace talks on the basis of the Madrid Peace Conference.

Firstly, they give the "Tunis people" an opportunity to bypass the talks in Washington and they weaken the most positive actors there—the inhabitants of the territories who are included in the Palestinian delegation. The "Tunis people" are the most extreme among the Palestinians who want a peace process, and they are preventing the more moderate actors from making progress in the negotiations with us. This fact was most clearly expressed at the ninth (last) round of the negotiations. Moreover, they are preventing members of the Palestinian delegation from departing for a dialogue with Foreign Ministry representatives in the United States.

It is quite possible that the intention of the "Tunis people" is to torpedo any chance of reaching a serious negotiation in Washington and to compel us to speak only to them, which would likely endanger the peace negotiations with Syria, Lebanon, and Jordan.

Furthermore, the proposals conveyed in the context of the "Oslo contacts" are completely unacceptable inasmuch as they speak of a "declaration of principles".

The document you forwarded to me includes an approach that would be completely unthinkable for us to adopt or see as a basis for discussion. That is so for two reasons: firstly, what it says; and secondly, what it does not say.

The approach expressed in the "declaration of principles" document is "give us the territories and the powers to control them, and then we'll negotiate with you over the details". Two clauses in this document—4 and 5—express this most clearly. Hence, whatever else is included in the other clauses is completely insignificant.

The attempts by the "Tunis people" to torpedo the talks are clear, and their proposals are disastrous and completely unacceptable.

I also regret that we submitted the ten-point document without your prior coordination with me.

Since the meeting we had arranged for the two of us today (07 June 1993) did not take place, I see no choice but to ask you to halt the contacts until the resumption of the negotiations on 15 June 1993 or until further clarification.

> *Regards,*
> *Yitzhak Rabin*

The letter threw Peres and his colleagues into depression. Personally, I thought it had some upsides. Rabin was setting conditions for the continuation of the talks, which meant that he accepted the principle of holding talks with the PLO. Our job was to find a way to meet Rabin's conditions. Peres answered Rabin with a letter of his own.[24] He defended the Oslo channel and made the argument that in the course of the discussions

the Palestinian side displayed a greater ability to compromise than in Washington ...
the Palestinian position is the Palestinian position, not ours, and there is no reason

to accept it a priori or as it is ... The ten points you raise in your letter were not handed over to the Palestinians; they were presented as private thoughts that deserved consideration.

It was clear that Peres was frustrated and angry. But he avoided a war of words with Rabin. He also conveniently presented him a ladder with which to come down from the tall tree he had climbed in his letter: "I believe that in our meeting tomorrow with Joel we will be able to formulate our position on the principles that they presented, as well as our approach to them." Peres even helped to allay Rabin's concerns that Oslo was helping to torpedo the Washington track: "It's possible for us to reach out to our interlocutors in Oslo only after the opening of the next round of talks in Washington."

Was the Oslo channel intended to help promote the Washington channel or substitute it? Here too, things were not planned in advance. Peres preferred to see the channel as a secret track supporting the Washington talks. In such a case, as Joel Singer explained in one of his reports, the agreement reached in Oslo would be signed in initials, or both sides could send a letter confirming their agreement to the Norwegian foreign minister, who would send the text of the agreement to the United States. Then the United States would present the proposal to the representatives from both sides in Washington as an American proposal. The PLO would instruct its representatives in Washington to sign the agreement as it was without changes. Israel would instruct its delegation to do the same. Joel explained that the PLO saw the Oslo talks as a parallel track that aided the talks in Washington, not as a substitute for them. The contacts with the PLO would remain secret unless Israel formally recognized the PLO.

Mutual Recognition between the PLO and Israel

The writing was on the wall for Israel's recognition of the PLO. Uri shortened the path for Rabin and Peres. Negotiations like Oslo are not conducted on a single channel. Uri negotiated with Ahmed Qurei, Peres with Rabin, and Uri with Peres. Uri was not the kind of negotiator who diligently implemented his superiors' instructions. He maneuvered them and spurred them into making their decision on mutual recognition by initiating discussions on a document on the principles of recognition (the "seven-point document") with Qurei.

These principles went on to form the basis of the letters that PLO chief Yasser Arafat and Prime Minister Rabin exchanged on September 9, 1993, in which Israel recognized the PLO as the representative of the Palestinian people and the PLO formally recognized the State of Israel. Peres was incensed when he was told that the document had been presented to the Palestinians. While Uri had discussed the idea with him earlier, and even explained later that it was a "non-binding presentation," Peres still feared Rabin's fury and even started having his own doubts about whether the timing of the move was right. "Uri made a mistake," he told me. I defended Uri as much as I could, but I did not need to make an effort. Peres did not really mean what he said. He considered Uri to be the best negotiator Israel could have sent. In retrospect, he also praised Uri for his initiative. He knew in his heart that his industrious disciple had acted as his teacher. The non-binding discussion on the mutual recognition document had become a reality.

No Love for Them, but We're Positively Romantic

In internal meetings, we analyzed the elements of the deal that had been put together and subjected them to a two-part test: how could we sell them to the Palestinians, and how could we sell them to Rabin? When we received a gloomy report from Oslo that Peres feared would depress Rabin, he ordered us not to burden him with the full document and asked us instead to write up and send him a short memo summarizing the achievements of the channel and the alternatives we faced.

The more realistic the possibility of signing a deal in Oslo looked, the more Peres grew frustrated that he would not receive the proper credit for his actions. I tried to encourage him:

> There'll be a day when it will be obvious to everyone that the real story of this period was your influence on the bilateral negotiations with the Palestinians. That's the central drama. The breaking of the ice and the opening of initial contacts with PLO officials, the channel that was developed in Oslo and made the one in Washington irrelevant, the main ideas you drove forward: "Gaza first", moving the PLO leadership from Tunis to Gaza. Nobody could ignore any of that.

Although my words were music to his ears, Peres refused to take comfort: "Rabin is already presenting himself as the owner of the 'Gaza first' idea. We need to keep a record of everything that happens." I promised him that I was already doing so.

Peres thought ahead and looked forward to the challenge of the day after the signing. He feared that without a section on economics, the signed papers would be insufficient. We had to commit ourselves to building a thriving Palestinian economy. Peres was driven by what he understood to be Israel's interests, not by some altruistic conception of a heavenly brotherhood of nations.

He explained his way of thinking to the Norwegian mediator, Terje Rød-Larsen:

> On the subject of the economy we propose ... that all countries with a foreign aid budget send a representative at a ministerial level to a meeting that both Faisal Husseini and I shall attend, where we shall ask them to give priority to Gaza from their existing budgets ... We'll also try to help Gaza through the World Bank, and I shall meet Jacques Delors, President of the European Commission, so the European Central Bank can help as well ... In the competition between the PLO and Hamas, Hamas has two advantages: bottomless demagoguery and a bottomless wallet. We don't want the PLO to lose. We have no love for them, but when we consider the alternative, we're positively romantic.

Without a little romance and a little vision, it was impossible with Peres. "I'm thinking of inviting someone from Singapore to Gaza," he added. "Gaza is the closest thing to Singapore. What happened there might be able to happen in Gaza too. I might suggest that the foreign presence mentioned in the declaration of principles be Singaporean."[25]

I Invite You to Kill the Whole Thing Off

Arafat's return to Gaza was a central plank of Peres's strategy. It was intended to serve two main purposes: firstly, Arafat could restore order and govern; and secondly, the move of Arafat and the PLO leadership to Gaza would relocate the Palestinians' center of gravity from the diaspora to the territories. Peres maintained that Israel did not have the means to solve the problem of the Palestinian diaspora. Despite the centrality of Arafat's return to Peres's grand theory, he did occasionally reveal doubts and even inklings of remorse. Peres's conviction was strengthened, however, when he was confronted with Rabin's own hesitations and then had to mobilize an entire repertoire of arguments supporting his initiative to persuade him. It was by being a supporting actor that Peres was in a stronger position to present and promote his daring ideas. The ever-organized and methodical Joel used to react with astonishment to the mixed signals he was getting from Peres.

As it became clear that we would soon strike an agreement, Uri began to reveal misgivings of his own. "I'm putting a gun on the table and I invite you to kill the whole thing off," he said in one of our last consultations. He used a fine-tooth comb to analyze the pros and cons of an agreement based on interim arrangements without a binding mutual understanding on the final destination. The difficult issues—Jerusalem, refugees, borders, and settlements—were all to be postponed. Without putting them off, there was no possibility of reaching a deal. We built the interim period in a way that would enhance mutual understanding and drop anchors of common interests, thereby paving the way for negotiations over a comprehensive agreement and a resolution of the difficult issues. But another scenario was also possible: that each side might hope to exploit the interim period to bolster its own position at the expense of the other ahead of the moment of truth. The conflict might only intensify.

On August 2, 1993, Rabin updated Peres that he was leaning toward taking the Syrian path. "We have made many compromises with the Palestinians but to no avail. There is a major problem in returning Arafat to Gaza."[26] But soon enough, Rabin gave up on Assad. The idea of "Syria first" had collapsed. In the wake of Secretary of State Christopher's meeting with Assad on August 4, 1993, Rabin understood that the Syrian president had no intention of meeting the demands that he had set for an Israeli withdrawal from the Golan Heights: full peace, strict security arrangements, a normalization of diplomatic relations, a scaled Israeli withdrawal, and tough action by Syria against Hezbollah in Lebanon. Assad even insisted on and demanded a clear commitment from Israel that the withdrawal be to the border of June 4, 1967—that is, to a line that would permit Syrian access to the Sea of Galilee.[27]

Rabin told Peres[28] that he had heard from Dennis Ross, the head of the American peace team, that Syria was unlikely to sign a genuine peace deal. Rabin was worried about going so far in one fell swoop. He stressed that he had refrained from promising a full withdrawal from the Golan Heights[29] and had reminded Christopher that Anwar Sadat had agreed, back in the 1970s, for an exchange of ambassadors even before Israel vacated the entire Sinai. Rabin argued that the question of normalization would need to be tested for a few years, such that it would be unthinkable for us to withdraw in one go and be left with no meaningful assets as collateral. Rabin explained that he wanted an early warning station on the Golan. Demilitarization would not be enough in itself because the area was so small. We needed an American presence in the territory and an American commitment in case the Syrians violated the agreement. Christopher was silent about such an American commitment. Rabin added that this was all complicated by the situation in Lebanon. The situation there was volatile and could combust at any moment.

Peres understood that this was the moment his wishes might come true and he bombarded Rabin with a whole host of arguments and condolences. Indeed, he told him, he couldn't expect much from Christopher at all. "When he says good morning, he immediately regrets he might have said too much." The situation with the Palestinians was even more complicated than with Syria, but the cost of the proposed agreement with them now was lighter. He stressed the advantages of the Oslo track: no dealing with Jerusalem and no discussion of settlements. Arafat's return to Gaza was important. Someone had to govern there: "Arafat may be crazy but he can govern. We'll have to hold our noses but it will work. The PLO *has* been weakened, but it would be a genuine loss for us if the PLO or Arafat disappeared."

Now that the Syrian option had collapsed, Rabin came around to sending an Israeli representative to Oslo. He explained that he preferred the seven-point document. He understood that we had no choice but to recognize the PLO. "And it wouldn't be the end of the world if Arafat visits Gaza." Rabin accepted Peres's assessment that if we agreed to conduct talks on the mutual recognition document, Arafat would be able to concede more in the declaration of principles. Peres now felt comfortable enough to tell Rabin that it had been Uri's initiative to start talks on the seven-point document. He then took advantage of Rabin's positive attitude to raise his desire to meet Arafat personally.

"Don't give him that now," Rabin replied. "We should wait on that."

How to Involve the United States?

The Americans were not a party to the Oslo talks. They received hints and snippets but remained outside the room where it happened. About a month and a half before the secret signing, Peres spoke to the American diplomat Dennis Ross.[30] He did not explicitly mention Oslo, but since he assumed that Ross was aware of the process, he dropped some heavy hints: "There needs to be a paper, but the thinner the better. If we get bogged down in discussions on formulations, we won't make progress. We need less paper, but more concrete action on the ground. We must be wary of an ocean of words that would be difficult to cross."

Peres urged the Americans to bring the Europeans on board to funnel economic aid into the territories.

> The real meat is in Gaza. The problem there is not as complicated as in the West Bank. There's no Jerusalem in Gaza and there aren't that many settlers. Gaza can rescue the PLO from being an organisation of exiles. Its leadership would gain some territory and move from the world of rhetoric to the world of reality. If we reach a deal with the Palestinians, take it upon yourselves to mobilise a large bloc of Arab states to support it. Tunisia, Morocco, and even Libya could be witnesses to the signing.

Ross wanted to know whether "Gaza first" included steps in the West Bank. "Of course," Peres replied.

Peres exercised great caution when speaking with Ross. He had concerns about the United States and still bore the scars from the torpedoing of the London Agreement. He blamed Ronald Reagan's secretary of state, George Shultz, for the failure that helped to sink the agreement and for cooperating with the rejectionist Yitzhak Shamir. Peres considered it an advantage of the Oslo talks that they were not run by the Americans. But he was still careful to give them respect, knowing that the United States could hinder and even foil its execution. For the deal to proceed, Washington's assistance was vital.

"For now we want each channel to work separately, and we might connect them in future," Peres explained to the Norwegian mediator, Rød-Larsen.[31]

> We want the Americans to receive the credit but our fear is that if we give it to them too early, they'll mismanage it like they ruined the agreement with Hussein. We don't doubt the Americans' good intentions, but let's first get to the final station. We want to be cautious. We'll coordinate with you and keep you informed and tell you before we update the Americans, and we expect the same from you.

As the Oslo process ripened, Peres agonized over the best way to involve the United States. He once explained to his Norwegian counterpart, Johan Jørgen Holst, that he was afraid the Americans would be jealous.[32] "They're in shock," he told Rød-Larsen. "When Christopher told you to go ahead, he didn't believe you'd actually succeed. They'll criticise the agreement. They'll say they could have cut a better deal."

Larsen: "What could make it up to them?"
Peres: "If they can present the agreement in Washington."
Larsen: "But the real process will leak and then their embarrassment will be twofold."
Peres: "They could say they were in the picture the whole time. Christopher spoke to Holst. Rabin spoke to Christopher. I also spoke to Christopher.

But the bureaucrats around them believe they know about everything. They'll feel hurt. That's part of the reason why I'm not in a rush on the seven-point document. We can 'consult' with the Americans about the seven points. People can't forgive success."

The talks in Oslo progressed and left only a few points open. They were solved at the end of an all-nighter in Stockholm on August 17, 1993, in negotiations with Tunis over the phone with Norwegian mediation. At dawn, Peres called Rabin and told him everything was done. Rabin demanded a final few corrections to the text. We had earlier received news of the deaths of seven soldiers in the north of Israel. We were concerned that Rabin would be unavailable to deal with Oslo during such a difficult time. I put Peres through to Rabin again. Peres expressed an interest in the situation in the north and then told Rabin, "They've agreed to your revisions. I know you're preoccupied with another matter. I don't envy you. I shan't bother you today. I'll call you tomorrow or the day after. We'll need to discuss how to tie this business up with the Americans."

Peres continued talking noncommittally and then finally said, swallowing his words, "And they'll initial it tonight at 9pm." Then he added, "We'll need to remain tight-lipped." I was slightly stunned by Peres's nonchalance, as if making an aside in mentioning his intention to sign a historic agreement that very night.

The Midnight Signing in Oslo

We landed in Oslo on the morning of August 19, 1993. Holst welcomed us at the airport. We held a small meeting—just Peres, Holst, Mona Juul (the head of the Norwegian foreign minister's office and Rød-Larsen's wife) and me—to coordinate the signing ceremony that night. Since we had arrived in Oslo on the pretext of a regular diplomatic visit, we also had to hold a wider diplomatic meeting with the whole entourage while ignoring what was going to happen that night. Peres and Holst played their parts well, and each treated the other's entourage to political analysis that completely ignored the impending drama.

It was agreed that we would hold the ceremony after midnight at the guesthouse, when the members of our delegation would be asleep. The planning of the ceremony was hectic. Rød-Larsen, Holst, and their wives worked hard on the preparations. They dragged an ancient desk into the room for the signing. They told me that it had been used for the signing of Sweden's recognition of Norway as an independent state. "I didn't catch that," I told them, "and don't tell the Palestinians about that piece of history." Rød-Larsen told me that the Norwegians would want to leverage the signing for their own domestic political needs. Elections were planned for September. They also told me that their prime minister, party chairperson, and trade union chief were in on the secret. He added that he had warned the party chairperson not to make use of our matter for now, although the upcoming elections were creating a temptation to take credit for contributing to the promotion of the Middle East peace process.

The Norwegians were fussy about the ceremony. They explained that the Palestinians were sensitive. They accepted my suggestion that they film the ceremony and keep the material in Oslo, for the sides to receive only by mutual agreement. Rød-Larsen sat down with me and sketched out the division of the rooms for the different delegations and the structure of the ceremony. The question of Peres's role came up. The Norwegians wanted Peres to give a speech together with Holst and the heads of the delegations in the formal part of the event. Peres refused and explained that the agreement had not yet secured cabinet approval. I settled with the Norwegians that after the formal part, we would move to a side room, where Peres would deliver his remarks. The ever-meticulous Norwegians checked that the pens for the signing had ink and would not disappoint at the moment of truth. Rød-Larsen told me to expect tears. From him, too. He said that the Palestinians, especially Qurei, were very emotional.

I woke Peres up from his nap. I talked him through the details of the ceremony and walked him across the floor of the event. He decided that he would sit on one side of the hall and at a certain point would be photographed with the teams. I updated Hagai, the head of our squad of bodyguards, only at a later stage. I was worried that he would report back to his superiors at home, and I wanted to limit the timeframe for anyone in Israel to leak the signing before it happened. "As a one-off gesture, please try not to open fire tonight even if you clearly see PLO people in front of you," I told Hagai. We stationed a barricade of Norwegian security guards to block the stairs leading up to the hall, in case anyone from our sleeping entourage had a fit of insomnia.

The event opened with an emotional speech from Holst. He was followed by Qurei, who spoke with deep admiration about Peres as a man of peace. Peres shifted in his seat next to me, visibly moved, and he murmured in English, "Thank you." Qurei could not hold back his tears for the whole ceremony. It was clear that he and Uri were bound by a genuine friendship. Another similar speech from Uri, and we were ready to sign.

At the end of the formal ceremony, we moved to a side room. Peres spoke about peace and cooperation between the two nations. He exchanged a private word with Qurei, then left. We stayed together for a while, taking advantage of Peres and Holst's departure to crack some undiplomatic jokes with the Palestinians, which would have been inappropriate in front of the ministers. Peres's entourage remained asleep one floor down, oblivious to the bursts of laughter above their heads.

In the morning, we continued our tour as planned and flew to Iceland. Sitting on the plane, I could finally breathe a little. I was thrilled about the previous, emotional night and was also extremely tired. I played music by The Doors on my headphones, closed my eyes, and quietly sang along with Jim Morrison. But this pleasant sense of calm was interrupted by an air stewardess who tapped me on the shoulder. "Your loud singing is bothering the other passengers. Please stop."

In Iceland we were awaited by a rowdy demonstration of PLO supporters. They carried posters reading: "Peres is a terrorist." I left our entourage and slipped into the crowd of demonstrators. I felt their rage up close. If only I could have told them about the previous night, perhaps they would have rewritten their slogans. Peres was in excellent spirits. He accepted the invitation of the Icelandic prime minister, Davíð Oddsson, to join him for a tour of the pastoral island, even though it meant traveling on Shabbat—a taboo for Israeli dignitaries abroad. Our host heaped praise on Israel

Figure 8 The secret signing in Oslo, August 19, 1993 (photographed by the Norwegian secret service).

and made Peres laugh when he said, "We are the frozen people—you are the chosen people." Having realized a dream the previous night in Oslo, Peres developed an appetite to realize another dream in Iceland. "I want to eat whale meat," he said. "I hear it's a delicacy they serve in heaven." We found a restaurant and Peres chewed blissfully on a slab of the great sea mammal.

Peres suggested to Rabin that he would leave Iceland directly for the United States in order to update the Americans. He explained that this was a request from Holst, who feared that the signing would leak. This would have likely provoked hostility from the Americans for having left them to learn about this breakthrough from the press. "I have a good cover. I'm already abroad and the media in Israel are focused on the security tension in the north. Christopher will be flattered to have two foreign ministers coming to him, and that will help avoid any bitterness on the Americans' part. We'll explain that we rushed to update him. That we're interested in having the signing in Washington."

Rabin was not convinced. "First come back and we'll pass this by our colleagues in the cabinet." Peres chose not to argue. Rabin added that if the Americans were going to adopt the agreement as their own plan, it could be presented that way to the government. But he also said that he did not mind for the agreement to be presented as it really was: an agreement between us and the Palestinians. Peres said that Israel had to offer the Americans to adopt the "seven-point" document on mutual recognition between Israel and the PLO.

Flying to Update Christopher

After a short stay in Israel, we set out to meet Warren Christopher. The secretary of state was on holiday in California and so it was decided that we would meet at the nearby Point Mugu military base, where our plane could land. We picked up our Norwegian colleagues on the way. Peres was primed and ready for this decisive meeting. Our task was to persuade the US secretary of state, and through him also President Clinton, to adopt the agreement we had already signed in secret in Oslo. I promised our Scandinavian colleagues, who had been forced to get used to our unsubtle Middle Eastern sense of humor, that Christopher's first response would be: "Norwegians? Who needs Norwegians?" Rød-Larsen turned this ditty into the catchphrase of that tedious flight, and it later became the title of an academic article by a Norwegian historian.[33]

Awaiting us at the American base were also Dennis Ross and our ambassador in the United States, Itamar Rabinovich. Peres apologized for cutting the secretary's holiday short, and Christopher poured us a drink. Peres tried to stop him: "No way—I come from a kibbutz and you, the secretary of state of the United States, will pour me a drink?"

During the meeting, which lasted several hours, Peres and Holst described the history of the talks in Oslo. Joel chimed in with a professional explanation of the "declaration of principles." Peres emphasized that we had two agreements in front of us: a declaration of principles, which was signed in Oslo, and another agreement, which was still up in the air, regarding mutual recognition (the "seven-point" document). Peres wanted to give the Americans the impression that they still had a meaningful role to play in the process, besides staging the ceremony. He explained that the second agreement was not yet final because we were aware of the restrictions that Congress had imposed on the administration regarding ties with the PLO. He also tried to dangle some bait in front of the Americans: "If we reach an understanding on both documents, we'll be able to present them to the cabinet in Israel as a U.S. initiative."

As far as Peres was concerned, he was killing several birds with one stone: the agreement would receive more credit in Israel if it were presented as an initiative with the agreement of the United States, Rabin would be calmer and more cooperative, and the Americans—if they felt a sense of ownership over the agreement—would not jeopardize it and would assist in its execution.

"I learned my lesson from the London Agreement," Peres explained. There, Secretary of State Shultz got cold feet at the last minute. Shamir sent Moshe Arens and the whole thing collapsed. If we get American agreement for the seven-points business, we'll hold a week of talks in Washington and then we'll end up with an agreement that will represent a brilliant achievement for American diplomacy and for the whole Middle East ... Rabin and I are ready to take this heavy task on ourselves, assuming it's acceptable to and backed by Washington. If we reach an understanding that the agreement is an American proposal, you could even add the Russians as sponsors to the signing.

Peres continued making it clear that Israel was interested in obtaining the Americans' agreement at every stage: "We don't want there to be any disputes with you." He said the seven-point document met the spirit of the conditions that the United States had set the PLO. "You should go over the wording carefully, there might be something that's important to you, so we can ensure it's integrated into the document ... I suggest that you propose an American addition to the document. That would help you to get it through Congress." Peres, who was aware of the administration's sensitivities to the positions of the American Jewish community, added: "We have called a few Jewish leaders: Lester Pollack and Malcolm Hoenlein.[34] I told them the full story, but I said we were *likely* to agree to it. I didn't tell them we had already agreed. Their response was enthusiastic."

"I'm very happy you did that," Christopher remarked.

At the end of the talks, Christopher expressed his deep appreciation and warmly congratulated us on our achievement.

> My recommendation, and I have some confidence the president will accept it, is to go ahead ... My instinct tells me that the seven-point document is a very positive development, but it also has political and congressional implications. I'll need to discuss this not just with the president but also on Capitol Hill. My advice is that you agree on the wording, and then we'll think later how to present it and sign it in Washington.

Peres recommended holding a grand ceremony to send a message of peace to the whole world. He added, "The Palestinians are asking for the signatories on their side to be Abu Mazen, Faisal Husseini, and Hanan Ashrawi, and on our side—me."

Despite the positive conclusion of this set of talks with the secretary of state, Christopher was not inclined to take Peres's bait—primarily because it bore a strong whiff of a fabrication. "I don't think a 'declaration of principles' could be presented as an American idea, because that isn't entirely true," he said politely. "I have learned to be wary of such things. The press would expose it. We need to present things in a reliable way that will withstand scrutiny."

Peres had led the talks skillfully and eloquently. The American weight was lifted off his chest.

Paris Nights Aren't for Sleeping

Peres jumped straight into finishing the job: obtaining an agreement on mutual recognition between Israel and the PLO. He asked the Norwegian foreign minister to come to Paris to help to mediate with the Palestinians and rebuffed my suggestion that we call Singer. He was confident in his own abilities and wanted to prove that he was capable of closing a deal without him. Paris, as usual, contributed to his elevated mood. He loved that beautiful city with an intense passion, and every corner evoked memories of his past adventures there. We dined that evening in a fine restaurant with a live band. Peres and Holst joined their singing and burst into a duet of French chansons.

In Peres's bible, Paris nights were not for sleeping. When I left him to go to my room after an exhausting day's work, he shot me an almost pitiful glance and said, "At your age I spent whole days in Paris without sleeping. What is happening to the younger generation?" So we continued to a trendy nightclub. The bodyguards got nervous about the dense crowds, the music was deafeningly loud, and Peres danced happily till 3am with Mona Juul and the women from the Norwegian embassy. When we returned, exhausted, to our rooms at the luxurious Hôtel de Crillon, Uri swapped around all the breakfast orders that the guests had left on their doors. It was his way of breaking the tension. I noted that even this sophisticated negotiator suffered from an uncontrollable sense of childish mischief.

Peres returned to Israel and left Uri and Joel the task of completing the negotiations. He was careful to keep Yossi out of the picture. It pained him later that the media depicted Yossi as the architect of Oslo. At a dinner in honor of Egyptian Foreign Minister Amr Moussa, Peres noticed that Yossi had been given a bigger bowl of fruit. He could not resist the temptation and told Moussa, "These young people take all the fruits for themselves." He was angry at Yossi for saying in a press interview that Rabin and Peres would not run against each other again.

With the talks in Paris completed, the path was now clear for a public signing in Washington. It was obvious to Peres that if a big ceremony were in the works, "it will need a director like Hitchcock."[35] When I asked him what he meant, he answered sheepishly, "Hitchcock gradually builds up the tension, from light to heavy, that's why we're only starting with an earthquake." Peres very much liked the idea that he and Mahmoud Abbas should represent the sides at the signing. He also had a reasonable argument: it was too early to give Arafat so much legitimacy—he had to pay more to deserve it. Neither Arafat nor Rabin, therefore, needed to come to Washington. But Peres feared that the structure of the ceremony could yet change, and he asked me not to start organizing the trip to Washington until Rabin clarified that he was indeed not going.

On a Friday afternoon, the director of the Prime Minister's Office, Eitan Haber,[36] called to say that Rabin had made the final decision not to go. I worked till nearly midnight to arrange the flights.

Rabin Wants Credit Too

Early in the morning, I received a phone call from Ruth Yaron, the spokeswoman at the Israeli embassy in Washington. She said that she had understood from administration officials that the Palestinians were pushing to bring Arafat as well, and that the administration would not object. In such a case, it would be natural for Rabin to come as well. I called Uri. He had also heard a similar report. We agreed that I would update Peres. I called him just before 06:00. The pillows he was covered in contributed somewhat to his relatively muffled response: "Do I or do I not need to write a speech?" I told him not to exert himself for now.

At 07:30, I received a call from Eitan Haber. He said that he had wanted to let me sleep, which was why he was only calling now. He told me that Christopher had called

Rabin at 06:00, informed him that Arafat was coming, and invited Rabin to join. Rabin had responded in the affirmative.

I updated Yossi by phone and asked him what he thought. He advised that Peres say, "I'll gladly go to the ceremony, but it's more important that I stay here in order not to leave the country in the hands of Minister Yisrael Kessar." (Peres loathed Kessar, who was supposed to be acting prime minister in the absence of both Peres and Rabin.)

After a telephone consultation with Yossi and Uri, I called Peres again (it was now 08:00). This time Peres sounded very much alert. The two hours that had passed since I informed him that Rabin might attend the signing ceremony, and the media reports to that effect, had turned the news in Peres's mind into a humiliating and painful blow. Now he sounded disappointed and most profoundly hurt. The spotlight had been taken from him, along with the photograph that would have memorialized him as the chief architect of this historic breakthrough. He ranted and raved against Rabin and said that he would not go to the ceremony. He requested that I update Moshik Theumim, a close associate, and ask him to call around 12:00. I spoke to Moshik and advised him not to wait because I was afraid that Peres was thinking of resigning. I then spoke to Haber and suggested that he persuade Rabin to call Peres directly. I apprised him of the severity of the crisis. Haber understood that we were entering a difficult day and made great efforts to stop the crisis from escalating. I knew that he had doubts about Rabin's participation in the ceremony and was revolted by the thought of meeting Arafat.

At 10:40, Haber called me and said: "They had a really stormy conversation. There's been a big falling-out." Immediately afterward, Moshik called me to share what Peres had told him about his conversation with Rabin:

> I shouted at Rabin: How are you not ashamed to say on TV that there were additional channels of talks with the Palestinians?[37] He replied: Didn't you know? There was a channel between [Environment Minister] Yossi Sarid and Nabil Shaath. I told him: But you told me that that was Yossi's own responsibility! Why don't you consult anyone after Christopher talks to you? Is he God? What's the point of me going with you to America? To hold your bag? To be your gofer? Rabin answered: Anywhere I go, you're coming too. He suggested that we meet to straighten things out. I refused.

I learned from Peres that Rabin had told him in their difficult conversation that he was sorry. "What am I supposed to with your apology?!" Peres had responded angrily. I consulted with Moshik, who had already come up with a few ideas for a compromise to put Peres's mind at ease. I called Eitan Haber and suggested, "Let's agree on a few rules to facilitate Peres's trip and end this crisis between them: Peres gives a speech at the ceremony, Peres signs the agreement next to Rabin, they're together in every meeting, both of them speak at the event organised by the Jewish community, no insults, we arrange a meeting between the two to straighten things out, and they'll both instruct their aides to set up a joint staff to arrange the travel to the ceremony." Haber replied firmly that he was on his way to Rabin and would raise the matter with him.

Peres asked me to make contact with him at 17:00. I called from the office. I reasoned that he was hanging Rabin out to dry until then and would eventually agree to fly with him to Washington. I called at the appointed time and discovered that I had been mistaken.

"I'm going to resign," Peres told me in an emotional voice.

"I'm on my way," I said. I found him agitated and angry. He cursed Rabin. How had he made the mistake of giving Arafat a stage? How had he received an order from Christopher at 06:00 to come to the ceremony and immediately said yes? How had he not bothered to consult anyone before answering? Agitated Peres had talked to Giora Eini, who duly arrived for another round of mediation between Peres and Rabin. I took advantage of the opportunity to have a long conversation with Sonia in the kitchen. She wanted Peres to resign. She had been pressuring him to do so for a while already. "Why?" I asked her. She said that Rabin was not letting him work. That he was a bad man and a liar.

I launched into a long and emotional speech:

The reality is the complete opposite. Rabin let Peres work on the most sensitive subject and Peres succeeded. Without Peres's involvement, the process would have been over. The public was calm because Peres and Rabin were working together. My children will not understand, and history will not understand, why Peres is dropping out at this moment, when his contribution is still critical to the success of the peace process. They'll say he left out of regard for his own honour, like David Levy during the Madrid Conference.

Sonia seemed to understand the logic of my remarks and was inclined to agree, but her heart was not ready to follow her head.

We moved to the living room. Peres asked me for my opinion. I decided to take a gamble and said, "Let's hear first what Sonia thinks."

"Right now, I'm not entirely sure you should resign," Sonia said. I repeated my arguments and Giora added his own. Peres agreed to see Rabin, and Rabin, as a gesture, made the journey to Jerusalem for a reconciliation meeting. Peres called me afterward and said that they had agreed that from now on, Warren Christopher would not be allowed to bypass Peres and speak directly to Rabin, and that the Foreign Ministry would play a meaningful role in the remainder of the process.

When Peres left his home to meet Rabin, we had already agreed that I would continue coordinating the flights. Peres did not want us to take Hirschfeld and Pundak. He explained that the participation of the pair, who were perceived as "leftists," would damage his ability to sell the deal to the public, and said that this was also the position of the Prime Minister's Office. I felt that this was simply unfair. "If we leave them at home, the papers will write—the Moor has done his duty, the Moor can go," I told Peres. I convinced him that the pair should take a commercial flight to Washington, and that I would make arrangements through our embassy to bring them into the ceremony. And that's what happened.

A few years later, Peres summarized to a journalist that nerve-racking Saturday when he had threatened to resign: "He [Rabin] didn't want [to go to Washington].

He asked me to go and sign it with Abu Mazen. I agreed. When President Clinton pressured him, he changed his mind but did not bother to update me. I heard about it by chance. Of course I was in favour of him going. And that's what he said sorry for."[38]

Three Kisses from Arafat

Yossi, Uri, and I nearly missed the ceremony at the White House. When we arrived in Washington, I was told that Mahmoud Abbas was asking for a meeting with Peres. It was 06:00. I called Abbas, who told me that he was not at all convinced that we would be signing that afternoon. "There's a crisis," he said. He wanted time to get ready and said that he would be in touch.

About half an hour later I received a call from Ahmed Tibi, who was working as Arafat's advisor. He said that he was in Arafat's suite, gave me a phone number, and asked me to call the bedroom from now on "because everyone's sitting in the living room, and we're alone with Arafat here." He told me that they had demands regarding the wording of the declaration of principles. Since the secret signing in Oslo, we had also reached an agreement on mutual recognition between Israel and the PLO, but this fact was not mentioned at all in the declaration of principles. Tibi insisted that the term "Palestinian team" in the document be replaced with "PLO team," and the term "Jordanian-Palestinian delegation" be scrapped altogether.

I told him that the fact they were asking for changes three hours before the ceremony would prove to the Israeli public and the world that the PLO was still the same old PLO and that its word was meaningless. The government had approved the wording of the declaration of principles and we were not allowed to change a single word. If we accepted the logic that elements from the recognition agreement had to be transplanted into the declaration of principles, then we should be expected to demand in return that the promises Arafat had made in his letters to Rabin and Holst also be transplanted there.

Tibi said that he understood the logic behind my remarks but that Arafat had an internal political problem. He was unable to explain why, despite the recognition agreement, the PLO was still not mentioned in the document. "Arafat has already instructed his people to pack their suitcases, and he won't come to the ceremony."

I said that we were in an even better position: "We haven't even unpacked yet, so there's no problem for us to go home." Before we left Israel, we reasoned that Arafat would make such demands and we had no objection to accepting them. But Peres instructed us to respond harshly until the very last minute. He feared that if we were to acquiesce immediately, the Palestinians would develop an appetite and rush to make additional demands that would likely complicate the situation.

Tibi called and said that the chairman was requesting that Peres meet him for a conversation. Peres agreed, but with nerves of steel instructed me to keep Tibi waiting in my room. The ceremony was planned for 11:30. Time was running out. At the last minute, Peres made himself available for Tibi. We went to his room and Peres agreed to have "PLO team" written at the top of the document instead of "Palestinian team."

Tibi was quick to call Arafat, told him Israel's final position, and listened keenly to the chairman's response: "The chairman says: See you at the White House. He says he's sending me three kisses, one on each of my cheeks and another for me to give you on your forehead, Mr Peres."

Peres was taken by his bodyguards to his car on the way to the White House lawn. But the transportation for the regular people had left long ago. Yossi remained calm as usual and suggested, "Instead of the ceremony, let's go to a matinée." We ran down the roads around the hotel looking for a way out and then, as if by magic, managed to get into a decoy car in Rabin's motorcade. "This is the car that's meant to deceive assailants," I told Uri and Yossi, who were out of breath. "If we're shot—we'll have served a national mission, missed the ceremony, and not made Yossi's matinée either."

I spotted a few figures from the Jewish community on the festive lawn, who were known for their vigorous opposition to any Israeli concessions and ties with the PLO. Now they looked like dedicated, longtime partners in the peace process. An invitation to a festive event at the White House, it seems, is an ideological argument of great persuasive power.

The Wizard's Syndrome

The world applauded the heroes from the Middle East. Peres loved going to Broadway shows on his trips to New York. Exhausted and jet-lagged, I generally fell asleep next to him a few minutes after the curtains went up but not before seeing the effect of his regal entrance into the theater. Our bodyguards used to take us to our seats after the rest of the audience had already sat down. We could sense the whispers rippling through the auditorium when someone noticed that Shimon Peres was gracing the theater with his presence. Soon enough the crowds stood on their feet and applauded for several minutes in his honor. Peres used to stand straight and wave back in gratitude at the excited audience. "I'm embarrassed," he used to whisper to me. I knew that he wanted this embarrassment to last forever.

Riding the waves of admiration flowing out of the signing ceremony at the White House, Peres could be derisive toward mere mortals. I asked him to meet my old teacher, Professor Herbert Kelman from Harvard. The man had long worked to promote ties between Jews and Arabs. "So, have I shown you academics that all your talking is misguided?" Peres snapped at him mockingly. I liked to say that Peres was suffering from "wizard's syndrome." He was treated around the world as a deity who performed diplomatic wonders. Sometimes he got carried away with that image and was tempted to believe that even his most delusional, inane ideas had come to him on a direct line from God almighty.

Peres saw himself as the leader responsible for the historic agreement with the PLO. He was troubled by attempts by other participants in the Oslo process to take credit for themselves and downplay his own part in it. He added a chapter on Oslo to his book *The New Middle East*. Since he had asked for my comments, I advised him to be magnanimous and elaborate a little on the people who had helped him reach the agreement. Peres replied that this was not a book of fiction but a "diplomatic programme," so there was no room for names. His inability to be magnanimous toward his own staff and his voracious appetite for credit affected the mood in his office and produced an endless series of sketches and impersonations. We joked that of all his advisors and acquaintances, Peres had chosen in his "diplomatic programme" to mention only his friend, the gossip columnist Mira Avrech.

Our criticism made its way up to Peres. When the Hebrew edition of his book was published, he showed me that he had mentioned Uri, Joel, Yossi, and me and asked me self-righteously, "Why do people claim that I didn't mention my advisors?"

"Because there's no such mention in the English version, which was published first," I replied.

"Really?" Peres answered. "That's strange. How did that get edited out?"

Peres sent Uri and Joel letters of thanks and appreciation for their work. He wrote that future historians would elaborate on their role in the story. In other words: the future is a long way away, so keep quiet for now. He asked me to send Hirschfeld and Pundak a written instruction: "In the course of the Oslo negotiations there were many meetings in Israel and abroad of which you surely kept your own records. Please take note that this is sensitive material that must not be published or shown to anyone else without clear authorisation." Peres also refused for the video of the secret signing in Oslo to be released. After all, he was not the star of the show.

After reading an interview that Uri had given a newspaper, Peres said to me, "Uri doesn't mention my name. Dennis Ross would have mentioned his boss five times in every line." But he reserved the thrust of his rage for Yossi. He was convinced that Yossi was trying to bolster the public's perception that he had been the true architect of Oslo. That Peres and Rabin were brought into the loop at a later stage and were essentially pawns in the realization of Yossi's great plan.

At Peres's request, I prepared a timeline that attested to his role and refuted the common assumption that Beilin had brought Peres into the picture at a very late stage:

- November 16, 1992: Peres plants the "Gaza first" idea in Egypt;
- December 4, 1992: Hirschfeld meets Ahmed Qurei for the first time in London;
- January 8, 1993: Peres presents Rabin the concept of "Gaza first," a big step toward the PLO, and Arafat's return.
- January 20–22, 1993: Beginning of a series of talks between Hirschfeld and Pundak with the Palestinians in Sarpsborg, Norway.
- February 9, 1993: Peres updates Rabin on these talks based on a report he received earlier from Beilin.

Furious, Peres did not mince his words: "Yossi betrayed me. He's flattering Rabin. He should be careful, I can be brutal." He was not happy about Yossi's left-wing politics. "He's going to trip me up big time one of these days." In conversations with guests, Peres gave Yossi the cold shoulder and sometimes interrupted him dismissively. He once told Foreign Ministry staff in his deputy's presence: "There will only be one Foreign Ministry here, and it won't belong to the Left." He instructed his secretaries that "there's no need to invite Yossi" to briefings with the heads of the intelligence agencies, as in the past. He asked me to join him instead.

Nobel Prize

The ultimate credit, of course, depended on the Nobel Peace Prize committee. Peres demurred in the press and said that he had no interest in a Nobel Prize. He had already received his prize in having had the honor of bringing peace to Israel. He said that the words of praise he had received from a young girl from the Galilee were enough. But to me, he said,

> Rabin's getting everything. Now he'll also get the Nobel Prize. His people have worked for him, and ours—nothing! We need to be less restrained against him in the press. We need to expose how he and his people have got half the world working for him to get him that prize. I don't expect anything. I didn't expect any help from my acquaintances, but I expected them not to ruin things for me. Yossi is taking Oslo from me. Pundak is saying that Yossi gave me Oslo and the ideas for Oslo. I'm not stupid and I know what's happening around me. At Rabin's— everyone put in work for him.[39]

I showed Peres the copy of a letter that arrived from our embassy in Riga, sent by the speaker of the Latvian parliament to his Israeli counterpart, Knesset Speaker Shevach Weiss.[40] He was confirming that he had acceded to the request to recommend that Rabin be given the Nobel Prize. "I told you," Peres snapped. "Rabin's guys are working methodically on getting him a Nobel Prize—and mine are all preoccupied with themselves." When I asked him whether he wanted us to lobby for him, he replied, "I don't want to be involved in that." Or in plain English: "Of course, Einstein. Why don't you understand that by yourself?"

I learned that Rød-Larsen had ensured that Peres's name would make the list of nominees. Lest the Nobel Prize committee overlook his role, Rød-Larsen even recommended that Peres also fly to Oslo for a concert marking Norway's role in securing a peace agreement between Israel and the PLO. *Yediot Aharonot* had reported on tension between Rabin and Peres's offices concerning who would win the Nobel Prize. Peres's acquaintances were quoted as saying that "contrary to the denials from the Prime Minister's office, a small taskforce has been set up around Rabin that is working to get him the prize. Knesset Speaker Shevach Weiss has asked parliamentary speakers around the world to pressure the prize committee to give it to Rabin." Rabin's people, the report went on, "are claiming that Peres is operating a vast network of lobbyists, headed by Terje Rod-Larsen and Uri Savir, to get him the prize." The article also said that "sources around Rabin are pointing to Peres's visit to Oslo on Tuesday to attend the concert as a milestone in efforts by Peres and his advisors to persuade the Nobel Prize committee to give him the Nobel Peace Prize. Sources in Peres's office claim that the Norwegian government had applied tremendous pressure to persuade Peres to come." And indeed, there was pressure. But we were behind the bulk of it. We explained that Israeli–Norwegian relations were likely to suffer greatly if Peres did not show up. Zubin Mehta, who was set to conduct Norway's national symphony orchestra, would carry out his threat and absent himself if Israel were not represented at the event by Rabin or Peres. The donors would demand their money back, the event would be called off—it would be a disaster.

The fierce opposition from Rabin's office to his trip made Peres think twice. He asked me to meet his devoted mediator, Giora Eini. Giora could not understand why the event was so important. I explained that the heart of the matter right now was not the event itself but how far Israel might offend a friendly Norwegian government. Peres spoke to me afterward: "I've spoken to Giora and I understand that you're not thrilled about me flying to Oslo." That was his way of saying: *Roll up your sleeves, because I'm flying.* I did not want it on my conscience that I had spoiled Peres's last chance to show his face in Oslo on the eve of the Nobel Prize committee's decision. So I asked for a written assessment from our colleagues in Oslo of the expected damage to the relations with Norway if Peres did not go. I said that if the Norwegian foreign minister truly wanted to make his concerns known, there was no reason why he should not make his distress clear to Rabin and that it was entirely "legitimate" for the organizers to send the sternest letter of protest possible.

The harsh reactions from Oslo—both requested and orchestrated—came quickly. I bundled them together and faxed them to Peres, straight to the cabinet meeting. Peres passed them on to Rabin, who said he would consider it. And after consideration, he gave Peres the green light to depart for Oslo.

On the flight,[41] Peres confided in me his disappointment in "my friends, who spoiled my chances of getting a Nobel Prize." But in the meantime, the ever-creative Uri had turned the event in Oslo into a diplomatic encounter with Arafat, in a bid to solve the crisis in the economic talks in Paris. We ended up signing another document, a joint "Oslo declaration"—festive but meaningless. Dennis Ross and representatives of the World Bank were invited but did not show up. Rød-Larsen told me that they had no interest in giving Norway credit on the anniversary of the agreement, and I felt relieved to learn that this preoccupation with credit was not exclusive to us. "When will we know already who the winners are and put an end to this saga?" Peres asked me, stressed, on the way back home. The subject even came up in a meeting with Rabin. Peres told Rabin that he had heard that he (Rabin) had complained that he (Peres) was busy promoting his own candidacy for a Nobel Prize. Rabin denied it. Peres, for his part, made it clear that he was not preoccupied with the matter.[42]

The suspense grew as the date of the committee's announcement drew near. A few days before, I received reassuring messages from Jewish community figures in Oslo that Peres was on the list of winners. These messages received a powerful reinforcement when a member of the Norwegian embassy in Tel Aviv called me. He wanted to know, discreetly, how Peres could be reached quickly if it turned out that he was on the list of laureates. I decided not to tell Peres. I was worried that the news would raise his expectations to new heights, and I didn't want to be responsible if those heights crashed down on all of us.

Peres welcomed the announcement of his win, jointly with Rabin and Arafat, coolly. The punctilious organizers of the Nobel Prize ceremony sent us a video of the previous year's ceremony with Nelson Mandela and Frederik Willem de Klerk, so we could know what to prepare for. I screened Peres the film. He watched, concentrating, then suddenly glanced at me and said, "You should know that all this adoration for me makes me embarrassed." The Norwegian mediator, Rød-Larsen, later said that the committee had briefly considered giving the prize to the teams who were involved in actually negotiating the agreement. I was amused to think what the implications of that decision might have been, and I felt that the final decision was the more sensible option.

The prize-giving ceremony was, to my mind, a clear testament to Peres's status as a supporting actor. On the Palestinian side, there was only one laureate; on the Israeli side, two. The necessary symmetry was broken by the singularity of Peres. I was glad to see him happy on the stage, but I enjoyed the button-down musical event the next evening even more. I was seated close to Rabin. He fidgeted nervously in his seat when he saw the singer Sinéad O'Connor, who took to the stage barefoot and with a shaved head. But when she began to sing, "Thank you for breaking my heart," Rabin stared at her, engrossed. He was clearly moved and swept away by her magical voice. I watched him now without any hostility. He had been dragged to Oslo and to this occasion grudgingly and haltingly. But during his journey to this agreement, he had made his peace with his own direction. He and Peres had become partners. I knew that without his go-ahead, there would not have been an agreement. But I also knew that Peres, the supporting actor, whom he loathed so much, was the one who had brought him there.

The Letter about Jerusalem

In order to reach the Oslo Accords, Peres had needed to cloak the process in a smokescreen of sorts. Peres believed that ambiguity was constructive, because it helped the sides to overcome obstacles without being asked to declare concessions on their most fundamental positions. But a lack of clarity can sometimes come at a painful price—as in the episode of the letter about Jerusalem.

Israeli leaders saw dealing with the future of Jerusalem as a dangerous minefield that anyone who cared for their own safety would avoid. No wonder that the idea of an interim agreement, promising a final-status agreement whose details were unknown, enchanted Peres and Rabin. But even so, without dealing with the difficult questions— Jerusalem, borders, settlements, refugees—they were confronted by a mighty task: breaking the taboo on talks with the PLO, recognition of the Palestinian nationality, and navigating a peace process without bringing their government to the point of collapse. They were well aware of the Israeli public's mental barriers when confronted with the terrifying visage of Yasser Arafat. They knew that the Knesset majority supporting the process was shaky. Any concession over the holy city would be the straw that would break the camel's back and bring the whole edifice crashing down.

Immediately after the formation of the Rabin government in 1992, and even before the Oslo contacts started, Egyptian Foreign Minister Moussa tried to put out feelers to Peres about the possibility of the Arabs of Jerusalem voting in churches and mosques in Palestinian elections. Peres gave a definitive "no": "Jerusalem is not in the game," he said firmly.[43] He explained to Faisal Husseini, in a secret meeting whose contents were relayed to the PLO headquarters in Tunis, "You have to understand that if we conduct negotiations about Jerusalem now, our government will lose its majority."[44]

But the Palestinians cared little for the Israeli leaders' domestic woes. They too had their own hopes and they too were coming under pressure. And indeed, as soon as the secret talks started in Oslo, Arafat demanded that his envoys not neglect the fate of Jerusalem. He sent a letter to the participants in Oslo and demanded, among other things, recognition of the ties between the Palestinian institutions in Jerusalem and the temporary Palestinian council that would be established.[45] In that spirit, Ahmed Qurei, the head of the Palestinian negotiating team, asked to include a paragraph stating that all Palestinian institutions in East Jerusalem should be subordinate to the Palestinian Council. Peres was horrified and even suspected that the Norwegians might give the Palestinians unrealistic expectations about Jerusalem. "I don't want you to negotiate in our name," Peres warned Rød-Larsen, the Norwegian mediator, in a meeting. "We will not be able to compromise over Jerusalem because if we do, we won't get a majority in the Knesset."

Rød-Larsen tried his luck: "But perhaps you'll agree for the Palestinian Council to hold meetings in Jerusalem?" Here too, Peres responded in the absolute negative.[46]

Arafat did not give up. He pressured the Norwegian foreign minister in a meeting in Tunis[47] to get a response from Israel, and Holst wrote to Peres that Arafat was asking for at least "something vague" on Jerusalem. A mention to the holy sites and free access to them by Jews, Muslims, and Christians. Peres updated Rabin and asked me to write that he had raised the issue with him and had even won his approval to accede to the request.[48]

In Oslo, meanwhile, Qurei repeated his demand for a clause in the agreement guaranteeing the continued functioning of the Palestinian institutions in Jerusalem. He justified his demand by explaining his fear that after signing the accords, Israel would shutter these institutions, chiefly Orient House. But as alternative to such a clause, the Palestinians would be willing to suffice with a letter from Foreign Minister Peres to Faisal Husseini—whom the PLO regarded as responsible for the "Jerusalem portfolio"—committing Israel not to prejudice the continued operations of the Palestinian institutions in the city.

The Palestinians' request appears in the summary of the talks that was received from Oslo and communicated by Peres to Rabin.[49] Rabin read it and asked Peres to take the papers back. He did not want to keep them. Perhaps he feared that they would be picked up by his own people, who had not been brought into the loop about the Oslo contacts. I assume that Rabin never received an independent, organized, running analysis of the documents that he had been given to read, so it is difficult to assess how attentive and aware he was of the significance of every detail in the reports he received.

Peres explained to Rabin that Arafat's tactics were clear: he was afraid that he would bear the brunt of bitter domestic criticism for the concessions made at Oslo. But he still wanted a deal and very much wanted to return to Gaza. "He inserted the issue about Jerusalem to pave his own way to Gaza," Peres explained.

The question of "the letter" cropped up again two days before the secret signing of the agreement in Oslo on August 19, 1993. Peres was staying in Stockholm as part of a seemingly innocent foreign tour. The Norwegians joined us at the Swedish government's guesthouse, which was now hosting the last marathon of late-night talks mediated by Holst and Rød-Larsen.[50]

The manageress of the guesthouse was furious that we had not updated her about this high-level meeting, which meant that she could not prepare the food that protocol required. She had it written down that Peres was dining at the Swedish foreign minister's home, so was supposed to return to the guesthouse sated. I told her that although she was hosting two foreign ministers that night, some simple sandwiches would be enough for their excellencies Holst and Peres. But the woman, most offended, was completely unwilling to compromise on her high standards. She refused to just bring sandwiches and even threatened to complain to the Swedish Foreign Ministry. We were concerned about a possible diplomatic crisis because the Swedish Foreign Ministry did not know about Holst's arrival and of course did not know about the purpose of his visit. Just to be safe, we agreed on a cover story. If the need arose, we would say that Holst had come to prepare Peres's visit in Norway and to resolve in advance some of the misunderstandings and tensions that remained between the states over the "heavy water" needed for the nuclear reactors that Israel had bought from Norway in 1959. But luckily for us, the hostess was satisfied with our unctuous flattery. After she left, we raided the pantry for whiskey, cake, and a giant chunk of cheese, which kept the ministers and their staff nourished till daybreak.

Arafat and his people gathered in the PLO headquarters in Tunis. They were extremely excited. Holst tried to deceive his Palestinian interlocutors into thinking that he was sitting in a different room from us. He was so devoted to the rules of fair mediation that he was not averse to a tiny lie to demonstrate how honest and unbiased he was. At Rød-Larsen's advice, he tried to prevent spy agencies from understanding the meaning of the phone calls he conducted next to us throughout the night. He made an effort to speak in codes. Instead of "Israel," he said "bleep." But the burden was too great for him and his tongue occasionally slipped. A few times he blurted, "Israel … sorry, bleep," and revealed the meaning of "bleep." Peres joined in our gales of laughter in front of an embarrassed Holst.

Ahmed Qurei reminded Holst that Uri Savir had promised that Peres would send him a letter committing not to harm the Palestinian institutions in Jerusalem. For Qurei, this was a compromise. He would have preferred that the letter be signed by Rabin. Holst asked for Peres's approval, explaining that this would enable him to obtain the Palestinians' agreement for the final revisions to the text that we wanted. Peres gave his approval. He had received authorization in principle from Rabin and did not believe that an Israeli commitment to guarantee the operations of the Palestinian institutions in Jerusalem deviated from Israel's traditional position. He said he had even heard from Elyakim Rubinstein—who was handling the talks with the Palestinians in Washington and whom nobody suspected of being quick to make concessions—that he himself had told Faisal Husseini that the Palestinians could continue administering the institutions in East Jerusalem, although they could not be connected to the institutions of the Palestinian autonomous entity.

Holst updated Qurei by phone, again careful to use codes. "They approve the writing of the letter. Will that help with the revision they're asking for? From my conversation with the father, I understand that it's a matter of necessity for the grandfather. It's connected to their ability to sell the matter at home." The father was Peres and the grandfather was Rabin. The matter of necessity: our demand for having the agreement stipulate that the institutions of the Palestinian Council would be established in Gaza and the Jericho area. The Palestinians agreed. The father received what the grandfather had demanded. The price: the letter about Jerusalem.

A few days after the secret signing in Oslo, Rød-Larsen said that the Palestinians were disappointed that they had not received the letter that night already. But Peres was in no hurry to sign it. He refused to see it as part of the agreement or for it to be presented as such. As he saw it, what the Palestinians were essentially asking from Israel was to clarify what had been existing Israeli policy for years. To his mind, Israel had neither made any changes nor made any concessions to the Palestinians over Jerusalem.

In the days left till the public signing in Washington, negotiations were held in Paris over mutual recognition between Israel and the PLO. I conveyed to our delegation Peres's instructions regarding "the letter": the letter on Jerusalem would not be sent for now. As far as we were concerned, it was not part of the agreement. It was an expression of existing policy, not a product of the negotiations. There would be an announcement about Jerusalem in the Knesset instead and only afterward, in about a week, would a letter "similar in principle and substance to the letter that Uri read out" be sent. It was not clear to me from Peres's remarks at the time whether the purpose of the announcement in the Knesset was to give public cover for the letter he was supposed to sign, or to act as a substitute for the letter the Palestinians were expecting. In any case, Peres was convinced that evening that he was executing a brilliant diplomatic maneuver. One that earned its masters the title of "diplomatic *akrut*," a term that Peres had coined and which described—besides Peres himself—outstanding individuals who had proven their mettle with the finest of diplomatic ruses. (*Akrut* is an Arabic slang term, meant to jokingly describe a clever and shrewd person.)

Peres feared that appending the letter on Jerusalem to the Oslo Accords, even if its content was nothing new, would expose the entire venture to attacks that could bring it down. He was adamant that Jerusalem was not part of the agreement reached with the Palestinians. He also sincerely believed it. On September 8, 1993, Peres summoned the religious affairs minister's advisor Israel Lippel, the head of the Foreign Ministry churches department Eitan Margalit, and the ambassador Oded Eran—all experienced experts on the question of Jerusalem. He asked them to draft him an announcement to be read out in the Knesset, detailing Israeli policy. Peres read their draft the following day:

> Israel has always recognised the importance and religious significance of Jerusalem to adherents of the monotheistic faiths, and it will continue to honour the unique value of the city and its sites in the spiritual and daily lives of Jews, Muslims, and Christians, as the Prophet Isaiah says: 'For My house shall be called a house of prayer for all peoples' (Isaiah 56:7). We are and shall remain committed to freedom of worship and to the proper running of the various religious institutions in the city. We shall continue to respect the aspects of free religious life in the city, and we shall aspire to enhance our dialogue with the institutions of the different faiths.
>
> We shall refrain, as in the past, from any action or activity that could hinder freedom of worship and freedom of access to the holy sites, or which could offend the feelings and sensitivities of members of the different faiths. This commitment applies both to residents of the city and to people visiting it and its holy sites.

Jerusalem is a multifaceted city of people, religions, and cultures. Jews, Muslims, and Christians live there together with each group managing to preserve its own cultural heritage, special characteristics, and social, religious and other institutions, including their special education systems. Coexistence in Jerusalem is a matter of mutual respect between all its inhabitants and of the proper functioning of the relevant institutions and systems.[51]

Nothing to Do with the Other Letters

The Paris talks concluded at the same time and the Norwegians set out for Tunis and then Jerusalem to get the sides to sign the letters of recognition. Before his departure, Holst sent from the Hôtel Le Bristol in Paris the four letters of recognition that he said had been agreed between the sides, including the letter on Jerusalem. The headline on the fax: "Attached: copies of the 4 letters agreed by the sides." One of the drafts we had received earlier from Paris stated in a footnote that the letter on Jerusalem would be classified until both sides agreed to its publication. It also said that the letter would be transmitted on September 13 in Washington. But Peres refused to treat the letter on Jerusalem as part of the agreement that had been hashed out with the PLO. He asked me to forward the letters to Rabin without the letter on Jerusalem. "This letter has nothing to do with the other letters," he said. I did as he instructed.

On Friday, September 10, the day after Peres made his announcement in the Knesset, Holst came to Israel bearing the letters of recognition signed by Arafat in Tunis. We held a signing ceremony in the Prime Minister's Office and then Peres hosted the Norwegian foreign minister and his entourage for lunch in Mishkenot Sha'ananim. After the meal, Holst had a private word with Peres in my presence, and asked for the letter he had promised on Jerusalem. Peres hesitated but Holst insisted. Peres ultimately retrieved a pen and signed the letter—but only with his initials:[52]

Dear Minister Holst,

I wish to confirm that the Palestinian institutions of East Jerusalem and the interests and well-being of the Palestinians of East Jerusalem are of great importance and will be preserved.

Therefore, all the Palestinian institutions of East Jerusalem, including the economic, social, education and cultural, and the holy Christian and Moslem places, are performing an essential task for the Palestinian population.

Needless to say, we will not hamper their activity; on the contrary, the fulfilment of this important mission is to be encouraged.

Sincerely,
Shimon Peres
Foreign Minister of Israel

The text that Peres read out in the Knesset had not elicited much public interest. It did not deviate from Israel's conventional statements. Neither was there anything revolutionary about the contents of the letter, which instilled Peres with such fear. But the content was not what mattered. At the heart of the matter was a politically explosive question: was Israel sending this letter as part of political negotiations with the PLO over Jerusalem while publicly announcing that Jerusalem was not on the negotiating table? The letter was not presented in the Knesset debate on the declaration of principles with the PLO. The stormy debate had ended with a speech by Peres, who promised that everything included in the agreements had been brought to the attention of the members of Knesset, and that there was no secret document "about Jerusalem."[53]

But for now, the Norwegian foreign minister would not let go. He asked for the letter to be signed properly. He wrote to Peres:

> Shimon, I must urge you to sign the letter that you initialled in Jerusalem. As Uri will confirm, the letter is the product of a careful negotiation as part of a whole package. It was agreed that the letter would be transmitted to me as a signed letter on 13 September 1993 in the presence of PLO representatives at the signing ceremony in Washington.

Holst added that several PLO representatives had asked him in writing and in person whether he could promise that he had received the signed letter. "I could not do so and I fear that as a result their confidence in me and in you will take a serious blow, which would likely cause a major crisis in the implementation of the declaration of principles."[54]

According to Peres's reports of his conversation with Rabin, the prime minister was apprised of the matter and even asked for the text of the letter that would be sent to Holst to approximate what Peres had said in the Knesset.[55] On October 11, Peres finally sent the letter to Holst. Uri Savir, who had left for a trip to Oslo, was responsible for handing it over. Peres emphasized that the letter was a response to Holst's letter from October 8 (that is, after the Knesset debate in which the Oslo Accords were ratified). He quoted his own remarks to the Knesset and also appended the signed letter that Holst was expecting, whose text we had accepted before the signing in Washington and before the debate and vote in the Knesset.

This affair made me uneasy and I raised my concerns in the discussions of our inner forum. I warned that the letter was bound to leak and extract a high price. I was surprised that Arafat had not publicized it yet. Whenever anyone doubted Arafat's sanity, I used to point out to his credit that he did not leak this letter. I repeated my warning that hiding the letter on Jerusalem, while claiming in the Knesset that the agreement contained no secret annexes, would cause major damage.

Peres dismissed my remarks again and again. He argued that I was being paranoid and that this was a standard and essentially insignificant letter between foreign ministers. "It's my letter to a foreign minister colleague. Like dozens and hundreds of other letters." I said that when the letter leaked, it would be easy to see that the wording had been the result of bargaining, not his free will. Peres dismissed my comments. Yossi Beilin recommended that we leak the letter. He explained that it contained nothing of substance, so it would be a pity to pay a price for hiding it. He even suggested that the leak be performed on a Friday, to minimize the levels of media attention. In the professional literature on leaks, such a maneuver is called an "inoculative leak": you inject a little bit of the virus into your body in order to produce antibodies and become immune to the full force of the illness. Peres was not convinced that we needed the inoculation that Yossi had prescribed and rejected his suggestion. As far as he was concerned, the letter on Jerusalem had nothing to do with the negotiations, was not addressed to the Palestinians, and had been sent to the Norwegian foreign minister to clarify for him, at his request, Israel's traditional positions on Jerusalem.

All in all, however, members of Knesset did not need the "letter on Jerusalem" to claim that Oslo had put the future of Israeli sovereignty in a united, undivided Jerusalem in question. In the agreement submitted to the Knesset, there was explicit reference to Israel's consent to discuss final-status solutions later on, chief among Jerusalem. Furthermore, the agreement stipulated that Palestinian residents of Jerusalem could take part in the elections that the Palestinians would hold in the West Bank and Gaza Strip for their governing council.

Jihad of the Soul

The hope that Arafat would forever keep our letter a secret was of course fanciful. On May 10, 1994, Arafat gave a speech in a Johannesburg mosque, calling on Muslims to "wage *jihad* to liberate Jerusalem" and revealing that Israel had given him a letter in Cairo stating that Jerusalem was part of the negotiations that would begin within three years. By referring to the agreement signed between Prophet Muhammad and the Quraysh tribe,[56] Arafat was implying that the agreement with Israel was no more than a temporary tactical step. We heard the news during a visit to Oslo. Peres had come to the Norwegian capital to receive another peace prize with Arafat, in the presence of former US President Jimmy Carter. Alon Liel, our ambassador in South Africa, sent us a fax of a handwritten note. He quoted Arafat, speaking in English:

> The Jihad[57] will continue ... Our main battle is Jerusalem ... I was insisting before signing to have a letter from them ... I did not publish it till now. In this letter, we are responsible for all the Christian and Muslim and the Islamic holy sacred places ... I cannot do it alone ... You have to come, and to fight and to start the Jihad to liberate Jerusalem ... It is not their capital, it is our capital ... I am not considering this agreement more than the agreement which had been signed between our prophet Muhammad and Quraysh.

An anxious Peres took advantage of his meeting with Arafat to register his protest.

Peres: "Your remarks in South Africa were very poorly received in Israel."
Arafat: "I was misunderstood. I was speaking in a mosque to Iranian Shiites who were criticising me harshly."
Peres: "You said that in the view of the Prophet Muhammad, there are second-tier agreements."
Arafat: "No, I didn't say that."
Peres: "Even Shulamit Aloni [the left-wing leader of Meretz] has called for the talks with you to stop. It's important that you make unambiguous comments on the matter to the media tomorrow."
Arafat: "Muhammad spoke about a lesser *jihad* and a greater *jihad*. The greater *jihad* is the *jihad* of the soul, not a violent *jihad*."

Is There or Isn't There a Letter?

Arafat's remarks caused a public storm in Israel. The initial focus was not on the letter but on the meaning of Arafat's comments about the validity of the agreement with Israel. Peres was forced to explain in a radio interview: "I'm not sure that Arafat and Muhammad are so similar ... Arafat explained to me that the Quraysh tribe was the side that violated the agreement, so Muhammad violated the agreement with the Quraysh. That's his explanation. But there's no doubt that Arafat was drawn to a speech that caused damage."[58] And the damage was indeed further compounded when media attention turned to focus on the letter that Arafat alluded to.

While we were still abroad, the opposition submitted a no-confidence motion in light of Arafat's speech. Minister Moshe Shahal replied on behalf of the government: "In his speech in Johannesburg, Arafat made a call for the Muslim nation to wage *jihad* to liberate Jerusalem and mentioned an imaginary letter about the future of Jerusalem that he supposedly received."

> **MK Dan Meridor** rushed to respond: "Don't be so sure. Don't state that it's imaginary."
> **Shahal:** "There's no letter about Jerusalem and there's no need for such a letter beyond what the agreement with the PLO states."

The sharp-tongued Benny Begin mocked him: "Arafat claimed in Johannesburg that he had an additional commitment from the Israeli government about Jerusalem. Knowing Arafat, it's difficult to believe his claim. But knowing Shimon Peres, better not to hurry to rule it out." I later learned that various figures in Israel had come to know about the letter through King Hussein. Arafat had relayed him the contents of the letter, provoking his rage because he concluded that Israel was prejudicing Jordan's own status in the holy city.

The pressure to clarify the controversy around the letter grew. Rabin hinted that there was something to it, and Peres finally confirmed that there was a letter "but it contains no political guarantees to the Palestinians about Jerusalem." "The letter is identical word for word with a speech that I delivered in the Knesset," he explained.

"I sent a letter to the foreign minister of Norway, in response to a letter that he sent me. My letter wasn't even marked as secret. The letter is completely open ... When I addressed the Knesset, nobody from the opposition said a single word." But he was in no hurry to publish the letter itself.

"There's no rush," he said again to his spokeswoman Behira, who was under heavy pressure from reporters.

I suspected that Peres was hesitating because of Rabin. I asked him again, "Does Rabin know about the letter and is he familiar with it?"

"Rabin knows," he replied, as usual.

The reporters were given a fanciful excuse: "There is no possibility of releasing the letter until the agreement of its Norwegian recipient is received." We had suddenly come around to observing the niceties of diplomacy.

On Monday, July 6, 1994, Peres asked me to send Rabin the text of the statement that would accompany the release of the letter for his approval. He waited nervously for the prime minister's reply. After a few nerve-racking hours, Rabin's approval came through with a request that we add a sentence to the statement saying that the letter was written after the Knesset debate that ratified the declaration of principles with the Palestinians. Did Rabin know that Peres had initialed the letter on September 10 in Mishkenot Sha'ananim? Did he know and still make that request? Maybe he had simply forgotten?

I told Peres that under no circumstances could he agree to Rabin's request. We would be knowingly lying. Peres hesitated for a second and decided: We would release the letter without any additions, and the spokeswoman Behira would provide oral explanations. The press release included both Peres's remarks to the Knesset and the original letter that Holst requested. The beginning of the press statement said: "Israel insisted that the institutions of the Palestinian Authority be in Jericho and not Jerusalem. Israel also clarified that there would be no change to the status of the Palestinian residents of Jerusalem. Foreign Minister Shimon Peres, with the consent of the prime minister, made this matter clear to the late foreign minister of Norway."[59] Poor Behira had to deal with the pressure from the journalists, who did not mince words in tearing our credibility to shreds. She called me that night in tears: "I want to resign." I convinced her to wait.

The publication of the letter set off a storm. Benny Begin argued,

This publication proves that the government is trying to lead the public astray until the very last minute. Just a few hours before this letter was released, government spokespeople were arguing that the letter was just a copy of the foreign minister's speech in the Knesset in September. That is untrue ... Given this imbecilic government has zero credibility, one can assume that other such grave documents that this government gave, directly or indirectly, to the PLO will come to light!

The columnist Nahum Barnea wrote in *Yediot Aharonot*, "Whatever the reasons, whether ineptitude or malice, negligence or manipulativeness, one thing is hardly in doubt: our government has been caught with its pants down. Peres sent a letter, and Rabin sent Shahal to the Knesset plenum to deny it. This is an embarrassing incident, perhaps the most embarrassing since this government was formed."

Dan Meridor, a Likud MK, declared in a fiery speech, "This government has acted in an unacceptable manner on three fronts: the concealment of the truth, the collapse of its credibility, and danger to the status of Jerusalem. This government must go home."

Peres tried to correct the damage. He was interviewed by the journalist Dan Margalit on Channel 2:

Margalit: "An agreement was signed with Yasser Arafat in September. Why do you need to send him a letter in October guaranteeing the existence of Palestinian institutions in Jerusalem and even promising to encourage them?"

Peres: "Because I said that I would do so before the negotiations. We had a very dramatic night, and I insisted that the institutions of the Palestinian autonomous entity be in Jericho. Holst asked me: Would that prejudice the existing position of the Palestinian institutions in Jerusalem? I told him: They won't be harmed. He asked me whether I was willing to put that in writing. I said: I'll be willing to put it in writing after the accords are signed, and without any connection to them. It wasn't addressed to Arafat, Arafat isn't mentioned, it doesn't say 'PLO'. I had addressed the Knesset two days earlier, and I said exactly what's in that letter in my remarks to the Knesset, that we would maintain the religious, spiritual, and other institutions. This letter does not contain a single promise that deviates from the existing reality, and it doesn't diverge at all from the present situation—the purpose of this promise was to remove any spark, any sign of [Palestinian] autonomy from Jerusalem. What Arafat said in Johannesburg was pure fiction. First he said that he was not willing to sign the agreement in Cairo till he got the letter. The letter had already been in Holst's possession for about a month. Second, he said that he had received a letter about Jerusalem. He did not receive any letter about Jerusalem … Minister Shahal was one hundred percent correct."

"The letter was sent to the Norwegian foreign minister after the remarks had been made in the Knesset," Peres told *Maariv*, "and therefore there was no need to place it on the Knesset's agenda."

Peres had feared that adding the question of Jerusalem to the agreement would torpedo the chances of getting it through the Knesset. He had worked hard for an agreement and believed that the very fact of its signing would generate fresh momentum. The new reality would matter; the words of the agreement itself would be forgotten. So he was allowed to leave some loose ends and proceed with the benefit of ambiguity. Each side had its own limitations and constraints. The Palestinians needed a fig leaf to prove that they had not abandoned Jerusalem, while Israel needed a fig leaf to prove that it had secured the agreement without prejudicing the holy city. After all, the Palestinian institutions were already active in Jerusalem. Why permit legalistic pedantry to obstruct the quest for peace?

And to what extent had Rabin been in the picture? When the "letter crisis" broke, we heard from Yoel Marcus at *Haaretz* that people close to Rabin were trying to encourage the impression that he had never even seen the letter. We rushed to complain to Eitan Haber, who promised to correct this impression. Rabin himself made clear in the cabinet: "Peres's letter was written with my full knowledge."

Maariv reported that MK Yehoshua Matza had called out to Peres in the Knesset: "In Japan people commit suicide over such things. Go kill yourself." I suggested to Peres that his ministry spokesman should respond that the minister had given serious consideration to the suggestion and decided to reject it. From the way he looked, I could tell that Peres was not in the mood for jokes. He was completely sick of the small-time politicians making his life a misery. As a man who felt at home among the most powerful people in the world and strode across continents, Peres felt that the political arena that awaited him in Israel was full of evil little pygmies. They could neither conceive of nor advance the spectacular political constructions he was engineering. They could not look boldly into the future, understand where things were going, and seize the opportunities that had opened up for Israel. All they wanted was to get in the way. Peres's soul had set course on a dramatic adventure. He was searching for the big levers that could change the face of the Middle East and Israel's fate. He had no patience for petty routine. After storming the Palestinian barrier, he set his sights on the next breakthrough. It awaited him over the river—in Jordan.

Peace with Jordan: Remember November 2

After the signing of the Oslo Accords in Washington, Peres looked glum. The dialogue with the Palestinians now turned to the dry details of the execution of the Declaration of Principles. There was nothing in it to excite his spirits. The negotiations were taking place in Taba under the direction of the Prime Minister's Office, and Peres let things progress without him. He made no attempts to maneuver inside, as he normally did, and he was in no hurry to convene the Israeli–Palestinian liaison committee, which he was meant to chair. After breathing the air of making history in Oslo, he struggled to acclimatize to the greyness of routine. Instead, he hoped to harness the momentum created in Oslo for another great stride. He longed to bring Jordan into the circle of peace. As he put it: "We have to storm Jordan."

Peres's romance with the "Jordanian option" had a history of fascinating twists and turns. In his book *David's Sling* (1970), he described King Hussein as "a weak candidate for peace." Peres analyzed his position and found that "there are basic domestic obstacles which he must overcome, and it is doubtful whether he is able to do this": the hereditary nature of his title; his reliance on the Bedouin tribal minority; and the fact that "the gap between his demands and the ability of Israel to respond to them is particularly wide." He wrote:

> The return of the West Bank to Jordan, for example, would mean the siting of Jordanian artillery along the whole of Israel's Mediterranean coastal strip, the most densely populated area in the country. These guns could again try to do what they did before—shell Israel's cities and villages from short range whenever the Jordanians felt like it. Even if there were an agreement to demilitarize the West Bank, the value of such an agreement would depend upon the power of the signatory—or indeed upon his very existence.

Peres's conclusion was that "monarchs are not immortal," and that "Jordan may be able to base her security on the words of a document, but Israel cannot base hers on a king."[1]

Over the years, the clearer it became that Israel could not avoid dealing with Palestinian nationalism and that the Palestinians would not accept the Israeli occupation forever, Peres changed his position and invested his energies in promoting the "Jordanian option." He had been left bruised and frustrated in April 1987, when Shamir scuppered the London Agreement, which would have aimed to resolve the Palestinian issue in a framework involving Jordan. On the eve of Oslo, Peres still adhered to this preference. As far as he was concerned, an independent Palestinian state was neither the desired end-goal nor a necessary product of the agreement signed on the White House lawn. Monarchs are not immortal, but the "Palestinian option" was also riddled with its own faults.

Peres was free to weave dreams of peace storming the Jordan River, but as a supporting actor he still needed the prime minister's approval. He persuaded Rabin that they had to exhaust the opportunity with Jordan, pressed him to let him go and meet with King Hussein, and secured his approval. The two agreed that ahead of the expected visit of Secretary of State Christopher, they would "turn him east instead of north."[2] Peres dedicated time to putting together a package of incentives for Jordan: security guarantees for Jordan's wellbeing if its neighbor Syria tried to sabotage the reconciliation with Israel; the cancellation of its debts; a regional economic summit in Amman; and joint development projects with international funding. Parallel to these inducements, there was also a warning: in the absence of progress with Jordan, Israel would divert its efforts to achieving an accord with Damascus. And if we made concessions over the Golan Heights, we would be unable to make concessions to Amman for quite some time. Public opinion in Israel would not allow it.

American Skepticism

The package of incentives that Peres wanted to equip himself with on his way to King Hussein required Washington's agreement. But the Americans were not an easy nut to crack. They believed that after Oslo, Israel should turn to Syria, not Jordan. Peres took advantage of the presence in Israel of Dennis Ross and his team for an in-depth strategic discussion.[3] He presented his comprehensive diplomatic vision and tried to persuade them the Jordanian option was likely to succeed. Ross reported that the Palestinians, Egyptians, and many others had recommended a strenuous attempt to make progress on the Syrian track. The Americans were worried about how Damascus might react when it realized that it had been knocked off the regional priority list. Martin Indyk[4] predicted a "catastrophe" if it looked like we were neglecting the Syrians. He argued that leaving Assad out of the game was a recipe for disaster. The Americans also expressed serious misgivings about whether Hussein would be willing to move ahead before Assad. They argued that if Assad suspected that he was being isolated, he would work to disrupt the peace process—with both the Palestinians and the Jordanians. The Americans' assessments were very similar to those of the Israeli intelligence community.

Peres fought against this wall of American skepticism and refused to give in. Even in such desperate situations, he knew how to muster the mental strength to remain optimistic. He used to explain that life had taught him that "a short time before great victories, there are flops and disappointments. You mustn't sink into a state of despair.

You mustn't give up." He insisted, therefore, that we had to complete the construction of the natural Israeli-Jordanian-Palestinian triangle. We could not waste time: we had to hurry up and sprint along the Jordanian track. If we managed, this would make it easier for Israeli public opinion and for the Israeli government to move toward an agreement with the Syrians as well. An accord with Jordan, for which it was easy to form consensus in Israel, would energize the rest of the journey. Peres urged his American interlocutors not to belittle the possibility of peace with Jordan. They must not forget that Hussein had already surprised them in the past by reaching the London Agreement without receiving Assad's green light. The king might yet surprise again. Peres's arguments were clearly beginning to trickle down. Ross agreed that the Jordanian option was worth a shot, even if the prospects were dim.

Ross was brought on board for this process and secured the US support for Peres's package of incentives for King Hussein: President Clinton would attend the regional economic summit that Peres was planning to hold in Jordan; the Americans give us approval to hint to the king that a peace agreement with Israel would release Jordan from a billion-dollar debt to the United States; and the United States could also restate its commitment to Jordan's security in the eventuality that its northern neighbor threatened it.[5]

Peres updated Rabin about his conversation with Ross.[6] He suggested that he would tell the king that Israel would respect the Mandate-era border as the basis for a territorial agreement with Jordan. That meant Israeli concessions over land in the Arava in the desert area between Jordan and Israel. "I'll also tell him that if we have to pay a high price in the north, we'll have no option of paying one in the east." Rabin accepted Peres's proposal.

Efraim Halevy, the deputy head of Mossad and veteran liaison to the Jordanian royal court, joined the trip to Jordan. To my delight, Peres asked me to accompany him. Yossi—his traditional partner on Jordanian affairs—was left at home. Peres was convinced that Yossi had been lobbying journalists to present him as the architect of Oslo. He was determined not to let that happen again with Jordan.

The Visit in Amman

The day before our departure, we met in Peres's house to familiarize ourselves with our cover stories and try on the disguises prepared for us by Mossad. Peres called Sonia down from the top floor so she could see Israel's most senior diplomat preparing for a mission in a wig, a moustache, and thick horn-rimmed glasses. Sonia, with her customary lack of diplomacy, dryly observed, "You look like a retard."

Efraim Halevy suggested that we announce in Israel that Peres was sick and therefore housebound. I knew from past experience that Peres disliked using sickness as a cover story. He believed that true leaders did not sleep, take holidays, or let poor health defeat them. Peres suggested saying that he had traveled abroad. I thought it would be illogical for him to have left the country on the day of municipal elections. I proposed that we say that he had wrapped up a few weeks of intensive campaigning for

Figure 9 Wearing wigs, Peres and Gil on their secret trip to Jordan, November 2, 1993 (photo by one of the people accompanying staff).

his party's candidates, and was now taking advantage of his day off to stay at home and finish writing his book. He would react to the elections only after the official results were released. And so we agreed.

On the way to the Allenby Bridge, we stopped to don our costumes. We switched to talking in English, but it quickly became clear that Peres's voice would be recognizable even if he spoke Sanskrit. He was asked to keep quiet. We crossed the bridge by foot. The river beneath us flowed slowly, barely a narrow stream. We each carried our own belongings and I also carried a gift for the king: a huge, limited-edition book about King David and Bathsheba. Peres had had a hand in writing it.[7]

Peres and Efraim were taken to the official car, and I was invited to enter the escort vehicle. At my feet lay a loaded submachine gun. There was another weapon at the driver's feet. I didn't know whether he was in on the secret, so I chose to make do with casual remarks about the scenery. The road to Amman is not exactly breathtaking but I was excited to see the Dead Sea from an unfamiliar angle. During my army service, I had spent many long hours patrolling the waterfront on the Israeli side, looking out onto the Jordanian coastline. Now Jordan, stripped of its mystery, looked completely unthreatening. We arrived at noon at the guest house of Crown Prince Hassan, adjacent to his palace. The prince and Prime Minister Abdelsalam al-Majali were waiting for us at the doorway. When he saw Peres in disguise, Prince Hassan burst into loud and uncontrollable laughter. Peres was clearly embarrassed.

The long discussion that unfolded after our arrival turned into a brilliant display of diplomacy by Peres. The king, his brother, and Prime Minister Majali listened attentively to his sweeping lecture on strategy, economics, and culture, highlighting dilemmas about the region, and laying down some operative conclusions at the doorstep of its leaders. Peres put on an impressive display of his erudition, accumulated international experience, creativity, and political daring. He demonstrated his rhetorical powers and his abilities to draw practical imperatives for action.

Sometimes, we walk around with a jumble of ideas and feelings in our heads until someone comes along to order them into coherent sentences and arrange them in a logical structure. Peres was adept at helping others, including kings, make sense of and navigate a confusing world. Their amazement at Peres's power, however, was obviously impaired whenever reality veered off the path that Peres had assigned it. There were also occasions when Peres's political derring-do caused him to cross a fine line. Whenever he captivated others with his sweeping diplomatic overviews, his strategic vision, and his insightful conclusions, we always feared that he would spoil this good impression by making a further proposal that would be seen as just one step too far.

At the talks in Jordan, Peres displayed tremendous charm, wit, and determination to finish the evening with a signed document. But at the same time, he left little time for his interlocutors to speak. Whenever they started talking, he found a reason to interrupt them. He rushed to guess what bothered them, phrased their questions for them, and was quick to provide detailed answers. Peres described at length the global developments that were transforming education, science, and technology into the real source of wealth. The problems facing us required a fresh approach: rivers did not stop at customs booths. Road networks and energy infrastructure had to be installed with a view to the regional picture. The full realization of our economic potential required cooperation. This was also the secret to successfully confronting the main challenges facing us: the arms race impoverishing the peoples of the Middle East, the fight against desertification, and the development of modern infrastructure.

But of course, pure theory was not enough. Peres had prepared himself for a practical test. He recognized that King Hussein was concerned about the agreement Israel had signed with the PLO. The king revealed what was on his mind: "We were not in on the secret. We provided the umbrella for the joint Jordanian-Palestinian delegation, and we were not updated by our Palestinian friends. I have nothing against you, of course. We have our own internal problems about the agreement, just like you do too."

Peres endeavored to convince the king that Israel still saw Jordan as its preferred partner. He presented him the package of incentives that he had prepared in coordination with the Americans. He proposed holding the regional economic summit in Amman: "The event is likely to be bigger and more important than the one at the White House in September." Clinton was willing to come with other heads of state, as were global economic leaders and representatives of the largest companies in the world. Peres listed a series of joint projects that would strengthen the kingdom's economy, from Israel's use of Aqaba's airport, through to the digging of a canal from the Red Sea to the Dead Sea dotted with desalination plants, and finally to transforming the Kalia area north of the Dead Sea into a joint medical tourism area.

Peres also came bearing good news about Jordan's external debt. He proved that he was on top of his brief and listed Jordan's main creditors: Japan was owed $2 billion; the United States, $1 billion; the World Bank, $1 billion; France, $350 million.

I've spoken to the foreign minister of Japan and asked him, "What's the problem with Japan rescheduling Jordan's debt?" He gave an encouraging reply. Clinton even told me that he knew the Japanese prime minister, and he'd help. If we two make progress, the Americans will forgive your debts. They wiped $7 billion off Egypt's debt after the Gulf War … If you want, I can also discuss the matter with my friend [François] Mitterrand.

Peres stressed that Israel accepted that the border in the Arava region would be based on the Mandate-era lines,[8] such that Israel would transfer Jordan some territory. He confirmed that he had checked with the United States and its security guarantees toward Jordan were still valid. Israel was also on board in that regard.

The idea that had seemingly been dealt another death blow in Oslo—that of a Jordanian-Palestinian confederation—cropped up again. "We're considering the idea of a three-way economic framework and a political framework between you and the Palestinians," Peres told the king. He strove to allay the Jordanians' concerns that Israel might have given the Palestinians a secret commitment that they would gain responsibility for the mosques on the Temple Mount. "Nothing was done that might prejudice your rights and your status. All we promised the foreign minister of Norway was not to harm existing Palestinian institutions. We know what your relationship is with the holy sites—we're not children, and we won't harm your status."

Alongside this package of incentives, Peres warned the Jordanians that if the Israeli government signed an agreement with Syria before doing so with Jordan, it would be left without the power or public support to pay the price that Jordan was expecting. "The Americans are very interested for us to reach a peace agreement with Syria," he said, swallowing his words. "From their perspective, it's also a question of political credit. They too were surprised by Oslo."

Peres avoided threatening language. He warned of the logical consequences if Jordan failed to hurry up and sign an agreement with Israel—not because of Israel's strength, but precisely because of its weakness. He summarized his arguments thus: "We and you both need to make a strategic decision … experts specialise in the past— but we must design the future."

The king thanked Peres for his wide-ranging lecture and said, "We've all grown up." He praised the idea of a regional economic summit and expressed a commitment "to do everything to see change … to give the young generation a chance of living in a different state—a state of security, a state of peace, a reality they have never experienced." We knew that the king was seriously ill. "I wish to clarify my basic position," he said at one point in the conversation, surprising us. "In 1951, my grandfather was murdered. I shall do everything to fulfil his legacy and bequeath it onwards. Even if I only have two years left."

Agreement in Initials

Peres suggested summarizing their understandings in a joint paper. "Rabin and I are coordinated. We want to pull this wagon quickly and together." The king gave his approval. Both he and Peres signed their initials on the joint paper. Four pages long it comprised the key components of the peace treaty that Israel and Jordan would later sign in October 1994. Peres dictated the document to Efraim Halevy in a single breath without relying on records and without omitting a single detail from their long deliberations. I was amazed by how he operated, and I felt fortunate to be working with him and witnessing his exploits. The Jordanians accepted his text as a fait accompli without demanding the insertion of any meaningful changes.

The document expressed the commitment of Israel and Jordan to act immediately to achieve a full peace treaty between the two states, to promote a comprehensive regional peace, to prepare the economic summit, to advance a solution for Jordan's external debt, to jointly develop common resources (the Jordan River, Dead Sea, Jordan Valley, and Red Sea), to coordinate on connecting electricity grids, to pave highways, to establish a financial fund, and to develop a regional economic infrastructure. The sides also undertook to enhance their cooperation and commitments on security, to foil attempts to harm the peace process, to protect Jordan's status at the holy sites, to promote interreligious relations among adherents of the three monotheistic faiths, and to strive towards economic cooperation in the framework of a Jordanian-Israeli-Palestinian triangle, including the establishment of a free trade zone.

Unlike King Hussein, however, who always projected a regal air of seriousness, his brother, Crown Prince Hassan, turned out to have a sense of humor. In our conversations, he spoke about the importance of interreligious dialogue and the need to invest in "human capital development" and cultivating young leaders. He came across to me as a man whose feet were floating slightly above the ground; but during our talks, he and the king still used to step aside on occasion for a private word.

The prince proudly showed me his private library at home. He was especially proud of a corner that contained Hebrew books and a Torah scroll in a grand silver case. He had little affection for the Palestinians: "The residence where you're staying now was mine in 1970. Your friend—Arafat—his people launched a rocket at the house, going straight through the window. I have left the bullet holes as a memento on the wall of the room where Mr Gil is staying."

We dined with the king and his brother, Prince Hassan, at the latter's home. Our hostess, the prince's wife, was born in Calcutta. Peres did not miss the opportunity to charm her too. "I have just finished reading Vikram Seth's book *A Suitable Boy*. It's a wonderful saga about family life in India. The quality of the writing would not have shamed Tolstoy."

The princess's tender face lit up. "Mr Peres," she said, "I am so happy to hear that from you. I'm reading the book now myself. But it's so big and so heavy that I own three copies—one at the palace here in Amman, another at our summer palace in Aqaba, and the third on our plane." Peres clearly identified with the fragile princess's difficult predicament.

After midnight, we listened to the radio. Peres's face fell when he heard the bad news from Israel about the Likud's breakthroughs in the municipal elections. Personally, I couldn't fall asleep. My thoughts about our exciting day, the monotonous noise of a water pump, and later the call of muezzin did not let me sleep. After breakfast, and before going home, we were taken for a tour around the streets of Amman by car. The city looked arid, devoid of greenery. Shaaban, my Circassian driver, managed to tune into a radio broadcast from Israel. I listened to the reports of the elections and even

translated for Shaaban an interview between the journalist Zuhair Bahloul and Tawfiq
Ziad, the mayor of Nazareth. It suddenly seemed so natural to me that two Israeli
Arabs were talking in Hebrew about elections in Israel, and I was translating them
into English for the Jordanian officer driving me from Amman to the Allenby Bridge.

Remember November 2

On our return to Jerusalem, Peres rushed to update Rabin on the talks. When he
returned, he told me that having heard the good news, Rabin was in seventh heaven. I
advised Peres to act quickly: I would call Joel Singer to update him, and he should sit
down at once to start writing a treaty with Jordan. Peres said yes. I summoned Joel and
told him about the developments. It quickly became clear to both of us that writing a
full peace treaty would take a while. If we wanted to move quickly, we should make do
initially with a declaration of principles. But Peres and Rabin preferred a full treaty.

Peres wanted to consult on how to move forward. "It's enough for you and Joel to
be there." Uri was abroad. I updated Yossi and gave him my written summary of the
discussions. Yossi expressed an interest in coming to the meeting. I told him to come.
I secured Peres's agreement after the fact.

I spoke to Peres again about our commitment to keep the meeting secret. I had
learned from past experience that he was often too clever for his own good and dropped
hints about secret developments. He wanted to be seen in hindsight as having known
all along about these developments and being responsible for them. I described at the
outset of this book how Peres pushed the limits at a meeting of the Foreign Ministry's
senior management when he asked them, shortly after returning from the meeting in
Jordan, whether they thought such a meeting would be possible. That same evening,
he succumbed to the temptation and his tongue slipped. In the makeup room before
a TV interview, he divulged that November 2 would be remembered as an important
day—and immediately set off a wave of rumors that soon enough led to the revelation
of his secret visit to Amman. Seeing these press reports, Peres asked the staff at his
office, "Who's the leaker here?" The spokeswoman Behira, who had been kept in the
dark about the visit, had more courage than all of us and replied in a heartbeat, "It was
you, Mr Peres."

Unlike similar cases in the past, when I had stoically resigned myself to politicians'
inevitable lust for publicity, I was furious at Peres this time. I was concerned that he had
given ammunition to the enemies of the peace process, who would now try to torpedo
it. But more than that, I was pained that we had proven ourselves untrustworthy and
ungrateful to the Jordanians. On the eve of our visit, the Jordanians had rejected Peres's
request for the meeting to take place in the open. They explained that they were facing
parliamentary elections on November 8, 1993 and were worried that the Islamist parties
would grow in strength. I asked Peres why he could not have just bitten his tongue. "I
wanted to raise public morale," he replied apologetically. "The enthusiasm about the
peace process has waned since the signing ceremony in Washington." I was curious
what he had told Rabin and he replied, "I told him it just slipped out. It happens."

Of course, this never had to happen. But that was Peres. The same qualities that led him to great achievements also betrayed him. His passion for realizing his mighty, fantastical, daring dreams. His confidence that he had the power to turn them into reality. His desire to win endless love and admiration for these achievements. His difficulty delaying gratification. His ever-insatiable appetite to see his own picture in the newspaper.

One month after our visit to Amman, Efraim Halevy met King Hussein again. He reported back to Peres that the king had made it clear that he was in no hurry to reach a peace treaty, because such an agreement had to solve, among other things, the refugee problem and the question of Jerusalem. Peres looked disappointed. Efraim rubbed more salt into his wounds. He emphasized that the king had taken the leak about Peres's visit in Amman exceptionally badly. "But he was photographed with me," Peres muttered to himself despairingly. "He gave me the picture with a signed dedication."

Peres paid a heavy price for his short slip of the tongue: "Remember November 2." He had offended the Jordanian king and given lethal ammunition to Rabin's team with which to keep Peres away from the remainder of the process with Jordan. They were determined not to let the Oslo pattern repeat itself. This time they would be in the picture and Rabin would appear as the sole leader. The supporting actor would be escorted off the stage and left in the shadows. And indeed—that's what happened.

What Would Happen if We Boarded the Plane and Went Home?

In July 1994, we were informed of an upcoming meeting between Rabin and King Hussein in Washington. In our internal consultations, my suggestion that we act respectfully and stay home was rejected. I was concerned that Peres would be forced to play second fiddle and we would all suffer the consequences. I could not have imagined that our suffering would be so great.

We had heard nothing from Rabin's office. Reluctantly, I called Eitan Haber. I explained that I had to plan Peres's schedule. I asked what was happening with the journey to Washington. Haber said that he did not know, and also that he could not see what exactly Peres would do in Washington given the nature of the ceremony under discussion. I told him that reporters were pressing me for an answer on whether or not Peres was going. It was better for us to decide now, calmly and collectively, or else a sudden decision would be forced on us under media pressure.

There had already begun to appear leaks in the press about "anger in Peres's office." Haber called me and explained dryly, "If Peres wants to go, he can go."

I told him there was no chance that "such a friendly and warm invitation" would be accepted. I asked him directly, "Is Rabin inviting Peres to join him?"

"I can't exactly say so," Haber replied.

After a while, Haber called back and said that if Peres agreed not to give a speech at the ceremony, he would make sure that Rabin invited him to join. I told him that if Peres were invited, he would not turn it down. "Such a diplomatic answer," Haber replied, "I'm writing it down."

I told him that he had to ensure there would be no problems. Peres was not going to give a speech, but in exchange he would take part in all the meetings. Afterward, in his meeting with Rabin, Peres agreed to a template whereby he would participate in all meetings with more than two participants. I was frustrated. I felt that we were investing energies in trivial questions of honor. I recalled a quote by Moshe Dayan that Peres liked to repeat: "Questions of honour don't concern me. Especially other people's honour." I asked Eitan whether he needed any help with the travel arrangements. Haber replied with his characteristic directness: "Of course. Don't come."

On the plane to Washington, the seating arrangement was conspicuous: Peres and Rabin did not sit together. After taking off, Rabin explained the nature of the visit to the press pack: "At the end of the day, we're talking about a three-way meeting: Clinton, the king, and me." At the dinner hosted by Ambassador Itamar Rabinovich at his home, Rabin announced, "The whole story with Jordan began two months ago with my meeting with Hussein—there was no Jordanian option till then. Anyone who claims otherwise—that's just idle chatter." Peres gritted his teeth. The London Agreement, the breakthrough at Oslo that had paved the way to Jordan, and the document he had signed with King Hussein on November 2 had all just been erased from history. Speaking to journalists, Rabin sneered at Peres. He mockingly nicknamed him "the prophet" and "the visionary." Even the experienced and cynical Israeli journalists appeared stunned by his derision. In the joint meetings with Hussein and later also with Warren Christopher, Peres had to fight to get a word in edgeways. Whenever he managed to speak, Rabin waved his hand dismissively. Peres told me with palpable pain that Rabin had let him read the document agreed with the Jordanians—the "Washington Declaration" of July 1994 terminating the state of war—only moments before the ceremony.

Pale and most profoundly humiliated, Peres came back and asked me, "What would happen if we boarded the plane and went home? I have a feeling that Rabin is planning a new *Service Book* against me.[9] I won't let that happen. Write everything down." I did.

A Palestinian State?

The agreement that Peres reached with King Hussein made me question more seriously Peres's commitment to establishing an independent Palestinian state. The phrase "Palestinian state" does not appear in the Declaration of Principles signed on the White House lawn in September 1993. Nevertheless, people normally assume that the minds behind Oslo were aiming for this goal even if they never said so explicitly. The agreement reached in Oslo defined the West Bank and Gaza Strip as a single territorial unit and recognized the Palestinian people. It also said that future negotiations on a final-status agreement would settle the question of borders, and since these negotiations would be conducted with the Palestinians, it was naturally assumed that these should be the borders between Israel and an independent Palestinian state. It is difficult, therefore, to totally refute the claim that Oslo laid the foundations of a Palestinian state.

And indeed, at the failed talks at Camp David in 2000, the sides discussed an agreement based on the establishment of a Palestinian state—a recipe proposed by Israel itself. Two years later, and in contrast to the position that his father had committed to as president, President George W. Bush announced that a final-status solution should be based on the principle of two states for two peoples. The "road map for peace" agreed in April 2003 as a binding political plan sets the establishment of a Palestinian state as the ultimate objective of the peace process. Bush even demanded that the sides officially endorse this position—and in Israel, it was a right-wing government headed by Ariel Sharon that gave its approval. It was seemingly a meaningful development on the path to fulfilling Peres's vision. But only seemingly so.

In contrast to the widespread perception, however, Peres did not consider Palestinian statehood his preferred political vision, a necessary solution, or the automatic and logical conclusion of the Oslo Accords. In his public statements, he expressed his opposition to a Palestinian state in Judea, Samaria, and Gaza. He protested when people close to him argued that, on the contrary, this was the only possible interpretation of Oslo.

Peres remained faithful to the idea of a Jordanian-Palestinian confederation; in his mind's eye, he imagined that this political partnership would be joined by a three-way economic structure including Israel. This was the perception with which he armed himself when a short while after the signing of the Oslo Accords, he "stormed" Jordan.

The precedence that he had given the Palestinians before the signing of the Oslo Accords waned. When we returned from the secret talks in Amman, I told Peres that his steps would likely leave the Palestinians feeling betrayed. Peres was not concerned. He even looked amused by the possibility of ensnaring the wily Arafat in his web of tricks. In his eyes, statecraft was a complicated game of scheming and there was nothing wrong with paving the road to realizing one's dreams with a couple of tricks.

Peres preferred to see Jordan as the political anchor that would stabilize any agreement. An independent Palestinian state would struggle to cope economically, and Arafat and his friends had not been sending positive signals about their ability to run a country. In contrast, Jordan was well run and its leadership had proven its efficacy and ability to impose law and order. For these reasons and more, Peres reasoned that the framework of a confederation would render the controversy over the West Bank less catastrophic. A decision on the difficult questions could be postponed. The pressure for a painful solution in Jerusalem would diminish.

Peres knew that he was being awaited in Amman by Jordanians who felt spurned by the Israeli–Palestinian deal that had been cooked up behind their backs. They feared that the fate of Palestinian refugees living in Jordan would be left unresolved, that the new Palestinian entity would develop an appetite for territory east of the Jordan River, and that they would be deprived of their control over the *waqf* and their special status on the Temple Mount.[10] The Palestinians had informed them of Peres's letter on Jerusalem and gave it a far-fetched interpretation. Prince Hassan told Peres with evident concern that he had understood from Mahmoud Abbas that there was a secret annex to the Declaration of Principles promising Palestinians' responsibility over the holy places in Jerusalem. Peres denied this, and explained that Abbas was talking about the innocent letter that he had sent Holst. "That's it?" replied the prince, relieved. "Unbelievable."

Peres worked hard to relieve the Jordanians' humiliation. He stressed Jordan's strategic centrality in any regional agreement. In the document he initialed with King Hussein, he added a guarantee not to prejudice Jordan's status in Jerusalem, and in order to reinforce this statement he invited Prince Hassan to visit the city. Upon his return, and on the basis of that same logic, Peres raised an idea in a conversation with Rabin: "Offer Hussein to come to Jerusalem when the repairs on the Dome of the Rock are finished. Let him land straight on the Temple Mount, so we can show Hussein we haven't sold Jerusalem to the Palestinians."[11]

But the implementation of this process was not so simple. While Arafat announced that he hoped for a confederation with Jordan, he said that this required a short period of Palestinian independence first, and then Palestine would be attached to Jordan as an independent state. Peres argued that Arafat had spoiled the broth. He put it like this to Christopher: "Arafat has made a grievous mistake. He offered Hussein a rotation agreement for the role of head of the confederation. Hussein heard this and decided that there was nothing to talk about."[12] One can safely assume that there were other difficulties along the way apart from Arafat's impoliteness toward His Majesty.

A Palestinian State in Gaza

Peres did not give up on the idea of a confederation; he just changed its emphasis. The path to the establishment of a Jordanian–Palestinian confederation would now run through the establishment of a Palestinian state in Gaza. Peres hoped that the creation of such a state would be considered a meaningful step on the road to solving the Palestinian question, which would remove the obstacle preventing the Arab world from recognizing Israel and would kick any discussion on the fate of Jerusalem into the long grass. With a state in Gaza, the Palestinians would be in a position to form a confederation with Jordan. The process that Peres envisaged required as short an interim period as possible of independent Palestinian statehood. Independence in Gaza.

Peres initiated a diplomatic assault. He needed Rabin's support. The Palestinians had to be convinced that this idea was good for them, and therefore Peres had to enlist the support of Egypt's president Hosni Mubarak and perhaps even the king of Morocco. He had to secure King Hussein's support, and of course he could not forget that the backing of the United States was vital for this process. If the Americans discovered that another diplomatic initiative was playing out without their knowledge, they would likely torpedo it.

Peres did not feel that he needed Israel's government bureaucracy to initiate and drive forward a daring diplomatic idea. Bureaucracies by their nature would create difficulties, behave conservatively, take ages to prepare organized staff work, and ultimately present him a paper that would contain little that was new. He was determined to push his ideas forward with his own bare hands. He believed that after they germinated, the bureaucracy would adapt and be propelled by their momentum.

Pushing a new diplomatic initiative requires mapping out the relevant actors and working with them with determination and grit. Peres preferred to create a whole whirlwind of parallel processes. In his eyes, a reality laden with contradictions was the nature of the human and political condition. People have to fumble around in the fog, navigating a confusing reality. These were the conditions in which he thrived. His eyes glinted with a mischievous smile when he quoted his teacher Ben-Gurion, who said that minor crises are difficult to solve—so they should be aggravated till they become major crises. Only then would a solution be possible. I asked him whether he thought we should indeed aggravate our small crises in order to prepare the ground for their successful resolution. "I prefer complicated situations," Peres replied. "And if they're not complicated enough, then we really do need to complicate them."

Peres explained his proposal regarding Gaza several times in meetings with Rabin:

A Palestinian state must be established in Gaza, because the West Bank cannot be divided. This process would enable the circle of peace to be expanded straight away, without getting bogged down on the question of Jerusalem—it would be better to reach agreements with the other Arab countries while there is still no comprehensive agreement with the Palestinians, because that's how we avoid a discussion on Jerusalem.[13]

Peres foresaw difficulties in reaching an agreement on all the final-status issues, especially Jerusalem and the refugee problem. He hoped to overcome the Arab world's hesitations about recognizing Israel, and he hoped to remove the achievement of a "full, comprehensive accord" with the Palestinians as a precondition for such recognition. Peres believed that the establishment of an independent state in Gaza would relieve the Arab leaders' pangs of conscience—both real and pretend—over the fate of their Palestinian brethren. After all, the Palestinian state in Gaza would recognize Israel and conduct normal relations with it.

Arafat was well acquainted with Peres's idea of a confederation and did not rule it out. In a meeting on the sidelines of the World Economic Forum in Davos,[14] he tried to placate Peres and create a positive atmosphere at the start of the meeting in preparation for the demands he would soon make:

We're all in the same movement. A movement for peace. Where there's a will, there's a way. I can understand your concerns. Your intelligence agencies are very worried about the crossings and the roads. Some claim we say it's a state, but it's not a state. Even in the longer run, there won't be a state because we decided at the session of the Palestinian National Council in 1983 on the solution of a confederation with Jordan. We are committed to this. The Palestinian leadership is committed to this. This resolution has been ratified at every meeting of the Council ever since. [George] Habash, [Nayef] Hawatmeh, and even Ahmed Jibril are also committed to this.[15]

Even though he had explained to Peres in an earlier conversation that he was not an expert in economics, Arafat told him now, "The economic subject is most important.

We can create in our region a similar structure to Benelux: Jordan, Lebanon, Israel, Palestine, and Egypt. We're not opposed to Syria's participation." Peres did not know whether to believe what he was hearing when Arafat joined the community of believers in the "New Middle East." Arafat repeated, "After all, I have read what your book says and I admire it. We have no alternative in the long run but to live together. To live in good neighbourliness with open borders."

On another occasion, Arafat informed Peres that King Hussein had concerns about the Israeli–Palestinian agreement and feared negative consequences for Jordan. "I told him—let's calm things down by starting talks towards a Jordanian-Palestinian confederation. The king refused. He doesn't have good advisors."

A year passed, the implementation of the agreement was looking weary, and Peres was searching for creative shortcuts. He was increasingly convinced that the path to a confederation would pass through the realization of his idea for the creation of a Palestinian state in Gaza. He rolled up his sleeves and set out to make it happen. Peres sensed that Rabin was ready for the idea. He told him that he intended to travel to Egypt to "sell the idea to Mubarak so he can sell it to the Palestinians, like what happened with the Gaza-Jericho idea."[16] Rabin responded positively and asked Peres for a written proposal.

And indeed, Peres drew up a handwritten, preliminary twelve-point draft for the establishment of a Palestinian state in the Gaza Strip. This was a document about a sovereign, demilitarized state. The residents of the Israeli settlements in the Strip would have two years to decide whether to stay in place with guarantees for their security, under non-Israeli sovereignty, or to be voluntarily evacuated to Israel with state funding. This process would not reverse the rolling-out of autonomy in the West Bank. Residents of the West Bank who were not Israeli citizens would be able to choose Palestinian or Jordanian citizenship—or dual nationality. They would be able to vote in accordance with their citizenship without any particular sovereignty applying to the West Bank. No new settlements would be built, and no existing settlements would be dismantled.

Peres went to Jordan and spoke to the king.[17] He described to him a complaint that people in Israel made against Arafat: "If you can't impose your authority in Gaza, how can we transfer you control in the West Bank?" And he confessed to Hussein,

As for the West Bank, my position has always been that we must give the three orientations—Jordanian, Israeli, and Palestinian—an equal chance without deciding on definitive facts now and without cutting the West Bank up into pieces. And especially not Jerusalem. Why should we prevent any inhabitant from deciding for themselves which parliament to vote for? I'm reading a book now by Mao Zedong's doctor. He describes the role of contradictions in politics. There are no decisions without contradictions. We must identify them and make a decision. In our decisions with the Palestinians, the contradiction is not going away: on the one hand, our desire to move quickly; on the other, our concerns about the consequences. We are determined to make progress in increments. If they agree to our proposals, they'll get more in Gaza and less in the West Bank. There's no need for a perfect balance between the two areas.

Not One Law for Gaza and the West Bank

Hussein noticed Peres's heavy hint: there would not be one law for Gaza and the West Bank. The door in the West Bank was open to the "Jordanian option." "We'll refrain from doing anything that might be interpreted as a plot on our part," the king replied. "Arafat, however, could be a prime suspect when it comes to his intentions regarding Jordan." Peres reported back to Rabin and said that in a follow-up one-on-one conversation, King Hussein had reacted positively to the notion of establishing a Palestinian state in Gaza.[18]

Rabin authorized Peres to broach the idea with the Americans. And indeed, Peres met with President Clinton during a visit to the United States[19] and explained,

> This state is not the ultimate objective. After all, Arafat says he wants a confederation with Jordan after the Palestinians enjoy five minutes of independence. They should be granted independence in Gaza ... we must create a situation where the Palestinians and Jordanians are working together. There's no need for conflict between them. In this scenario, if this idea becomes reality, there would be a distinction in the West Bank between residency and citizenship. The Palestinians in the West Bank would be able to choose between citizenship in Gaza or Jordan. Citizenship also means voting rights. A key advantage of this process would be reduced pressure for a final-status agreement over the West Bank. There would also be less pressure over Jerusalem.

Peres informed Clinton that the Palestinians' initial reaction had not been encouraging. He would travel to Egypt, therefore, to try to mobilize the Egyptians to sell the idea to the Palestinians and thus play a similar role to the one they had played in the Oslo Accords. Peres noted that he had discussed the idea with King Hussein, who welcomed the premise. Clinton replied that it was a good and promising idea, as long as it were clear to the Palestinians that this would be a supplement to the Oslo Accords and not an attempt to erode it.

The report on the conversation was written up by the Israeli ambassador to the United States, Itamar Rabinovich. Peres asked me to send Rabin the handwritten version, not the typed-up copy. This would convince Rabin that he was receiving an original record that was not edited for Peres's own ends.

Next came Mubarak's turn. In their conversations, the Egyptian president usually listened with astonishment to Peres's detailed analysis of the wonderful future awaiting the region. Since I was highly familiar with this monologue, I sometimes let myself spend this conversation time in private reveries, imagining I was watching a comedy sketch and the man listening to Peres's vision was not really Mubarak but the comedian Eli Yatzpan doing an excellent impersonation. I used to wake up from my daydreaming to write down Mubarak's remarks when he started speaking. But on one occasion, the Egyptian president seemed to choose to take part in the skit running through my head and recalled with evident glee how he had hosted the Libyan ruler Muammar Gaddafi on a flight from Jordan to the Sinai Peninsula and invited him to sit with him in the cockpit. "I told Gaddafi to look down, because we were now above Eilat and I intended to land the plane at the city's airport." In Mubarak's bemused recollection, Gaddafi completely lost his senses and begged him in abject fear not to land in Israel.

But this time[20] the conversation in Cairo had a defined objective, and Peres was focused and to-the-point. "It's time to establish a demilitarised state in Gaza," he told Mubarak. "In the long run, there needs to be a Jordanian-Palestinian agreement. Arafat said he needs one day of independence before forming a confederation. This isn't instead of autonomy. It's in addition." Mubarak wanted to know what would happen with the settlements and Peres replied, "The choice will ultimately be in the settlers' hands—to live under non-Jewish sovereignty or to reach their own conclusions." As for the mission that Peres tried to delegate him—to convince the Palestinians—Mubarak refused to make a commitment. Before speaking to Arafat, he had to consult King Fahd of Saudi Arabia.

Peres did not leave Mubarak much time to act. In his own meeting with Arafat in Gaza,[21] he raised the idea of establishing a state in the Gaza Strip, stressing that it was not in lieu of autonomy in the West Bank but in addition to it. He explained to Arafat that it was important that the process be over before elections in Israel. "You've always said that you need a day of independence before forming a confederation with Jordan. Here is your day of independence and a state. The residents of the West Bank would be able to opt for Palestinian citizenship and vote for the Palestinian parliament."

Arafat asked whether the state that Peres was offering included Jericho. Peres replied that he had not thought about it. Arafat asked for time to think. Peres inferred from Arafat's question about Jericho that he was not ruling the idea out and even took it as evidence that Mubarak must have played his part and raised the idea, "because the Egyptian president also asked me about Jericho."

The campaign to establish a Palestinian state in Gaza also brought Peres to the palace of the king of Morocco.[22] "I have come to seek your advice on a most discreet matter. I shall raise it only between the two of us," Peres said first, then set out his ideas.

The king lavished Peres with praise. "The fact that you're the foreign minister of Israel is the best thing that has happened to the Middle East. There's a great deal of trust for you in the region; people are pinning high hopes on you." But as for Peres's idea itself, the king was more skeptical, saying that he could see many problems with it. "The Palestinians will likely suspect that you're only talking about Gaza. That is also likely to be the sense across the whole Arab world. The idea will therefore meet stiff resistance. King Hussein will likely be appalled by the idea."

The diplomatic blitz had failed. A blitz that illustrated Peres's diplomatic modus operandi and revealed, moreover, that he had never abandoned the idea of a Jordanian–Palestinian confederation. Unlike some of his advisors, Peres did not see the establishment of an independent Palestinian state as the preferred destination, and it was certainly not an ideal motivated by a sense of duty to performing an act of historic justice with the Palestinians. The "Jordanian option" looked like the best one and continued to stimulate his political imagination whenever he sensed that an opportunity was opening up to implement it. He supported the establishment of a

Palestinian state as a second-best option—as the corollary of a failure to get Jordan on board, and based on a cold calculation of Israeli interests.

Peres set his sights on a broad, inclusive vision of the future. He did so based on his understanding of major geopolitical developments, trends in the global economy, advances in science and technology, and even changes in culture and society. His worldview was generally dictated by his optimistic outlook on the development of history and his positive conception of human nature. Peres was frustrated not to find another leader in Israel's political scene who could see so far ahead, or who acted in accordance with any broader worldview whatsoever. Even if Peres never admitted as such, he saw himself as a kind of "philosopher king"—a man skilled in both devising great ideas and putting them into practice.

But Peres was almost never the king. He was forced to maneuver under prime ministers who resisted his great vision, feared him, or doubted him.

Peres did not like these prime ministers. The only one he admired and was completely loyal to was of course David Ben-Gurion. In June 2012, Peres spent time writing his acceptance speech for the ceremony in which President Obama awarded him the Presidential Medal of Freedom. His first draft was overflowing with references to "my teacher and mentor" Ben-Gurion. I told Peres that it might be time to stop wallowing in the dust around Ben-Gurion's feet. "You're already mature, you're 89, you can say what you think without having to salute the supreme leader in every paragraph." I sensed that Peres accepted the logic of my remarks but was finding it emotionally difficult to internalize them. He evaluated every prime minister he served under with reference to Ben-Gurion's leadership, and his conclusions were always grim.

6

Rabin's Spell

"I don't have a partner anymore. It's so hard for me. I'm all alone." I heard Peres repeat this over and over on the night when Yitzhak Rabin was murdered. Peres looked desperate. He was so submerged in grief that I feared he might lack the strength to bear the heavy burden that Rabin, his rival and partner, had left him. I shut myself away with him in a side room in the Ministry of Defence in Tel Aviv as we waited for the other government ministers to arrive. "I'm totally alone," he whispered. I knew him well enough to know that there was nothing fake about him that night.

In his speech after Rabin's assassination in November 1995, Peres spoke of the great reconciliation with his "partner Yitzhak" after years of bitter rivalry, and about how they had recognized together that they had to make painful decisions to pave Israel's way to a long-awaited peace. They knew there would be a heavy price, but they felt it was their duty to the nation before handing over to Israel's next generation of leaders.

Peres explained that as he and Rabin had matured and got used to each other, their sense of historic mission had sidelined their rivalry. In his more overstated eulogies, Peres went as far as to call Rabin "my older brother." In his ever-dialectical mind, he managed to feel profound sorrow for the loss of a man he despised. At times he was willing to suppress his own feelings in order to make a good impression through his elegies for Rabin.

In 1992, the two men had charted a new course. Rabin as prime minister, and Peres as foreign minister. Behind them were many years of animosity and political rivalry. Rabin was seen as the ultimate *tzabar*—a native Israeli. A soldier from the Palmach, a warrior, IDF chief of staff during the Six-Day War—emotionally restrained, straight-talking, no funny business. Peres, in contrast, never shook off the specter of the Diaspora—in his accent, his cultural richness, and his intellectual complexity. One was perceived as a King David-like figure, taken against his will from shepherding to rulership; the other, as having enjoyed wading through the political swamp his entire life. As mentioned previously, in his memoirs, *Service Book*, Rabin had dubbed Peres a "tireless schemer." As far as Peres was concerned, this nickname was only a small taste of the curse that Rabin placed on him, an enchantment that could never be lifted.

It might seem odd to associate Peres with magic. But somewhere in his complicated soul, there was a small corner that allowed for the modest existence of a metaphysical world. After Rabin's murder, we received a letter at the office from Michael Drosnin, the author of *The Bible Code*. He claimed to be able to predict the future using a hidden code in the Bible, and lo and behold—over a year earlier, he had sent Rabin a letter warning that he would be assassinated. Now he was warning of a much greater danger facing Israel. He wanted to meet Peres to alert him to the severity of the coming catastrophe. I told Peres about the letter when I sensed that he required comic relief, but to my utter surprise he asked me to invite the man for a meeting. "What do I have to lose by listening to him?"

I told him I would not permit such a meeting. "They'll say the prime minister of Israel is consulting magicians." Peres conceded. I remembered that Peres had met several times before with Yossi Gil, an astrologer who had promised him that the stars were aligned for his path to the Prime Minister's Office. When I learned of their relationship, I instructed that no more astrologers be allowed anywhere near the foreign minister's bureau.

And indeed, there was something spell-like in the way Peres saw himself as the victim of Rabin's epithet—"the tireless schemer." Only after Rabin's death could I try to joke with him about that hurtful moniker. I discovered that my kayaking instructor was a fan of Peres's. I convinced him to write her a dedication in one of his books: "To a tireless rower—from a tireless schemer."[1] He hesitated for a moment and then, with a surge of courage, wrote it down.

When Peres started penning his memoirs in December 1994, I warned him against coming across as settling a score with Rabin. In order to successfully implement the Oslo Accords, I argued, we had to keep industrial peace with Rabin. "But Rabin is still selling copies of *Service Book* and handing them out to his guests," Peres protested. "That man ruined my life when he lumbered me with that epithet—'tireless schemer.'"

"And yet," I told him, "you've managed quite a few accomplishments in that ruined life of yours." Peres refused to take comfort.

Industrial Peace

As the director of the foreign minister's bureau, I endeavored to keep things calm and avert any crises between Rabin and Peres. I believed that without industrial peace, we would lose our ability to influence the policies of Rabin's government. In the early months of their partnership, Peres held back from responding to the humiliations to which Rabin and his people subjected him. We discussed this at length. Peres often used to vent: "I'm fed up. How much longer? How long can I restrain myself?"

"Shimon, I know the situation's tough and you're gritting your teeth," I tried to encourage him.

> But you mustn't break now. You have to wait for the peace process to develop, for the moment the Israeli people face a real historic decision—only then can you impose the full force of your weight. The Likud will soon start to recover from its defeat in the [1992] elections, and people in your party will start to feel that time's flying by and there's so much we've yet to achieve. The public will say: you promised peace, there's no peace; you promised employment, there's no employment; you promised security, there's no security. Rabin will come under heavy pressure to

prove results, and then the peace processes you're planning and pushing will gain added momentum. You should wait.

Peres became sensitive and touchy whenever it came to Rabin. He interpreted almost every move by Rabin as an attempt to hurt and humiliate him—from Rabin's failure to include him in the growing ties with Syria to his insignificant, passing remarks at a dinner he hosted for the US secretary of state on his first visit to Israel. "I was really offended and felt embarrassed," Peres told me, agitated. "Listen to what an intelligent dialogue I had to sit through.

Christopher: 'This wine is excellent. Is it Israeli wine?'
Rabin: 'Yes, it's made on the Golan Heights.'
Christopher: 'It tastes wonderful.'
Rabin: 'Well, it's not really an Israeli wine. Two experts from California came and did most of the work.'"

I struggled to get to the bottom of Peres's impassioned objections and asked him, "So what was so terrible with what Rabin said?"

"It's such outrageously bad taste," Peres replied bluntly. "It's a testament to Rabin's enslavement to America. The whole conversation he's trying to show what a boss he is, and all the secretary hears from him is: I said this, I did that. Me, me, me. I'm fed up."

It became much more difficult for Peres to maintain discipline toward Rabin given the criticism of him in the press. Israeli journalists seemed to be competing with each other to emphasize Peres's irrelevance in matters of dispute with Rabin. Rabin's specter also haunted Peres on questions that should have been his exclusive domain. He told me a rumor had reached him that "Rabin does not like the plan to appoint Uri Savir as director-general of the Foreign Ministry." I wanted Uri to get the appointment and replied, "So for Rabin to be happy, maybe appoint his loyal advisor Shimon Sheves to the job?"

"Yes, it's ridiculous," Peres said, laughing. "I need to hold my nerve, but I'm fed up of Rabin's paranoia. I'm tired of justifying myself. He and his people are always leaking against me."

I told him that he had to make his peace with Rabin's office blaming him for everything, even faulty traffic lights in random towns. I advised him that we should act firmly against Rabin's aides but not say a bad word against Rabin himself. Peres agreed and promised that, in his next conversation with Rabin, he put his foot down and demand that Rabin keep his aides on a tight leash. "Just like in the Cold War," I joked. "The United States and Soviet Union didn't spill each other's blood, only their proxies' blood. There's another job for political advisors: to bleed for the boss."

The Junta

Many of our discussions about the Rabin–Peres relationship took place in a small group that started convening in early 1993. The forum changed its name a few times: it was "Team Beilin" at one point; Behira, the spokeswoman, dubbed it "the junta." Besides Peres, it also included Yossi Beilin, Uri Savir, the advertising executive and Peres's friend Moshik Theumim, and me. This limited forum was designed to guarantee that the conversations would not leak. The general feeling was that we should wait and grit our teeth. The time was not right for a battle, and there was no single issue over which Peres had to fight.

Peres spoke freely. He was angry at the unsatisfactory diplomatic momentum in the peace process and frustrated that the public was protesting the government's stagnation. He often mocked Rabin: "After the Goldstein[2] massacre at the Cave of the Patriarchs [in Hebron], this hero accepted my proposal to evict the settlers from Tel Rumeida.[3] But he quickly got fright and backtracked. He feared they'd take up arms against the IDF. He and his brave generals in the IDF are afraid to clash with the settlers."

Whenever anyone in the "junta" proposed manufacturing a crisis with Rabin, I came out completely against it:

> There won't be a future for the peace process unless Rabin and Peres are in sync. A spat between the two would place Peres on the left-wing margins of the political map, weaken him, and not produce any practical results. The only metric for our decisions is the peace process. Any shake-up now would threaten our ability to make progress with the Palestinians. He needs to put up with all the grief Rabin gives him.

When Yossi wanted to invite a few Labour Party members who were uncomfortable with Rabin to Peres's home to discuss the situation in the party, I asked Peres to stop the gathering. "There's a battle now for your place in the Palestinian and Jordanian tracks, and you mustn't open a partisan front against Rabin at such a time." Peres accepted my advice.[4] Sometimes it drove Peres's impulsive mind crazy keeping such tactical discipline—but it was as a supporting actor that he could afford himself more creativity in his diplomatic thinking and more freedom in promoting his ideas. The prime minister, meanwhile, was weighed down by preserving his coalition's survival, the country's economic and social problems, and the conservative positions of the security establishment. Whenever Peres protested that the newspapers were "only talking about Rabin," I argued back, "As prime minister, you wouldn't allow the foreign minister one tenth of the freedom of action that you have now." And indeed, Peres made progress turning his dreams into reality.

The Casablanca Economic Summit

In October 1994, we could have held a cabinet meeting aboard an El Al jumbo jet en route to Morocco. Israel's cabinet ministers were joining the foreign minister and his large business delegation on their way to the regional economic summit in Casablanca. Nobody wanted to stay behind in Israel. It turned out later that the Arabs were peeved by this large Israeli presence. They saw it as proof of the threat Israel supposedly posed to the Arab character of the Middle East, as if the Jews were conspiring to take over the regional economy. Egypt's Foreign Minister Moussa went as far as to say that the Casablanca Summit exposed Israel's ploy: it was not ready to pay the price for reconciliation with the Arab world. It was trying to skip straight to the pay-off. And in so doing, it was acting arrogantly and imperiously.

But even if we had erred and been insensitive, no one can erase Peres's mighty personal achievement. He had conceived of the idea of a regional economic summit as part of his broader worldview: that diplomatic accords needed to be stabilized by an economic anchor to guarantee their survival. The Arabs would sense the arrival of economic progress; the Israelis would emerge from their forced regional isolation and know that despite the heavy price, peace had paid off.

World and regional leaders crammed into the Moroccan coastal town, washed ashore by the dreams of one man—Peres. The celebration should have been his and his alone. Peres felt at home walking through crowds of people in gold-embroidered galabeyas and expensive Western suits—but as usual, something went wrong. Rabin, who had belittled Peres's idea, could not resist the temptation to arrive for a short visit in the middle of the summit. "He came to take the credit that did not belong to him," Peres complained.

Some Jews Are Calling for My Murder

Rabin and Peres had a meeting with Arafat together. Rabin warned him that the Palestinian terror attacks at the time were endangering the peace process. Arafat blamed radical Islamic terrorists trained on the battlefields of Afghanistan who, spurred by Iran, were now setting their sights on Israel in order to foil Israeli–Palestinian peace. "I know you're committed to the peace process with us, and I thank you for it," said Arafat.

> Please release Hamas leader Ahmed Yassin for me. It will help me in my efforts to neutralise the organisation. Yassin is a moderate, and his release will cause a split in Hamas. Hamas's leaders abroad won't be able to give instructions from outside if Yassin is freed. I know him well, back from when we were students. He won't order acts of violence.

Rabin explained that he would have been ready to accept such a deal during the abduction of the soldier Nahshon Waxman,[5] but the law now tied his hands and he could not accede to the request. "You should know, some Jews are calling for my murder."

"I also receive such threats," replied Arafat.

"If so," concluded Rabin, "we're in the same boat, and we must cooperate."

When it was Peres's turn to speak, Rabin announced that he had to run and left the meeting. Peres outlined his economic ideas to Arafat. But it was clear that Arafat was distracted and had little interest in the details of how to found a regional bank and build desalination plants that would turn Gaza into a vegetable garden. Rabin, who was supposedly in a rush, held an extended press conference just outside. The microphone carried his deep voice into the room, and it was clear Peres and Arafat felt offended.

On the plane back to Israel, Peres looked a little sad to me. "You scored a massive achievement in Morocco," I told him. "Why do you look depressed?"

"I don't want to appear euphoric," he answered at first. Then he added with a sigh, "It's hard for me to work with Rabin. I'm tired of him, emotionally. He suffers from chronic suspicion and he shares less with me than Assad shares with his foreign minister." This pattern repeated itself on a loop. Peres was frustrated. He felt that he was taking the initiative, blazing a path, fighting against Rabin's suspicion and indecision—and lo and behold, when at last there was a moment of joy, along came Rabin to pick fruits that were not his. One night in Cairo, for example, after an exhausting day of talks with the Palestinians about the implementation of the Oslo Accords,[6] I patched Peres through to Rabin, who wanted an update. Lying drained on his hotel bed in his underpants and a scruffy undershirt, Peres described the day's events to the prime minister. "I build these successes for him from scratch every time," he snapped angrily after putting the receiver down. "I make decisions for him. I do everything alone. Without me, he wouldn't make decisions. He's a coward."

Rabin had an aura of security experience around him, which drove Peres crazy. Although he had never worn uniform or held a rank, he felt that Rabin could not compete with him on courage, and he was frustrated that the Israeli public overlooked this fact. "If I were prime minister, things would look different," he said. "The public needs to be shown optimism. Rabin's taking over the media. He gives endless speeches with no strategy and he's making people depressed."[7]

Sometimes Peres suggested that he might throw in the towel and quit. "Sonia's pressuring me to resign and devote more time to home and our grandchildren." We talked at length on the plane journey home. Peres asked me what I thought about the option of taking the role of secretary-general of the United Nations. "You haven't stopped being Israeli, so there's no chance in the world," I told him. "Besides, my children need you here. We haven't finished making peace yet."

"I'm tired," he replied. "I'm fed up of working with Rabin. He's impossible. Why is he the one who's given all the praise? The whole story that he prepared the IDF for the Six-Day War, it's bullshit. That war got us into trouble. If it hadn't broken out, the Arabs would have reconciled themselves to our existence in the region."

"But the war gave Israel the cards it needs to make peace," I said.

"The war got us into trouble," Peres repeated. "The conquest of East Jerusalem created a problem that will be extremely difficult to solve in negotiations. I suggested before the war that we perform an act of deterrence. The cave was already ready in the Negev. But Dayan and Eshkol could smell the spoils of war. We could have spared ourselves the Yom Kippur War and the Lebanon War."

Haggling over Peres's Status

Rabin's people did not believe that the supporting actor deserved the same status as the prime minister. They were offended by how Peres had maneuvered Rabin into Oslo without their knowledge. Sometimes they enjoyed attacking him through the media. The battle over Peres's place next to Rabin in political meetings and peace ceremonies became my central mission. It seemed important not only for reasons of political substance, but also given the ongoing deliberations of the Nobel Peace Prize committee. We wanted it to stick in the committee members' minds that Rabin and Peres were an inseparable pair. If they awarded the prize to one, they had to award it to the other. Officially, Peres had the supporting role; but in reality, he had played the part of a leading actor.

Peres was gripped with envy whenever he heard Rabin give a speech. He wanted to have his own speechwriter, as skilled as Eitan Haber. But every attempt to find one failed. He struggled to read speeches written by others and usually ended up writing them by himself. I had to haggle with Haber like a petty peddler. Sometimes he felt magnanimous, wanting to safeguard the partnership with Peres; other times, he felt vengeful. Before we traveled to meet King Hussein in Aqaba, I found myself deconstructing the trip based on one deciding principle: where was Peres likely to be offended? I demanded from Haber that Peres not be separated from Rabin on arrival, that they travel in the same car, that they sail together on the royal yacht, that they appear side-by-side at the press conference, and of course that Peres not be left out of the meeting with the king. It was humiliating enough to see Peres walk toward the canopy where the king and Rabin were talking and sit next to them uninvited, when it looked like they did not even want him there.

At times, especially after arguments, Rabin seemed to make an effort to be friendly to Peres. But even then, his personality and feelings frustrated his own intentions. He struggled to conceal his almost chronic allergy to Peres. In one meeting with the Jordanian king, this time in Amman,[8] Rabin made sure that his foreign minister would also have time to speak; but his impulses got the better of him and he interrupted Peres to explain the situation better. Peres did not give up and fought for his right to finish his lecture to the king. The pair then recycled the same well-worn anecdotes they had already presented in previous talks. The Jordanians, astonished, were forced to watch as Rabin and Peres prevented the king from playing any meaningful role in the discussions in his own palace.

When we landed in Jerusalem, Peres invited Uri and me to his home for a drink. And again, he started bitterly complaining about Rabin and his own predicament. "Rabin doesn't know how to negotiate," he said. "He sold everything cheaply to the Jordanians, and yet *he's* the one the public sees as tough and *he's* the one who'll win the Nobel Prize." The next morning he told me, "After you left, I found it hard to sleep. I felt humiliated in Jordan. Rabin won't stop insulting me."

"You've known him for so many years," I said. "Why are you surprised every time as if it's new?"

"You're right," he answered. "Every incident with him is like a new and painful experience for me."

When we flew to the signing ceremony for the peace treaty with Jordan in the Arava, Peres asked me, "Do you think I'm happy today?"

"You have a good reason to be happy," I said. "You created the momentum, you defined the terminology, you pushed for this, you wrote the script everyone's reciting. The playwright might not be always on the stage, but the actors are reading the lines he put in their mouths, and events are happening just as he wrote them."

Peres was encouraged by my therapy, and I imagine it helped him to hold back and praise Rabin in his excellent, extemporaneous speech. On our way back, he asked why we were not responding in kind to the smears against him coming out of Rabin's office. I explained that we were adhering to our strategy of industrial peace. "So maybe don't be so strict and relax those strategies of yours a bit," he replied with his usual smile.

Self-pity

As a result of the tensions in his relationship with Rabin, Peres outwardly displayed the sort of soul-searching that he usually kept secret. His tiredness and favorite cognac eased the process. In moments of emotional turmoil, he engaged in introspection as if preparing for a purification ritual before his own funeral. During the Taba talks in June 1995, despite the late hour, he asked me to join him for a drink in his room. He felt he needed to discuss the day's events. He almost always ended up speaking about Rabin:

> He's frightened. He can't make decisions, can't give compliments. I treat him nobly and ask for nothing for myself. I'm completely at peace with my own work. I don't care if I die tomorrow morning. I'm not afraid of death. Death doesn't scare me. Rabin gets all the credit. Soon he'll say he built the nuclear reactor. He's a coward. My whole life, I've learned generals wet themselves out of fear. I'm an exceptional politician. My integrity is unimpeachable. I don't care if I die tomorrow morning. I'm not afraid of death. Sometimes I wake up and regret I'm not dead. I'm fed up. But I understand that nobody could step into my shoes.

Whenever Peres got so carried away with self-pity, I ordered him to go to sleep and he acquiesced. The next morning, he rose like a lion and went for a power walk on the beach by the Red Sea. He did not have sportswear or trainers. His bodyguards, astonished by his energy, sweated as they caught up with him. When I asked him why he was not wearing trainers for a more comfortable walk, he replied, "I can't feel the difference."

The Lone Toothbrush

Our security guards were a part of us. A small family. We got to know them more on our many trips abroad. They seemed to me to be a proud and impressive group. Many of them were graduates of elite military units, brimming with confidence, and they treated their role with great responsibility. Yigal Amir's bullets killed Rabin, but they also hit the Shin Bet, and especially members of its dignitary protection unit. They had failed in their primary mission: to protect the prime minister's life. A veteran member of the unit, Yizhar, called me after the murder and asked me to help him meet Peres in secret. He wanted to talk him through the need to wear a protective vest during public events. The vest had to be fitted to his measurements. "There are threats to his life," he said, "and we mustn't lose another prime minister."

Yizhar, a tough, veteran commander in the unit, was in an emotional state. I had seen him once at the doorway of a meeting between Peres and President Mubarak, who was staying at a New York hotel, engaged in a brutal confrontation with the massive Egyptian bodyguard who was trying unsuccessfully to keep him away from the president's room. When I told him about the uproar he had created, he replied sternly, "My job is to protect Shimon. I must be by his side at any price." Now, at the entrance to Peres's office, he told me in a trembling voice, "I know I'll start crying when I go in." And indeed, when he told Peres about his love for Rabin and his heart-breaking conversation with Leah, he could not hold back the tears.

On the night of the murder, at the end of an emotional cabinet meeting, I forced myself to think calmly about how to organize ourselves for Peres's new mission. I prepared a memo with points for discussion and met Uri to brainstorm about what would come next. In the morning, I updated Peres about our thinking and asked him whether we should add Yossi to the small group that would accompany him in his new role. "Not for now," Peres replied. I asked him not to sit in Rabin's office until after the funeral. I entered the inner sanctum. There was a picture of the Palmach commander Yigal Allon on the wall. It struck me as strange that Rabin's esteemed commander bore the same name as the murderer who took his life. In the bathroom, my eye was caught by a lone toothbrush—of the cheap variety given to passengers on flights. For some reason, I had expected the prime minister to have had a slightly more luxurious toothbrush.

Peres convened Rabin's grieving office staff. He spoke to them with great sensitivity, consoled them, and promised that nobody would lose their job. Eitan Haber, the director of the prime minister's bureau, resisted the temptation to hang on and handed me his office and his job.

As the days went by, Peres grew increasingly troubled by the abundance of mourning ceremonies for Rabin. He was even a little bit jealous. He detested the burden of demands for speeches, interviews, and letters in which he had to lavish Rabin with unctuous praise and celebrate their partnership. In earlier years, whenever he had asked me to draft a speech and I asked about the structure he preferred, he replied with a smile, "What's the problem, Avi? A good speech is built around three parts: the situation in the world, the situation in the country, and the situation in the party."

Now that he was so bitterly complaining about being asked to deliver ever more eulogies, I repaid him in kind: "What's the problem, Shimon? A good eulogy is built around three parts: the deceased, the deceased and me, and me."

"So write it yourself," he snapped.

We received reams of letters from citizens hoping to console Peres over Rabin's death, and I gave him a draft template to sign. "The illustrious warrior has fallen in the battle for peace," I had written.

Peres looked at me, astonished. "Where did 'illustrious' suddenly come from?"

Peres knew that for my own part, I kept well away from these tiresome mourning ceremonies. I promised him that I was watching his riveting speeches on TV. Whenever I had no choice but to show up, I passed the time exchanging scraps of poetry with my fellow advisors. At one eulogy-laden ceremony in Oslo, Shimon Shiffer snatched one of these notes off me and published my rhymes in the paper:

A Speech—Friends (The Undelivered Speech)

I've come to say, "Goodbye, my friends,"
And given our friendship, to tie up some ends.

It's hard without Eitan[9] to muster the words,
My head is still spinning from speeches I've heard;
And Sheves was left off the guest list you shared.

At first I was pleased by the ritual grief,
I never quite knew I was such a great chief
And Oslo would welcome such stunned disbelief.

But if you write speeches, name roads and a square,
You're likely to miss the most vital thing there.

You're making your vows to finish this stuff—
To me that just sounds like a joke or a bluff,
And I'm close to boiling point, having enough.

And facing your salmon and flutes of champagne,
I think that it's time that you grasp this refrain:

If a brave man's peace is the mission that calls,
Then speeches are great, but you've got to have balls.

The Same Sense of Isolation

Peres lost sleep over the horror of Rabin's murder and the burden of his new role as prime minister. He told me that he was tormented by troubling thoughts at night and often grappled with them till daybreak. "I'm all alone," he used to repeat to me. Sometimes it looked like age had caught up with him since the murder. He used to close his eyes in important meetings at the Defence Ministry. It was hard to tell whether he was losing consciousness or merely napping. I was afraid this would leak. Mitka, the veteran stenographer, told me that the heads of the Mossad and Shin Bet, who were used to Rabin's close attention and careful listening, were having to sit through short and sleepy meetings. It was clear that Peres's mind was troubled and tormented. Sometimes he found solace by writing his thoughts down in a yellow-covered notebook: ideas, impressions, and even fragments of poems he composed.[10]

He described ironically how Ehud Barak had rushed to capture the room he had vacated in the Knesset "in a brilliant military operation." He voiced his concerns about building a barrier along the Green Line, "which would likely turn the Green Line into the future border." He wrote about the body searches to which the Shin Bet subjected guests at a memorial ceremony for Ben-Gurion: "Ben-Gurion could not have dreamt that they'd have to take such internal security measures in Israel ... Now I am standing above his grave as prime minister and defence minister. I have the same sense of loneliness, but not the same power. He has no replacement."

After a while, Peres pulled himself together and started promoting a daring diplomatic agenda. He was skeptical about the possibility of reaching a permanent, comprehensive, and definitive solution with the Palestinians. Arafat had not done enough to stifle terrorism, and the questions of Jerusalem, refugees, and settlements would be difficult to resolve. Apart from the sensitive flashpoint of Hebron, Peres transferred the Palestinian towns and villages in the territories to Palestinian control. He was committed to promoting the Oslo process but came to see the Syrian track as the key to a dramatic change in Israel's situation and reality in the whole Middle East. This concept had already crystallized in his mind in the months before Rabin's murder, when he sensed that the government was hemorrhaging public support. He pinned the bulk of the blame on Rabin: "Rabin will ruin everything: he has ruined the party, lost the Jerusalem mayoralty, destroyed the Histadrut,[11] and he'll also lose the elections to Bibi [Benjamin Netanyahu]."

New Momentum with Syria

In the months before Rabin's assassination, Peres had pressured him to make progress toward a peace deal with Syria. "The Labour Party may lose power," he warned him in a nighttime meeting on March 8, 1995. "That would be a loss in itself, but it would be even worse if we lost the peace process. There's no great chance of reviving the Histadrut; there's no confidence in the government on the economy. There is one way to get out of this mess: to change the agenda by creating new momentum that won't focus on small things." Peres was proposing a complete change in the approach to Syria.

> The price we have to pay Syria is known. We have to be creative to boost what we get in return. We must propose that the treaty with Syria also include reconciliation with all members of the Arab League, a full and comprehensive commitment to end violence and terrorism, the cessation of Hezbollah's operations, and the removal of the headquarters of the Rejectionist Front from Damascus.

Peres suggested that he and Rabin meet with Warren Christopher and propose the "Eshkol Formula": a withdrawal to the Israeli–Syrian international border, with guarantees for Israel's security and water needs. Rabin asked whether this meant a complete withdrawal from the Golan Heights and the dismantling of the settlements there. Peres responded in the affirmative, saying that meant either a referendum or elections. "We're both old enough, and I believe that you believe the same as I do— peace comes first." In Peres's words, Rabin was "quite positive" and asked to think the suggestion over.

Peres took advantage of a meeting with Christopher[12] to explain how he saw things:

> In the negotiations with Syria, we're focusing on questions of territory—but that's not the substance. Peace with Syria needs to bring with it a comprehensive regional peace. Syria must fight terrorism, because otherwise what's the point of peace? It's important to offer Syria an aid package. Perhaps we could think about an American-Russian package. The Russians could forgive Syria's debts.

Peres said that he had raised the subject with Russian Foreign Minister Andrei Kozyrev and had offered to talk to him again during his planned visit to Israel at the end of the month.

"We need to take the talks with Syria up a level—to national leaders or ministers," Peres said.

> If all our demands are accepted, we shall consider a withdrawal to the international border alongside vital arrangements for our security and necessary guarantees regarding water flows from the sources of the Jordan River. I propose that President Clinton be involved in presenting the issue to Assad. That would add to the effectiveness of the plan and introduce the necessary drama.

Dennis Ross replied that the beauty of Peres's proposal was in the fact we were telling Assad: in contrast to Arafat, Sadat, and Hussein—you're the only one who holds the keys to a comprehensive regional peace.

After Rabin's assassination, Peres continued pushing for an agreement with Damascus. When it became clear to him what verbal "deposit" Rabin had given the Americans—a promise to withdraw to the 1967 lines if Syria met all of Israel's demands—he told Clinton in a conversation: "I shall honour whatever Rabin committed to, in writing or orally."[13] Peres found it convenient to base himself on Rabin's willingness to pay the heavy price for peace with Syria.

A Letter to Assad

Peres sent Hafez Assad a letter via Dennis Ross.[14] He wrote that he was aware of the commitment that Rabin had made in the interests of peace with Syria and called it "a commitment I shall honour." Peres said that he and Assad could be partners in a great, historic development. He visited Washington a week later and exhorted the secretary of state:

> We're ready for a quick process with Syria. But if the Syrians want to slow dance— we'll dance slowly. The advantage of a quick jump is that the whole thing would be over before the elections. Nine months is not long. Three or four Islamic Jihad or Hamas bombs could do a lot ... One thing is clear. We're not prepared to accept an "Egyptian payoff" ...[15] We'll want a meeting with 20 Arab leaders, with a declaration of the end of the history of wars in our region ... If we want to move towards a big bang, background music isn't enough—we need an almighty din. It was provincial on Assad's part not to send condolences to Leah. If Assad is polite, we will be too ... If he doesn't crack down on Hezbollah, I'll destroy them. Assad will be surprised by my response. I may well be tougher than my predecessor on this. Tell Assad that I view a meeting with him as a good first step.

Warren Christopher flew to Damascus, and Peres, waiting impatiently, invited him and his staff for Friday night dinner at his Jerusalem home as soon as he landed back in Israel.[16] On the table was Sonia's famous honey-glazed roast chicken. Sitting on the

Israeli side were Ehud Barak, Uri Savir, Yossi Beilin, Itamar Rabinovich, Danny Yatom, and I. Christopher briefed us on his conversation with Assad. I wrote his words down keenly, but it was clear that nothing foretold of a breakthrough. Assad appeared to be in no hurry to join the big bang that Peres was planning. His evasive answers did not constitute a sufficiently positive response to Peres's wishes, that Syria give Israel a meaningful return in exchange for a withdrawal from the Golan Heights: cooperation on turning the bilateral treaty into a comprehensive peace with the Arab world; security arrangements; guarantees regarding the water sources of the Jordan River and the Sea of Galilee; a commitment to hinder Hezbollah's terror activities; a ban on the presence of the Palestinian Rejectionist Front in Damascus; the commencement of normal economic relations; and a meeting between the two leaders in order to guarantee speedy progress toward these goals and demonstrate this historic turnaround to the world.

But Peres refused to let such trifles bother him. "I propose convening the government on Saturday night, and I'll invite the secretary of state to present the breakthrough with Syria to the ministers. What do you think?" The attendees were taken aback. Nobody replied. In the absence of volunteers, I asked Peres, "Would you like me to answer in Hebrew or in English?" I thought that he would understand that way that his proposal was problematic.

"English," Peres said.

I said that a cold analysis showed there was no breakthrough in Assad's reply to the US secretary of state, so it would be a mistake to invite Christopher to the cabinet. "We would create baseless expectations and embarrass Assad."

Peres cut me off angrily and said in Hebrew, "*Al te-bal-bel li et ha-bei-tzim*." This crude Israeli slang defies English translation. The plain translation is: "Don't confuse my balls." It means something like "don't give me that bullshit," but the English phrase is far milder than the Hebrew original. I knew that some of Christopher's staff understood basic Hebrew, and I gathered that I was party to an unprecedented development in the history of international diplomacy. Had a US secretary of state ever seen a prime minister asking his advisors not to confuse his balls before?

I sensed that the others agreed with me and even admired my willingness to put myself on the line and anger my boss. Peres explained that "we need to ensnare Assad with enthusiasm for peace and thereby make him publicly committed to the process," but he canceled his invitation for Secretary Christopher to attend the cabinet. He explained later that he "didn't want to create unnecessary drama."

Get Me a Meeting with Assad

Peres tapped Uri Savir to lead the talks with the Syrians. He was pinning his hopes on the skills and experience that Uri had acquired in Oslo. But at the same time, he also hoped to meet Assad himself. He explained to US Ambassador Martin Indyk:[17]

> I don't want to be manoeuvred into a situation where people say I'm returning the Golan up to the Sea of Galilee and getting no meat in return. You need to try to get me a meeting with Assad. It's not a condition, but I have to show some sort of achievement. There needs to be some commitment on the matter

of a comprehensive [regional] settlement; the treaty with Syria must also include reconciliation with the whole Arab world. I don't want the election campaign to be about Syria alone. I'm concerned we won't be able to solve the problems of the security arrangements, borders, and water by October. I don't want to get to the elections on 29 October with my hands tied, because otherwise we're better off with early elections. If Assad agrees, I'm ready for an interim agreement—over Lebanon, for example. I'm also willing to discuss a partial withdrawal, including Majdal Shams.[18]

Indyk said that the Americans were getting signals that Assad was thinking of taking the talks up to the level of foreign ministers, Farouk al-Sharaa and Ehud Barak. "I think that's a waste of time," Peres replied. "They'll both play tough. I'm willing to travel to Damascus, Washington, or anywhere else to meet Assad."

Damascus interpreted the rumors about the possibility of early elections in Israel as a conspiracy to pressure Syria to open up to concessions and move more quickly. Assad was as suspicious as always and maneuvered carefully. Peres understood that he would not reach a breakthrough before the elections. The Americans reached the same conclusion. Peres decided to hold early elections. He proposed that Indyk tell the Syrians: "Let's take a month for a methodical break in the talks, and Peres will come back later with full and renewed energies. We can continue negotiating until a few weeks before the elections and renew them immediately afterwards. Better for Peres to go to elections with hope ahead of him, not a crisis behind him."

Indyk sent a message through me: the United States would accept any decision Peres made, but there was concern in Washington that Christopher might return from Damascus and that we would announce early elections based on his report. The Americans asked that Peres not present his decision to call snap elections as a response to Christopher's failure to advance an Israeli–Syrian treaty. Christopher's visit had to be separated from any decision to have early elections.[19]

Uri, who was handling the talks with the Syrians in Washington, was still trying to give his interlocutors the sense that the elections would not necessarily be brought forward, and reported progress. But Peres had already made up his mind. He sent Assad a letter,[20] in which he expressed satisfaction with the results of the talks to date.

> I wish to restate my determination to work with you and the United States with the objective of reaching a treaty in 1996. I have explained the political picture in Israel to Secretary Christopher, and for reasons that are not connected to our negotiations, I may call early elections. I must make a decision in the near future. In any case, this need not influence our ongoing negotiations. This decision will not obviate the possibility of realising the historic opportunity facing us—I hope it will even strengthen it.

Peres announced early elections. He sought a new mandate from the people. But in a twist of irony, this man of peace was forced to run an election campaign in the shadow of the devastating terrorism of Palestinian suicide bombers and of a fresh military campaign in Lebanon, once Hezbollah started raining Katyusha rockets on northern Israel.

Arafat Will Remove Us from Power

Since Oslo, the Palestinians had failed to make the requisite efforts to stop terrorism. After one of the more deadly terror attacks, Peres received a call from Osama El-Baz, an advisor to the Egyptian president, to convey Mubarak's condolences. "Arafat will remove us from power," Peres told him with intense frustration.

What would you say to me if I paid a condolence call at the home of Goldstein, who committed that massacre at the Cave of the Patriarchs? And now Arafat's gone to condole the family of the "Engineer", Yahya Ayyash,[21] who was responsible for the murder of so many innocents. We asked him to jail Ayyash, and he replied that he knew for certain that he had fled through a tunnel to Sudan. He arrests terrorists and then immediately lets them go. Treats us like we're idiots. We demand that he outlaw terrorist organisations, that he not allow them to carry arms. We've given him the names of the terrorists but he doesn't arrest them. They're taking advantage of the VIP vehicles[22] we've authorised them, to smuggle weapons. I'm truly ashamed. I won't commit suicide for Arafat's sake. You must know, the Likud will kill this all off if it comes to power. They'll start building settlements again. At Bibi's side you'll find Arik Sharon and Raful [Rafael Eitan].[23] You know what will happen. Rabin was assassinated physically—I don't plan on being assassinated politically. There's nobody around me calling for restraint and moderation. Farouk Kaddoumi[24] said Arafat was more an anarchist than a terrorist. Perhaps he's right.

A frustrated Peres had realized that his partner was a slippery character who was not delivering the goods. Arafat had revealed his peculiarities in many of their conversations. When we returned from a meeting with Arafat in Taba,[25] for example, I told Peres that I was also making a record of their small talk: "Maybe they'll help us understand the soul of the partner you've found yourself." I read him a section of the text:

Arafat: There's also the question of Rachel's Tomb, which we need to solve. Of course you know, Rachel was my grandmother. When will Abu Ala [Ahmed Qurei] and Abed Rabbo stop smoking around me?

Qurei: I stopped smoking two years ago!

Arafat: Abed Rabbo is smoking your share now.

Peres: Let's agree we'll turn the air conditioning off and open the doors for some fresh air from outside.

Arafat: Yes, yes.
(Ahmed Qurei struggles to open the doors.)

Arafat: I hope Abu Ala [Qurei] is better at conducting negotiations than opening doors.
(Uzi Dayan[26] reads out Israel's proposals for Hebron.)

Peres: My head hurts. (Takes a paracetamol.)

Arafat: Your excellency, I recommend you also take some vitamin C. I can give you some. I have a whole pharmacy here with me. In many places around the world, I'm depicted as a traitorous Arab. I need some relief. To solve the problem of the prisoners. To release them.

Peres: It makes things difficult for us that you haven't caught the hardened killers who've found refuge in Gaza. The Engineer, for example.

Arafat: The Engineer is no longer in Gaza. We received information about him about two months ago. We arrived at the house where he was staying and the woman living there admitted, on the basis of our description, that the man had indeed lived in her house for ten days and then fled to Sudan through the tunnels at Rafah.

Peres: According to the information we have, he's still in Gaza.

Arafat: We want to build a safe passage between Gaza and the West Bank. I'm thinking of an elevated road or a train on an elevated lane. The cost would be $1.8m per kilometre. The project could be carried out quickly, and I'm speaking as a professional in this field. As an engineer, I built countless projects in Saudi Arabia. I could have been a billionaire. What General Uzi Dayan is offering is to turn us into his mercenaries. I say this as a general. I have no need for this, I'm not a mercenary. If General Dayan wants to rule, let him rule without me. Moshe Dayan and I were together in Jerusalem in our childhood.

Peres: Why did you not sort everything out back then already?

Arafat: One of my relatives was the head of the police and responsible for East Jerusalem. Uzi Dayan's uncle and my uncle were in the same unit under Abdullah's command.

Peres listened without responding. I told him that some of our Palestinian interlocutors had admitted in private conversations that in their leader's world, fragments of facts, fables, Quranic tales, and plain old fantasies coexisted in perfect harmony. "Take him for a polygraph test, and he'll come out as telling the truth. He generally believes the stories he comes up with." On the eve of the fateful 1996 elections, an unlucky Peres would be dependent on this man and his behavior. There was little we could do to change it.

Operation Grapes of Wrath

In the north, Hezbollah launched an attack and residents of northern Israel were forced to hide in bomb shelters because of the Katyusha rockets. After some hesitations and delays, Peres decided to embark upon Operation Grapes of Wrath. Uri and I had tried to persuade him to give diplomatic action another chance. The IDF had suggested a surgical aerial operation without a ground offensive. According to the plan, residents of Israel's north would have sat in bomb shelters for about a week, waiting for the threat of the Katyushas to be lifted.

During the cabinet deliberations, Ami Ayalon—the director of the Shin Bet at the time—wrote me a note: "As minister of defence he must ask the army: how do we intend to end the war? Derive the next military steps from that, and give instructions for diplomatic action right at the beginning." I passed the note to Peres. He felt that Hezbollah's aggression left him no choice, and he was also counting on the confidence the army inspired.

Peres met Arafat and his people at the Erez Crossing during the operation to implore them again to fight Hamas's suicide bombing terrorism. "Make no mistake," he warned Arafat. "You're a target for them no less than we are. Your complacency over Hamas will ruin the peace process. I remember well how Ben-Gurion confronted our dissidents. Without his grit, we would not have established a state. You must learn from our experience. To prove you're capable of asserting your authority."

"I will not compromise on 'one authority, one gun,'" Arafat replied. "But I must do it my way. I'll disarm both Hamas and Fatah."[27]

Arafat instructed Muhammad Dahlan,[28] the head of the Preventive Security Force in the Gaza Strip, to present his plans. Dahlan gave us a professional briefing, together with charts on a board. And indeed, in the months after that meeting, Arafat fought Hamas. He arrested many of its operatives, shaved their beards off, and proved that he could act effectively. But his actions, which bore fruit, came too late to fix the damage to Peres's chances in the upcoming elections. The Likud was able to make effective use of the punchy slogan: "No security. No peace. No reason to vote Peres."

Upon our return to the Defence Ministry from this meeting with Arafat, we were informed about the disaster in the Lebanese village of Qana. IDF artillery had killed over 100 civilians who had taken refuge there. (The papers later reported that the shells were fired to rescue a unit operating deep inside Lebanon under the command of Naftali Bennett.[29]) I was late to the meeting Peres was chairing. When I entered his office, I saw the IDF top brass looking grim and confused. An operation that had been planned as surgical had gone horribly wrong. I was told that a decision had been made to declare a unilateral ceasefire. Peres was sitting at his desk, away from the meeting table. I approached him and said,

> I was in favour of restraint and holding back. But now the war has started, we have to win. You went to war to eliminate the threat of the Katyusha rockets facing the residents of the north. They're still in their bomb shelters and the Katyushas are still landing on our population centres. You haven't achieved your objective, and you're abandoning the campaign. You must appear determined to win the war; hold a press conference, express regret for the victims, and place the blame on Hezbollah.

At this point we were joined by the chief of staff, Amnon Lipkin-Shahak. Peres asked me to present my position. I did so and added, "Amnon, what legacy are you leaving the IDF? The army under your command was given a mission and failed to carry it out." Peres told Amnon that he could see the logic in my remarks. Amnon was convinced.

"Postpone the announcement of a unilateral ceasefire," Peres decided. Lipkin-Shahak explained that he had already given the order to halt military operations. "So cancel it!" Peres snapped. The cabinet was convened that evening and Peres explained that a unilateral ceasefire was a terrible idea. At the end of the meeting,

Lipkin-Shahak turned to me, gave me a hug, and said, "We prevented a mistake today." The fighting continued, but Israel's air force and artillery could not stop the Katyusha attacks. Peres was forced to compromise on a political arrangement—the "Grapes of Wrath understanding"—which did not put an end to Hezbollah's ability to threaten our population centers. In briefings and interviews, Peres of course stressed the contributions made by the understandings, but when the television lights were switched off, he told me: "The army got me into trouble. They promised they would silence the Katyushas in a week or two. I'm all alone."

Again, Defeat

I discovered just how alone Peres could feel when he arrived at the office looking grim-faced after the election results were announced. I sat down with him in his office and he said in a pained voice, "It's over. You're a Foreign Ministry man. Pick one of our embassies around the world and I'll make sure you get the appointment."

I told him that I had no interest in representing the Netanyahu government as an ambassador. "All I need is a week's holiday on a faraway beach," I said.

Peres looked at me almost imploringly. "Not now, Avi," he said. "Stay here. I'm all alone." I stayed, struggling to keep the images of that day of defeat out of my mind.

The day looked like this. After voting in Jerusalem, I joined Peres for lunch in Herzliya. He looked worried. He was troubled by a rumor doing the rounds among journalists, that he had collapsed. One reporter tipped us off that MK Avraham Ravitz of the ultra-Orthodox Degel Hatorah Party was the source of the story. Peres called him and a loud argument broke out. "Bibi is not your rabbi," Peres shouted. "For the love of God, what are you doing?" He begged him to stop. I passed Peres a note saying the conversation would leak and people would say he was panicking. But Peres was convinced he was right.

We arrived later at the Labour Party's election headquarters. In a sad little room, without any tools to control the campaign or visual aids, sat the campaigners Moshe Shahal and Meir Nitzan. They had two telephones, with one cord stretching across the middle of the room, at risk of getting disconnected by anyone who crossed the floor. Meir Nitzan was holding a mobile phone and started dialing. "Don't you have a telephone operator?" I asked him.

"No need," he answered. "Peres is winning," he said calmly.

We started receiving news that Arab voters were not turning up at the polling stations at the levels we had expected. Peres started fervently calling key figures in the Arab community. The HQ had no voter rolls. I summoned two secretaries and asked them to bring two more telephones. Unable to bite my tongue, I told Peres that a short hop to Cyprus gets planned in greater detail than his election campaign. In the evening, watching TV at home, Peres looked exhausted. Throughout the night I received phone calls from President Clinton's office, saying that based on early polls, the president wanted to make an announcement congratulating Peres on his win. I advised them to wait and not do anything silly.

When I left Peres's house toward 02:00, we were still talking about victory. There was a two-point gap. "It looks like it's over," Peres told me. "We've won." He went to bed. Hours later, when it became clear that he had been defeated, I called his daughter Tsvia and suggested that she and Raphi, her doctor husband, be with Peres when he woke up. I asked the Shin Bet to make sure they also had a doctor in the area. I was extremely worried for him. I waited for daybreak, unable to shake off what a journalist friend had told me just before the elections. He said that the Likud HQ had one nightmare: that Peres would appoint Ehud Barak as minister of defense. I raised the matter with Peres and he replied, "Back in the day, in a similar situation, when I replaced Bar-Lev with Rabin as a candidate, it made no difference. There's no basis for the claim that appointing Barak will change anything."

I did not relent and called Moshik Theumim. I told him that some polls indicated that appointing Barak as defense minister would add two to three percentage points to Peres's support and decide the elections. "The matter has already been raised with Peres and he rejected it outright," Moshik replied. After Rabin's assassination, when Peres was forming his government, I joined those who recommending him to appoint Barak as minister of defense. "That way you'll put a buffer between you and the next terror attack," I told him. Peres would not listen.

And indeed, Peres served his short tenure as prime minister after Rabin's murder in the shadows of Rabin's memory. Prime Minister Shimon Peres made every decision with Rabin's ghost hovering in the background. Rabin's specter loomed over Peres when he formulated his moves on Syria, when he decided to embark on a military operation against Hezbollah, and also when he decided to hold early elections, partly to prove that the legitimacy of his leadership was not rooted in Rabin's murder but an electoral mandate. In his death, Rabin had raised the bar, and Peres had to surpass it or at least meet it. The bar he had raised on security was among the most sensitive. On the one hand—Rabin, Mr Security, the celebrated army chief of staff from the Six-Day War; and on the other—Peres, the man people argued had never worn a uniform. The decision not to put Ehud Barak in charge of the Defence Ministry, which would have likely saved the elections for Peres, was a clear testament to the influence Rabin's specter had on Peres. If Rabin had been good enough to serve in the two roles, how could Peres admit that *he* was not? Especially now, when Rabin was no longer with us, the evil spell that he placed on Peres should have disappeared with him.

Barak's Cold Shoulder

I went a long way with Peres. I stayed with him after he lost the 1996 elections to Benjamin Netanyahu, and I helped him found the Peres Centre for Peace, with the hope of continuing to contribute to Israeli–Palestinian reconciliation from there. I accompanied Peres around the world to raise funds for the center's activities. Peres gave lectures for payment and then donated a great deal of money to the center. On our travels we also met world leaders, who thirsted for his political analysis. Peres proved able to seamlessly adapt to different circumstances and find purpose and hope in any situation he was thrown into. He found a common language with members of all cultures.

After only a few hours in Seoul, he was already able to present his Korean guests with a comprehensive strategy for handling the threat posed by the communist North. South Korea's president listened to him, rapt, and was rewarded with a new and improved version of Peres "eggs and omelette" analogy. In order to definitively clarify the logic behind the Oslo process, Peres gave the following explanation: "Rabin and I tried to turn the omelette back into eggs, in order to let each egg live its life separately from the other eggs."

In Hungary he accepted his socialist hosts' invitation to don camouflage and set out to hunt some ducks. Fortunately for the birds, he missed.

Peres also met Arafat on occasion. The Palestinian leader knew that "His Excellency, Shimon" had lost his political power, but he still respected him. Arafat vented about the Netanyahu government. "Nothing from the agreements is happening. Your electoral loss is a loss for the Palestinians, for the Arabs, and for the whole region." He surprised Peres in one such meeting with a present: a Hebrew-to-Arabic dictionary. He even proved that he had read some of the heavy tome: "How are you, my love, I love you," he said in Hebrew.

For us, these trips abroad sweetened the depressing atmosphere in Israel. Peres delivered terrific speeches and was welcomed enthusiastically. At a speakers' forum in San Diego, he was voted the best speaker, leaving Mikhail Gorbachev, Jimmy Carter, Leah Rabin, and many other famous figures behind him. Peres adapted quickly to his new world. One moment he was a widely admired prime minister, and the next he was forced like everyone else to submit to a body search by a burly security guard working by the book at a remote American airport. Peres's escorts were shocked by the incident, but he accepted it with indifference and was perhaps even a little bemused.

Peres had an optimistic spirit and a tough character. He did not break, and he was quick to find meaning in activities that he was pushed into by his election defeat. He believed that luck would favor him in due course, as in the joke he enjoyed about the cinemagoers who remain in their seats, hoping that something will change in the next screening and their hero will prevail. Peres never reconciled himself to the assumption that the script was final and that he was always fated to lose. To anyone who raised an eyebrow over his persistence, he explained, "Winners don't quit, and quitters don't win."

At the time of the fateful discussions in Israel about a withdrawal from Hebron in early 1997,[1] we visited distant towns in the United States to raise money for the Peres Centre. Peres, who had led to the decision on Hebron, was not involved in the passionate debate in Israel. Instead, wearing an old tuxedo, he was giving speeches and taking questions from excited audiences. He responded patiently, never leaving a question without a detailed answer. He gladly obliged anyone who asked for a photo with him. At one press conference, he was asked to describe his impressions from the three hours he had spent at one of these far-flung towns. "A charming and admirable place that gives individuals a life of dignity," he said into the microphone, and the crowd melted. Shortly earlier, when we saw the town from the plane, he had told me, "What a shithole. I hope you're not going to leave me here for more than one night."

Bob, the dedicated American security officer who accompanied us on our travels, was forced to listen to Peres's speeches over and over again and particularly loved the story about the "Zionist cow." In every speech, whenever the audience seemed to be getting bored, this cow would be rudely awoken. "You know," Peres revealed,

> when Moscow started trading with Israel, they wanted to buy cows from us. It turns out that a capitalist Zionist cow produces four times more milk than a communist cow. Both cows have the same horns, the same tail. The difference is in the system. If you change the system, there'll be enough for everyone. In the end, you'll be able to leave the cows alone and just milk the system.

Whenever Peres ploughed on through a speech and failed to mention the cow, Bob used to signal to me anxiously from his post. We calmed down only once Peres mentioned the cow, toward the end of his speech, to the sound of laughter from the crowd. As far as the audiences were concerned, it did not matter either way that Peres was in the opposition. He was the face of Israel.

A Moment of Humiliation

My many years at Peres's side allowed me to be with him at moments of success and satisfaction, but also no less so at moments of defeat and dismay. One of the most painful low points was after Ehud Barak's victory in the elections of May 1999. I joined

Peres in his meeting with Barak a short while before he announced the composition of his government. Peres was going to be appointed "Minister for Regional Cooperation." It was a title that lacked any defined substance. Peres wanted to settle with Barak on the new ministry's areas of responsibility. He swallowed his pride and made a pilgrimage to a man who used to knock diligently on his own door. The wheel turns in politics; Peres accepted the verdict, gritted his teeth, and adapted. He believed that if he did not break, fortune would smile on him again.

I met Barak at his home before the elections to try to reach an understanding that would guarantee Peres's role in the government. I planned to get Barak angry right at the outset of our conversation, to nudge him to prove his admiration for Peres through tangible action. After his wife Nava left the room, I told him, "I know your time is short, so I'll say this without much introduction—I can read your attitude towards Peres very clearly: you're working to eliminate him politically. It doesn't suit you to have such a strong character in your surroundings." In my plan, Barak should have reacted angrily and pounced at me in a fit of rage and denial, expressed his admiration for Peres in order to refute my accusations and then—I hoped—translated that into practical promises. But Barak was not much fussed by my remarks and displayed neither displeasure nor anger. Instead, he asked me matter-of-factly, "So what do you propose?"

I warned him that Peres, if frustrated, would likely form a rival party. "It would be a disaster," I said. "You've got to create a positive connection between the two of you." Barak requested that Peres publicly support his candidacy for the premiership. I told him that would happen if he made sure to secure Peres a spot on his Knesset list, and if he promised that Peres would serve in a senior ministerial position involved in promoting the peace process, in his government or in any government he joined. Barak agreed and even kept his word—formally. Peres was placed on the Knesset list and given the role of Minister for Regional Cooperation.

Peres could not hide his agitation when confronted with the winner's hubris. He asked Barak to clarify what areas of responsibility he would be assigned. Barak answered that he had not thought about it yet. "We'll form a committee with a representative of the Prime Minister's Office and the ministries of Finance and Foreign Affairs, and a representative of yours too. The committee will discuss and make recommendations for this new ministry's fields of responsibility." Peres, who had already served in almost every possible role in past Israeli governments, now made a modest request: responsibility for the regional economic summits and any cooperation or development projects with our neighbors. But Barak put his foot down and refused to approve anything. Whenever Peres raised an idea, he was met with the same chilly response: "I can't grant your requests, because they fall under the responsibility of the Foreign Ministry. We need to look into it."

I had never seen Peres so hurt and humiliated. He glanced at me and asked, "What do you think?" I said that it was sad to see how the prime minister-designate was appointing Shimon Peres to a ministerial office without having given any thought to the substance or content of the role. My emotional appeal had failed to bother Barak in the least.

I Need Your Help

I struggled to understand Barak. The first time this limitation got in my way was immediately after Rabin's assassination. Barak applied some pressure and got Peres to appoint him foreign minister. On one of his visits to the Prime Minister's Office, he entered my office and told me with demonstrable friendliness, "I need your help. I have no clue how the Foreign Ministry works." I answered that I would help him as much as I could. "So give me some advice," he said. "Who should I appoint as my diplomatic advisor?" I advised him to appoint someone from within the ministry itself. That would send the organization a positive message, and there were also some suitable candidates for the role in the ministry.

Barak replied that he had not thought about this angle at all and could see how much he would need my advice later on. "Who would you recommend?" he asked, interested. I answered that he would find Mark Sofer in the minister's office. "He served as my deputy, but he's better than me. He's a consummate professional and a wonderful man. From my year in the cadets' course. A graduate of the London School of Economics. Give him a trial period and you won't regret it." Barak thanked me warmly.

Mark called me during the night, in shock. "Barak summoned me and said I have to clear my things from the minister's office by the morning and leave my position," he said.

I turned to the military secretary, Danny Yatom, and asked him to explain Barak's decision, as one who had served as Barak's deputy in the elite Sayeret Matkal unit of the Israel Defense Forces. Danny looked at me, amused. "You're such an ass. Barak must have played a basic trick on you to find out who you left behind to spy on him." I was left with Yatom's speculation without knowing whether it was the real reason for Barak's decision.

The Regional Cooperation Ministry

Humiliated, Peres held his pain in, and off we went. I found myself building a whole new government ministry, fighting for manpower and budgets, and gnawing at areas of responsibility that naturally belonged to the Foreign Ministry, my original home. In order to solve the political problem posed by Peres, Barak had authorized the creation of a ministry whose entire existence ran counter to good governance. To my shame, I served as the director-general, a partner, and founder of a shameful governmental error, which continues to bloom in the soil of Israel's cynical politics. This error—the Ministry of Regional Cooperation—has not been corrected to this day.

Barak made sure to minimize Peres's stature and role. He neither consulted him nor involved him in diplomatic activity. I tried to persuade Peres to keep his lips sealed. "The rapprochement between you and Barak will be slow. He'll keep on banging his head against the wall until he stops fearing you'll undermine him and learns you can help him. You're used to these situations—it didn't come easily with Rabin either."

I reminded Peres that when he was prime minister after Rabin's murder, we met with Barak, who was courting him religiously. In the course of the meeting, Barak decided to pay me a compliment: "Shimon, you must be grateful that a man like Avi is working with you." Peres looked at Barak, expecting to hear an explanation. Barak hesitated briefly, then said, "Even if you turn your back to Avi, he won't knife you." This was the first compliment that came to his mind. I reminded a frustrated Peres of these remarks. "The man's obsessively suspicious. You have to be patient with him." I chimed in with what Eitan Haber had explained to me: Barak's nightmare was that one day, he would collect the Nobel Prize that obviously awaited him and suddenly find Shimon Peres popping up next to him to receive the prize as well, "just like what happened to Rabin."

Months passed and my hopes faded. The gulf between Barak and Peres deepened. There were clashes in the territories, the peace process was collapsing, and Israel's regional and international position was deteriorating. I believed in Peres's ability to reach creative understandings with the Palestinian side. To make a difference. I was familiar with his persistence and his ability to speak with Arafat, but Barak made no use of any of this. Instead, Peres was asked to go on "hasbara trips" around world capitals. A convenient way to get rid of his bothersome presence. Peres gladly acquiesced. He was always willing to report for duty to defend Israel's name abroad, and he was not averse to staying abroad in the company of world leaders and in the lights of television cameras. Peres ploughed his way through Europe and won plaudits for his level-headed and hopeful performances, and for his devotion to peace and reconciliation despite the intense violence. European leaders were happy to meet him, reveled in hearing his analysis, and lathered him with affection.

I tried, without success, to convince Peres that his addiction to these foreign hasbara missions led to him being identified with Barak's policies—while in our conversations he called Barak an "un-ideological opportunist" and claimed that he, in his hubris and deafness, was responsible for the deterioration of the situation with the Palestinians.

Leah's Letter

As I saw things, the whole point of Peres's entry to Barak's government was to enable him to influence the peace process. We did not succeed. Peres was kept away from the diplomatic arena, the violence intensified, and there seemed to be no way out. In my despair, I also looked for less conventional options. The opportunity arose in a conversation with Amnon Abramovich, a commentator on Channel 1 at the time.[2] I told him that the media should cover the fact that Barak had forgotten to enlist Peres to help solve the crisis with the Palestinians. "He promised to leave no stone unturned," I told him, "and he hasn't turned Peres's stone." Abramovich asked whether anyone of stature had appealed to Barak. I decided to engineer such an appeal and reasoned that the most suitable figure would be Leah Rabin.

Leah was hospitalized with cancer at the time. I wrote a draft letter for her to sign and presented the text to Peres, Uri, and Yossi. But who should ask Leah? Peres suggested that I ask Shimon Sheves to do it. Uri volunteered to ask Dalia Rabin. But I decided to go to the hospital myself.

I had joined Peres to visit Leah a week earlier. I had never had any real acquaintance with her until then. She told us about the difficult moments immediately after Rabin's assassination, when she was still in the dark about what had happened. She was driven to the Shin Bet building, and to her surprise discovered that Peres had been driven there as well. "You should know, Yitzhak greatly respected Shimon," she told me. "Whenever he phoned on weekends, Yitzhak would get angry if the call wasn't transferred to him immediately. He didn't want Shimon to feel that he was belittling him."

I told Leah that before revealing the purpose of my visit, I wanted to take the opportunity to describe two minor encounters I had had with her late husband. It was the small, seemingly insignificant events, I said, that had left an impression on me. "Rabin was always a rival for me, as were you," I said. "He struck me as cold, and it took me a long time to learn to appreciate him. I got to know you, Leah, only after the murder. I was impressed by your fortitude, by your adherence to your principles."

The first incident that I described to her took place in Beit Gabriel, on the banks of the Sea of Galilee, as we waited for the arrival of King Hussein for the ceremony ratifying the peace treaty with Jordan.[3] I entered a room and found Peres and Rabin and a few other close advisors sitting around a table. I saw that there were no empty seats and turned to leave, when suddenly I heard Rabin's deep and phlegmatic voice: "Avi, don't cause a fuss, find yourself a chair and come sit with us." Before then, I hadn't known that Rabin knew my name. The fact that he addressed me, out of everyone in the room, moved me and dented some of my more bitter feelings toward him.

The second incident was on a plane returning from talks in Cairo. Peres, Rabin, Uri Savir, and I sat facing each other. Rabin was not a party to the lively conversation and perhaps felt a little sidelined. Our eyes met and I sensed that he was lonely and wanted to be involved in the discussion. To break the ice, I told a joke. Rabin burst into laughter. He got up and walked past the dividing curtain, to where the other passengers were seated. "I have to tell you an amazing joke I just heard from Avi," he said. I can't remember the joke, but I felt again that there were human layers to Rabin's personality that did not fit in the stereotype I had had of him: cold, irascible, and aloof. "These are small stories and they don't mean anything, but for some reason they've always touched my heart," I told Leah. "I wanted to tell you about them."

I sensed that Leah was touched. Most of her body was covered with a blanket, but I could tell that she had shrunk since the previous week's visit. She had looked better when I accompanied Peres to visit her. It was also clear that she had made an effort to look her best. Her hair had been neatly combed and she was wearing gold and diamond jewelry. After her husband's murder, her connection with Peres had deepened. Despite their hate-filled history, next to her bed and close to her death the two seemed to be closer. Genuinely close. Peres gave her a book as a present. He admired her love of reading and mentioned this in his remarks over her grave.

I explained to Leah why I had come. "The situation in the territories is terrible. The peace process that Yitzhak and Shimon created and led is collapsing. Barak can't and won't talk to Arafat." I said that I admired Yitzhak's leadership and self-confidence. "He was aware of his weak points and knew he wasn't good at negotiating, so he preferred for Shimon to do the job and reserved the authority to accept or reject things and give instructions. Barak, unlike Rabin, cannot see his own limitations and is afraid of Peres's involvement."

Leah replied that my remarks about Barak were too kind on him. "That man is a disappointment," she said. "I do not believe, as you do, that his problem is simply one of management. In my opinion, he doesn't want to pay the necessary price for a permanent agreement with the Palestinians."

I told her that Barak responded to pressure. That was why I proposed she make a dramatic request to Barak to enlist Peres for the task of negotiating with Arafat. She could ask him through an open letter, and, in order to make things easier, I had already drafted a text. Leah asked me to read it to her. I did:

27 October 2000

To: The Prime Minister

Dear Ehud,

I was happy to hear you speak last night about your commitment to the path of Oslo, the path of peace. To move away from this path and the spirit of Oslo would mean moving away from the hope of creating peace here and taking a conscious step towards a national disaster and the danger of war.

You used to say that you felt a duty to leave no stone unturned to bring peace to Israel. And all the more so, that you were committed to leaving no stone unturned to avoid war. Only then, as you said, could you look the mothers whose sons are being called to the battlefield in the eye.

There is at least one stone, Ehud, that you have still left unturned: Shimon Peres.

Shimon has a rare ability to speak with the Palestinian side. He has an international stature and a moral authority owing to his commitment to peace. Yitzhak was able to get over their past disputes, recognised Shimon's special virtues, and managed to work shoulder-to-shoulder with him during difficult times of decision-making. The present situation requires that Shimon be enlisted for the task of negotiations with Arafat.

I am convinced that this is the advice Yitzhak would have given you at this difficult time. I am convinced that if you manage to work together, the chances are we shall mark the anniversary of Yitzhak's murder in an atmosphere of calm and renewed hope for peace.

Out of loyalty to Yitzhak's legacy, please consider my request.

> *Regards,*
> *Leah Rabin*

> *—I owe it to myself to make my request to you public.*

Leah listened excitedly. She looked straight at me and said, "I'm signing onto every word. You have surprised me, I didn't think this was what you'd ask. I can fulfil your request, but I have serious doubts whether these words will make any impression on Barak." I told her we had to try. I explained that the plan was to send Barak the letter and circulate it to the media simultaneously. She asked to consult her daughter Dalia about the wording. I later learned that Dalia asked to remove one sentence from the letter: "I am convinced that this is the advice Yitzhak would have given you at this difficult time." She disapproved of pretending to speak in Yitzhak's name.

Abramovich's report on TV caused a stir. In parallel, we arranged for Arafat to request to meet Peres. On this occasion, perhaps also thanks to Leah's letter, Barak acquiesced.

We departed for Gaza accompanied by Gilead Sher, Barak's head of bureau.[4] The conversation in Arafat's office did not go well. Gilead forcefully attacked the Palestinian leader and refused to allow Peres to direct the conversation as he wanted. We finished without results and were called to the dining table to eat dinner together. I knew that our failed mission had ended. I turned to Arafat and told him, "Mr President, I can't go home to my children without you and Mr Peres reaching an agreement about an end to the violence. How shall I explain to them that we returned empty handed? I am asking you and Shimon to go back into that room and together find a way to a ceasefire." Arafat acquiesced, and the two returned to his office.

Muhammad Rashid,[5] Arafat's economic advisor, noticed my efforts to have Peres and Arafat left alone. "I'll take Gili [Gilead] for a walk around Gaza until Abu Ammar and Peres finish," he suggested mischievously. After a short while, Arafat and Peres left the room smiling and announced that they had agreed on a ceasefire plan. Peres stressed to Arafat that we were honoring Rabin's memory. The fifth anniversary of the murder was upon us.

We returned to Jerusalem to update Barak. He placed a hand on Peres's shoulder in an unusual embrace and told him, "If this works, you should know you've made a big contribution tonight." Gilead coordinated with Arafat's office on a timetable leading to a simultaneous declaration by Barak and Arafat of their commitment to a ceasefire. Beforehand, the IDF would withdraw its tanks to their former positions, and the security forces would hold coordination meetings. It was also agreed that after a few days' quiet, the sides would renew talks "in commemoration of Yitzhak Rabin." I reached home toward dawn. I was extremely tired but happy. I felt that if there was really going to be a ceasefire, I had been a party to reaching it.

The following morning proved that my happiness had been premature. Arafat failed to meet the commitments he had undertaken or make the declaration he had promised to make. That same day, Islamic Jihad committed a major terror attack in Jerusalem. Two Israelis were murdered in a car bomb explosion. The Palestinians had not held their fire, and the violence had not ceased.

The endeavor had failed but "Leah's letter" continued to preoccupy the media. When she was asked in a press interview[6] what had prompted her to write to Barak, she replied,

I am angry and hurt. I'm outraged by all of Barak's behaviour. It started with his handling of the negotiations with the Palestinians and continued with this emergency government of his, and after that the agreement with Shas. His delusions are unacceptable to me. I doubt his political zig-zagging will bring peace. I know that Israel wants peace, and without the prime minister's tricks. None of the people around him have stood up and said this openly, so I felt I had to send him the letter.

The commentator Sima Kadmon reported:

Peres's people came to the hospital where she is being treated, had her sign the letter, and faxed it to the television stations … Rabin signed the letter gladly. She saw it as her final mission on Yitzhak's behalf. There is a legal term for a document brought for an ill person's signature on their deathbed. It's called a "deathbed will". In such a will, sometimes doubts are cast about whether the person signing is sound of mind. That was not the case here. In this case, the sick person was lucid, focused, and as mobilised as ever. She has not changed. Neither has Shimon.[7]

For Barak's part, his reaction was obviously different. "Barak never forgets a thing, but there are some things he remembers in particular," wrote the journalist Nahum Barnea. "One of them is how Peres's people went to Leah Rabin to get out of her— under the influence of tranquilisers and on her deathbed—a letter against Barak."[8]

Breakfast at the President's Residence

Barak might not "forget a thing," but his troubled past with Peres did not impede good working relations after Peres was elected president. As minister of defense, Barak joined President Peres for a regular breakfast every Sunday before the weekly cabinet meeting. Peres felt that Barak was an important partner in his efforts to influence Netanyahu to move toward a historic compromise with the Palestinians. In this context, I met Barak a number of times in his home, and at his request, I formulated a peace plan that he could adopt and whose content he could promote to Netanyahu. Barak impressed me with his sharpness, the depth of his analysis, his strategic vision, and his sense of humor. I have not found many in Israeli politics to be as clever or as well read as he.

The time that passed, however, taught me that Barak would not risk his own skin to push for peace with the Palestinians. There gradually also developed tension between him and Peres over the latter's opposition to an Israeli strike on Iran's nuclear sites. Peres believed that Israeli military action against the will of the United States would surely bring catastrophe. In private conversations, he described Barak as an arrogant, self-centered, and dangerous man "who thinks even Churchill is dwarfed by his shadow."

Peres believed that Barak was telling one story to Netanyahu and a different story on his frequent trips to Washington. "Do the Americans not understand Barak's double game?" he asked me in astonishment. Peres is considered the person who incited Israel's security chiefs against a military operation. At one point, Netanyahu and Barak approached him together to warn him that he was overstepping his role as president.

Peres withstood the pressure. He argued that he had been elected by the Knesset, not appointed by the two of them. His duties were to the public, and he would act as he saw fit. His relationship with Barak suffered, and Barak stopped coming for breakfast at the President's Residence; Peres said Barak stopped senior military officers meeting him too. But Peres laughed it off. He said he wouldn't be surprised if down the road, when the political calculus changed, Barak came back to give him a big, friendly hug.

Sharon's Charm

The UNESCO summit in December 1993, at the ancient royal palace in Granada in Spain, was the site of the first working meeting between Peres and Arafat.[1] The festive atmosphere at the signing ceremony on the White House lawn had made way for the harsh reality of the implementation of the accords. In a public speech, Arafat spoke with elation about how Granada was a symbol of coexistence between the descendants of our common patriarch, Abraham. But later, in front of the burning fireplace and the masterpieces of Andalusian art, he seemed depressed to hear Peres's rigid positions.

Arafat was especially angry when he was informed that Israel would not transfer responsibility for control of the border crossings with Jordan. "I cannot agree for you to control the crossings," he said.

It will be the end of me. I can't go for a Bantustan.[2] Don't push me into a corner, my back's already against the wall. How will I tell my people that you control every entry, from every direction? I'm not in power because of a popular majority, but thanks to the personal credit I've accumulated. For me this is a disaster, a catastrophe.

Peres explained that this had been agreed at Oslo. We could not change the treaty, nor would we agree to an American or European presence at the crossings—the compromise that Arafat suggested. Arafat's legs started twitching even more nervously, and he shouted at Peres angrily, "I won't be able to govern like this, you're destroying my trinity!"

Until that point, I had been careful to write down every word. I sensed that the conversation was of great operative and even historic importance, and I had intended to hand Rabin the whole text upon our return. But I suddenly stopped writing. I did not know how to translate "trinity," and I didn't really understand what Arafat meant. Yasser Abed Rabbo was sitting next to Arafat. I signaled to him that I required an explanation. He spoke to Arafat in Arabic, and after hearing his reply, the two burst out laughing. Abed Rabbo explained, "It's not his trinity that's been destroyed. His *dignity* has been destroyed!"

When we returned to Israel, I could not resist the temptation and re-enacted this moment to Yossi and Uri, mimicking Arafat's offence-stricken voice: "Not trinity ... dignity!" But what started between us as cheap humor turned into a basic rule in later negotiations with Arafat. The Palestinian leader often grumbled, "All I hear from the Israeli side is: security, security, security." We, who insisted primarily on matters of security, discovered soon enough that if we wanted security from Arafat, we had to give him in exchange his trinity. Put simply, whoever belittled and injured Arafat's honor greatly diminished any prospects of securing his cooperation.

Arafat made a critical and central contribution to the failure of the peace process, which must not be obscured. But Israel's habit of ignoring the equation of "honour for security" played its own part. Arafat absorbed countless humiliations from his Israeli interlocutors—as above all, from Sharon.

Admiration for Sharon the Bulldozer

For many years, I regarded Sharon as the declared enemy of Peres's efforts toward peace. The settlement enterprise, which had his name all over it, seemed to be designed to foil any chances of a future agreement between Israel and the Palestinians.

Peres took a different attitude toward Sharon. He admired his bulldozer character, his ability to put things into action, and of course his achievements as a military commander. When Peres was finance minister in the late 1980s, he wanted to lead a bus tour of the directors-general of the various ministries and solve problems in one stroke "like Sharon." The pair knew each other for decades. After the establishment of the Netanyahu government in 1996, Peres, who was left battered and defeated in the opposition, made sure to hold low-key meetings with Sharon. He tried to find common ground with him about a resolution of the Palestinian issue. Peres had reached the conclusion that peace could not rest on the shoulders of the Israeli Left alone. He needed to bring the political Right on board, and to that end, Sharon would be a key asset.

Peres did not share the dominant attitude in Israeli left-wing circles that deemed Sharon persona non grata on moral grounds. In order to co-opt the political Right into the peace camp, he was willing to twist the commitments we had undertaken in the Declaration of Principles at Oslo. Nor did he oppose attempts during the Rabin government to hatch plans to bring Sharon into a unity government. At the start of 1995, Peres asked Yossi, Uri, and me for our opinion about such a possibility. He had previously expressed a lack of faith in Rabin's willingness to move forward with implementing the Oslo Accords, but now his words reflected a bitter disappointment in the Arabs as well: "They pocket everything they gain from us and demand more."

From his tone, it sounded like Peres was sobering up. "What would you think about Arik Sharon, David Levy, and maybe the whole Likud joining the government?" he asked. "I've had secret talks with Sharon and Levy and have reached some surprising agreements with them."

Uri said he thought no such option existed. "You have to stick to this effort, however frustrating: to point out solutions and persuade Rabin to accept them."

"This government is formed of nobodies," Peres went on. "Everyone's sucking up to Rabin, and the public will forgive him for anything. Believe me, it'd be easier for me to work with Arik. I formed the unity government with him in 1984 and I've never regretted it. We pulled the IDF out of Lebanon, we withdrew from Taba."[3]

I said that the decision had to be considered in light of a single question: what would best advance the implementation of the interim accord with the Palestinians? "The Right could probably join until we reach the stage of a final-status agreement. I believe there would be great educational and political value in Netanyahu and Sharon shaking hands with Arafat."

Yossi dismissed the idea. "The Likud will not join a unity government because it's not worth it for Bibi—even if I'd also like to see the spectacle of a Sharon-Arafat handshake."[4]

Peres's idea for unity was never put into practice. After the Likud victory in 1996, with Peres in the opposition, he and Sharon swapped roles. This time, they explored the option of having Peres and *his* party join a unity government. In their conversations, Peres listed a number of basic principles around which he thought a national consensus could be forged: Jerusalem would remain united, no foreign army would cross the Jordan River, and no settlements would be dismantled. He even suggested "to permit immediate Palestinian sovereignty over Gaza, and to make efforts at the same time for the West Bank to remain under no formal sovereignty for a long time ahead."

"It will be difficult to move David Levy out of the Foreign Ministry," Sharon replied matter-of-factly, "so I would suggest you go to Defence and Ehud Barak to Finance." He explained that the current electoral system was problematic and made it difficult to get things going. "We need to change the system, to form a government of the two large parties, without the small ones, and to go for a peace treaty." He said that he was conducting talks with the Palestinians and "they were listening." The Oslo agenda could not presently be implemented, he believed, and it was impossible to reach a permanent accord. Sharon proposed interim accords instead. Both Ahmed Qurei and Mahmoud Abbas, Sharon said, were practical men.

Peres replied that if Israel continued to dither and play for time, it would aggravate the Arabs' hatred. "You too are perceived as an Arab-hater," he said.

Sharon was offended. "But I respect the Arabs," he said, "and they respect me as a man who fulfils his promises."

Peres described to Sharon how globalization was creating dangers but also new opportunities. "The world has changed. Enter an Arab village, and you'll find even young Arab women want a smaller bottom that will fit into a fashionable pair of jeans."

Sharon said that he agreed with Peres's analysis but there was nobody to talk to. "I have an image problem," he confessed. "What will people say about me?"

"The world has changed, and so have you," Peres reassured him. "I'm prepared for both of us to set out with a joint plan: changing the electoral system, a two-party government, a comprehensive peace based on recognising a Palestinian state on constructive borders,[5] involving the Arab states in the reconciliation efforts, and mobilising economic resources."

Sharon: "It's very exciting. I want time to think about it. Will we form a
movement?"
Peres: "Let's first come out with a plan. The plan can form the movement."
Sharon: "Give me a week to think about it."

Political Partnership—A Natural Step

The establishment of a political partnership with Peres after Sharon's victory in the
2001 elections was, therefore, a natural step for the pair. It was based, besides coalition-
building calculations, also on friendship, a long-standing acquaintance, mutual
respect, and no few political conversations and attempts to find common ground.
Their partnership, once it took off, also obviously gave expression to the fundamental
differences, both between their positions and dispositions. One basic bone of
contention was their respective attitudes to Arafat.

Despite spending a lifetime in the cynical field of politics, Peres was optimistic about
human nature. People could change. Their paths could be influenced. They are not
immune to the upheavals of modernity. Arafat was to be judged by his deeds and not
necessarily by his speeches. His rhetoric reflected an internal dissonance: fragments
of dreams that would never come true, a desire to retain the affections of the entire
Palestinian people, and an attempt to balance out tangible concessions with fiery words.

Even at moments of growing consensus that Arafat was "not a partner," Peres still
argued that they could not diminish what he had done by recognizing Israel and
agreeing to peace and coexistence with it. Peres told Secretary Christopher, "You can
be angry at Arafat, but you can't ignore the fact that he made a historic decision that
no Palestinian leader before him had ever dared make. Arafat's demise would be a
failure for all of us, so we must support him by any means possible."[6] Peres believed
that Israel had to be cool-headed in its attitude toward him. Arafat was not a man like
King Hussein, who could conquer people's hearts. But he was still a leader who could
serve Israel's interests. He was an address and had proven he could compromise on his
nation's behalf. That was why we had to be smart and sophisticated in our dealings with
him. Above all—we could not hurt his pride.

President George W. Bush asked Peres in one meeting, "Does Arafat want an
agreement, or does he want to eliminate the State of Israel?"[7]

"He wants it all," Peres replied. The American president, who saw the world in
black and white, was baffled by Peres's reply. But this was the essence of how Peres saw
Arafat. For Peres, the meaning of the observation "he wants it all" was that Arafat's
mind was home to both a desire to be the hero of a "peace of the braves," as he put it,
and a hunger to throw Israel into the sea. Peres felt at ease working with a man who
accommodated contradictory positions in the space between his two ears. He himself
was a statesman full of contradictions, and he believed this was the expression of a side
of human nature that had to be reconciled with and respected.

Peres believed that Arafat's path would not be the automatic consequence of a
coherent, basic strategy. It depended, to a great deal, on Israel. "We made a mistake
during the talks at Camp David," Peres told President Bush. "We gave Arafat the feeling

that he could get more. We wanted negotiations to end the conflict, and we put the question of Jerusalem on the agenda. The time is not yet ripe for a discussion on this subject."

In Peres's opinion, the talks at Camp David lacked sensitivity to the range of options that the other side could permit itself; creativity in designing political options that served our interests without provoking a negative response; and chemistry and the ability to forge a connection with our partners.

Peres was not surprised, and perhaps felt a certain satisfaction, when Bill Clinton told him about events at Camp David:[8] "Barak is a genius and in his heart he wants peace, but he has as much understanding and sensitivity towards people as this wooden table." Peres believed that if he had been the Israeli negotiator at Camp David, the talks would not have ended so miserably. He would have salvaged an agreement. I believe so too.

Nobel Prize or Oscar?

When dealing with Arafat, Peres displayed the best of his talents. He knew how to console, instill hope, propose solutions, and give attention and respect. He could also attack, threaten, and be—in his own words—"brutal." He tended to reveal his more severe side only in one-on-one meetings with the Palestinian leader. Peres did not want to embarrass Arafat in front of his own people, and Arafat appreciated it. During their conversations, Peres adopted whatever facial expressions and manners of speech suited his negotiating needs. Even the experienced Joel Singer once fell prey to Peres's deft hand, during one of the rounds of talks in Cairo.[9]

The tactic that Peres had planned for that night was to place Arafat and his people on the defensive. Peres took the floor before anyone else could open their mouths. Instead of the usual courtesies and greetings, he launched into a frenzy, berating his Palestinian interlocutors, and rebuking them in the harshest of terms. They had expected a business-like negotiation on a few matters that required an orderly discussion, but Peres chose to lash out at them. He assailed their irresponsible behavior and failure to fulfil their commitments. "You're creating disappointment in Israeli public opinion and you're weakening the government and its ability to help you," he shouted angrily, thumping the table with his hand.

Joel, sitting next to me, was overwhelmed by embarrassment and frustration. "Peres isn't talking sense," he told me. "He's attacking them unfairly. He's being ridiculous." I tried to explain the tactics, but he refused to take comfort. Akram Haniyeh, Arafat's advisor, whispered to me, "Your boss deserves a prize. But not a Nobel Prize. He deserves an Oscar." Although Arafat and his people were experienced in the secrets of negotiations, and were sophisticated enough to deduce that Peres was going overboard on purpose, his performance still had a positive result. It put Arafat in a position of being forced to try to conciliate his Israeli interlocutor.

At the end of the evening, I told Peres how Joel had been horrified by his performance, and how Haniyeh had awarded him an Oscar. "I think you begin your performance acting but get sucked into it quite quickly, and identify with the character you're playing. You start believing what you're saying, you start being genuinely angry and enraged. It stops being just a show."

Peres looked at me with a smile. "There might be something in that, but the most important thing is that it works." That night, he played the same trick in a phone call with Rabin. In order to continue the talks, Peres needed some more rope. Before explaining his request, he attacked IDF Chief of Staff Ehud Barak, saying he was causing problems and opposing several concessions. As Peres got carried away with his own speech, his anger became genuine, his hands started shaking, and his voice started quaking till he nearly cried. "That Barak, that insolent man, he'll ruin everything for us!" Peres was being true to his heart, but he was also laying the groundwork for getting what he wanted from Rabin.

The Attitude toward Arafat

"Don't destroy my trinity." That desperate plea by the PLO chairman at our first working meeting in Granada always echoed in Peres's mind whenever he dealt with Arafat. When the Israelis made a mistake at the Taba talks[10] and conceded territory in Hebron that they intended to keep in Israel's hands, Peres went to Arafat's room and told him, "There's a basic lack of fairness in our talks. They're not balanced. I have no professional skills, and you're both a general and an engineer. We conceded a certain

Figure 10 A pleasant atmosphere at the talks in Taba. From right to left: Peres, Gil, Stella Shustak (MFA), Maj. Gen. Oren Shachor, and Arafat. September 1995.

piece of territory by mistake." Arafat responded immediately, "It doesn't matter what the territory is, take it back."

Despite the differences between the two, Arafat fascinated Peres with his complex personality and the challenges he presented him. Peres neither hated him nor recoiled from shaking his hand and embracing him. He appreciated Arafat's achievements in keeping the Palestinians as a people in the cruel arena of the family of nations, despite the heavy blows they had suffered.

Sharon, in contrast, loathed Arafat. He saw him as a bloodthirsty terrorist and a key obstacle to any Israeli–Palestinian reconciliation process. Members of the Israeli delegation that joined Netanyahu at the Wye Plantation talks[11] joked that Sharon would find it easier to hand Arafat territory than to shake his hand. The minister Natan Sharansky even told him that he should reverse his order of priorities. In the talks at Sharon's ranch I noted to Sharon's credit his paternal and loving attitude to his dog Schwartz—which was why it was strange for me to discover that he called Arafat "the dog" in disgust. During the Second Intifada, Sharon seemed to take pleasure in giving the order to tighten the siege around Arafat's headquarters in Ramallah and to toughen the conditions of his detention. It appeared that Sharon saw the siege as a settling of historic accounts and as a direct continuation of the siege he had imposed on Arafat in Beirut in 1982. Sharon seemed to be keen to finish the job.

As a graduate of the Peres–Rabin partnership, I approached the Peres–Sharon partnership with preconceptions about how to influence the government's direction whenever Peres was a supporting actor under the prime minister. First and foremost, it was vital to preserve industrial peace with Sharon. We could not slip into arguments about petty matters or respond to provocations, and we had to fight only for what truly mattered. Through it all, we also had to maintain a measure of deterrence and send the message: "Peres is not in your pocket."

On the eve of Peres's departure for his first working meeting with Prime Minister Sharon, I wrote him a memo that articulated what I understood to be the key points of his position, which I thought he should present to Sharon.[12] Among them:

> The continuation of our harsh rhetoric with Arafat and the Palestinian Authority is likely to swiftly eliminate our political room for manoeuvre. We would lose our ability to act with our interlocutor on the Palestinian side (problematic as he is) because we would become victims of our own propaganda, which says: Arafat is not a partner. We must agree to a basic, strategic premise: Arafat and the Palestinian Authority are *the* partner. We must emphasise this point in public. No action (in security, economics, diplomacy, or hasbara) may contradict this premise.

But Sharon did not back down, unconvinced by Peres's learned arguments. He refused to meet Arafat and sufficed with sending envoys, including his son Omri. The central message was: no negotiations under fire, and talks only after a month of complete quiet. Peres was frustrated and tried to operate within the rigid constraints that Sharon had set. He told US Secretary of State Colin Powell, "I know Sharon. He doesn't want to end his term surrounded by fire and columns of smoke. But still, he won't negotiate under fire."[13]

Peres remained loyal to Sharon's guidelines but tried to find loopholes to make progress. Powell asked once, "I understand that Israel will not establish new settlements. But is it possible to reach an understanding on the reasonable scope of the development of the existing ones?" Peres gave him an opening: "Perhaps a quiet verbal understanding, but not in writing."

Peres believed that only dialogue with the Palestinians could bring salvation. While Sharon fought against the various political initiatives and subjected them to conditions and constraints, Peres tried to get a foothold on every initiative in order to create engagement. He believed that the plans themselves were less important than the cultivation of a partner.

At outset of our journey with Sharon, the Egyptian–Jordanian initiative[14] and Mitchell Report,[15] both in 2001, served Peres in this approach. For him, they were levers for dialogue. But when US envoy Bill Burns came to explore how to get the Mitchell plan going through dialogue, Sharon reacted harshly. "We will not discuss anything but security, and through meetings between security officials. We will not negotiate with Arafat, directly or indirectly, on political matters. We have to first secure an end to the violence. Arafat is playing with us. He is behind the terrorism."[16]

Those present at this discussion admired the diligence of whoever had taken the care to place American and Israeli flags on the table. Without them, one could have been easily confused about which of the two speakers represented the superpower: the slim, delicate, and soft-spoken Bill Burns or Sharon, the large man with the booming voice, who hijacked the conversation and acted like a teacher giving a telling-off to a naughty child.

Sharon used to begin deliberations in his office, especially after major terror attacks, by making a hard-line statement that made it clear which positions he would be happy to hear and what he would reject. In one such meeting, he watched a presentation by the IDF Planning Directorate. The officers, accustomed to the regimented methods of the army, thought about the Israeli–Palestinian clashes in terms of a need to define an overarching objective from which they could logically assess the advantages and disadvantages of possible courses of action. They struggled to adjust to our political reality, in which the leader—Sharon—refrained from revealing his objectives and forced military planners to simply guess the direction or act on instructions that were neither written nor explicit but conveyed with a wink. Instructions that if needed, and without paying a political price, he could simply deny.

The officers' methodical presentation noted that Israel's main objective was to defeat Palestinian terrorism in order to create conditions for resuming the peace process. "Who set you objectives like that?" Sharon asked furiously, interrupting the presentation. "Beat Palestinian terrorism—yes. The rest of the sentence—delete!" The message was passed on.

The IDF was talking about erecting a barrier, stopping the Palestinians from making gains, and reversing the cost-benefit calculus in Arafat's mind. Arafat had to reach the conclusion that in the final analysis, the cost of continuing the conflict was greater than the cost of ending it. Some in the IDF said that the absence of a political horizon was encouraging Arafat to continue fighting. Sharon of course rejected this criticism. As far as he was concerned, "that dog simply enjoys killing Jews."

What stood out in the IDF's analysis was its mechanistic understanding of the inner workings of Arafat's mind. Intelligence services, which require a model to predict and elegantly explain political behavior, draw mainly on rationalist models and neglect other possible explanatory theories.

I considered it a grave error to let soldiers deal with political analysis. They are no better trained than others in interpreting political behavior—perhaps the reverse. Their military upbringing primes them to misunderstand politics. Moreover, entrusting policy in the hands of military officers is inconsistent with democratic values. In Israel, the army encroaches into civilian political matters by exploiting its strength, resources, and public prestige.

In our many conversations with the chiefs of the security forces, I argued that they mistakenly assumed that underneath Arafat's keffiyeh was a sophisticated computer. As if his brain defined interests, ranked them according to importance, absorbed all the information without losing any details, evaluated every option through a precise cost-benefit analysis, reached a rational conclusion about the optimal course of action, and then raised or lowered the flames as needed. If he really acted in such a rational manner, why had he not managed to foresee that his actions would lead to imprisonment in his headquarters? How had he not discerned that the Palestinian Authority, which he had founded, was crumbling, that his forces were being destroyed, and that his political and maybe even physical end was nigh?

Another idea kept coming up in our discussions: not just that Arafat was in control of the situation, but that he was also acting in accordance with a "phased plan." This interpretation completely minimized any possibility of a diplomatic solution to the violence, and in fact left the military option as the only recourse. Even if Arafat had taken steps toward a ceasefire and reconciliation, this would have aroused the suspicion that his actions were ultimately aimed at the phased elimination of the State of Israel.

This is a tautologous argument, which can be neither proven nor disproven. But one thing is clear: if Arafat had been assassinated following the signing of the Oslo Accords, he would not have gone down in history—or even in military intelligence briefings—as having paid a personal price for his adherence to the Phased Plan, but as having fallen victim on the altar of peace. I told army officers that if we could reach a long-term ceasefire deal with Arafat, that would have been enough. We would walk the rest of the way to peace with his successors.

The matter continued to crop up in memos written by the Foreign Ministry at the time, but nobody listened. These memos argued that Arafat was the only actor who could impose order, which was why he was an "asset" for Israel. Israel had to be creative in prodding him in a positive direction. And since the ramifications of the military option would likely be severe, we had to ask ourselves: Have we done everything possible—without prejudicing Israel's key interests—to cause Arafat to change direction? To answer this question, we first had to answer another one: Do we know what would influence Arafat to abandon the path of violence? Military pressure? Political pressure? Some combination of these pressures while marking out a political horizon? The creation of some basis for trust? Dialogue with Sharon?

Arafat's associates claimed in multiple conversations that what Israel was offering him made it difficult for him to embark on a "mini-civil war," which would be the only way of ending the violence. They argued that Israel was demanding that they fight their own brothers in an atmosphere of bitter hostility toward Israel, while Sharon refused to commit to talking and even reserved the right to end all dialogue in response to every rock thrown. "Sharon calls Arafat 'bin Laden', and Arafat draws his own conclusions," they said. "He knows you eliminate bin Laden, you don't make peace with him."

Arafat's associates outlined a "package of reinforcements" to make it easier for him to work toward a ceasefire: the improvement of living conditions, the lifting of the siege, employment in Israel, free movement within the territories, the rehabilitation of the economy, the transfer of tax revenues held by Israel, an end to collective punishments, a settlement freeze, a return to the peace process, and a fixed calendar for the start and end of final-status negotiations. Sharon responded with his fixed mantra: first—the Palestinians had to put a stop to terrorism.

Pushing for Dialogue with Arafat

Peres tried to breach Sharon's impermeable preconditions. He and the Foreign Ministry tried to persuade him that the collapse of the Mitchell Plan would aggravate the security situation. They also argued that it would leave a vacuum that would give rise to an alternative political plan that would be even worse for Israel. Peres took advantage of a meeting of the Socialist International in Lisbon to steal a meeting with Arafat.[17] Although Sharon had asked him not to do so, Peres did not intend to miss his chance. At the event I made sure, through our Norwegian friends, to obtain an invitation to a joint meeting with the Portuguese prime minister to which Arafat would also be invited. On our return, we could explain that it would have been impolite to reject an invitation from our host.

After the fact, we spun the meeting as a dinner, although we were barely served a single sandwich and the talks took the format of a full-fledged diplomatic meeting. Peres demanded seven days of quiet. "You must imprison anyone who's planning an attack," he told Arafat. "You must speak clearly with the commanders."

"I've made my decision," Arafat replied. "I'll make a greater effort. Help me."

Peres stressed to Arafat that it was important that his speech the next day point to a change in direction and instill hope that we were going to change this miserable situation. Arafat nodded understandingly and promised that this was indeed his intention. "Don't repeat your Davos speech," Peres demanded.[18]

The next day, Arafat delivered an exceptionally hard-line speech. Among other things, he accused Israel of using weapons against the Palestinian people that were forbidden under international law: hand grenades loaded with poison gas, and uranium bullets. Muhammad Dahlan—who was also shocked by the speech and was sure he had convinced the chairman to change his tune following the meeting with Peres—told me in the fluent Hebrew that he had acquired in Israeli jail: "Wait and see, Avi, I'll settle the score with whoever wrote this speech."

Back home, Sharon came under pressure from his partners on the Right. They demanded that the government treat Arafat as an enemy, not a partner. They claimed that Peres was making a mockery of government policy. The Yesha Council, the umbrella organization of Israeli settlements, declared that Peres's meeting with Arafat was tantamount to a green light to continue the terror attacks. Sharon found himself between Peres's rock and the Right's hard place. He knew that Peres's activities overseas gave him opportunities to meet with Arafat, and he tried, to no avail, to preempt him. Ahead of our departure to a Mediterranean leaders' forum in Palma de Mallorca,[19] Sharon told Peres, "A meeting between you and Arafat now would be received badly in Israel. There are still funerals here, he's doing nothing against the terrorism."

Sharon suspected that Mubarak, who was also attending the event, would sneak Arafat into his meeting planned with Peres. "If you're photographed, of course, then there's no choice," he told Peres, "but there had better not be a meeting in a separate room."

Peres made no commitments. "Diplomacy has rules of its own," he replied, "and Israel scores points in international public opinion by not turning its back on its partners." And indeed, such a meeting took place, attended by both the Spanish prime minister and the Egyptian president. When the question of Jerusalem came up, Peres told Arafat, "The present situation isn't bad for you. The Al-Aqsa Mosque is under your control. The mufti effectively controls the Temple Mount, Jews won't enter till the Messiah comes, and the Messiah is a consummate diplomat—he never comes."

A further opportunity for a meeting with Arafat arose in Brussels.[20] But there too, we discovered a man for whom the less balanced parts of his personality dominated a great part of his behavior. In a meeting attended by Belgian Prime Minister Guy Verhofstadt and EU foreign policy chief Javier Solana, Arafat found himself under concerted attack from his friends. They demanded that he fight terrorism. "Don't treat Europe and Shimon as if we're in your pocket," Solana warned him. "Whoever replaces us will be worse for you."

"Your people," Peres added, "are giving us the impression that you're not giving unequivocal orders to fight terrorism."

Arafat looked agitated and his lips trembled. "I am one of the greatest leaders alive today in the Arab world, in the world of non-aligned states, and in the whole wide world!" he said. "I am a general who has never lost a single campaign. I know how to give orders and how to take control. In Beirut, I faced down Sharon for 88 days. All my phone calls are under your surveillance. You can listen to the instructions I give."

Peres swallowed his pride. While he wanted to be the one to hold a running dialogue with Arafat, he understood the importance of a meeting between Arafat and Sharon and tried to persuade the prime minister to authorize a formal but discreet line of communication with Arafat. On August 21, 2001, Sharon finally agreed to attempt such a dialogue. It was decided that the Israeli side would be represented by Peres and the head of the IDF's Planning Directorate, Giora Eiland. The defined purpose of the talks was to exhaust the possibilities of reaching a ceasefire, and to initiate seven days of quiet as a gateway for implementing the Mitchell-Tenet plan.[21] But at the same time as giving his authorization in principle to the meeting, Sharon postponed it, and his office gave political instructions that completely contradicted the logic of the talks to which he had agreed: "We must, gradually and with the requisite caution, paint the true picture that an agreement cannot be reached with Arafat, and we need to prepare for negotiations with more pragmatic leaders."[22]

Al Qaeda's terror attack on September 11, 2001 handed Sharon a new excuse to demand that Peres delay his planned meeting with Arafat. He explained that the Americans would not appreciate such a meeting at the present time. We had heard the opposite from the Americans. "Everyone here has his own American!" Peres replied with a bitter laugh.

No Difference if It's Shimon or You and Omri

Officials in the Prime Minister's Office briefed reporters that Peres and his staff were maneuvering the United States into applying pressure for a meeting with Arafat. Moshe Kaplinsky, Sharon's military secretary, told me, "Arik asked me to look you in the eye and ask whether you're behind these feelers from the Americans."

It was agreed to postpone the meeting with Arafat by a week, but in a meeting at his ranch,[23] Sharon asked for a further postponement. This time, he demanded that Arafat proclaim, in person and in Arabic, an end to terrorism. "He must order the terror organisations to hold their fire and enforce his orders," he said. "Otherwise, there's no meeting."

Frustrated and grumpy, Peres announced that he was opposed to Sharon's approach. He complained to Sharon that his staff and certain actors in the IDF were inciting against him in the press. There was a crisis atmosphere in the room. I tried to find a way out, and after checking with Peres, I proposed that Sharon's son Omri and I go to the meeting with Arafat. Sharon said no. "It makes no difference whether it's Shimon or you and Omri," he said. Peres despaired and walked out, but Sharon asked me to stay. When we were alone, he tried to placate me with his usual explanations. "Shimon and I have no disagreements about the objectives," he said. "But you're running too quickly. You're forgetting there's also the public here."

"Peres won't stand with you at the gallows when you execute Oslo," I told him. "He won't participate in the funeral you're planning for his baby. Peres has no chance of succeeding with the Palestinians unless you help him, but you're making him fail."

Sharon replied that I should make no mistake: he loved and respected Peres and his enormous contributions to Israel's defense. "I am one of the few people who know what this nation owes him," he said. Sharon, suffering from a cold, apologized for needing to rest and went up to his room on the top floor. "You're welcome to stay," he told me. I stayed in the kitchen with Uri Shani, the head of Sharon's bureau and Omri. On the rough-hewn wooden table were slices of dark bread and an open tin of spicy Thai sardines, which Sharon had taken a liking to after being invited to taste them by the Thai workers on his ranch. Uri Shani urged Omri to go upstairs and check whether his father had changed his mind about my proposal. Omri came back and reported, "The Caucasian wants to sleep on it tonight."[24]

The following day, September 16, Sharon announced in the Knesset—without coordinating with Peres—that a meeting with Arafat would be permitted only after

48 hours of calm. At the same time, he called me and said, "I accept your proposal. You see, I'm not so rigid. I want you to come to me with Omri so we can outline the positions you'll present to Arafat. I want you to go there tonight."[25] I told Sharon that Peres had to be present at the preparatory meeting, and he quickly obliged.

It was agreed in this meeting that we would make clear to Arafat that he needed to make an indisputable decision: either the path of violence, or the path of peace. If we could see that he had made a strategic decision and was seeing it through, we would help him and could take a big step toward him. A strategic decision, as far as we were concerned, meant peaceful rhetoric, preventing incitement, clear orders to his security organizations, and the consistent implementation of counter-terror measures by his security forces. If all this were to happen, the IDF would receive orders to completely halt operations, and a meeting would take place within days between Peres and Arafat, who would agree to draw up a detailed timetable for putting the Tenet Plan into action and getting the Mitchell Plan rolling. After Peres left, Sharon turned to us as if he had caught us red-handed and said in a teacherly tone, "Don't forget, you're a young men and Arafat's a grown-up. Don't interrupt him, let him speak first. Be polite to him."

On the way to the Gaza crossing, I asked Omri, "What's your father thinking? Has he turned into Hannah Bavli?[26] He despises Arafat and calls him a dog, and suddenly it's important for him that we be polite." Omri was hunched over the wheel, excitedly testing out the government-owned Honda's ability to reach speeds that exceeded the recommendations of its Japanese manufacturers. All he said was: "That's what it's like with the Caucasian."

Arafat welcomed us with a hug and plates of fruits and nuts. He was especially proud of the high-calorie kanafeh[27] that we were served. "This is Gaza-made kanafeh, the best there is," he attested in a pique of regional patriotism.

"Is it better than what you get in Nablus?" I inquired.

Arafat shot me a forgiving glance, half-offended: "How can you even compare?" I noticed that his eyes lit up at the sight of Omri, who was energetically chewing the sweet pastry, as if taking seriously his father's instructions to be polite to the PLO chairman.

We made it clear to Arafat that we had come on a joint mission from Sharon and Peres. We conveyed the messages that had been prepared in advance, and we explained that the terror attack against the United States had created a new global reality. It was in the interests of both our nations to be on the right side of the world map. This was a moment of truth for our two peoples, there would be no more opportunities, and the world would not forgive anyone who tried to combine violence with diplomacy. We were completely committed to the Tenet and Mitchell plans. We wanted them to be implemented, not only for the sake of Israel's security, but also in order to progress to a resumption of the political negotiations and the peace process. We stressed that the Israeli public had to see that Arafat and the Palestinian Authority were returning to the path of peace. Without popular support, Sharon and Peres would struggle to move forward. More violence would not hasten a solution; it would only push it further away. Both nations were hoping to see results on the ground. The specific details would be elucidated in a meeting between Peres and Arafat.

"I have given clear orders for a ceasefire," Arafat said. "I'm very grateful that you've come together. I see it as an important message, and it touches my heart." He pushed for the meeting with Peres to take place as quickly as possible and expressed an interest in also meeting Sharon. When we suggested that both sides declare a ceasefire in parallel the following day, Arafat recoiled. "I am prepared to make such a declaration, but only after a meeting with Peres," he said. He obviously had no interest in wasting on us what he could give someone else higher up.

On the way home, Omri asked me, "Will you and Peres be willing to finally admit that Arafat has chosen the path of violence and not the path of peace?" I told him that while we had no tangible achievements apart from the kanafeh, we still had to wait for the Peres–Arafat talks and should not rush to despair. After all—we knew what the alternative was.

Ahead of the long-postponed meeting between Peres and Arafat, the prime minister held a consultation.

Sharon: "We are entering an unbearable situation. Arafat is making a mockery of us. I'm in favour of a meeting, but I'm against having one under fire."

Peres: "But the whole point of dialogue is to produce a ceasefire. Not the other way around. I didn't know that you'd announce in the Knesset a new condition for the meeting—48 hours of calm. We can't keep presenting a new ultimatum every morning. I give you back-up, and you give me surprises. The head of the Shin Bet says that there has been a dramatic drop in terror attacks in the last few days."

Sharon: "Are you imagining a meeting when the terrorist who murdered that woman from Tekoa[28] is still on the loose? I don't think we need to have this meeting."

I'll Call a Faction Meeting

Peres was incensed. His voice betrayed a profound anger and offence. "You are acting against everything we agreed on," he told Sharon. "I shall call a meeting of my party MPs." The meaning was clear. Peres was threatening to sever their political partnership. He had taken enough grief from Sharon. The repeated postponement of his meeting with Arafat was a symptom of the clash between their most basic positions.

Sharon returned fire. He spoke about Peres in the third person in front of him and said angrily, "I heard that Shimon said in a meeting in New York that I'm a bumpkin with a narrow vision and limited comprehension. You should know that I'm proud to be that—a bumpkin who won't let anyone kill Jews." He hauled himself up from the table and walked out.

Peres turned to Uri Shani. "It's clear to you, this is the end of the unity government," he said.

Shani, who had worked tirelessly to preserve the partnership between Sharon and Peres, took pains to convince Sharon to reauthorize the meeting with Arafat. It was scheduled for September 26, 2001, at the inactive Palestinian airport in Dahaniya in the

Gaza Strip. Ahead of the meeting, I met Saeb Erekat to draft the concluding statement in advance. When I showed Sharon the text, which mainly expressed a commitment to a ceasefire, one problematic line caught his eye. It read: "Both sides wish to express their gratitude to all states and leaders encouraging our efforts to revive the peace process." Sharon demanded that I strike out the word "revive." I asked Erekat to not even try asking me what stood behind this request. Erekat asked if instead of "revive" we wrote "facilitate the peace process," that would eliminate the threat to the future of the Jewish state. "It would," I told him, "and I owe you one."

Erekat shrugged and said, "So why do people claim our leader's the only strange one?"

On our way to Dahaniya, we stopped off at Sharon's ranch for a final consultation. Sharon greeted us angrily and gloomily. Overnight, the Termit army post on the southern border of the Gaza Strip was blown up. A large bomb had been placed under the post through a tunnel and destroyed it, wounding several soldiers. Sharon was furious at the army's complacency and claimed that he had warned of such an attack. He later turned to Peres and said, "When you get out of there, we'll respond. And have no doubts: I'm happy to send Arafat to hell." I knew that I was about to be the object of Sharon's rage, but I asked to speak and said that if our forces went in, it would cause a conflagration and there would be casualties. If we wanted to give the upcoming talks with Arafat a real chance, I proposed restraint. Sharon ripped into me angrily: "Do you think I'd let IDF soldiers be there for a single second without cover? The army post must be rebuilt tonight already."

And indeed, after we left Gaza, there was a military operation that left Palestinian casualties. Rebuilding the army post took a long time. The meeting itself made no meaningful difference to the violent situation. Peres absorbed growing criticism from IDF officers for his pursuit of Arafat. I also received my fair share of criticism. Amir Oren wrote in *Haaretz*: "It is not worth declaring a day of love at the IDF for foreign ministries. The officers have doubts about the Foreign Ministry in Jerusalem—they treat its director-general, Avi Gil, as if he were the director-general of Peres's meetings with Arafat, who does not invest his time, as he should, in giving diplomatic back-up to the military's operations."[29]

Peres remained loyal to his beliefs and wrote to Sharon, "The alternative in which security measures are not combined with negotiations leaves the path of conflict as the only possible path in the Arabs' eyes. It will also lead to fundamentalist players joining forces with Fatah."[30]

Sharon continued to point to Arafat as the main obstacle to a breakthrough. After the murder of the government minister Rehavam Ze'evi,[31] he announced at a cabinet mourning session,[32] "The entire responsibility for this murder is on Arafat. He is responsible, and that is how we must present and explain the matter." The cabinet resolution stated: "By his deeds, and by his failure to fight terrorism, knowing that this failure to take steps against the terrorist organisations would cause terrible acts of murder, Arafat is the one responsible for the terrorism and for this bloody attack. This message will be conveyed to the whole world through our hasbara channels. We shall send a group of ministers for a hasbara offensive in the United States in the coming days."

The Importance of Hasbara

Sharon attached great importance to hasbara abroad, and he had plenty of criticism about how the Foreign Ministry's hasbara operations worked. In one meeting on the subject, I told him that he—for better or worse—personally reflected Israel's image. "Why not go to one of the checkpoints in person," I asked him, "and be filmed explaining to the soldiers how to treat the Palestinians waiting there more humanely?" Sharon looked at me in amazement. He cut me off when I added that improving Israel's image required us to combine a determined fight against terrorism with a credible outreach for peace.

Later, after the government decided to blame Arafat for Ze'evi's murder, I was invited for a meeting at the Prime Minister's Office on the implications of the possible collapse of the Palestinian Authority and potential alternatives. I prepared an alarming brief that foresaw harsh repercussions: a crisis with the United States, possible sanctions from Europe, the severing of ties with Egypt and Jordan, and diplomatic crises in Asia, with international organizations, and elsewhere.

Sharon preferred to advance toward his target in a gradual manner. He believed that the world was getting increasingly used to the new reality on the ground, and that Israel could now lengthen its list of preconditions for implementing the Mitchell Plan. Sharon's office articulated the latest version of these conditions in its published talking points: "The complete cessation of terrorism and incitements, the rendition of Minister Ze'evi's killers and their handlers, the dismantlement and outlawing of all terrorist organisations, and the arrest of their personnel."[33] The document emphasized: "The comparison between Arafat and the Taliban is apt. The Palestinian Authority must be depicted as a regime that gives immunity to terrorism and is implicated in terrorism."

But talking points did not stop the violence. The appalling terror attacks continued, and the government decided to declare the Palestinian Authority "a terror-supporting entity, which must be counteracted accordingly."[34] Arafat was declared directly responsible for these terror attacks, and all contact with him was suspended.[35] The government later decided that "Arafat must be prevented from leaving Ramallah to participate in ceremonies in Bethlehem or for any other reason, until Minister Ze'evi's killers and their handlers are arrested."[36]

Peres's expression attested to his despair. He passed me a note during the meeting: "There's nothing for us to do here." But as always, he regained his composure and tried to speak to Sharon's heart again during a breakfast together:[37] "If the current situation continues, the terrorism won't cease. Your term in office will have been wasted. The economic situation won't have improved. Everyone in the country will be furious. You don't have long left. I say so as your friend and partner."

But Sharon stuck to his guns. "We need to diminish Arafat's stature and for something else to come along."

Sharon's firmness and the international pressure spurred Arafat into action. On his orders, most of those involved in Minister Ze'evi's murder were caught. I took advantage of a break in one of the meetings to meet privately with Sharon. I handed him a written plan that I had devised for a dramatic diplomatic initiative and told him,

Your pressure on Arafat has worked. He has caught most of the terrorists who participated in Minister Ze'evi's murder. You can declare victory. This is the moment you can create a turnaround from a position of strength. Announce you're about to fulfil your promise and lift the restrictions on Arafat's movement. Say you have one condition: before Arafat goes anywhere, he must come to your house. Invite him for a weekend on the ranch. The entire world media will gather around the perimeter fence. Your image in the world will be completely transformed. Arafat will be beside himself with excitement. You'll be able to get anything you want from him. It's the highest honour he's dreaming of. Give him the honour, and get any genuine asset you choose from him in return.

Sharon listened and replied, "You know the day will come. But you're like Shimon. Always in too much of a hurry. He needs to sweat it out some more, that Arafat of yours." He later looked at me, amused, and said: "On that weekend you're talking about, when Arafat comes to the ranch, we'll have to ensure my son Gilad's not around. He's quite extreme and would probably shoot him."

Instead of a dramatic gesture, the cabinet decided to let Arafat roam free within the boundaries of Ramallah alone:[38] "Arafat's departure from Ramallah shall be subject to a decision made in a forum of the prime minister's choosing after his consultation with the minister of defence." Ahmed Qurei called Peres, angry and hurt, to protest this insult: "The chairman throws the murderers in jail, and all you give him in return is the right to walk around Ramallah?"

Peres could only apologize: "Unfortunately I'm not the cabinet majority."[39] Later, despairing, he interrupted a meeting of the inner ("kitchenette") cabinet:[40]

I would not have entered this government had I known that we would come to this. A decision just to lash out, so close to a strategic catastrophe. The Palestinians are showing a sense of daring and sacrifice. They'll neither crawl nor surrender. We're losing the public's confidence, and the Palestinians aren't oblivious to that fact. I'm against the IDF entering the refugee camps. I'm against airstrikes. These things cause us immense damage. Our moral stature has diminished. We're mobilising the entire world against us. We're belittling the world, and we shall pay a price for it.

"Arik, who on the Palestinian side will be influenced by your pressure and will translate it into quiet?" Peres implored Sharon. "Not only is there no one—they have no reason to do so. The public also have feelings. We should be troubled about a reality in which after a young child perpetrates a suicide attack, his father says he hopes his other sons will follow his path. You don't want to partition the land between the two nations, only because of the settlements. What you're proposing, Arik—there's no chance."

Sharon: "I may speak quietly, but the voices of the children murdered last night in Jerusalem are crying out."[41]

Peres: "We are starving them and giving them no hope. We can fight
terrorism, but not the whole Palestinian people. You propose hurting
the Palestinians, the same ones you want to act against terrorism. I'm
not a fan of Arafat. But if Arafat is relevant—talk to him. And if he's not
relevant—leave him alone."

Arafat's acquaintances described to Peres the chairman's grim predicament. "Arafat feels betrayed by everyone," explained Erekat. "He recognised Israel on 80 percent of the territory of historical Palestine. He knows that Sharon is counting on ousting him. Why should he take a risk? Why should I take a risk?"

Peres did not abandon his conviction that Arafat was the right negotiating partner for Israel. He tried to explain to his ministerial colleagues that the key question, as far as he was concerned, was how to spur Arafat into action. Our strategy to date had failed. We had eroded his power. None of the Palestinians came close to Arafat's ability to work toward de-escalation. Only he could bestow national legitimacy on de-escalation and reconciliation with Israel. We had to work *with* Arafat and the Palestinian Authority, instead of ousting Arafat and dismantling the Palestinian Authority.

Peres tried to convince his colleagues that Israel must not expel Arafat:

He would be more effective from the outside. He'd travel the world a hero. The
problem is not the guns they were given under the Oslo Accords but the suicide
bombers. What's the terrorist infrastructure of the young suicide bombers? Their
mother and father? We have to fight terrorism, not the Palestinians. We're pushing
the Palestinians towards terrorism. We need to change the reality in the territories,
a reality of hunger and crisis. We are leading an entire people to hatred, against
all logic.

Minister Shlomo Benizri protested Peres's remarks: The Oslo Accords created
the suicide bombers!"
Peres retorted: "And I can say, the settlers created the suicide bombers."

Peres discovered that US Secretary of State Colin Powell's position on Arafat was similar to his own. "Powell told me on the way from the airport that they're concerned about Arafat," he told Sharon in a late-night meeting. "Nobody will move without him. Without Arafat, there's no alternative."[42]

Sharon knew that the secretary's standing in the White House was shaky. "We won't deal with Arafat," he replied to Peres. "It's impossible to reach an agreement with him."

Peres did not relent. "If *you* were to meet Arafat, you could make a lot of headway. You'd discover he's the most moderate of them all."

But Sharon stuck to his guns. "I shall explain to the secretary that Arafat is not a partner. The Palestinian Authority must be reformed in a way that will eventually produce a Palestinian government without Arafat."[43]

Peres's political partnership with Sharon gave him a fistful of bitter pills to swallow and much humiliation. Sharon sent emissaries to the United States without Peres's knowledge, surprised him with his conditions for progress, deliberately undermined the symbols of Palestinian self-rule, trampled on Arafat's honor, and worked systematically to overthrow the Palestinian Authority.

Peres read in the newspapers that unlike him, Sharon believed that Israel should not embark on a diplomatic initiative and should rather wait for the Palestinian Authority to reform itself and shunt Arafat aside. Sources in the Prime Minister's Office briefed the press: "Political success is not measured in terms of hyperactivity. Arafat is under immense pressure, and it would be a shame to embark on an initiative that would give him a lifeline." The headline: "Peres presented ideas—Sharon unimpressed."[44]

Leaving Dung with Your Reporters

Sharon and his staff were convinced that Peres and I were running a sophisticated media operation against them. During one of our visits to Washington, Sharon called me to give me an earful: "Make no mistake. I know that before you left Israel, you left piles of dung with your reporters so it would all be published when you're away." He was referring to an article by Ben Caspit in *Maariv* about a crisis between Sharon and the United States. I told Sharon over the phone that he was wrong. Uri Dan, Sharon's mouthpiece, later published an article reviewing the headlines that were intended to damage the prime minister. "They come from a single factory of disinformation run by Foreign Minister Shimon Peres and mainly his right-hand man, Foreign Ministry Director-General Avi Gil, who is in charge of production and sales," it explained. "So where are you, Civil Service Commissioner Mr Shmuel Hollander, when a state employee, Avi Gil, is disseminating these lies against the prime minister to his faithful reporters?"[45]

Upon our return, we had a meeting with Sharon in his office. Toward the end, Sharon turned to me and said, "Avi looks grumpy tonight. Perhaps he'll explain why?"

"That's right," I snapped. "I'm angry at you." Sharon signaled to me to stay back with him alone and asked to delay the helicopter that was waiting to fly him to his ranch. I said that he had accused me unjustly. "I'm working with Peres in your government to try to have an influence. Leaks against you don't serve that objective. I'm actually working to maintain industrial peace between the two of you."

Sharon swallowed his pride, apologized repeatedly, and asked to put the incident behind us. He stressed the importance he attached to his partnership with Peres. "I love Shimon, I greatly value his contributions to this country, the nuclear reactor, the Suez campaign, Entebbe. We don't have the tension that existed between Shimon and Rabin." He then had some critical words for IDF Chief of Staff Shaul Mofaz and his manner of writing down everything he was told. "Personally, I've never acted that way," he said. "Unfortunately, there's no one in the army who is to me what I was in my youth to this country's leaders. The army is slow and clunky, and I have to spend ages with the generals to explain to them what to do."

Peres often advised me not to waste energy on revenge, but I still felt a certain satisfaction when the opportunity once arose. Sharon and his staff had asked us to allow Uri Dan to be sent abroad as a consul-general. They even spun this as a personal favor I should do them, "so he'll be as far away from here as possible." I answered back rudely to Sharon, "No problem, prime minister, as soon as we have an opening at our consulate on Mars."

This was not the only request of Sharon's that I enjoyed rejecting. In 2000, when the Austrian Freedom Party headed by the racist Jorg Haider rose to power, the Israeli government decided, on the advice of the Foreign Ministry, to recall our ambassador from Vienna in protest. Now Sharon asked me to return the ambassador to his post. I was surprised by the theatrical manner in which he depicted the situation: "Avi, you're a very busy man, you're the director-general of the Foreign Ministry. You probably don't have time, like me, to watch foreign television networks. It's just terrible. Israeli soldiers are shooting indiscriminately, heavy tanks are advancing towards defenceless children. These are harsh scenes of a brutal and merciless occupation." I looked at Sharon incredulously, and then he clarified the purpose of this emotional introduction: "Given these difficult scenes, we must understand that it is not at all easy to be a friend of Israel. And there's one place in Europe where, despite everything, we have friends. And it's *there*—Austria—where the Foreign Ministry does not have an ambassador. I mean, we'll lose the friends we still have this way."

I was charmed by Sharon's acting skills. The voice of the bleeding-heart Left was crying out from his throat. But I had no intention of granting his request. I ordered a written opinion from the professional echelon in the Foreign Ministry. I knew what their position was, and it was no surprise when they came up with a litany of reasons against normalizing relations with Austria. "The professional echelon is warning in writing that returning the ambassador, without any change in Vienna, would likely encourage the growth of extremist and antisemitic elements across the whole of Europe," I told Sharon. "My hands are tied." Sharon did not appreciate the bureaucratic trick we had concocted at the Foreign Ministry, but both of us knew that he would have many further opportunities to settle the score.

Sharon could be captivating. I arrived at my first working meeting with him, uncharacteristically, in a jacket and tie. Vigilantly, I entered the office of a man who, for me, represented the aggressive and heartless side of Israel. He looked at me with a smile and asked, "Why the fancy dress? Have you come to a wedding?" The ice was quickly broken. I felt that he respected me. He identified me as belonging to the rival camp—the dreaded leftists—but he tried to win me over. I visited his ranch and enjoyed the company of his associates, especially his son Omri and Uri Shani. We found a common language, and despite seeing things differently, we were committed to preserving the political partnership between Sharon and Peres.

I enjoyed seeing Sharon, as a father, looking fondly at his son. "Without him, I wouldn't be prime minister," he told me. Omri used to play chess on a tiny computer during meetings and sometimes fall asleep. It was amusing to see his father waking him up from his reveries with a teacherly rebuke: "How many times do I have to tell you, Omri? When you sleep at night, you don't fall asleep during the day." Omri used to nod in agreement and go back to sleep.

The Ground There is Soaked with Jewish Blood

As time went on, I discovered even more fascinating aspects of Sharon's personality—his sharp sense of humor, his great sensitivity diluted by a healthy dose of cynicism, and his unconventional and sometimes poetic modes of expression. He phoned me during a working visit to Poland once. "Where are you?" he asked.

"I've come home," I told him. "I'm in Warsaw."

He burst into laughter, and suddenly his tone changed: "Avi, never forget, the ground there is soaked with Jewish blood."

He was speaking from the heart. I knew it was not a reaction for public relations purposes. His sensitivity to the fate of the Jewish people, and his brutality at the same time, produced painful results, and I felt their sting. The European Union threatened to cancel customs exemptions on Israeli products unless we reported separately on goods originating in the territories. The Europeans do not recognize the territories as legally part of Israel, and they had no interest in incentivizing factories there. In a series of inter-ministerial meetings, we reached the conclusion that it was best to accede to the demand and label the origin of the produce. The loss of customs relief on goods originating in the territories was negligible compared to our potential losses if the relief had been canceled for all Israeli goods.

I presented the arguments to Sharon and planned for representatives of the economy-related ministries to speak after me to support my position. But they were deterred after Sharon cut me off mid-argument and scolded me, "I understand that you want to give the Europeans a list of names. You know, Avi, throughout history we've also had Jews like who passed on lists of names."

You're Not Coming Back without Eating Umm Ali

Sharon's addiction to food was fascinating. Whenever meetings dragged on till noon, he looked increasingly worried as lunchtime approached. He used to sniff and say, "The smell of a cooked meal means food is ready. We shouldn't delay and cause the chef any grief." On the eve of a visit to Cairo with Peres, after we finished a preparatory meeting in his office, he called me over and said, "With all due respect to your meeting with Mubarak, promise me you won't come back without having a plate of Umm Ali. I want you to tell me when you return what it's like to eat that wonderful delicacy." At a later occasion in Cairo, I told Mubarak's advisor, Osama El-Baz, about Sharon's love for the local dessert. That night, on the eve of my return to Israel, El-Baz's emissaries handed me two large ceramic bowls filled with large quantities of high-quality Umm-Ali for the prime minister. The security guards in Israel did not let him taste the delicacy, and the secretaries told me that Sharon, frustrated, circled it like a caged lion.

Marit, Sharon's dedicated office manager, told me wonders about Sharon's personal approach to his staff. I knew Marit, and she was neither flattering him nor exaggerating. Marit happened to be at the Pat Junction in Jerusalem exactly at the moment of a terrible terror attack there. She returned to the office shocked by the horrible scenes. But I heard about her experiences of that horrific episode not from her, but from Sharon. He had listened to her, consoled her, and felt a need to share her story in detail with me. Once again, he undermined the image I had had of him before I got to know him.

Many of Peres's friends struggled to understand why he was committed to continuing his partnership with Sharon. "I'm staying in this government because if I sing songs about peace in the opposition, I might be recognised as a singer, but I won't achieve anything," Peres said. "For the sake of peace, we need to form a majority, and for that we need the Likud." And indeed, Peres felt that despite the bumpy and humiliating road, he had managed to influence Sharon. In particular—he noticed such a development when he tried to promote the memorandum of understanding known as the "Peres-Abu Ala document."

The Peres-Abu Ala Document

Although the 1993 Declaration of Principles determined that the West Bank and Gaza Strip were a single territorial unit, Peres did not feel bound by the text that had been signed with such fanfare and proceeded to push for the establishment of a Palestinian state in Gaza alone. Peres believed that this was more practical than giving the Palestinians independence in one fell swoop. It would also obviate the need to grapple with problems that he believed had no solution at this stage: Jerusalem, refugees, and the settlements. The Palestinians rejected the idea, and Peres was forced to scrap his plan.

But after the failure of the final-status talks at Camp David, Peres was all the more convinced that progress should be incremental and that unsolvable problems should not be placed on the table. He believed that this had been Barak's fundamental mistake. Peres therefore proposed establishing a Palestinian state with temporary borders. Its territory would be based on the Gaza Strip and Areas A and B of the West Bank.[46] He felt that an opportunity had been created to reach a formulation that would be acceptable both to Sharon and to the Palestinians. During a visit to Prague for a the Forum 2000 Conference, he explored his ideas in a late-night meeting with former president Bill Clinton and Arafat's economic advisor, Muhammad Rashid.[47]

When we entered Clinton's room at midnight, he was playing cards with his bodyguards. Peres valued Clinton's wisdom and rare combination of charisma, intellect, erudition, and political nous. He was impressed by, and perhaps a little jealous of, Clinton's ability to quickly break down barriers and radiate a human warmth in a way that looked totally natural. Clinton had five books in his hotel suite, all of which were about Islam. He explained excitedly that he was reading all of them in parallel, because since the 9/11 attacks, he had felt an irresistible urge to understand Islamist extremist terrorism in depth. Clinton also revealed that as president, he was once given the opportunity to order the assassination of Osama bin Laden. The Al Qaeda leader had been identified from the air, but since he was surrounded by dozens of innocent civilians, Clinton decided to hold off the attack, and he agonized over whether he had made the right call.

The following night, Clinton met Peres alone. We waited in the adjacent room for the meeting to end. We heard Clinton in the corridor wishing a good night to Peres, who headed to his room. I peeked into the corridor and discovered that Clinton had not moved and was listening to us speaking. It was clear that he craved company. I told him that Peres was already in bed but we, his advisors, would be delighted for him to join us. I apologized for wearing a tracksuit and Clinton said, "Who cares what you're wearing?" His eyes lit up and he joined us for a chat like a regular Joe. He was not concerned by the late hour. We were exhausted, but Clinton did not retire to his room until he had finished eating our entire supply of peanuts.

In their conversation the previous night, joined by Muhammad Rashid, Clinton had warned Peres that the Palestinians would be wary of receiving a state that did not include Jerusalem without a commitment for an agreed end-date for final-status talks. Rashid, who had not forgotten to bring Clinton a fine box of expensive cigars, explained that the Palestinians would demand a number of basic clarifications about the idea of a temporary state: where its borders would run and who would control them, how the West Bank and Gaza would be connected, and who would receive responsibility for the territories that would not be transferred to the Palestinians (such that it would be clear that this land—and especially East Jerusalem—did not belong to Israel).

Given these difficult questions, it would obviously have been tremendously difficult to obtain the Palestinians' consent for the idea of a Palestinian state with temporary borders, but such difficulties never put Peres off. He hoped to reconcile the Palestinians' positions with Sharon's. He emerged encouraged from meetings in which he tried to persuade Sharon of the idea. Sharon accepted the principle of establishing a Palestinian state with provisional borders. On November 25, 2001, Sharon even wrote his plan down in his own hand and gave it to Peres. I held onto this document tightly. If it had leaked, it would have caused a big political crisis. This is what it said:

The objective is to reach a comprehensive peace settlement between the State of Israel and a Palestinian state (which will afford the citizens of Israel and the citizens of the Palestinian state quiet and peaceful lives).

The agreement will be based on two stages:

Stage one: A ceasefire agreement to create a state of non-belligerence. In this stage, a demilitarised Palestinian state will, by agreement, be established in the Gaza Strip and in Judea and Samaria on provisional borders.

Stage two: The final borders of the Palestinian state will be determined in a final-status agreement[48] that will be the result of a future relationship forged between the two sides.

A ceasefire and cessation of incitement are a condition for the beginning of the stage involving political negotiations.

Both states will guarantee freedom of worship to all religions in the holy places under their control.

Infrastructure works to minimise points of friction and create territorial contiguity, in coordination with the United States and with a grant for their implementation, will begin immediately.

There will be no international observers.

We will form a committee in the Prime Minister's Office headed by you and me, together with the minister of defence, which will handle the negotiations. First, negotiations for a ceasefire, and once there is a ceasefire, the committee will begin negotiations for a final-status settlement.

The composition of the committee under our leadership (prime minister, foreign minister, defence minister)—[National Security Adviser] Meir Dagan, team leader; a senior representative of the Foreign Ministry; [former UN ambassador] Dore Gold; [Defence Ministry Deputy Director-General] Moshe Kochanovsky; Danny Ayalon + military officials and experts to prepare the material and different options for an accord.

Peres added the following in his own words, which he said Sharon had accepted:

Additions to Sharon's document—

A territorial addition is possible;
Instead of a timetable—a set of expectations;

The talks with Abu Ala [Ahmed Qurei] will be secret. If reported, we will deny them.

Sharon will tell the U.S. president about this.
I said I'd present a counterproposal.
The talks will take place outside the country.
No objection to my participation at the donors' conference[49] and meetings with Arafat.
Regarding Syria, the answer will be: willing to enter negotiations without preconditions. Each side may raise any subject.

The composition of the committee—for a 30-day trial.

Sharon remained loyal to his traditional belief that long-term interim accords were preferable. But he gave Peres, the supporting actor, meaningful space to work with, given his willingness to accept the establishment of a Palestinian state as early as the first stage of the process. Reading this document today, one might not be surprised by the fact that Sharon eventually led the Disengagement from the Gaza Strip and the dismantling of all the Jewish settlements there—but at the time, this draft for a working political agreement between Sharon and Peres would have destabilized the Likud if it had leaked.

Peres progressed in his usual way. He put Uri Savir in charge of negotiating with Ahmed Qurei for a draft agreement, and even flew in person to Italy to help to

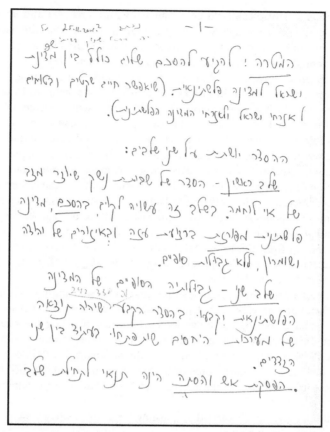

Figure 11 Excerpt from the peace plan that Ariel Sharon wrote in Peres's house on November 25, 2001. (Photo: Avi Gil, 2001)

promote the contacts. The talks took place in an ancient castle not far from Rome. Peres did everything he could to promote the plan to the right world leaders and made an effort to create momentum to translate his ideas into a political reality. He traded in ambiguity and was wary of clear formulations. "There's an opportunity emerging for the Palestinians to agree to the immediate establishment of a state in the territory under their control," he told the US secretary of state. "There are signs, which must be treated with extreme caution, that they might agree to postpone the difficult issues: Jerusalem, refugees, settlements."[50]

A draft of the plan, which had not yet been agreed, found its way to the press. The leak caused a major problem for Sharon in the Israeli right-wing camp. The key points of the plan flatly contradicted the Likud's own stance. It said that after two months of a ceasefire and the implementation of a security plan, Israel would recognize a Palestinian state in the West Bank and Gaza and would attend negotiations for a final-status agreement that would be completed within one year and implemented within another year. Although Sharon had confirmed to us that the basic idea of the plan reflected his position, he was forced to publicly denounce it and define it as "fantastical and dangerous to Israel … a plan full of problems."[51]

Sharon promised his party colleagues that the reports ran completely counter to his own position. The Prime Minister's Office released a statement, in response to Minister Benny Alon's question about the foreign minister's contacts with Ahmed Qurei, clarifying as follows: "Discussions on political matters—including on the matter of a Palestinian state—cannot be held without being debated in the cabinet and receiving government approval. The agreement on this matter still applies. Contacts with Palestinian Authority figures, further to government decisions, can only touch on a cessation of terrorism, violence, and incitement."[52] The official statement further said, "Foreign Minister Shimon Peres has said that his mandate is to reach a ceasefire, and if we move to political negotiations, the matter will be brought before the prime minister and government."

This statement from the Prime Minister's Office did not reflect the truth, but it certainly remained loyal to the spirit of paragraph 3: *"The talks with Abu Ala will be secret. If reported, we will deny them."*

When Peres arrived for a meeting with him, Sharon said angrily, "We could have gone together, but you leaked the document and created a situation that has caused me major damage. We cannot move forward without bringing the matter before the cabinet. This document has a central problem. Contrary to my position—it sets timetables. We've been left with the Tenet and Mitchell plans!"[53] After Peres attempted to salvage the initiative, Sharon softened a little: "Now my hands are tied because I'd have to present the initiative to the government. We all have our own lunatics. Maybe later, in a few weeks' time."

Peres did not give up. He carried on pushing for his plan. On a visit to the United States, he explained to Powell,

> I'm trying to bring the Palestinians as close as possible to Sharon's position, and I'm also trying to bring Sharon to understand the Palestinians' positions … As for borders, the Palestinians want it to be said that they'll be based on the 1967 lines with adjustments. We say—[Resolution] 242.[54] Abu Ala hopes you'll help to explain what 242 is. Sharon says we won't conduct negotiations under fire. I've added the formulation that we'll conduct negotiations towards a ceasefire, and that in addition we'd offer a political horizon. The most tangible thing you can give Arafat is a political horizon.[55]

Peres pointed out to the secretary of state what the Palestinians considered to be the main weakness of the plan. They were afraid that the temporary borders would become permanent over time, and that their cause would recede from the international agenda. And indeed, Ahmed Qurei insisted on including a reference in the document to the 1967 lines. Peres explained that there was no chance of obtaining Sharon's approval. Qurei was open to a compromise: the United States would provide a written guarantee. And indeed, Peres subtly hinted to Powell, "Abu Ala hopes you'll help to explain what 242 means." In a conversation with EU envoy Miguel Moratinos, Peres said, "Europe needs to adopt the Peres-Abu Ala document. If the plan is acceptable to the Palestinians, I shall even be willing to leave the government. I have no reason to do so now."[56]

The Americans were in no rush to pick a fight with Sharon and did not provide the letter of guarantee as the Palestinians requested. Uri Savir wrote to Peres, urging him, "The entire accord is conditional on a U.S. letter of interpretation, in which the United States adopts the initiative and repeats its traditional position on borders (1967 with mutual adjustments)."[57]

Ahmed Qurei reminded Peres, "We wanted to receive a letter of guarantee from the Americans."[58]

"Israel will not agree to conclude negotiations before they have even begun," Peres replied, "which is why '242' will have to suffice. It's acceptable in the international and Arab jargon, it appears in the government's basic guidelines, and it's the foundation of the treaties with Jordan and Egypt. You could ask for a letter like that only at the end of the negotiations."

Qurei, who had led the Palestinian team in Oslo, looked like he was staring at the shattered remains of hopes he had nurtured for a historic breakthrough. His deep disappointment was clear in his voice. "Our goal was to persuade the Palestinian public that there's a genuine political horizon. As far as we're concerned, the novelty of this document is the mutual recognition of the 1967 borders with minor adjustments and land swaps."

Since my first meeting with Ahmed Qurei, on the night of the secret signing in Oslo, I had learned to like him and appreciate his sense of humor, the negotiating skills, and his habit of always seeing the comprehensive strategic picture. In one of our conversations, before he returned from his exile in Tunis to his home in Abu Dis, he spoke longingly of the smell of the citrus fruits of Palestine. During one of our rounds of follow-up talks in Cairo, I brought him some pomelos that I had bought for him in Jericho. The tough negotiator was surprised by the gesture and held onto the fruit tightly, unable to hide his glee. I also remembered how I had accompanied him in the ambulance when he felt unwell during the talks in Taba and was whisked away for treatment in the hospital in Eilat. These were some of the moments in which the conflict between our nations paused briefly to make way for simple and natural human friendship. Now that the Peres-Abu Ala document seemed to be collapsing, I felt I was a full party to his disappointment.

Peres, as usual, did not concede and continued pressing on the Americans. Powell explained that Sharon was opposed to timetables: "Sharon doesn't want Israel to be subjected to time pressure."

Peres did not give up: "He'll have to backtrack." He headed from the State Department to the White House and updated National Security Advisor Condoleezza Rice,

We have proposed that the principle for the border be 242. They want the basis to be 1967 lines plus land swaps. Abu Ala wanted a side letter. He did not receive one from you. I told him, you might be able to receive such a letter, but not at the first stage. Sharon was in the loop the whole time. He told me that this plan was the closest to his own stance. He even accused me of stealing his positions. I told him—I tried to bring the Palestinians closer to your positions. The only thing he opposed was the timetable … Sharon fears that his government will fall and he's also worried I might leave.[59]

Peres urged Rice to convene a regional conference, an idea to which Sharon had agreed: "If there's a conference, there'll be a decision. The conference matters because it will be a place for Sharon and Arafat to meet even though they don't like each other. We must combine three elements: American vision, the Saudi initiative,[60] and the Peres-Abu Ala plan."

Despite our mighty efforts, the Peres-Abu Ala plan, which gave Peres a reason to remain in Sharon's government, never took off. The media fixated on the phrase "the Peres-Abu Ala Agreement." But there was no agreement. The sides, Peres and Qurei, never managed to bridge their differences, and the United States was never called on to help them. But the idea of establishing a Palestinian state on temporary borders did not disappear. It resurfaced in the "Road Map," which became a binding political plan. This state, with provisional borders according to the document, could be established as an intermediate step toward a final-status agreement.

I Believe There'll Be a Breakthrough

During this time, I frequently asked Peres what his red lines were: "How far will you accompany Sharon on Oslo's funeral procession?" Peres was charged up with boundless optimism and still believed that he would find a breakthrough. He saw fit to fight for the peace process and dialogue with the Palestinians from inside the government, to wage an all-out war against Sharon's attempts to topple the Palestinian Authority, and to try to persuade others of Arafat's political relevance to Israeli interests.

He latched onto the fact that Sharon was willing to establish a Palestinian state and spotted his chance to promote the Peres-Abu Ala Plan, as he had done earlier with the Jordanian–Egyptian initiative, the Mitchell Report, and the Tenet Plan. Peres was a man of action and saw no point sitting in the opposition and engaging in futile shouting matches in the Knesset. He also believed that it was necessary to have a meaningful majority to move toward a historic compromise with the Palestinians. And to that end—the right-wing camp had to be brought on board.

But Peres's faith in Arafat's abilities to meet our expectations gradually waned, until he himself despaired and pushed for the chairman—the *Rais*—to be moved aside into a symbolic position "like the Queen of England" and for a prime minister with the bulk of the executive power to be appointed alongside him. But besides the manifold reasons that caused Peres to stand by Sharon despite the grim reality, we must add one more important element—Sharon himself.

Project Partnership Preservation

In his wisdom, guile, and great charm, Sharon knew how to keep a hold on Peres. And on the occasions he dropped his guard, his associates—and especially Uri Shani—immediately jumped into action to help. Sharon needed his partnership with Peres for political reasons, but he also had a substantive interest. The gulf between their respective worldviews guaranteed that their partnership would be fraught with tension, and Sharon succeeded in transforming the institution of their meals together at his home into a highly valuable tool for preserving their partnership.

Whenever an argument broke out or tension emerged, we were invited to dine with Sharon. He was normally joined by Uri Shani, Omri, the military secretary, and later Dovi Weisglass, who replaced Uri Shani when he resigned as head of Sharon's bureau. This was a common ritual. At first Sharon focused the conversation on the food. He enticed Peres into sharing his culinary experiences and understanding of fine wines, also pitching in with his own. I discovered that Sharon was not above the most basic foods. A bowl of falafel was enough to cheer him up, and he was always happy to gorge on a bowl of sausages wrapped in puff pastry. A mango was enough to fill him with memories of his childhood in Kfar Malal. Sharon could launch into long, lyrical, nostalgic recollections of a specific mango tree on his childhood moshav, whose location he could remember precisely and whose fruits had a magical smell that had since vanished from this earth, but not from the worlds in which this great bear of a man resided.

The meals progressed, and Sharon invited Peres to describe the changes that China was undergoing and their global implications, and even nudging him to expand on the importance of nanotechnology. Peres used to describe to Sharon the wonders of the latest technology, and how the entire *Encyclopaedia Britannica* could be stored on the head of a pin. The pair enjoyed being buffeted between visions of the distant future to memories of the past, indulging in juicy gossip about the people who had built the country and had long since been buried.

Sharon used to encourage Peres to delve deeper into history. He laid these traps with evident glee and gladly leapt into them together with his prey. Sometimes he wound up quoting the children's rhymes he used to sing on the moshav. "Do you know the song?" he asked. "*There was an old mufti, all angry and grumpy?*"

Jokes, wordplay, and impersonations were an inseparable element of their reconciliation ceremonies. Dovi Weisglass's devastating sense of humor made Sharon roar with laughter. Whenever someone's name came up for discussion, Dovi always had useful information at hand. Like when the name of a member of Knesset whom Sharon and Peres detested came up, and Dovi immediately tore into them: "Arik, did you know the Darwin Institute in London is awarding its annual prize to the MK you mentioned?"

"For what?" Sharon asked, keenly awaiting the punchline.

"For being discovered as the missing link in the evolution between gorillas and humans."

Nobody cared that the humor was bawdy and undiplomatic. Everyone laughed. But when we came to the reason for the meeting, both Sharon and Peres were too tired, and too reconciled, to fight. Sharon always offered his apologies. Peres, the ever-gallant, accepted them. On other occasions, Sharon used to playfully reproach a staff member, "Next time don't forget to update Shimon and ask his advice." His aides accepted his rebukes with humility.

I was so wary of the encounter between Sharon's charm and Peres's gentlemanly spirit, that I heard alarm bells when Sharon invited himself over for dinner: "Shimon, I miss the taste of Sonia's cooking." I warned Peres that Sharon was bound to lure him into making concessions. Peres promised me that he would be on his guard. After the meeting he called me and told me gloomily that in a moment of weakness he had acceded to Sharon's request for his associate Meir Dagan to head the team negotiating with the Palestinians.

"I can't believe it—that's your role!" I replied. "We have that approved in writing." There was nothing Peres could say in his own defense.

I called Uri Shani immediately and told him that we had to restore the status quo ante. Uri wisely understood that Sharon could not push his luck with Peres if he wanted to keep him as a partner. "I knew they mustn't be allowed to meet without us," he told me, half joking. "We'll deal with it." And indeed, no such team headed by Dagan was ever formed.

I learned the secrets of Sharon's reconciliation rituals and advised Peres not to fall into the trap and to begin their next meeting with the subject of the meeting, and only then to make time for the "social part." They certainly had meetings that began with heightened emotions:

Peres: "I want to get this off my chest. I've had a difficult week. You sent the military secretary [Moshe Kaplinsky] to the United States without informing me. You later said two or three people knew about the plan. That is—I didn't know about it. You're sending your friend, the businessman Arie Genger, to talk to the White House. That's improper governance. As the foreign minister, I *must* be in the picture."

Sharon: "I don't want to go back to the things you did behind Golda Meir's back. I remember how furious she was about the relationships you cultivated around the world. Prime ministers have always had their own liaisons."

Peres: "You keep repeating that story, and you're wrong. Everything I did was on the instructions of the prime minister, Ben-Gurion."

After Peres got his troubles off his chest, the pair returned to a calm and conciliatory spirit. But Peres's partnership with Sharon was soon broken off, to his dismay, by Labour Party chairman Binyamin Ben-Eliezer.

Something Has Gone Seriously and Dangerously Wrong in Your Zionist Education

After the Labour Party quit the government in October 2002, Sharon asked me to remain in my job as director-general of the Foreign Ministry. "I don't intend to appoint a new foreign minister. We're on the way to elections, and I'm asking you to show some national responsibility and stay in the role. I've offered the job [of foreign minister] to Bibi, but he'll turn it down. I'll be the only one above you." I told him I would consider it, but I did not need to deliberate for long. Netanyahu surprised Sharon and accepted his offer.

I went to Netanyahu and told him, "I believe that a minister deserves a director-general who will be loyal to him and his path. Since I cannot meet these demands with you, I'm leaving."

I kept in touch with Peres the whole time. We met frequently, and it was clear to both of us that whenever he needed me, I would be glad to help him. After many years in government service, I had decided to add some variety to my day and opted to engage in a few issues as a consultant and researcher. I served as a consultant to the Washington-based Center for Middle East Peace and Economic Cooperation. One of the fellows, Dan Rothem, had developed a digital map to understand the territorial situation in the small stretch between the Mediterranean Sea and the Jordan River. You could see the region from a bird's eye view and zoom in to make out the cars waiting at West Bank checkpoints. The program allowed users to draw borders and understand their demographic implications, to explore options for land swaps, and use other tools to inform their decisions. Prime Minister Sharon expressed an interest in this digital map, and soon enough Rothem and I came to his office.

Sharon welcomed me with a usual rebuke: "I'm impressed by the intelligence I receive that the Arabs actually like you. I deeply appreciate that you've found time to meet with Jews as well." As one who knew the situation on the ground well, he was fascinated by the digital map, and he let us leave only after an hour and a half. When Dan took us on a virtual flight above the Gaza Strip, I mentioned the futility of our continued presence there. Less than 1 percent of the population was taking up nearly 20 percent of a territory with some of the highest population density and fertility rates in the world.

"So what do you suggest we do?" Sharon asked. I replied that in the first instance, we should evacuate the three isolated settlements—Netzarim, Morag, and Kfar Darom. This was only one month before Sharon went on to announce that Israel would evacuate all the settlements in the Gaza Strip. He looked at me and said reprovingly, "I like you, Avi, but if you're willing to talk about evacuating Kfar Darom,[61] something has gone seriously and dangerously wrong in your Zionist education. I think that's a shame."[62]

Peres did not personally see the Disengagement Plan as the pinnacle of his own political dreams, but he backed it and rationalized his support with pragmatic arguments: better the implementation of a "mediocre plan" than a "genius plan" that had no majority. Peres believed that Israel's settlement of the Gaza Strip was a mistake and had already tried, to no avail, to promote a political initiative in which Palestinian independence would be realized first of all in the Gaza Strip. In later days, as president, Peres publicly admitted that he had made a mistake in supporting the Disengagement Plan[63] and that it should have been executed differently, in full and careful coordination with the Palestinian Authority.

Olmert and the Valley of Peace Disappointment

A short while after the evacuation of the Gaza Strip was completed, Peres suffered a humiliating setback when he lost the Labour Party leadership elections to Amir Peretz (November 9, 2005). Again I saw Peres at the peak of his distress, and again I saw him regain his composure, collect his strengths, and act out of a profound inner conviction that there was always a hidden way to extricate himself from a crisis. This time, the path meant leaving Labour and joining the Kadima Party, which Ariel Sharon had just established,[64] having quit the Likud in the wake of an internal revolt over the Disengagement.

I was used to cynical maneuvers in politics, but I struggled to digest Peres's resignation from the Labour Party. I was discomfited both by his leaving what had been his political and spiritual home for decades, and by his violation of the rules of fair play by not accepting his defeat and abandoning the party colleagues who had given him their trust. I did not hide my feelings from Peres, and he justified his move to me by claiming that there was nothing sacred in partisan frameworks and that together with Sharon he could advance the cause of peace more successfully. In this spirit, he posed this rhetorical question to an audience of students: "When you buy a picture, do you buy it for the frame or the painting."[65]

Peres pinned his hopes on his alliance with Sharon, but he was forced to limit his aspirations when Ehud Olmert became Israel's prime minister after Sharon suffered a stroke in January 2006. During the Olmert administration, Peres was pushed out of the negotiations with the Palestinians and was not party to the most important diplomatic developments. In desperation, he asked for some space to promote the Valley of Peace initiative. It did not seem to have had any political significance, other than in Peres's mind. The years of violence and frustration after Oslo had brought Peres to the brink of despairing of the Palestinians. He also felt personally hurt, because he believed that he had sacrificed a great deal for their success and that they were being ungrateful. He blamed his loss in the 1996 elections on their incompetence in stopping terrorism. "They ruined me," he used to vent to me when he got his bitter feelings off his chest.

Peres's conduct showed that he really was on the brink of despairing of the Palestinians' abilities to build a state of their own. The seemingly innocent Valley of Peace initiative contained the hidden premise that Gaza and the West Bank would not necessarily be a single, consolidated polity. Peres hoped to concentrate Palestinian economic activity on the borders between the West Bank and Jordan and between the Gaza Strip and Egypt. He had moved on from the vision of Israel and the Palestinians living together in a single, borderless economic union. "Instead of having the Palestinians dependent on trade routes that pass through Israel and are subject to Israeli security checks, better for them to do it through Jordan and Egypt." The Gaza Strip's economic dependence on Egypt would eventually have implications for the political situation, as would the West Bank's economic dependence on Jordan.

Peres, therefore, was returning to his ideas for a New Middle East, but this time with a more limited version. He endeavored to transform the stretch of land between the Red Sea and the Sea of Galilee into an area of joint economic development involving

Israel, Jordan, and the Palestinians. Once again he launched an "assault" to establish the Valley of Peace. He explained that for years Israel had been dealing with questions of politics and neglecting the power of economic leverage. Development, modernization, employment, the creation of common commercial interests—these would be the alternative to the reactionary violence offered by radical Islam. Peres strove to enlist the support of world leaders; traveled to persuade officials in neighboring countries; labored to construct a leadership team headed by Clinton, James Baker, and other notables; and tried to recruit the press and the business community to add momentum to his endeavor.

I did not join Peres's efforts. I feared that a focus on economic peace served the right-wing camp in Israel, which opposed the two-state solution, because it would make it easier for them to dodge the real challenge facing Israel—one that would require a political solution and involve painful costs. I did not believe, and I still do not believe, that economic peace can prevail without political peace.

I did not hide my opinions from Peres, and we got into bitter arguments. Our relationship was strong enough that I felt free to tell him exactly what I felt. But it was the Second Lebanon War that sparked the most bitter dispute between us. Perhaps it was because of the painful memories I still bear from the 1982 Lebanon War serving as a young soldier in the reserves.

When it became known that Hezbollah had abducted Israeli soldiers on July 12, 2006, Peres called me and said that he was on his way to an urgent cabinet meeting. He asked what I thought about how Israel should retaliate. I told him that an operational mishap could not be allowed to drag us into war. "You're right," Peres replied, "so how do you propose we retaliate?"

"If you've got big balls," I said half-jokingly, "fire the chief of staff."

"And if we have only tiny balls?" Peres persisted.

"Make do with firing the head of the northern command," I answered. I later learned that Peres had voted in favor of going to war. I was stunned. He explained his move by saying that there was a decisive majority for war anyway, and he did not want to prejudice unity and morale at such a critical hour. I told him that he had let me down and there was no absolution for political leaders who voted against their conscience in matters of life and death. He dropped a hint that suggested that he feared that a rupture in his relations with Olmert would sink his vision for the Valley of Peace.

Although the Israeli government eventually authorized Peres's project in March 2007, its most aspirational elements remained only on paper: the construction of a joint Israeli–Jordanian airport, a canal linking the Red Sea and Dead Sea, tourist sites and industrial zones along the Arava and Jordan Valleys, and more. Peres claimed that Olmert broke his promise on this matter. He was especially angry that Olmert had let the minister Binyamin Ben-Eliezer work on advancing the Red-Dead Canal, a key component of Peres's vision. Even after Olmert was forced to leave office, Peres still bore a grudge against him for the disappointment of the Valley of Peace.

Netanyahu's Trap

On June 13, 2007, Peres ran for president for the second time. This time he won, and I was asked to help draft his speech for his inauguration. As a private joke of sorts, I added to the text a paragraph that I had written for a speech that was never delivered—the one Peres was supposed to have delivered when he ran against Moshe Katsav for the presidency seven years earlier:

> In late 1992, when I served as foreign minister of Israel, I had a chance to return for the first time to Vishnyeva, the town of my birth in Belarus. I did not find any Jews there. Next to the municipality building was a pile of stones. A modest memorial to mark the mass grave of the inhabitants who failed to flee for their lives from the German invaders. The Nazis packed the Jews who stayed behind into the town's synagogue, and in their great cruelty, they set them on fire. Nobody survived. Among those killed in the flames were also my beloved grandfather and grandmother. I stood facing the heap of stones with a broken heart.
>
> I felt inside me the bitter cry of my grandfather and grandmother. If only I could have whispered to them about our independence, about the IDF, about Dimona, about Entebbe. About the enormous privilege that their grandson had been given, to help rebuild the ruins of our people, to give substance to the promise of the vow of "never again". And now—to be elected to the most demanding of roles, the one that symbolises the heart of the state and the nation—president of the State of Israel.[1]

The records of Peres's visit to the town had served me in drafting the speech. This was the speech that was never delivered, because Peres suffered a surprise defeat in the vote against Katsav. Before giving Peres the draft, I tested it out on my family at home. "But, Dad," my daughter Yael asked worriedly, "If Shimon loses again, what will you do with the speech?"

My eldest son, Yotam, preempted me and answered her spitefully, "Don't worry, Dad will give it to Katsav."

I was used to a reality in which the texts I wrote in my role involved a mixture of genuine feelings and more cynical considerations. Peres's visit to his forlorn birthplace was indeed touching. Peres had stepped out of the car briskly and begun a fervent search for his parents' house, accompanied by television cameras. Shortly before we had to leave, he found the place where the building had stood. There was no trace of the old house, its place taken by a relatively new building. But Peres insisted that the taste of the water, which he drank from the well in a dramatic gesture, at once flooded him with memories of the taste of his childhood. At the cemetery in neighboring Volozhin, he stood very emotionally facing the remains of his relatives' headstones. He gave the cemetery guard there all the cash he had in his pockets, some $800, to help with the upkeep of the graveyard.

The addition of this unctuous section to Peres's new inauguration speech was, for me, a form of twofold revenge: for the injustice inflicted on Peres when he was defeated by Katsav in his first battle for the presidency, and to a lesser extent against Peres himself, whose life's dramas still exhausted me.

Peres was enamored by the written word. He had an authorial pride that made it difficult for him to recite words that he had not written himself. I used to write the first draft for his speeches. That made the writing easier for him. He used to take ideas and phrases from my drafts, but at the end of the process, he usually threw my proposal in the bin. From his own pen there always emerged, for better or worse, his personal creation. But Peres still left the section I drafted about his visit to his birthplace in his inauguration speech—both in the version he did not get to read, and in the one that he read seven years later, when he became president.

Defeat to Katsav

I was by his side in the Knesset when the results of the vote came in, on the day of his defeat to Moshe Katsav.[2] He was overwhelmed with pain. He lamented the treachery of the party colleagues who had voted for his rival and were now joining the ranks of those filing quietly to the doleful mourners' room to offer their condolences.

The day before, Peres had signed a letter resigning from the government. That was the only way he could swear an oath as president the next day. Forty-eight hours had to pass between the submission of his letter and the entry into force of his resignation, and Peres did not want to lose a single moment on his way to the President's Residence. If he ended up not winning, he knew, he could withdraw the letter.

I had assumed that defeat in the battle for the presidency would mean the end of Peres's political career. Tsvia, his daughter, was with us at the most difficult moments. I asked her what she thought. "Dad needs to go home and not withdraw the letter," she told me.

I turned to Peres and he gave us his response, surprised by the question: "Recall the letter, of course," he ordered. I decided not to rush. Peres went home. I assessed that the pressure from his wife Sonia and the children would overcome his resistance this time. We met toward the evening in his Tel Aviv office. "So what are we doing about the letter?" I asked him. Peres looked at me surprised: "You haven't withdrawn it yet?" His wonderment was apt. I should have predicted his response. After all, this was not the first defeat I had experienced with him. And I had already learned that such defeats broke the hearts of his associates, and mine too, but they could not break him. Peres felt hurt, offended, humiliated, and victimized, but he knew immediately how to summon new strengths and move on, unable to understand the depression and paralysis that gripped his staff.

In the speech that was never delivered, Peres was meant to have made a festive commitment:

> This, for me, is also the moment of leaving this house, whose benches I have saddled for 41 years, more than half of my life. I have loved the powerful rivers and calm waters here, their deafening volume, and the streams that run so deep. I am leaving the routine of my former life, moving from the executive arm and onto a different challenge—to be the unifying shoulder. I am no longer the messenger of a party but a trustee of the nation.

It was easy for Peres to drop his cloak and join a new world, just as it was easy for him, after his defeat, to take a step backward. In this case, to revert from the role of a "trustee of the nation" back to being a "messenger of a party."

Finally President

After he was elected president in July 2007, Peres offered me to serve as the director-general of the President's Office. I was alarmed by the thought of having to accompany him to all the ceremonies that the president must attend. Peres accepted my negative answer understandingly and made do with a promise that I would help him with whatever he wanted.

For my first task, I was asked to prepare his transition into the new role. In one of the preparatory meetings at the President's Residence, Moshe Katsav, who had come to collect his personal possessions, asked to speak with me. For more than an hour, he laid bare his soul to me and denied the rape allegations against him, which had forced him to resign and triggered the special presidential election that Peres won. He dragged me to every corner in his office to prove that every point faced a window and was therefore visible from the outside—and how was it conceivable that he might have done what was being attributed to him when he was so exposed for all to see? He spoke from a powerful inner conviction that I told Peres afterward that in my opinion, he would successfully pass a polygraph test.

The knowledge that the president's official functions were extremely limited did not deter Peres from aspiring to transform the presidency into a means of influencing what was happening in Israel. In this respect, Peres continued to be a supporting actor even as president—a position with which he was well acquainted, and which required a special modus operandi that he had perfected over the years. But this time, the price that Peres would have to pay for his overt political activity was somewhat different: the erosion of the great esteem with which the public held its president, a phenomenon that moved Peres and filled him with joy. And indeed, once Peres entered the presidency, he was torn between two contradictory aspirations: on the one hand, the impulse to cultivate and preserve the public's admiration for him; and on the other, the urge to promote his positions on two key issues—achieving a peace treaty with the Palestinians, and preventing an Israeli attack on Iran's nuclear facilities.

They're Convinced They're Better than Churchill

Peres deemed these issues existentially important for Israel. He told me repeatedly that he could not sleep at night, for fear that Netanyahu and Barak would decide to attack Iran. He thought plans to strike Iran's nuclear facilities evinced a complete lack of judgment, which would likely bring about Israel's destruction. The more time went by, the more extreme his pronouncements in closed circles became: "Netanyahu and Barak are drunk on grandeur. They're acting completely illogically. They're convinced they're better than Churchill."

He chose not to fight the prime minister and defense minister publicly. "If I come out against them publicly, I'll have fired the only bullet in my gun. I'll lose the influence I have from my public esteem and my excellent ties with the heads of the security establishment. It's better that I operate patiently, without a visible clash." I understood him. After all, he had been the target of searing hatred from so many people throughout the many years of his political life. The sense that he was the victim of injustice did not leave him in the presidency either, and he continued to blame Begin and Rabin "who ruined my life" by spreading lies and aspersions about him.

The tremendous hatred that confronted Peres throughout his public life victimized a man who needed a great deal of love and attention. And now, as president, Peres was at long last widely admired. He had suddenly become a character within the Israeli national consensus. It seemed the nation needed a wise, elder statesman, whose wisdom could be trusted, and Peres performed that role with devotion: he was well known and admired internationally and among Diaspora Jewry. He was familiar with how the world functioned and felt at home among world leaders.

His image became even more popular in light of the reservations that many in the international community had about Israel's leaders—chiefly Benjamin Netanyahu and Avigdor Lieberman. Citizens wrote Peres letters apologizing for their contemptuous attitude toward him in the past. And whenever a favorable opinion poll was published, he told me, "I'm just embarrassed. I don't understand where this love for me is coming from." But nobody was happier than he was to memorize the results of the polls and to read the articles favorably reporting on his deeds. He was crowned in various polls as the most popular person in the State of Israel. One poll published in *Haaretz* (April 21, 2011) found that 72 percent of the public were satisfied with his performance as president, as opposed to only 20 percent who were dissatisfied. Peres's office was so devoted to cultivating his public standing that I sometimes accused his staff of so slavishly guarding his image that they were stopping him from being a president of any substance.

One of Peres's common sayings echoed in my ears: "No leader is great unless he fights the good fight." Rather brutally, I reminded him on occasion that he was indeed refraining from fighting the good fight. In our conversations, I told Peres that history would write little about his public popularity. I argued that the true test of his presidency lay in a clash between him and Netanyahu. Peres tried to drag Netanyahu into an accord with the Palestinians. He used the techniques he had used in the past as a supporting actor and tried to adapt them to his status as president. He tried to cajole him, to promise him a place in history, to mobilize political support, to appeal to those close to him, and to flatter Netanyahu in his public pronouncements—but of course, he was not averse to overstepping his authority to kick-start moves that would sweep the doubters toward the goal that he had set them.

Peres understood well that his support for Netanyahu was an asset for the prime minister. Netanyahu, however, had identified Peres's soft underbelly. He gave him space for the diplomatic activities he so enjoyed, swayed him with public words of appreciation, and devoted many hours to meetings with him, joined in some of them by his wife Sara.

I used to tell Peres that in the confrontation between them, for now, Netanyahu was winning. I put it to him that he was Netanyahu's fig leaf. Peres reacted angrily. He had a whole set of arguments in mind proving that his actions were correct and bearing fruit. Thus, for example, he explained that he had persuaded Netanyahu to pursue economic peace in the West Bank. And Netanyahu had indeed removed many checkpoints and eased economic activity in the territories, which had produced—at the time—an improvement in the Palestinian Authority's economy.

Netanyahu Accepts the Two-state Principle

Peres claimed that he had convinced Netanyahu to publicly accept the principle of two states for two peoples. "Even if he doesn't implement this solution, the fact of a public declaration is of historic importance because from now on—the Likud has accepted the principle of two states." Peres saw Netanyahu's declaration as evidence of a moral victory for the Oslo school. I cannot say for certain how much weight Peres's arguments had in Netanyahu's decision, but in their many conversations, Peres beseeched him to repeat the magic words.

On the eve of Netanyahu's Bar Ilan speech on June 14, 2009, the "Beilin Team" had a meeting. In the forum, Peres's most senior former advisers debated whether Peres should use the full force of his weight to pressure Netanyahu to say the words "two states." Beilin argued that there was no chance of this happening, and Moshik Theumim suggested that Peres formulate a creative sentence that would not directly refer to "two states" but would nevertheless imply it. Peres liked Moshik's suggestion and started playing around with alternative formulations, such as "the solution will end the Israeli occupation." I told Peres that the whole affair reminded me of his unforgivable behavior when the government decided to embark on the Second Lebanon War. "You were against the war but voted in favour," I said. "There are moments when you have to act according to principle, not petty considerations—and now is such a moment."

Peres was palpably angry, but he decided not to appeal for Netanyahu to use alternative formulations, and he did not soften his demands till the moment of the speech. At the end of Netanyahu's speech, in which he uttered the magic words, Peres called me feeling evidently satisfied: "This is a historic night. I want to thank you for helping me in this important mission." I thought to myself: *Peres doesn't usually go out of his way to give thanks or credit to others.* But this weakness was dwarfed by his openness and his willingness to listen and adapt to criticism, no matter how stinging and painful. He listened, let his anger or disappointment show, reacted forcefully, and vigorously defended his own beliefs—but he let different arguments incubate in his mind. He mulled over the logic of various criticisms, and he was always willing to let himself be convinced and to change his mind.

A Jewish State

In his Bar Ilan speech, Netanyahu stressed: "The fundamental condition for ending the conflict is the public, binding and sincere Palestinian recognition of Israel as the national homeland of the Jewish people."

Peres scoffed at Netanyahu's demand. His vision was practical, not declarative. "If we have a substantial Jewish majority, we'll have a state with a Jewish character. What do I need a Palestinian declaration for without a Jewish majority? And what will we do if after they make that declaration they walk back on it? Would we thereby stop being a Jewish state?"

Peres also dismissed my remarks that there was historic value in having the Muslim world recognize Jewish sovereignty in the Holy Land. He saw our need for recognition of our identity from "the other" as evidence of our lack of self-confidence and weakness. He had put this position to me long before Netanyahu's Bar Ilan speech. But despite his approach, I tried to get a statement on the subject out of the Palestinians. An opportunity arose in June 2004, when one of Arafat's associates asked for my advice ahead of an interview by the Palestinian leader in *Haaretz*. Asked what it was important for Arafat to say in the interview, I replied: "That he accepts that Israel is the Jewish state." I was promised that my advice would be relayed to Arafat.

At the same time, I advised people at *Haaretz* to raise the matter in the interview. And indeed, when Akiva Eldar and David Landau asked whether he understood and accepted that Israel had to be and remain a Jewish state, Arafat replied, "Absolutely." He even added that the Palestinians "had accepted this openly and officially in 1988, at the Palestinian National Council" and remained completely committed to this position.[3] A cursory read of the Palestinian Declaration of Independence, as drafted by Palestinian national poet Mahmoud Darwish and signed in Algiers on November 15, 1988, indeed shows that it considered the partition plan "which partitioned Palestine into an Arab and a Jewish State" to be the resolution that "continues to attach conditions to international legitimacy that guarantee the Palestinian Arab people the right to sovereignty and national independence."[4]

I put it to Peres that Netanyahu's demand could be satisfied with a statement in the final treaty that rested on what was already written in the Palestinian Declaration on Independence. The formulation would have to take account of the Palestinians' sensitivities, since they saw Netanyahu's demand as a ruse designed to prejudice the rights of the refugees and the status of Israeli Arabs. For example: "This peace treaty expresses the rights of the Jewish people and the Palestinian people to national self-determination in their own independent states, while being fully committed to the rights of minorities living in the territory under their sovereignty."

Peres generally treated my comments on the matter as sophistry, but after he understood that the Americans were taking Netanyahu's demand seriously, he asked me to suggest my ideas to Secretary of State Hillary Clinton, who was coming to meet him at the President's Office. When I did so, Clinton expressed a great interest and asked for the material in writing, but Peres remained apathetic and told me after she left, "The demand for them to recognise us as a Jewish state is just a silly excuse."

Peres and Mahmoud Abbas

During his efforts to drag Netanyahu into an agreement with the Palestinians, Peres met frequently with the key Palestinian figures whom I brought over for secret dinners at his residence: Saeb Erekat, Ahmed Qurei, Jibril Rajoub, Munib al-Masri, and others. I personally also met Mahmoud Abbas and his people from time to time. In informal discussions, we scratched layers usually not reached in formal talks, including internal rivalries and power struggles. Sometimes our Palestinian guests strayed from the accepted line and voiced some exceptionally brave positions. Thus, for example, one official told me that for an accord to be successfully implemented, a Jordanian–Palestinian confederation would have to be founded, with responsibility for security and foreign policy falling on the Jordanian king: "Because we've failed to give you the core of your demands: security." The Palestinians had no faith in Netanyahu's intentions and continued to pin their hopes on Peres. Although they had no great illusions about the powers of the president in the Israeli system, they believed in the sincerity of his intentions and hoped that he might manage to influence the prime minister.

Peres had known Mahmoud Abbas since they signed the Declaration of Principles together at the White House in 1993. He believed that Abbas was a genuine partner, who wanted reconciliation and compromise. In a leisurely meeting on the banks of Lake Como in Italy on the margins of an international conference,[5] Abbas spoke empathetically about Olmert's domestic problems. He said that in their last meeting, a few days earlier on August 31, 2008, the prime minister had presented him an Israeli map for the first time, although he did not let him keep it:

> Israel is asking for 6.8 percent of the West Bank and is willing to give 5.5 percent in return. I believe that this is a good start. It's an important change that we're talking about the border and drawing a line on the map. But it's extremely difficult for us to accept you taking such a large section of our land. We don't understand why Israel is demanding 6.8 percent of the West Bank when the built-up Israeli area beyond the Green Line is only 1.2 percent. We have proposed a map with land swaps of 1.9 percent. The border you have proposed with 6.8 percent does not afford us contiguity in our own territory. The West Bank will be divided into cantons because of the Ariel, Gush Etzion, and Maale Adumim settlement blocs.
>
> It's very difficult for us to "sell" such a border to our people: without contiguity, without ownership of the water, and with 55,000 West Bank Palestinians remaining in Israeli territory. Olmert proposed a committee of five or six states that would be

responsible for Jerusalem for a certain period. The idea sounds unclear to me, but it's a good start. I told Olmert that I'd give him an answer to his ideas.

There are very large differences between us on the matters of refugees and Jerusalem. I understand well that it's not realistic for five million refugees to return to their homes in Israel. It would mean the destruction of Israel. But in order to "close" the refugee file, I need us to agree on the number of refugees who could return to Israel over a few years. Otherwise—the agreement will not gain Palestinian public support. I know that Tzipi Livni is strongly against this demand.

I know that unless I solve the problem of Hamas, I won't manage to implement the agreement between us. The Arab Peace Initiative gives Israel an offer of the type that has never been since 1948. The Muslim states also support the initiative.

Peres replied that in his opinion, the differences over territory were not so great, and the gaps could be bridged. "Olmert very much wants to reach an agreement," he said.

I believe that he wants to leave behind a breakthrough and a meaningful achievement. You must understand that we have a real problem with the settlers and with evacuating them. When we insist on a particular border, that's meant to minimise the number of settlers who'd have to be evacuated, and so will in fact make it easier to achieve and implement an agreement. Even if you don't reach a complete agreement on all the issues, you can sign a document relating to the achievements in the negotiations so far and expressing a joint commitment to continue them until they reach a successful conclusion. For the sake of peace, it's important that you remain in your position.

These talks strengthened Peres's impression that this long-awaited peace agreement was within reach. After Netanyahu became prime minister, Peres sought to recruit him to continue Olmert's peace process, which was picking up steam. Publicly, he created the impression that he had faith in Netanyahu's peaceful intentions. This was a classic Peres step. It was based in part on his limitless optimism and natural tendency to have faith in other people, in part on his interpretation of the geopolitical trends that would force Netanyahu to go for an agreement against his will, and in part on his attempts to promote a positive, self-fulfilling atmosphere.

Peres tried to persuade the Palestinians that if they entered negotiations with Netanyahu, they would achieve their goals. As always in the face of adversity, Peres came up with abundant possible solutions, some fantastical and some creative: from building an island off the coast of Gaza ("to enable you in future to take over the Gaza Strip and liberate it from Hamas rule"), to his idea of one day offering the settlers to remain in place under Palestinian sovereignty. As he explained to Secretary of State Hillary Clinton (September 15, 2010): "There's no reason hundreds of thousands of Arabs should live in Israel and Palestine should be completely free of Jews." Peres even informed Netanyahu that the Palestinians he had spoken to on the matter had not rejected it outright.

Netanyahu Would Prefer History to Politics

Peres tried to convince Netanyahu that he had to choose between the leadership models of Menachem Begin and Yitzhak Shamir. "Although Shamir served as prime minister for a long time, nobody really remembers what he did. You need to be recorded in history as the person who brought peace to Israel and preserved it as a Jewish and democratic state."

Peres used his tricks from the past. On the eve of his first meeting in Washington with the newly inaugurated President Obama, he agreed with Netanyahu that he would present his ideas for an agreement with the Palestinians without committing Netanyahu to them. His intention was to convince the American president to jump-start a diplomatic initiative based on calling for the immediate establishment of a Palestinian state on provisional borders, and to continue holding negotiations on this basis. Peres argued that if Netanyahu did not present an Israeli plan, he would be dragged against his will into a worse plan promoted by someone else. Merely presenting an initiative would enable him to reach understandings with Obama that would strengthen Israel's position in the peace process and guarantee the support of the United States in case the Palestinian side failed to cooperate.

Peres, therefore, hurried to Washington to lay the ground for Netanyahu's meeting. He knew quite well that the Palestinians suspected that temporary borders would become permanent and that their cause would fall off the international agenda. He knew there were no buyers on the Palestinian side for such a plan, which was presented in the Road Map document as a mere possibility. Overcoming this obstacle required a commitment to the principle of drawing the final, permanent border on the basis of the 1967 lines with equal land swaps.

Netanyahu, of course, rejected this formulation. In the preparatory talks for his visit, he agreed for Peres to present his own positions while stressing that they did not commit the prime minister. This fuzzy approach was meant to signal to Obama that there was room for him to talk with Netanyahu, and to nudge him in the direction we preferred. Although it was not agreed with Netanyahu that Peres would present Obama a written memo, Peres instructed me to prepare one at the last minute. Owing to time pressure, he only managed to read half of it before stepping into the White House.

Toward the end of his meeting with Obama,[6] Peres asked to speak privately with the president and signaled for me to stay. Then he whipped out the memo, presented it to Obama, and asked him to keep it confidential. Obama nodded, folded the memo, and slipped it into the inner pocket of his jacket. The document also contained the sentence that Netanyahu found hard to accept, but Peres considered indispensable: "The United States may guarantee the Palestinians the principles for the delineation of a permanent status border (the full scope of '67 areas including agreed land swaps)."

The memo contained a further clause that was problematic for Netanyahu: "Both sides will implement the articles of the Roadmap, including a commitment to a Two State Solution, the Palestinian commitment to fight terror, Israel's commitments regarding settlement activity in the West Bank, etc." This clause was difficult for Israel because fulfilling Israel's commitments under the Road Map meant freezing settlement construction, including natural growth, and evacuating unauthorized outposts.

In order to explain to President Obama how credible his proposals were and the manner in which they reflected Netanyahu's positions, Peres used a humorous story about the Yiddish translation of *Romeo and Juliet*, which says: "The original version was written by Shakespeare and the Yiddish version before you was improved by the translator."

"While I'm not presenting you Netanyahu's official position," Peres explained, "I'm saying these things with his knowledge. From my familiarity with him, I believe that they also will be acceptable to him, otherwise I wouldn't be saying them."

That was Peres's way. As a supporting actor who aspired to a leading role, he acted with gumption, overstepped his formal authorities, and preferred to speak in ambiguous turns of phrase. What seemed natural and logical to Peres was not always interpreted as such by the people he was speaking with, who struggled to comprehend how a certain position could simultaneously be acceptable to Netanyahu and also not be Netanyahu's position. "Netanyahu would prefer history to politics," Peres promised Obama. "He'll take the path of Menachem Begin, not of prime ministers who preferred a long tenure to historic action. Netanyahu is ready to begin negotiations with the Palestinians immediately. He doesn't want to rule over the Palestinians. He and his government will be obligated to the decisions made by previous Israeli governments, including the Road Map."

Peres made an effort to explain to Obama the constraints that Netanyahu had to deal with because of the coalition make-up in Israel. "Netanyahu is at pains to sustain his political coalition. He needs a little constructive ambiguity. It's true he hasn't expressed support for a Palestinian state, but neither has he come out against the idea since he was elected."

Although Peres promised Obama that Netanyahu would raise the plan for jump-starting the negotiations with the Palestinians in their upcoming meeting, Obama's staffers told us afterward that Netanyahu had not done so. When Peres asked Netanyahu what had happened, the prime minister replied that he had expected Obama to raise the subject himself.

Peres gritted his teeth but did not despair. Even when Netanyahu did not meet his expectations, he never tired of trying to drag him into negotiations based on the 1967 lines. Peres himself had adopted the position, having angrily rejected it for years, that land swaps should be equal. And as always, when he changed his mind, he was adept at adopting a new position as if it had been his all along, and to lobby for it with all his heart. Thus, for example, he explained his revised position to Secretary of State Hillary Clinton:

> In my opinion, it's not fair to demand from the Palestinians to concede a single inch of the total area of the 1967 territories. Arafat made an enormous concession, for them, when he renounced the original Palestinian dream of 100 percent, and in Oslo he also conceded the territory allocated to the Palestinians by the 1947 UN Partition Plan, leaving him with less than a quarter of the territory. We must be fair and pragmatic. It's important to preserve 100 percent of the 1967 territories

through equal and mutually agreed land swaps that will help resolve the issue of the settlers and security.[7]

In meetings with Netanyahu, Peres never tired of explaining that the absence of a genuine peace process with the Palestinians was causing Israel's increasing isolation, and that we would wind up being subjected to sanctions. In a meeting in February 2011, Peres warned Netanyahu that if he persisted in his refusal to make concessions on Jerusalem in its current borders, failed to promise that the Palestinian state would encompass an area no smaller than the original size of the West Bank, and insisted on the IDF's continued presence in the Jordan Valley, nothing would happen. After his conversations with Netanyahu, Peres excitedly told me that Netanyahu (and his wife Sara) had relished his analysis, and that he was encouraged about the chances for an imminent resumption of the peace process.

Meeting Mahmoud Abbas in London

Peres sought Netanyahu's consent to meet Mahmoud Abbas—"with your knowledge but not as your envoy"—in order to check the possible parameters for an agreement. Peres hoped to enlist President Obama, King Abdullah, and President Mubarak to support his plan. After Netanyahu acquiesced, Peres spoke by phone with Abbas, who agreed to a secret meeting in London. Peres updated Netanyahu[8] that he would present the Palestinian leader a comprehensive plan based on the principle that the size of the territory allocated for his state would be similar to the original size of the West Bank in 1967. On the matter of Jerusalem, Peres suggested that the Arab neighborhoods go to the Palestinians, and the Jewish neighborhoods to Israel.

When I inquired about Netanyahu's response Peres replied, "His response was unclear. A kind of semi-agreement." I persisted: and what about his insistence that the IDF remain a long time along the Jordan River? Peres said that Netanyahu had indeed insisted on that and claimed that the absence of an IDF presence would endanger our security. "He's claiming the Iranians will come and take over the whole region."

The meeting with Abbas took place at the home of a friend of Peres's, the businessman Poju Zabludowicz. We arrived in London on a private jet for just a few hours, and Peres was in high spirits: a secret flight, classified negotiations, grand plans—I could not but admire his energies. Aged 88, and still focused, alert, and full of confidence in his powers to steer Israel toward a long-awaited peace. Peres described his ideas during a dinner with Abbas: as usual, he summarized the plethora of possibilities that the future held for a Palestinian state that would be, as he defined it, "science-oriented and democratic." My many attempts to convince him that Abbas was entirely unimpressed by these descriptions were in vain. On the final-status issues, Peres presented the following positions:

- The territory of the Palestinian state would be equivalent in size to the 1967 territories, with mutually agreed land swaps;

- Jerusalem—the Arab neighborhoods would be under Palestinian sovereignty and the Jewish neighborhoods would be under Israeli sovereignty. A joint municipal framework would be possible with both sides' agreement;
- The holy basin—the existing framework would continue, whereby each side was responsible for its own holy sites. Discussions about sovereignty in the holy basin would be postponed to a later stage;
- Refugees—there would be a quota of refugees that Israel would agree to absorb into its territory, but the precise number would be the subject of special negotiations later on;
- Settlements—the sides would agree to a "political ceasefire." Israel would stop building in the Arab neighborhoods of Jerusalem and would limit itself to construction within the built-up areas of the settlements;
- Security—Israel and the Palestinians would cooperate in a manner similar to the model of Israeli–Jordanian cooperation.

Abbas replied that he agreed with the wording about the 1967 territories and land swaps. "If we agree on this principle, I believe that we will also agree on the details and percentages." The wording on the refugee question was also acceptable to him. As for Jerusalem, he said, "I have proposed that the Arab neighbourhoods come under a separate municipal framework, and the same for the Jewish neighbourhoods, but the city as a whole would not be divided. Your capital would be on your side, and the same would go for our capital." On the security, Abbas explained, "The basis, as far as I'm concerned, is Israeli recognition of Palestinian sovereignty over the entire territory of the Palestinian state. We'll explore together what the threats are and how we confront them. Perhaps the right framework will be a multilateral one. We propose deploying NATO forces on our territory, to preserve our security and yours too. I also agree to forgo having an army."

Peres returned from his meeting encouraged, and decided to bring King Abdullah of Jordan on board. We departed for a secret trip to the king's palace.[9] Peres told the king that he had come with the knowledge of the prime minister, who was also aware of the messages he would convey. But still, his remarks did not commit Netanyahu. The king expressed support for the principles of the agreement that he presented, and Peres believed that the time was right to bring the United States in the loop. He was interested in having the Americans invite the sides to renew negotiations, with an invitation enumerating a number of principles regarding the future treaty. The Palestinians would thereby be convinced that the process was serious.

Peres knew that Netanyahu could not stomach the formulations that represented the Palestinians' absolute minimum. The idea, therefore, was for the Americans to present them, and for Netanyahu to accept their invitation while still being able to claim that he had not agreed to everything written in it. Peres and I drafted a memo that would be passed to the Americans after receiving Netanyahu's approval. The core of the document included a statement that the territory of the Palestinian state would be equal in size to the territory that existed before June 4, 1967. In the course of several meetings with Netanyahu and Yitzhak Molcho, the prime minister's liaison to the Palestinians, we held exhausting negotiations over the precise wording. Netanyahu demanded that the clause concerning Jerusalem (which said that the

Arab neighborhoods would be under Palestinian sovereignty) be removed, and also insisted on an IDF presence along the Jordan River (in the spirit of what Peres had said to Abbas in London, we wrote in the memo: "Special security arrangements will be made along the Jordan River between Israeli, Jordanian, and Palestinian forces"). The original memo also included a clause that said that during negotiations, Israeli construction in Jerusalem would be limited to the Jewish neighborhoods alone. In the settlements in Judea and Samaria, construction would be limited to the existing built-up areas.

Shimon Believes Abbas but it's a Grave Mistake

Netanyahu must have felt that it would be easier to persuade Peres through me, because he asked me to come to his home with Molcho.[10] He preferred for us to sit on the patio so he could enjoy the sunshine and his aromatic cigar. Netanyahu said straight away that he had thought hard about the matter before we came, and that he could not sugarcoat the situation and ignore a tough reality: "We need to tell the truth. It's the right thing to do, and also the most natural." He spoke darkly about what would likely happen in the West Bank if we transferred control to the Palestinians. "Abu Mazen [Mahmoud Abbas] won't last. The Iranians will fill the vacuum. They'll threaten the airport and sit on the outskirts of Petah Tikva. Abu Mazen doesn't want negotiations and he's also incapable of delivering anything. Even if he enters negotiations, he'll quickly blow them up." Netanyahu did not conceal his fears about the political ramifications of our proposed undertaking: "I'll pay a heavy price just for beginning negotiations, and Abu Mazen will quit them before we reach any results."

He spoke calmly, but had some harsh words: "Shimon believes in Abu Mazen and his abilities. But that's a grave mistake." I responded by explaining the logic of Peres's proposal: he would tell Obama how an American invitation could be worded to facilitate Israel's participation in negotiations with the Palestinians. Netanyahu could say, of course, that this was the Americans' proposed basis for talks and that he did not agree with every dot and comma. I said that if we failed to take this course, the Europeans and Americans would soon force us into an agreement much worse than the option he had now: to design the principles himself and to dictate the rules for moving ahead.

Netanyahu read the draft memo and asked to completely remove the matter of Jerusalem. "You've divided Jerusalem for me," he scolded me. He made clear that he was not open to having a multinational force stationed along the Jordan River, insisting on an IDF presence along its entire length. As for the Palestinians' abilities to put the agreement into practice, I said that we had to distinguish between the treaty and its implementation. The implementation could be conditioned on a timetable and performance tests. I read to him the relevant clause in the Annapolis Declaration, in which the Palestinians had effectively agreed to the logic that Israel would not honor all its commitments until the Palestinians already had an effective government in Gaza. I said that they would understand us if we insisted on the rule of "one government, one gun." No Israeli leader, from right to left, could evacuate settlers while Sderot was being pounded by rockets fired from Gaza.

Netanyahu nodded and asked us to add this position to the text. He then asked what I thought about Molcho's ideas for an interim agreement, based on the phased transfer of limited swathes of territory to Palestinian control. I said there was no chance and no strategic reason for interim steps if they were not connected to a vision of our final destination—especially on territory. I said that if the Americans were allowed to act on the format that Peres was proposing, Israel could reach meaningful side-agreements with the United States that could also be presented to the Israeli public as an achievement. The termination of the Palestinians' campaign at the United Nations, for example, or the cessation of calls for a boycott and suchlike. Alongside the negotiations, we could initiate a gradual process of confidence-building measures in the spirit of Molcho's proposal. We could also plan in advance with the Americans for the possibility that the Palestinians would indeed abandon the negotiations, as Netanyahu predicted, and try to secure their support for a partial agreement.

Netanyahu replied that the whole of Israel was within range of missiles, and that we did not understand the threat level. "Only 20 percent of Israelis think like you and Shimon." I told him that even if he was right, and we were entering a volatile and dangerous period, it was better to do so with one clenched fist, and one open hand extended to peace. Only thus would we secure assistance from the United States and other Western states. Given the Arab Spring, it was important to reach a breakthrough with the Palestinians before the Egyptians formed a permanent government.

Netanyahu asked Molcho and me to prepare a shorter memo taking into account his notes, and we would meet again. The text included Netanyahu's demand for the IDF to remain along the Jordan for a "prolonged period." After further meetings involving Netanyahu and Peres, the document that Peres would present Obama was finally agreed. The territorial core was phrased thus: "Territory—the territory of the Palestinian state will be similar in size to the territory that prevailed prior to 4 June 1967. The delineation of the border including territorial swaps will be agreed upon by the parties, and will take into consideration both sides' security needs, demographic realities, and developments on the ground." According to the memo, the solution for the refugee question would not be on Israeli soil, Jerusalem would remain open and united, and a full agreement on it would be reached in the course of negotiations. Settlement construction would be limited to the existing footprint of built-up areas in the settlements. In Jerusalem, the same policy from the last forty years would be continued. The memo thereby recognized the principle that the Palestinians' sovereignty over their areas (to be agreed in the negotiations) would be recognized at the time of the treaty's signing, but that its implementation would take place gradually and in accordance with the fulfilment of both sides' commitments, including "effective control of the Palestinian government over the Gaza Strip and the disarming of terrorist organisations."

Both Agree and Don't Agree to 1967 Lines

But Netanyahu also insisted on including a clause in the memo that would comprehensively free him from any commitment to the other clauses. The memo, therefore, included the following line: "The U.S. recognizes that on some of the issues, the parties have different positions. The U.S. does not expect the parties to agree to all of its positions, but it does expect them to resume direct negotiations between them since direct bilateral talks are the only way to resolve the conflict." Netanyahu also insisted that we write "points for the Peres-Obama meeting," which would be agreed by him and Peres, including that "Israel will clarify that the language with regard to the position dealing with territory is not acceptable to it." The points would also say that Israel and the United States would agree from the outset what steps Israel would take if the Palestinians refused to join the negotiations.

In my follow-up talks with Peres, we differed on the importance that we attached to the document. I claimed that Netanyahu had not committed to anything and that our approach would raise eyebrows in the White House. In effect, we were proposing that the president of the United States formulate an invitation to the parties, whose content he should expect Israel to reject. Peres, as usual, saw the upsides: the fact that Netanyahu was personally involved in wording a document that touched on such sensitive questions, and the fact that we were allowed to continue our efforts. He believed in his own powers "to confuse everyone" and, amid the confusion, to pursue the cause of peace.

On the eve of another of Peres's meetings with President Obama,[11] we handed this document to his advisor Dennis Ross. And indeed, Obama informed Peres at the beginning of their meeting that he had read the memo and would be willing to invite the parties to renew negotiations, on the condition that it be clear in advance they were entering a genuine dialogue and that they accepted that the treaty should be the result of direct negotiations. Obama said that he had the impression that the Palestinians put a lot of faith in Peres, which was why he thought it best that Peres himself meet Abbas, present him with the revised document, and receive his consent to move ahead.

From my acquaintance with Ross's cautious approach, I gathered that President Obama would adopt his recommendations. The Americans had no intention of risking a negative response from the Palestinians, which was why they asked Peres to be the one to convince the Palestinians to accept the memo. Peres stressed that this was a draft invitation detailing the positions of the United States. The parties were meant to accept the invitation and resume talks, notwithstanding reservations about terms here and there. Netanyahu would thus clarify that he did not accept the position regarding the 1967 territories. He would also demand a long-term Israeli military presence along the Jordan—without denying the principle of Palestinian sovereignty, which would be agreed on. At the same time, it was expected that the Palestinians would clarify that the deal would be implemented gradually, but the principle of sovereignty would be made clear with the signing of the treaty. They would demand a quota of refugees to be allowed into Israel, insist that no new construction be permitted in the West Bank, and oppose a long-term Israeli military presence along the Jordan (but would agree to NATO forces).

Peres emphasized that Netanyahu was taking a substantial political risk. He feared that uncontrolled changes in the West Bank would likely bring Iran to Israel's doorstep. There was no ignoring that it was Netanyahu who had warned, before the withdrawal from Gaza Strip, that the area would serve as a base for rocket attacks on population centers in southern Israel. He was right. In this context, it was legitimate for him to insist on certain security demands.

While Peres was maneuvering Netanyahu into position, *Haaretz* published an editorial,[12] declaring that President Peres "has been working in recent days to defend the prime minister's domestic and international standing." I recalled similar things written in the same paper when Peres was secretly pushing the Oslo process, but I had no great illusions that we would succeed this time as in the past.

In my follow-up meetings with Saeb Erekat, I got the impression that beyond the various comments on the text itself, there was a complete lack of faith among the Palestinians that the Israelis were indeed interested in reaching a final-status agreement. They were also deeply disappointed by what they saw as the US one-sidedness. They thought they had a better political alternative at their disposal: applying for member-state status at the United Nations. They believed that they would win 137 "yes" votes at the General Assembly—a two-thirds majority. Such a resolution would change the political picture and would open up new opportunities for them. It would strengthen the impression that Israel's presence in the West Bank constituted an occupation of Palestinian territory, and that this was not "disputed territory" as Israel claimed.

Peres took advantage of his stay in New York during the General Assembly session to meet Mahmoud Abbas again[13] and implored him to resume negotiations. He explained Netanyahu's dilemmas. "For Netanyahu, it was a difficult journey to move from his native ideological base to where he is now ... He has accepted the principle of two states. Intellectually—he has made the shift. Emotionally—it's still tough." Peres tried to bolster the spirits of the desperate Abbas, and compared his situation to that of Ben-Gurion, who was "isolated like you at such historic moments of decision."

"Did he also consider resigning?" Abbas asked with a smile.

"Every other day," Peres replied. "But as with you, everyone on our side panicked and urged him to remain." Abbas was not much encouraged. He started speaking more often of his intention to dismantle the Palestinian Authority, give Israel responsibility for the entire territory, and resign.

Peres's Letter to Netanyahu

Sometimes even Peres lost his optimism about the possibility that Netanyahu might make progress toward an accord. After months in which nobody could point to a possible breakthrough, he started speaking in apocalyptic terms about Israel's future without a peace treaty. As one who kept an eye on the history books, Peres decided, with my encouragement, to put his thoughts in writing and send Netanyahu a personal letter on May 15, 2011. The date was the eve of Netanyahu's planned visit to the United States. Since Peres presented his beliefs in this letter in an organized and detailed fashion, I have decided to replicate his words in full:

Dear Bibi,

On the eve of your departure to the United States, I wish to summarise the main points that were raised in our discussions.

The dangers facing Israel:

The demographic danger has not passed. If a Palestinian state is not formed in Judea and Samaria and in Gaza—Israel will become a state with an Arab majority and will lose its Jewish identity.

The future that Israel is marching towards is going to be influenced by new weapons systems—missiles, nuclear, and cybernetics—which will greatly strengthen the security and defence challenges we shall have to confront. The answer to this danger cannot be limited to protective weaponry. The enmity must also be reduced.

Except for the new types of weapons, there are increasingly new modes of warfare that threaten Israel even without the deployment of firearms: protests on the border, a growing use of media and social media, etc.

The lack of progress towards an accord is strengthening the Arabs' argument and is causing many states to reduce their support for Israel and adopt the Palestinians' talking points. This phenomenon is being felt in Europe and Latin America. The United States' influence over these countries is lessening, and it is doubtful the American president is in full agreement with the present policies of the Israeli government.

The uprising in the Arab world was born as a protest against the domestic situation in the Arab states. But in the absence of a solution to the Israeli-Palestinian conflict— the extremist camp, which rejects Israel's existence, will place the Palestinian issue at the top of its agenda. The uprising that was supposed to bring democracy will be turned against Israel. This change is already evident on the streets of Cairo.

An anti-Israel regime in Cairo will help Hamas transform Gaza into a state of sorts, where terror will reign. If diplomatic relations are broken off—it's doubtful whether day-to-day security will be preserved.

In order to avert these dangers in large part, we need friends.

Our most meaningful friend is the United States. Washington sees the promotion of the Israeli-Palestinian peace process as serving the American interest well. But it is doubtful whether we shall be able to secure coordination with the United States without taking its opinions and positions into consideration.

The political options:

Based on the talks conducted in recent weeks, it seems to me that it is possible to reach the following agreement:

The Palestinians will be brought back to the negotiating table if they are invited to these talks by the president of the United States.

The Palestinians understand that there will be no agreement on a Palestinian state without the provision of an answer to Israel's security needs, and therefore the delineation of the border and the satisfaction of these security needs are one and the same thing.

The Palestinians are willing to accept our condition about the demilitarisation of their future state.

They accept that the basis for the discussion is the 1967 territories and not the 1967 borders, and that is in order to take into consideration the settlement blocs that will remain under Israeli sovereignty and Israel's security needs. (They agree for there to be land swaps in order to enable the continued existence of the three main settlement blocs in Judea and Samaria under Israeli sovereignty.)

They are willing to join the war against terrorism and terrorist organisations.

In order to meet Israel's demands, the Palestinians accept that an Israeli withdrawal from the territories will take place gradually and not before terrorism is defeated in those territories. That is, the redeployment of the IDF following the accord will also be carried out gradually and will also be conditional on performance tests of the Palestinian side's commitments.

Additional agreements:

The question of refugees—the Palestinians agree that this matter will be resolved in an agreed and just manner (this is the best wording ever achieved, because it requires Israel's consent and does not include reference to Resolution 194, which is mentioned in the Arab Peace Initiative). The violent incidents yesterday endanger this formulation. Protests by Palestinian refugees in Syria and Lebanon (who are neither Syrian citizens nor Lebanese citizens) will likely raise the right of return again to the top of the Palestinians' lists of demands, with a retreat from the wording that is possible today (which is the only wording that will enable an agreement).

On the question of settlements—the Palestinians will suffice with verbal agreements given by the prime minister to the president of the United States.

The question of Jerusalem will be postponed till later negotiations.

On the question of a Fatah-Hamas agreement—the government that will be formed will not be a unity government, but a technocratic government exclusively answerable to the president of the Palestinian Authority (who among other things, will also insist on [Salam] Fayyad continuing to serve as prime minister).

The negotiations will not be brought for the approval of the PLO or Palestinian National Council. Mahmoud Abbas will handle the talks with Israel by himself, independently. He is also committing to reach "one government, one gun", and it is clear to him that reunification [between the West Bank and Gaza] will not be completed without the fulfilment of this condition.

On the matter of the termination of the cash transfers—this money belongs to the Palestinian Authority. Stopping the transfer of this money will weaken the Palestinian camp that is responsible for effective security coordination with Israel, will destabilise the economic agreements, and will ultimately increase the terror level.

In summary:

We have little time left at our disposal. Unless there is movement, tensions will rise and the danger of a violent deterioration will increase. Our international situation will be weakened even more. Our relations with the United States will suffer. The economy will take a hit, and the delegitimisation (including non-violent protests) will escalate. A collapse into violence will serve Iran because, among other things, it will contribute to a rise in the price of petroleum. It's doubtful whether we'll be able to reach better conditions. Without a political agreement now, however, there is a real danger that the Arab side will go back to demanding the 1947 borders and the right of return. I see your upcoming meeting with the president of the United States

as a historic, one-off opportunity to coordinate positions on matters of substance as
above, which will enable the initiation of negotiations. Such a process would advance
a solution to Israel's security needs, strengthen our alliance with the United States
and our relations with the international community, and fortify our regional position
in the face of the changes taking place in the Middle East.

I wish you every success in your important mission to the United States.
This is the time for a historic decision.

> *Regards,*
> *Shimon Peres*

Netanyahu was not happy about this letter. And the tensions rose even further when Netanyahu learned, shortly before taking off to the United States, that President Obama was going to refer in a planned speech to the 1967 lines as the basis for a permanent border. Peres told me that Netanyahu had called him in a fury, suspecting that Obama's move was coming from things the Americans had heard from us.[14] He asked Peres to call the Americans and implore them to keep the question of the 1967 lines for a conversation between him and President Obama. Molcho called me later to communicate their reservations about Peres's letter—a letter that he said was inconsistent with the connection they had formed, based on quiet and informal conversations. He suggested that Peres tell Netanyahu that this was a "non-paper": a document with no official status. But Peres did not walk back on his letter.

Netanyahu's accusations found their way to the press. *Yediot Aharonot* reported that according to a senior minister, "Netanyahu claims that Shimon Peres is the one who planted with Obama the formula that Israel would offer the Palestinians territory identical to what it conquered in 1967 ... Peres and Barak played a double game, he said, supporting him publicly but behind his back encouraging the Americans to clash with him."[15]

Netanyahu returned from the United States after an enthusiastic reception by Congress and a clash with President Obama, who was forced to correct a number of his statements when he spoke at the conference of pro-Israel lobby group AIPAC. Peres reacted to Obama's speeches with excitement, and to Netanyahu's with scathing criticism. Although Obama was not much liked in Israel, Peres regarded him as an outstanding leader. He could see a certain wisdom and intellectual depth in him and admired his conduct. Peres thought that Obama exercised an impressive self-restraint, steered clear of embarrassing fights, and contributed to the prestige of his office. Peres even defended Obama's controversial decisions. Thus, for example, he did not accept my claims that the 2014 nuclear deal with Iran was not good enough and that Obama had made a grievous error in failing to carry out his threat and attack Syria when Bashar al-Assad crossed Obama's red line and used chemical weapons. In the ongoing clash between Obama and Netanyahu, there was no mistaking that the Israeli president's sympathies lay with Obama.

When Netanyahu returned from Washington, he met with Peres and told him that he had received confirmation that Obama had adopted Peres's line.[16] Peres replied that he had not even met the Americans recently. Maybe Avi Gil spoke to them, Netanyahu wondered. "Do you imagine that Avi would say anything different from the paper we agreed on?" Peres replied. "Avi is disciplined and punctilious, and knows every dot and comma in that memo." Netanyahu insisted that every idea that Obama had brought up must have come from Peres.

Despite the criticism, Peres drew encouragement from his conversation with Netanyahu. He called me and said in a celebratory tone that he had found Netanyahu to be business-like and not at all euphoric as expected of someone who had returned from a victory lap in Washington. "It was a good meeting, and there's something to work with," he said. "Come to me immediately, we have work to do." I went to his office and Peres asked me to read his notes from his conversation with Netanyahu. I could not understand from the document what encouraging news he had heard. He directed me to a sentence that he himself had told Netanyahu: "However, a new opportunity has emerged for us. Abu Mazen has accepted Obama's formula on the matter of the territories and borders. You have also accepted them. And so there's effectively agreement on one of the most sensitive subjects." I thought these remarks were baffling, and I told Peres that he could see mountains where there was not even a shadow of a hill. But Peres was insistent. He asked me to prepare a new memo based on speeches by Obama and Netanyahu, to see what points of agreement could be gleaned from them.

Having done so, I joined Peres for lunch with some senior staff. I explained what was written in the paper I had drafted, but I stressed that Netanyahu was deceiving him. The problem was not to bridge the texts. The problem was to move Netanyahu from his opposition toward the agreement whose price we all knew. I said that it was time for Peres to draw his own conclusions. "As president, you have an obligation to the nation to speak the truth as you see it, because you think we're careering towards a national tragedy." Peres replied that he would continue to "befuddle" everyone. That we had made progress with Netanyahu. After all, we had come to this far-reaching document. I told him: we have failed. Netanyahu had not honored the memo. He had neither discussed it nor built upon it. Peres said that we had special ties with the Arabs and the United States and had to take advantage of them. I told him that recent events had rendered us worthless and untrustworthy. We had been speaking for ourselves, without reflecting Netanyahu's positions at all. "History will judge you on whether you were loyal to your vision of peace," I told him, "or whether you gave it up for popularity and a connection with the prime minister. Do you not fear that people will conclude you effectively gave Netanyahu back-up for a policy that's leading to disaster? That you acted against the vision you had fought for your whole life?"

On Friday night, the journalist Rina Matzliah said on television that there were widespread reports of an understanding between Netanyahu and Peres. Netanyahu was allowing Peres to conduct diplomatic talks that were non-binding but bought him Peres's support. There were even rumors that Netanyahu had promised legislation that would extend Peres's term in office. Former Kadima party minister Haim Ramon called and asked sarcastically: Does Peres finally understand what's going on? In the Kadima Party, the anger at Peres was growing. In the view of Kadima's leaders, which was relayed to me many times, a shift in the popular president's attitude to Netanyahu would help their party, because it would undermine Prime Minister Netanyahu's public support.

We're Rushing Headlong into a Wall

Peres sought to take advantage of an upcoming visit to Rome to meet Mahmoud Abbas again. The two men had been invited to celebrate the 150th anniversary of Italy's unification. Before his departure, Peres met with Netanyahu and told me that he could not detect any positive movement. Netanyahu had even added a new condition: Israel would not come to talks with Abbas if Fatah reconciled with Hamas. In his record of their conversation, Peres wrote: "I had a heavy heart. How shall I convince Abu Mazen to give up on the agreement with Hamas? Avi Gil did not make things easier for me. If I had any doubts, he was certain that Bibi is toying with me and his intentions are not serious. I have nevertheless decided to try."

The meeting with Abbas in Rome on June 2, 2011, led nowhere. Peres's optimism was shaken. He allowed himself to speak most freely in private conversations that leaked to the press and contained criticism of Netanyahu. *Haaretz* published the headline: "President Shimon Peres: We're Rushing Headlong into a Wall."[17] It was also said that Peres had warned that Israel was in danger of ceasing to exist as a Jewish state. Peres told me that Netanyahu had phoned him angrily after the publication and said that no prime minister in Israeli history had given the president as much diplomatic room for action as he had. Peres replied that he too, for his own part, was helping the prime minister enormously. Netanyahu claimed that Peres was not being considerate of his electorate, while he (Netanyahu) was being considerate of him. Peres replied that he had no electoral constituency and was the president of the whole nation.

Netanyahu wrapped up the argument by saying that he was not in the mood to come for their scheduled meeting that day. I calmed Peres down and told him that I was happy about the headline. "You wouldn't have forgiven yourself if you hadn't gone on record as someone who spoke his mind, especially when in your view the situation is so grave. Netanyahu needs you. It's not good for him to get into an argument with you. He must understand that you have alternatives. That's the only way he'll respect you." Peres, agitated, looked like he needed some words of reassurance.

In parallel to Peres's efforts, the Quartet[18] was also trying to come up with a formula to resume negotiations. Erekat made clear to Peres during a meeting at his home that for Abbas, another failure in a fresh round of negotiations was not an option, and that he was considering directing his political efforts toward the United Nations.[19] "Our position is known: we recognise Israel. We are open to land swaps of 1.9 percent on the basis of the 1967 lines. It's not a sacred percentage and it doesn't appear in the Quran. We're willing to consider a counteroffer. But we won't be able to return to square one. Israel, under Olmert, already officially offered land swaps of 6.5 percent. We want to know what the United States' position is to bridge this gap. We will not enter talks with Israel without an American guarantee that the talks are serious."

Netanyahu Wants Me to Conduct Negotiations on Borders

The fact that the Palestinians intended to go to the United Nations to secure recognition of their statehood aroused concerns in Jerusalem. For Peres—it aroused new expectations. He met Netanyahu for a four-hour-long conversation[20] and updated me that he had found the prime minister to be very much interested in his help "to meet Abu Mazen quickly and negotiate with him on borders." According to Peres, Netanyahu asked for a map that would allow 90 percent of the settlers to remain in their homes.

I was surprised. Was Netanyahu really willing to open up a map and sketch borders? I recalled a dinner with him in Peres's house. I had gone to get a drink from the kitchen exactly when Peres raised the subject of borders. Netanyahu must have feared that I was going to get a map and said almost in panic: "Don't bring me any maps." And now he was asking us to talk to the Palestinians about borders?

My wall of skepticism had cracked. In our conversations, Peres as usual brought up ideas that he thought were creative and I thought were groundless. For example: to offer mutual Israeli autonomy over the Ariel bloc (under Palestinian sovereignty) and Palestinian autonomy over the Umm al-Fahm bloc (under Israeli sovereignty). I feared that such ideas would help Netanyahu veer off point. I told Peres that there was no symmetry between these settlements, and that most residents of Umm al-Fahm did not want a change in their legal status and that there was no chance that Abbas would accept the idea. Peres replied that we had to think outside the box. He thought that this would enable him to obtain Avigdor Lieberman's support. Lieberman supported exchanges of populated areas, and Peres cunningly tried to craft an agreement that would preserve the integrity of Netanyahu's coalition. He also repeatedly suggested that Europe build the Palestinians an island opposite Gaza. And after I scoffed that the Palestinians would be offended that he was giving them an island in water in the future in exchange for land on the ground now, he replied, "It would be a gesture. They'd have a port, a commercial centre, an airport—there'd be employment there for half a million workers. And it would also be a base from which Fatah could seize control of Gaza." I could not resist the temptation and wrote Peres some verses about his vision for an island:

Jazeerat Shamoun

Gaza's collapsing, and it needs a miracle,
Hamas isn't helping, as ever inimical.
The youth are enraged, the public's all gloom,
Unemployment and violence, it all could go boom.

We know that there's only one fix in existence,
It's close by to Gaza, a mere hopping distance.
An omelette will soon make an egg, never fear.
High up on the clouds, Arafat sheds a tear,
Rejoicing to see his friend Shimon, so dear.

Shimon, the miracle man, all the while,
The saviour of Gaza, who'll build it an isle.
An island of hope, a bright pearly sheen,
He'll build it an airport, hotels will be seen.
And in the new port, a ship's introduction—
Shimon's new island is under construction.

Peres read it and smiled but did not drop his idea for an island, and argued with me: "You also didn't believe that Bibi would agree for us to deal with borders. You were wrong about that and you're also wrong about the island." My wall of skepticism suffered another blow when Netanyahu recommended that Peres meet with his faithful cartographer, Danny Tirza. The mere suggestion seemed to me to be further confirmation that the development might be serious. In meetings with Tirza at the President's Office, Peres asked for options for a map based on land swaps of 4 percent. That was a figure that the Palestinians had told us was possible.

Peres wanted to arrange a meeting with Mahmoud Abbas. This time he would come armed with Netanyahu's permission to discuss territory and borders. I warned him against holding another meeting in which he would present a personal position that did not represent the prime minister's stance. I advised him to make his visit conditional on having Netanyahu approve the opening position that he would present. Peres promised that would indeed happen. I also suggested that Peres ask Netanyahu to have his confidant Yitzhak Molcho join the meeting, as a sign of his consent to Peres's offer. To my surprise, after checking with Netanyahu, Peres called me and said, "Bibi agrees."

I feared that I had treated Netanyahu unfairly. Here, for the sake of peace, the man was willing to take a meaningful risk with his voters. I recalled his promising remarks in a meeting with Peres at the beginning of his term: "I will reach an agreement that I believe in. I won't hesitate, and I'll be willing to take it to the public for early elections."

The meeting with Abbas was arranged for July 28, 2011, in Amman. Three days before, Peres hosted Erekat for dinner. Peres made it clear that he intended to present Abbas a tangible offer, and this time—with Netanyahu's consent. He decided not to detail the offer to Erekat, in order not to unnecessarily burden Abbas with doubts. "Better to lay down our cards directly in front of the Palestinian president and not mediators." After parting from Peres, Erekat told me, "I hope Peres won't let Bibi bullshit him again."

Canceling the Meeting in Amman

Netanyahu and Peres spoke the day before the planned meeting in Amman. Peres informed me glumly afterward that Netanyahu said there was a positive development in the contacts between Molcho and Tony Blair, the Quartet Middle East envoy. According to Netanyahu, the Quartet had put together a draft invitation for negotiations that looked relatively good, and this was a game-changer. Peres acknowledged bleakly that Netanyahu had backed down from the idea of having him present positions on the territorial issue in his meeting with Abbas. "Bibi asked for you to go to him. He'll explain the details to you." I rushed to the Prime Minister's Office. At first I spent two hours with Molcho, who explained that he knew nothing about the content of the talks between Peres and Netanyahu and was surprised to hear that he was meant to join Peres's meeting with Abbas. He described the progress in his talks with Tony Blair, the Quartet envoy, and said that Blair had sent a draft overnight that was starting to sound reasonable to Netanyahu.

The prime minister was at the Knesset at the time and asked for us to come to his office there. I said that it was a bad idea because reporters would see me and start sniffing around. I waited for Netanyahu at the Prime Minister's Office. I had learned not to underestimate how sharp he was. I remembered how he had left me speechless on a previous occasion, when I showed him a poll that proved that if he signed a peace treaty with the Palestinians and went to elections as the head of a new political alignment, he would remain prime minister. Netanyahu had inspected the data and asked me, "In such a case, would *you* vote for me?" Unable to force myself to give an affirmative answer, I reinforced his most basic conviction that he could not afford to betray his right-wing electoral base.

Netanyahu returned to his office, lit a cigar, and surprised me with his ease, despite the pressures and tensions surrounding the massive cost of living protests rocking Israel at the time. His thinking was sharp and lucid. I told him that I had read Blair's memo, and that we were faced with two completely different processes. One was an Israeli maneuver designed to isolate the Palestinians and to blunt their campaign at the United Nations by creating a European-American-Israeli axis. And the other, Peres's move, was meant to get to the point and was not a ploy. Peres wanted to produce a breakthrough for genuine, final-status negotiations. I said that in either case, we needed to decide what to do in tomorrow's meeting. Netanyahu said that it was important to have the meeting in order to keep that channel open. I asked him, "And what should Peres tell Abbas?" Netanyahu suggested that he explain to him why he should not appeal to the United Nations. I replied that in that case, it would be best to forgo the meeting, and that this would also be my recommendation to Peres—in order to keep the channel credible, we had to avoid fruitless meetings.

Returning to the President's Residence, I told Peres that there was a profound gulf between him and Netanyahu. You want genuine negotiations and a treaty, I told him, while Netanyahu wants to isolate the Palestinians and dissolve their support at the United Nations. I recommended that he put his foot down and not travel without a genuine mandate to present a position on borders. He asked me to return to him early in the morning[21] before he spoke with Netanyahu. I stressed the need for him to be insistent. Netanyahu needed him now, in light of the cost of living protests.

Peres was tempted to travel to Jordan. He believed that he would manage to pull a winning rabbit out of his hat at the last minute. I told him that if he went, he would justify the perception of Netanyahu's staff that his support could be bought at a low price: the right to play games on the diplomatic playing field.

Peres and Netanyahu spoke the following day, on the morning of the planned meeting with Abbas. It was ultimately agreed in their conversation that we would ask to postpone the meeting. Peres asked me to convey the message to Erekat. I insisted that he must speak personally with Abbas, since he was talking about postponing a meeting that might one day preoccupy future historians. Peres agreed. He explained to Abbas that he was still not ready for a meaningful conversation as promised, and that he did not want to waste his time. Abbas later explained to reporters that when Peres called him, he was already en route to Amman and had to turn around and drive back to Ramallah.

A few days later, I gave free rein to my feelings at a lunch with Peres: are you not afraid that by waiting for Netanyahu to come around and tortuously maintaining tactical discipline, you'll end your time in office full of remorse and regret for not having warned about the dangers you see? Peres told me that he thought he had brought Netanyahu closer to the right positions. Peace was more important than anything—even the personal considerations I had listed. "I will not take my popularity to the grave," he said. "I am convinced that reality will force Bibi to go for an agreement. Economic sanctions against Israel will soon grow stronger. That way Bibi will understand it's impossible to continue like this."

Nevertheless, at a certain stage something snapped in Peres's optimistic faith that Netanyahu would surprise him and make peace. Nothing came of another meeting with Abbas in Amman on February 26, 2012. Abbas spoke despairingly of the prospects for a breakthrough and warned that the Israeli prime minister would find himself responsible for the entire territory between the river and the sea. "I believe that if I were negotiating with you," he told Peres, "we would reach an agreement." Peres did not deny it. He also became more outspoken. In his speech at the official ceremony commemorating the Zionist visionary Theodor Herzl, Peres warned that Israel's settlement of the territories threatened to change Israel's demographic balance and endanger its Jewish character. In the wake of his statement, *Haaretz* printed a paid announcement signed by settler leaders: "Peres is endangering Israel." It called for him to be ousted and replaced by a "representative president who prefers the interests of the Jewish people and not those of the Arabs." I told Peres that I was happy about the announcement because it was evidence that he was willing to risk brutal attacks from the right, was sticking to his guns, and was not deterred from telling the public what he thought even at the cost of endangering his popularity.

We Can't Do This Alone

Peres's disillusionment with Netanyahu on the Palestinian issue also contributed to his increased boldness and audacity on the Iranian issue. There was a real turning point in mid-August 2012, when he addressed the possibility of an Israeli strike on Iran in a television interview: "Now, it's clear to us that we can't do it alone. We have to proceed together with America."[22] These remarks, which reflected what had been on his mind for months, provoked a backlash from Netanyahu's office. The press reported that "Peres is taking on Netanyahu and Barak on the Iranian issue—and says that Israel does not have the ability to attack Iran's nuclear facilities alone."[23] I called Peres to congratulate him on his remarks and I discovered that he felt relieved. He had finally relaxed his self-imposed discipline and told the public what he thought. The harsh reactions from the prime minister's bureau were swift to come. Peres was accused of having made "cardinal" mistakes with regard to national security:

He was wrong when he thought that after the Oslo Accords there would be a New Middle East here, when in reality that process claimed more than a thousand Israeli victims in terror attacks emanating from the territories that he handed to the Palestinians. He was wrong when he said that after the Disengagement there would be peace in Gaza, when in reality rockets are being fired from there at Israeli civilians. And his biggest mistake was in 1981, when he thought that bombing the reactor in Iraq was a mistake.

Peres stood steadfast against these attacks, and he was not put off when the papers reported on "an unprecedented crisis between the president and the prime minister," saying people close to Benjamin Netanyahu had said that "Peres has forgotten what the president's role is in the State of Israel."

"I believe there's a diminishing chance that we'd attack Iran alone," he later told me proudly.[24] Peres even told me with pride repeatedly how "the two gentlemen" (Netanyahu and Barak) had met with him to try to discourage him from making further pronouncements on the subject of Iran, accusing him of undermining the government's policy and messages. "They threatened me, and I told them that I had a duty to the truth."[25]

10

Final Words

Peres's methods did not change when he turned 90, but his strengths were not what they used to be. Relative to his age, he was of course a walking miracle. He had a jam-packed diary, made exhausting journeys in Israel and abroad, and wrote countless speeches. His curiosity was insatiable. He was a compulsive reader and was always eager to discuss the latest book he had read.

I tested him on the "Shimon Post," the collection of articles from the international press that I sent him every morning, and found that he rarely skipped a single piece. He never shook off the political bug. When I told him that some on the Left were contemplating suggesting that he resign his post and lead the peace camp in the 2013 elections, he replied, "I might do that." He complained to me sometimes that he felt lonely in the President's Residence, especially on weekends. "You, my friends, helped me board a luxury yacht and left me alone on the deck." I suggested that he come to Tel Aviv on Saturday, because most of his friends were there. Peres replied that as the president of the whole People of Israel, he refrained from traveling on Shabbat. He would not budge when I told him that even a president is entitled to a private life. Peres also explained that he felt obligated to pay back the religious MKs for supporting him in the vote for president. In my heart I suspected that perhaps his innate political instinct was instructing him, even at the age of 90, to maintain the rabbis' support in case he ran for prime minister again.

But alongside his untiring ambition, he also showed signs of ageing. When he was tired, he looked like an old man napping at an old age home. He declared that history was of no importance and that it was a shame to waste time on it, but this lesson did not apply to his own history. In his more difficult moments, he steered conversations toward petty score-settling with past rivals and the injustices inflicted on him by party leaders, chiefly Rabin. He never tired of saying that the Palestinians were to blame for his defeat in the 1996 elections by failing to stop terrorism and the suicide bombings. In diplomatic talks with world leaders, he scarcely let them get a word in edgeways.

He remained enchanted by the wonders of science and was convinced that the future would look completely different from the reality we know. The study of the brain captured his imagination. Given global problems and the ineffectiveness of global governance institutions, the study of the brain would allow for individual rule and self-restraint. He refused to listen when I presented him with the ethical problems inherent in connecting man and machine and attempting to change human nature. He intended to recommend to Obama to adopt the study of the brain as a central focus in his 2012 election campaign. "Just like Kennedy excited America with his vision of a moon landing, Obama can present his vision of cracking the greatest mystery of all—the human brain."

Sometimes I reproached myself: why was I still pestering Peres about the dying hope of Oslo? The presidency had been good for him, and I was spoiling the atmosphere of satisfaction. In the final year of his presidency, I even suggested—in vain—that he resign in order to cause a public drama that would communicate his feeling that Netanyahu was leading Israel toward disaster. I felt that by helping to produce the five Israeli Presidential Conferences, I was compensating somewhat for the occasional grief I had given him. I was the content manager for the conferences. It was obvious to me that an annual international conference under his sponsorship had to look toward tomorrow, and that was indeed how we built the agenda. I was delighted to see how happy Peres was during the conferences. He was charmed by the abundance of the assembled brilliant minds and listened to them speak with curiosity and excitement. They came because of him and for him. At the end of every conference, no decent person could avoid the question: who else but Peres could bring such people together in Jerusalem?

Peres relished the public's love. Even after he left office, he was in no rush to get involved in political scuffles that would have eroded the legacy of his presidency. I tried to persuade him several times to be more aggressive. "You're still acting in a statesmanlike manner, as if you were still president. The popularity you amassed is not the goal but a tool that must be used, even at the cost of eroding it. If, as you say, you don't sleep at night because you're so concerned for Israel's future—bang on all the drums."

"I have only one bullet in my gun," Peres used to reply. "I must shoot at the right time. The time is not yet ripe."

On the eve of Israel's 2015 elections, I convinced Peres to deliver a dramatic speech warning the public against Netanyahu. We decided at the last moment, in internal consultations, to cancel the speech. The fear was that the Likud would turn Peres into a target for all the old hatred toward him and thus excite dormant right-wing voters to head to the voting stations. We agreed that these sections of the public did not harbor the same hostility and hatred toward Labour leader Isaac (Bougie) Herzog as they might for Peres.

I later wondered about the extent to which public adoration for Peres, which so enchanted him and influenced his behavior, might have been only a fragile illusion, its existence conditional on never being put to the test. Peres wanted the public's love, but his challenging vision was not always consistent with this desire. He looked far ahead and was enthralled by the winds of change shaping our tomorrow. He was borne on the wings of his imagination into the future and struggled to understand why mere mortals felt threatened and could not comprehend the new and exciting reality taking shape before their eyes. When he explained that territory had lost its significance because the real source of wealth was in the human mind, few saw this as a justification for territorial compromise. When he argued that our Arab enemies could change their spots and live in peace, many sections of the Israeli public dismissed him as naively ignoring the most basic reflex, to be suspicious of foreigners and never trust their intentions.

I had my own thoughts about aspects of Peres's philosophy. I saw peace between nations as the desirable—if transient—product of balances of power in an unforgiving world ruled by interests, competition, and a rapacious and fickle human nature. But I remained enthralled by the sweeping worldview that propelled Peres. When he told Abbas that Palestine would be a "democratic and science-oriented state," I protested, "Why do you think Abbas will be impressed by the scientific future you've assigned Palestine?" But on second thought, I felt a profound admiration for his loyalty to his vision.

Peres was a leader of practical action. He knew how to build coalitions, make compromises, and sometimes even perform tactical retreats without losing direct line of sight with his greater vision. Peres was influenced by his advisors and revised his opinions in an ongoing process of dialogue with those close to him, but he was responsible for his overall conceptual outlook. And therefore the solutions that he often borrowed from others were meant to answer questions that followed from a great, comprehensive vision that was all his.

The "Peres Formula" was complex and had an inner logic: optimism about human nature, faith in human progress drawing on scientific and technological developments, Judaism as a moral base (with an emphasis on the Ten Commandments), and an adherence to the principles of a humanistic Zionism and social democracy. He was a unique leader, and I revered him for operating effectively in political swamp true to a vision—and true to his worldview.

I Loved Her Personality because She Was My Opposite

The closer Peres drew to his final day, the more conciliated I found him to be. He gave free rein to his sense of humor and expressed his affection for me in a manner that was freer and less stilted. Often when we had lunch together, he asked me to call my mother Aviva. Peres had learned to acknowledge and value her sharp tongue and merciless observations. To my shame, I never asked her permission and put her on speakerphone so Peres could listen to her scathing criticism of our country's leaders, whose names Peres whispered to me in the course of the conversation so I could direct her answers.

Peres did not escape her remarks either. "Mum, what should Shimon do?" I asked her once. "Bibi's making his life hell."

"Come on, seriously, Avi," she snapped, "are you blind? Can't you see for yourself? Bibi only does what Sara decides for him, and your Peres is an old man, he should go home. I love him, but enough already. How much longer can we hear that old man's Polish accent?" Peres, ever the gentleman, listened to her with bemusement. He loved this little break, in which the constraints of political correctness were completely lifted. He knew that Aviva's comments were the truth as she saw it, without any of the disguises and manipulations that so characterized the political world in which he had spent most of his life.

Peres mentioned my mother of his own accord in a prerecorded sixtieth birthday message arranged by my son Eliav:

> There's nothing funnier or more entertaining than a conversation between Avi and his mother. It's rare. It's an otherworldly business ... Aviva is a woman who wakes up every morning with her own sunshine. She doesn't accept the sky she's given. The sun that exists. She has fresh perspectives. And she's incapable of hiding or not saying her thoughts. It's not that her tongue says what's on her heart—it's that her tongue has no more patience to wait for her heart. She freely expresses remarkable opinions, which is sometimes embarrassing but always refreshing.

Only after Peres passed away did I connect the dots between how he spoke about my mother's candor and what he had told me about his wife Sonia. In interviews that I conducted with him before writing this book, the following was said:

> *Sonia told me once that she feels a certain anger towards you. She told me: he used to leave with his flock in the morning and come back with his flock in the evening. We lived a simple life, a life connected to the land. The life of kibbutzniks. That was exactly what I wanted. And then suddenly he was a leader, he was a politician, a minister—I didn't plan it this way. And she tells me, that's what she's angry about. Are you aware of that?*

Figure 12 Amused by a toy chicken at the President's Residence. January 23, 2012. (Photo: President's Office)

Of course. Of course I'm aware.

And what do you think of that? Is she right?

From her point of view, yes, she's right. Generally, between the two of us, I think she's right. I couldn't have gone for what was right personally. I was pulled away by other things.

But tell me, when you walked around with your cows on the meadows of Kibbutz Alumot, or when you spent your honeymoon in a tent on the banks of the Jordan, did you ever think that one day you might sit here in the President's Residence or you might be a political leader? What did you think you'd do when you grew up?

First of all, you have to understand I was in insanely love with Sonia. A true, deep love, the love of my life ... I loved her personality not because she suited me but because she was my opposite.

How was she your opposite?

With everything.

For example?

A simple life, a life of nature ... I wanted to seduce her, so I read her Karl Marx. What a fool. I was a complete fool. You get the misunderstanding? I thought romance meant this kind of sophistication, and she thought true beauty was in nature.

Re-reading these words, I remember our preparations for the secret visit to Jordan on November 2, 1993. As I said earlier, after Peres had donned on his wig, he called Sonia over and asked for her opinion on how he looked. Sonia did not hesitate for a second and replied, "You look like a retard." On another occasion, when he was fuming against Chabad's support for Netanyahu in the 1996 elections, Peres said, "In my opinion, they're like the Ku Klux Klan."[1]

"You're talking rubbish," replied Sonia with evident anger.

That was the language and style with which my mother reacted, too. The two women were similar in their directness. In their total honesty and the complete compatibility between their feelings and words. When Peres mentioned his profound love for Sonia to me, he longingly stressed how they had had different personalities. Peres, because of his character and the career he had chosen, was used to concealing no small part of what was on his mind. Strategy and pretenses are inseparable from politics and statecraft and the endless negotiations they involve. The need to win public support requires politicians to cultivate an image in the media that is appropriate for their mission, even if that image does not always reflect the inner truth in their hearts. Sometimes I wondered how many scabs had to be picked away from Peres to reach the man himself. I felt that I was among the few people Peres allowed to pierce through his scabs, through the armor of his pretenses.

Only after his death did I begin to think, and forgive me if I am being insufficiently modest, that Peres's affection for me might have also come from his affection for those who, besides their love and devotion for him, did not shy from telling him the truth and in language that was blunt, simple, and sometimes even hurtful. For my prerecorded birthday message, my son Eliav asked Peres to choose one stand-out negative quality and one positive quality that he saw in me. On the negative side, he accused me of "unnecessary skepticism." On the positive side he said, "He tells people to their face what he thinks." When he was asked to state his greeting in brief, he said, "I wish for you not to change. Keep saying the things people are afraid to say." Peres allowed me, completely naturally, to be myself. For his own part, he took great care over his wardrobe and reveled in the compliments he received for looking dapper in his tailored suits. At the end of one conversation with Bill Clinton, he asked me, "Did you notice his suit?" I had not, I admitted. "It's creased," he said. "He clearly has no one by his side to notice these things."

But despite the importance he attached to his attire, he was tolerant of my own appearance. Although he occasionally gave me elegant ties, he made his peace soon enough with the knowledge that he would find me by his side without them, and he never grumbled about how I came to meet him at the President's Residence without a buttoned-down shirt. "Maybe come for dinner with the French foreign minister tonight," he offered me once, before continuing with a mischievous look, "and maybe also consider, in honour of the occasion, coming with your festive black Crocs and not your usual blue ones."

The Right to Have the Final Word

I could have ended this book with a trenchant statement about Peres's greatness. A great, unique leader. A man who created two milestones that will long outlive him: Dimona and Oslo. One is a symbol of his contribution to Israel's security; the other, of his daring strides toward peace. A stride that had become possible after Israel's existence was already guaranteed, largely thanks to him.

I could have ended with an incisive comment on Peres's dying wish that we, the Israelis, continue the march to peace. I could also have ended on a personal note about our special connection—about how much I love and miss him. But instead, I have decided to give Peres the right to the final word. I had several long conversations with him before writing this book. We agreed on their purpose: I would present him some central issues in my book, some of which also raised critical questions about his actions; Peres would respond. He cooperated gladly and encouraged me to write and publish my impressions, whatever they may be. I have selected his main points from the transcript of our conversations. Here and there I have lightly edited his remarks to divide them by subject and render his interrupted speech more readable.

There were junctions at which I saw you making weighty decisions that confronted Rabin with a fait accompli. When you sent Uri Savir to Oslo, for example. Did you not overstep your authority?

That's a good question, and it's a question of style. It wasn't the first time I did that, and it wasn't the last. When there's a large part of an issue that's ready for a decision, at the last minute people are afraid to decide. At that last minute, I come in and take the risk.

Let me give you an example. On the eve of the Suez Campaign, Bourgès-Maunoury[2] called me over, showed me the plan, and started interrogating me. From my answer, he could tell that we were ready to go. When we left, I was with Yosef Nachmias,[3] who was a good friend of mine. He told me: "Shimon, the truth? We should have taken a tree, strung a rope, and hanged you. Based on what are you giving him this impression? Who gave you that right? Do you know what you're doing? Two world powers and you haven't even spoken to anyone."

I told him, "Listen, Yosef, it was said the government would decide, right? So what. So they'll tell me 'no'. But if they want to say 'yes', it'll be too late. That's why I take the risk and say 'yes'."

Now, I think I was being OK, because what could happen? I say "yes," the government decides "no." So what? But if I hadn't said "yes," the whole business would have been over. And I was in favour of the operation. Same thing here. I know Rabin. And I assume he would have moaned. If he had remembered everything precisely. Since I don't know, I imagine that my memory is more accurate than his ... He's got the temperament of a redhead [Hebrew slang for a hot temper]. That is, what he says first, that's the redhead talking. What he says second, that's less redheaded. So when the redhead talks to me, I think to myself: give it a minute, he'll calm down. Same thing with Arik [Sharon]. [When I proposed a diplomatic move with the Palestinians,] his initial reaction <mimicking Sharon's agitated voice with a smile>: "But they're killing Jews." I let him calm down and sat with him the next day, to tell him even more difficult things. I can work out what an initial reaction is ...

Rabin was miserable [on certain occasions, if] I went to him, he'd tell me—no. And he'd regret it inside. I reasoned that if I didn't ask him, I'd make things easier for him. Quite simply ... I knew I was clean. That I was serving the nation.

You're cutting corners a bit. He was the prime minister, you were the foreign minister, you picked a goal and latched onto it. And you wouldn't let anyone stand in your way. Including nobody above you?

Correct.

He was the prime minister, and he'd still be prime minister the next day. You were heading to your destination?

Correct.

And if while approaching your destination, he didn't know everything or found out later—so be it? Am I exaggerating?

No. I go for it all. I take a risk. It's not that I'm disparaging him. I think that losing a risk is a greater danger than taking it … I learnt with a man who really was the biggest genius there was. Do you think that he [Ben-Gurion] gave me clear instructions? Do you think he wanted to know everything? You don't think I kept a few steps ahead? But I'll tell you what, he was a great man, he loved it. He knew this was the advantage with me.

But he gave you the space.

He didn't stop me, and he didn't give me instructions …

You're basically saying: because I can see the goal, and I completely believe that this is the right thing to do, then it doesn't really matter what my role is?

Correct. Whenever I can serve a cause and I can defend it … Man is the most anti-administrative being there is. This whole division of labour is stupid. [In reality]—everyone steps on the others' toes … Hierarchies are only needed in the military. In politics, hierarchies are artificial. If I overstepped my authority and succeeded—that's fine … For a bird like me, sitting in an administrative cage is a waste of time. I'm not interested in whether the bars are made of gold or silver. Why would that interest me? I look at where I want to fly. The rest is less important. After all, I'm not doing it for personal reasons or for any personal profit.

The road to Oslo and the signing. Was that an attempt to influence history?

No. It was a historic opportunity that could either be missed or seized. It was up in the air. Look, not everyone was keen on Oslo at the time. The extremists said it was bloodshed, it was a disgrace. And those who were [in favour] of Oslo, don't defend it. They don't defend it, and they don't take pride in it.

Because they made two arguments. First, that Oslo did not bring peace like it claimed. Second, that Oslo cost 1,000 lives because there was an intifada afterwards.

And there wouldn't have been an intifada anyway? What's the connection? That's an old wives' tale. The difficulty with Oslo was the pairing-up with Arafat. Since people remember him as a deeply, deeply disliked character, any association with him is unpleasant, it's uncomfortable. And on the side in favour, Oslo's defenders are extremely cautious. They don't want to be depicted as having believed Arafat or been connected with Arafat, no way.

I wrote a chapter on Oslo in the book, and I gave it the temporary title: "Oslo—the battle for peace and for credit." Why? Because I'm convinced that Oslo was largely the creation of one man—you. There was one man who dragged Rabin to Oslo. Without that, this wouldn't have happened. And that man is called Shimon Peres. And therefore, for better or worse, Oslo was your creation … But on the other hand, there was work by other people … all of whom wanted the credit for themselves. How do you live in a world like that?

I think that I made Oslo and I lost the personal credit for it. I live with it.

Is my analysis right, do you think?

Yes … I'll tell you what happened like this. Rabin was under two impressions. One, he knew the Elyakim business[4] was coming to an end. Two, he thought that what I was offering had no chance. There's very simple proof for that … Asked why he didn't tell anyone, he answered honestly: I didn't think anything would come of it. That's why he gave me some rope, so to speak. But look, the person following this, and he wasn't stupid, was Terje.[5] Terje told me that they actually wanted to give the Nobel Prize just to me. Then they said, that's not good for the Palestinians, they were being political. But I saw the game very transparently.

As early as the 1970s, in a Knesset debate about the PLO, someone said: this leopard cannot change its spots. And you replied: if the leopard does change its spots and turns into a cat, then we'll pat the cat. We'll fight the leopard.

When most of my friends analysed Arafat, they analysed him as expert psychologists, and I analysed him in an amusing way … I found out that this bandit, this man, doesn't know what he wants. He wants to be everything. He wants to be a prophet, wants to be a king, wants to be Gandhi, wants to be president, wants to be everything—everything. So childish. There was something similar with Sadat. I thought for a moment, it's a game of shadows. We can play this right. How can we play this right? Not to tell him that he'd relinquish this or that, but there would be a group of people who would praise a couple of his traits and take him in. The job was done instinctively by the Europeans, the social democratic group. Kreisky, Willy Brandt. I was for it, I was connected to them. Kreisky told me that Arafat liked music. Music? He doesn't know who Beethoven is. It was nonsense. What do I care what he tells him? He told him, he must be a European. And you know his clothes as well, he was no longer wearing a keffiyeh. He was wearing a uniform, but still not civilian dress. Though if you ever saw Sadat like a marshal, one moment the most expensive European suits, the next a galabeya in his village. What are these clothes? It's three dreams, each is different.

In my opinion, Arafat could have dreamed two contradictory dreams in the same night and still wouldn't wake up from a nightmare. In one dream he's making peace, and in the other dream he's conquering and waging war.

Let me tell you something about Arafat. To his credit. Like we discovered Arafat's weaknesses, Arafat discovered the weaknesses of the West. He also played the game, let's be fair. And he knew how to play it not badly at all. Arafat did not respect any facts. He was certain that people would believe his fantasies, his lies, no less than they would believe facts from professors. He succeeded. He seduced the whole world.

But there's still a trail of murder and blood behind Arafat, and responsibility for terrible bereavement and terrorism. What does that do to you as a leader who negotiates with him, who shakes his hand?

I think he can be let off on that. Look, I think a fish out of water will act a lot worse than a fish in the water, and if you can't give it a sea, give it an aquarium, and I also thought, let's put the fish in that aquarium. Now Arafat in my opinion also wanted to be Gandhi.

Rabin found it very difficult to shake Arafat's hand.

It wasn't difficult for me. Because Rabin saw him as an enemy, and I saw him as a person.

How can you see him as a person with all that history?

He amused me. I thought he also had potential. Just like he did a lot of nonsense, he could also do some positive nonsense.

You're very forgiving.

Yes, it's a waste of my time, if you're going after offence. There are a few things that waste your life. Offence, rest, sleep.

The Arab states wanted to annihilate us. The conflict was existential. You're convinced that the existential nature of the conflict has changed?

Yes. It's changed not in terms of their will, but their ability. The Arabs know in their hearts that it'd be tough to annihilate us. There was a time they thought they'd annihilate us with ease. An international boycott, armies—till the Yom Kippur War, they were convinced that there was a chance of exterminating us. On Yom Kippur they started to have doubts, and then the situation changed.

But in their hearts, there's no love for our existence here?

Today yes, in their hearts, [but] this time their heads have kicked into action. Back then, their hearts and their heads were saying the same thing, that was possible to annihilate us. Today, the heart wants to destroy us, but the head says it mustn't. Quite simply. That's the major difference. Apart from that, I think the Arabs are also changing, they've changed, they don't have a choice. They can't be cross with history. I don't see a future for Islam. It will give in. The young generation will subdue it, science will subdue it.

You're both a political leader and a man of thinking and books. The first is decisive and full of confidence in where he's going, the second is meant to be skeptical. As a leader, you have to make decisions and convince others to follow you. How do you live with this internal contradiction?

I can't be a public figure and sow doubts. They don't go together. If I see a reason to doubt, no one will believe me. They won't understand, why's he causing a fuss? You have to appear decisive … A leader is someone who even if he has question marks, has to make exclamation marks. No one will follow question marks.

When there's something of a gamble in a decision. Or uncertainty. How do you decide?

There's a myth that man can decide between good and bad. There's no such choice, because good and bad are always mixed up. Therefore you need to decide about two cocktails of good and bad. The difference between them is not 100 percent [but] 51–49. Take for example the question of the release of Gilad Shalit. There's no doubt that it's a source of encouragement for Hamas. Hamas will gain materially, but we'll gain morally.

When you went to Oslo, when you decided to launch Operation Grapes of Wrath, or when you decided to go for the Dimona project—was that also 49 to 51?

Yes. I work on the basis of the alternatives.

On what basis do you decide?

Since you need to decide, you can't carry on without a decision. So how should you decide? I prefer the 51 to the 49.

Do you think there's a basic difference in human nature between a young Israeli soldier and the young men in Hamas?

They each represent their own nation's culture. For the Arabs in their culture, honour is the most important thing. Honour is more important than life. That's why if you take an Arab's honour, he's ready to die. That's how he was raised from the moment he tasted his mother's breast milk. Israeli soldiers aren't like that. They're from a different culture, that says you need to defend yourself but you don't need to attack. So there's a clash of cultures here, in that respect.

What drew you to politics? Why aren't you a banker, a scientist, an author, a contractor?

Admiration is more important than money. For politicians, admiration is their money. They need it like an actor needs an audience. It's the same principle, it's the same stage. A politician is like an actor who can't act without an audience. Look at Madonna at home, and look at Madonna on the stage. That's the difference. At home, she's a normal woman. But when she goes on stage, it's electric.

What's the meaning of this need for the public's love?

To reach a goal, I need support. Attitudes towards me went both ways, there was a lot of hatred for me but also a lot of love. There were people who from a young age admired me, and people who from a young age hated me. I didn't know how to behave with enemies, I didn't know either how to behave with those who loved me, with neither of them.

To what extent is politics a field where you always have to make compromises?

You have to make compromises to achieve the most important thing. If you compromise on the most important thing, then you don't have that most important thing. For the sake of that most important thing, you have to build coalitions. If you only go down one stream, you'll discover it's a narrow stream.

You have to make streams merge. The compromise is over the path, but not over the most important thing. I think that in my heart, when I decide on something, I insist on it like a bulldog. But to achieve it, I don't mind making compromises.

In the world of science, you can't make compromises in which you agree that water evaporates at 70 degrees so that someone else will agree that water freezes at 15 degrees.

It's not the same. It's the difference between a scientist and a politician. That a scientist is judged by elites, and a politician by the masses. Since their audiences are completely different, the rules are also different. In politics, the common denominator is the lowest standard—in science, it's the highest standard. I don't feel I can satisfy the masses at their standard. I think I can raise the standard. Politics is dialectic, not confrontational. I mean, you've got thesis and antithesis and you need to create synthesis. That's the art of politics, because politics combines negative and positive, there's no choice. That is, I don't think things are born separated—[as if] there's positive and negative. It's all mixed up. And if I want to transform it into energy, I have to use that mixture. Everything's mixed up, and politics is always a combination of the 49 percent and the 51 percent. It's not 100 percent, there's no politics of 100 percent. Just like human nature is built from a mixture of good and bad.

What do you feel about the popularity you enjoy today?

Today I'm the most popular man in the State of Israel, it's taken me 60 years. I had to pass through seven circles of hatred and contempt, and I didn't despair. You saw that even on the day I lost the elections, I got up the next day as if nothing had happened. You throw a stone in the water, and the water changes slowly-slowly. So I'm changing the topography.

If you had to take two or three friends to a desert island?

de Gaulle.

Why?

A giant. An intellectual giant.

And what would you talk to him about?

About everything. There's no subject you can't discuss with him.

From cheese to atom.

From cheese to women. There's no subject you can't talk to him about. [de Gaulle is] from the ones I knew. From the ones I didn't know, Mao Zedong made a huge impression on me. His writings ... his whole life.

Which of the American presidents you knew would you take to a desert island?

For leisure, Reagan, because he was modest and friendly. For business, I'd take Clinton. He hides a lot of fire inside him, he could get angry, we never saw it, but people who work with him did. He has positive qualities: he knows how to pay a compliment, he has a sense of humour, he's charismatic, he's a wonderful conversationalist.

And who from Israel gets a passport to this island?

Alive or dead?

Whatever you want.

Moshe Dayan, Amos Oz, [Nathan] Alterman. My opinion is subjective, because all of them thought highly of me. That's one of the reasons, by the way, why I speak of them like that. Alterman, from the day he met me, when I was still a nobody. Uri Zvi Greenberg, the poet—you know when I was 20, 22, he wrote I'd be prime minister?

Did you feel you were missing an academic education?

Autodidacts are disorganised. I lack method. Order. I've never learned how to write a memo. How to read a document. I didn't know any other language but Hebrew and Yiddish till I was 26, not a word of English.

What benefit do you derive from your advisors?

Experts can give me aspects I've missed. I'm short-sighted. I can't see everything. I'm grateful when someone tells me: "Listen, there's a step here, be careful you don't slip." I need facts I don't already know, because I see myself fundamentally as an ignorant boor, and that's my advantage. That is, I learn something in detail when I need it. I don't store knowledge for knowledge's sake. I think differently from most people. There are things that make others panic that don't make me panic at all.

Give me an example.

The nuclear issue. I didn't approach it in a panic.

Who panicked?

Who? The whole country. The whole government. Even Ben-Gurion hesitated. "What will the world say about it? What will America say? They'll boycott us. What insolence." Shaul Avigur[6] said I was a charlatan. The scientists said it was unattainable. I was almost alone … My answer was very simple: if we don't do this, we're in an even greater danger. We'll be led like sheep to slaughter. I was fed up of seeing us so vulnerable that we could be finished off. That's why I said: correct, I can see the dangers, that's the 49. But the 51 was [preferable] … to the alternative, my friends?

What are your strong points?

I can think outside the box, I'm endlessly imaginative, I'm brave enough to do it, to draw the right conclusions and not take fright. I'm tremendously curious and willing to learn. I treat people well. My relations with people are not the fruit of suffering, they're the fruit of love. I love people and I'm interested in them. I'm not greedy, and I think I'm also relatively good-hearted towards everyone. I mean, if there's no special reason, I'm good-hearted.

What are your weak points?

I'm reckless. I talk too much, reveal too much, everything that goes with recklessness. Like when we returned from Jordan, for example. When I said, "Remember November 2." I regretted it. But enough, I did it. I don't know whether I have enough of the brutality that leaders need. I don't have a killer instinct, and I don't want it either. After Rabin published his book,[7] I could have banished him from politics. Everyone in the party would have supported such a move but I avoided it …

I'm not educated enough. I never learned English. I can give speeches and I can talk, but I can't write because I don't make use of it. I'm missing it. It bothers me greatly. Sometimes when I need to sign a guestbook, I'm afraid of making a mistake. I'm not sure I act correctly with people, sometimes I offend them, hurt them unintentionally. I don't notice something, [or] I don't say the things I should have said. I don't say thanks enough. Don't appreciate things enough. I feel there's a deficiency in my interpersonal relations. They're not polished enough.

On that trip to Jordan, November 1993, I thought you acted like an amazing diplomatic virtuoso, but I criticised you because you didn't give the king enough time to talk.

You're right, the criticism is valid. You keep going back to it, and I keep thinking you're right. The same with Mitchell.[8]

So what do you do?

I get washed away, I can't. Listen, it's an addiction.

What's the difference between women and men?

There's a huge difference between women and men. Two worlds. Two different planets … Women are born mature, with good sense. Men will always remain babies. Because of their different biological roles in life, women see everything differently. There's a womanly wisdom that men can't begin to understand … A woman wants to feel that she's an angel.

Are you willing to give her that feeling?

I'm built to give her that feeling.

You said once that you need to be a bit blind to give such a feeling.

Yes of course, there's no romance without blindness. In general, since there's no perfection, there's only fabricated perfection.

Alcohol helps you see things more optimistically?

Yes, certainly.

Would you be interested in experimenting with other drugs?

No.

Why not?

Because it would mess with my mind. I can drink without it messing with my mind, I can drink and improves my mood.

You said you can be reckless. When you have a drink or two, don't you become even more reckless?

Yes, but not beyond what's allowed. I permit myself to be much more relaxed. I sing, I dance, I can do all sorts of nonsense. I love life.

What are you afraid of?

I'm not afraid to fail. And I'm not afraid to die. I know it will happen. That it's unavoidable.

What happens a minute after that?

There is no minute after that. It's all over.

Notes

Chapter 1

1 Conversation between Rabin and Peres, May 15, 1993.
2 Further the Madrid Conference of 1991, which brought together Israel, the Palestinians, and Arab countries in a bid to jump-start peace talks, Israel conducted negotiations with a Jordanian–Palestinian delegation in Washington. Israel had insisted that the Palestinians be represented in the framework of a joint mission with Jordan in order to avoid discussions with the PLO and in order not to appear to accept from the outset that the Palestinians had an independent standing, which could have had consequences for the results of the agreement.
3 "Dimona"—Israel's Nuclear Research Center is also known by its unofficial title: "Dimona," a southern city located near the secret facility. In August 2018, the installation was renamed after the late Shimon Peres.
4 "Astronaut"—Hebrew slang for a person who is detached from reality, head-in-the-clouds, hovering in a world of imagination and dreams.
5 Yossi Ben-Artzi, "Mapai's Settlement Plans in Anticipation of the Establishment of the State," *Contemporary Jewry*, 10 (1996), 230–1 [Hebrew].
6 The Second Intifada (2000–5) was the Palestinian uprising against Israel that erupted following the failure of the 2000 Camp David Summit to reach a final agreement on the Israeli–Palestinian peace process. About 3,200 Palestinians and 1,000 Israelis were killed during the uprising.
7 August 2001.
8 September 28, 1995.
9 September 8, 1993.
10 Occupation—Following the Six-Day War of 1967, Israel took control over the Palestinian-populated territories of the West Bank and the Gaza Strip. (Israel withdrew from the Gaza Strip in 2005.) Many on the Israeli Left maintain that Israel's ongoing domination of another people has a morally corrupting effect on Israel itself.
11 David Levy (b. 1937) is an Israeli politician who served as a member of the Knesset, representing the Likud party (1969–2006) most of his tenure. Levy headed various government ministries, among them the Ministry of Foreign Affairs.
12 Maariv, November 7, 1990 [Hebrew].
13 Al HaMishmar, November 9, 1990 [Hebrew].

Chapter 2

1 G. R. Berridge, "Diplomacy after Death: The Rise of the Working Funeral," *Diplomacy and Statecraft* (July 1993), 217.
2 The government that was formed in 1984 was a national unity government based on a rotation between the leaders of the Alignment (Labour) and Likud parties. They

agreed that Shimon Peres would serve first as prime minister with Yitzhak Shamir as foreign minister and that they would swap roles after two years.

3   *Haaretz*, February 13, 1987 [Hebrew].
4   Menachem Begin, "Foundations of Hasbara Abroad," *Maariv*, May 2, 1975 [Hebrew].
5   Knesset protocols, February 17, 1988, 1903 [Hebrew].
6   The Palestinian National Charter, the PLO's founding document, was written in 1967 and updated in 1968. It calls for abolishing the existence of the State of Israel through armed struggle.
7   Knesset protocols, December 31, 1986, 965 [Hebrew].
8   Knesset protocols, February 17, 1988, 1913–15 [Hebrew].
9   Davar, October 10, 1986 [Hebrew].
10 May 23, 1994.
11 June 2–3, 1994.
12 The United States presented the Road Map, a diplomatic plan for solving the Israeli–Palestinian conflict, to the sides in April 2003. The plan offered guidelines for progress in three stages leading to the signing of a permanent peace settlement between Israel and the Palestinians, based on the establishment of a Palestinian state and a peace agreement between Israel and all the other Arab states.
13 Netzarim was a Jewish settlement located in the middle of the Gaza Strip, between densely populated Palestinian areas.
14 Operation Defensive Shield (2002) took place against the backdrop of the growing wave of terror attacks in the Second Intifada. This broad operation was intended to stop Palestinian terrorism and damage its infrastructure. Owing to the operation, there was a substantial reduction in the number of Palestinian terror attacks.
15 http://www.nizarqabani.com/1/the-hasteners/
16 Shimon Peres, *Reading Journal: Letters to Authors* (Tel Aviv: Yediot Aharonot, 1994), 119.
17 Gideon Samet, "Letter to Shimon Peres," *Haaretz*, December 28, 1994.
18 Geo Bogza (1908–1993), "Any Human."
19 Shimon Peres, *Battling for Peace: Memoirs* (London: Orion, 1995).
20 October 4, 1995.
21 The woman's name and a few other details have been changed to protect her identity.
22 In 1986–1988, the Foreign Ministry had two directors-general: Avraham Tamir and Yossi Beilin, who was the director-general for political affairs.
23 Ami Ayalon (b. 1945), a recipient of Israel's highest military decoration, the Medal of Valor, was nominated to head Israel's internal security service (Shin Bet) following Yitzhak Rabin's assassination in 1995.
24 August 7, 1989.
25 Peres was referring to the relations he cultivated with France starting in 1955, which led to the French arms sales to Israel, collaboration during the Suez War in 1956, and French assistance for the construction of the nuclear reactor in Dimona.
26 The document is dated November 1, 1995.
27 "The State of Palestine shall be granted extra-territorial sovereignty over the Haram ash-Sharif under the administrations of Quds Awqaf."
28 Nabil Shaath (b. 1938) served in various senior Palestine Liberation Organization (PLO) positions, including chief negotiator, cabinet minister, and acting prime minister of the Palestinian National Authority (PNA).
29 The event took place on March 13, 1996.
30 October 20, 1989.

31 October 21, 1992.
32 Abba Eban, *The New Diplomacy: International Affairs in the Modern Age* (New York: Random House, 1983).
33 Kol Israel, Yoman Hashavua, June 19, 1993 [Hebrew].
34 July 14, 1992.
35 July 7, 1993.
36 Channel 1, *Moked*, August 11, 1993 [Hebrew].
37 August 2, 1993.
38 *Al Hamishmar,* June 2, 1993 [Hebrew].

Chapter 3

1 January 29, 1995.
2 Samuel Huntington, *The Third Wave: Democratization in the Late Twentieth Century* (Norman: University of Oklahoma Press, 1991).
3 Shimon Peres, *The New Middle East* (New York: Henry Holt and Company, 1993), 44.
4 Ibid., 73.
5 The international conference held in the Spanish capital in late 1991, which was intended to advance the peace process between Israel, the Palestinians, and the broader Arab world.
6 Shimon Peres, *The New Middle East* (New York: Henry Holt and Company, 1993), 64.
7 Rainer Maria Rilke (1875–1926), free translation.
8 Early 1990s.
9 E. F. Schumacher, *Small Is Beautiful: Economics as if People Mattered* (New York: Harper and Row, 1973).
10 Faisal Husseini (1940–2001) was a Palestinian leader who served in various senior positions, among them head of the Palestinian delegation to the Madrid Middle East Peace Conference (1991), head of the Fatah faction in the West Bank, and Palestinian Authority Minister for Jerusalem Affairs.
11 Hanan Ashrawi (b. 1946) is a Palestinian political leader and scholar who served as a spokesperson for the Palestinian delegation to the Middle East peace process. In 1996, she was appointed Palestinian Authority Minister of Higher Education and Research.
12 Yasser Abed Rabbo (b. 1944) was a member of the Palestine Liberation Organization's (PLO) Executive Committee. He served in several official positions, including Culture and Arts Minister of the Palestinian National Authority (1994–2003).
13 Ahmed Asmat Abdel-Meguid (1923–2013) was an Egyptian diplomat, who served as the Foreign Minister of Egypt (1984 and 1991) and Secretary-General of the Arab League (1991–2001).
14 An economic union comprising Belgium, the Netherlands, and Luxembourg.
15 The Presidential Medal of Freedom and the Congressional Gold Medal are the two highest civilian honors in the United States.
16 President Peres's remarks at the ceremony awarding him the Presidential Medal of Freedom at the White House, June 14, 2013.

Chapter 4

1   *Yediot Aharonot,* July 26, 2002 [Hebrew].
2   Ahmed Qurei (b. 1938) (also known as Abu Ala) served in various senior positions within the Palestine Liberation Organization (PLO), among them prime minister of the Palestinian National Authority (2003–6). He headed the Palestinian negotiating team in the secret talks with Israel that led to the Oslo Accord (1993).
3   *Getting to the Table—Oslo,* discussion at the Peres Center for Peace, March 20, 1998, 36 [Hebrew].
4   The law was amended on January 19, 1993.
5   Conversation between Rabin and Peres, January 8, 1993.
6   Yossi Beilin, *Touching Peace* (Tel Aviv: Yediot Aharonot, 1997), 167 [Hebrew].
7   *Getting to the Table—Oslo,* discussion at the Peres Center for Peace, March 20, 1998, 4 [Hebrew].
8   Ibid., 2–3.
9   Ibid., 11.
10   Knesset protocols, July 8, 1975 [Hebrew].
11   Ziad Abuzayyad (b. 1940), a Palestinian editor and columnist who served, over the years, as an advisor and a member of various Palestinian negotiating teams.
12   January 9, 1993 (Jerusalem).
13   Following the murder of border policeman Nissim Toledano by Hamas members, Israel expelled 415 Hamas and Islamic Jihad operatives to Lebanon (December 17, 1992).
14   Member of Knesset Yael Dayan met Yasser Arafat and his staff in Tunis at the end of January 1993. Her visit provoked public criticism in Israel, including from the leaders of the Labour Party, with Rabin foremost among them.
15   *Yediot Aharonot,* December 23, 1992 [Hebrew].
16   February 24, 1993.
17   Aliyah–a Hebrew word that literally means "ascent" and refers to Jewish immigration from the Diaspora to Israel (and signifies an ideological motivation behind the choice to immigrate).
18   Conversation between Rabin and Peres, February 9, 1993. The government struggled to meet the challenge of absorbing the massive wave of immigration from the former Soviet Union in the early 1990s, including problems relating to housing and income.
19   *Getting to the Table —Oslo,* discussion at the Peres Center for Peace, March 20, 1998, 36 [Hebrew].
20   This logic was also expressed in the memorandum signed later by Rabin and Peres (June 27, 1995), which was first revealed by *Yediot Aharonot* on May 30, 2017, twenty-two years after it was signed. According to the memo, Peres committed not to challenge Rabin for the premiership, securing for himself in return the role of foreign minister, the guarantee that the Foreign Ministry "bore full responsibility for foreign affairs," and Rabin's commitment that "the peace process, with all its elements, will be managed jointly" by them both. (Two weeks before the pair signed the deal, Peres told me that Rabin had offered him such a deal ahead of the 1996 elections, but he did not tell me that the deal had actually been signed.)

21   Yossi Beilin, *Touching Peace: From the Oslo Accord to a Final Agreement* (London: Weidenfeld and Nicolson, 1999), 136–7.

22   Conversation between Rabin and Peres, March 7, 1993.

23   Conversation between Rabin and Peres, May 26, 1993.

24   June 7, 1993.

25   Conversation between Peres and Terje Rød-Larsen, July 18, 1993 (Jerusalem).

26   Conversation between Rabin and Peres, August 2, 1993.

27   The Syrian version is according to Patrick Seale, The Middle East Media Research Centre, December 8, 1999.

28   Conversation between Rabin and Peres, August 7, 1993.

29   Rabin gave Warren Christopher a verbal, conditional promise—the "deposit"—in early August 1993, to withdraw to the 1967 lines if Syria met all his demands. The Americans rushed to report this to the Syrians. (From an interview with Danny Yatom, Rabin's military secretary, Maariv, May 24, 2008.)

30   July 9, 1993 (Jerusalem).

31   July 18, 1993 (Jerusalem).

32   August 23, 1993.

33   Hilde Henriksen Waage, "Norwegians? Who Needs Norwegians?" *Explaining the Oslo Back Channel: Norway's Political Past in the Middle East,* PRIO, October 2000.

34   The chairman and executive vice chairman of the Conference of Presidents of Major American Jewish Organizations.

35   Conversation between Peres and Terje Rød-Larsen, July 18, 1993 (Jerusalem).

36   Eitan Haber (b. 1940), an author and journalist on Israeli security issues, served as bureau chief and speechwriter for Prime Minister Yitzhak Rabin (1992–1995).

37   Rabin said in a television interview (September 11, 1993) that he had authorized other actors to explore lines of communication with the PLO: "I have decided to see in what direction there's more success. I had very much hoped that this one [the talks] would be with the PLO inside and not the PLO outside."

38   *Maariv*, November 3, 2000 [Hebrew].

39   October 11, 1994.

40   February 14, 1994.

41   September 13, 1994.

42   January 16, 1994.

43   November 16, 1992 (Cairo).

44   January 9, 1993 (Jerusalem).

45   July 11, 1993.

46   July 18, 1993 (Jerusalem).

47   July 20, 1993.

48   A meeting between Peres and Rabin, July 23, 1993.

49   August 1, 1993.

50   August 17, 1993 (Stockholm).

51   Knesset protocols, special sitting, September 9, 1993.

52   Menachem Klein, *Doves in the Skies of Jerusalem: The Peace Process and the City, 1977–1999* (Jerusalem: Jerusalem Institute, 1999), 109 [Hebrew].

53   September 23, 1993.

54   October 8, 1993.

55   Ibid.

56   The armistice agreement with the Quraysh tribe who controlled Mecca (628 AD) allowed Muhammad and his followers to pray in the Holy City. The rival sides (the

polytheistic Quraysh vs. the monotheistic Muslims) committed to a ten-year period of peace. However, two years later, as the Muslims had gained strength, the agreement was abrogated (the cause for this is still disputed) and Muhammad seized Mecca.
57 Jihad—Islamic holy war.
58 May 23, 1994.
59 Norwegian Foreign Minister Holst passed away on January 13, 1994, after a stroke.

Chapter 5

1   Shimon Peres, *David's Sling* (London: Weidenfeld and Nicolson, 1970), 259–61.
2   Conversation between Rabin and Peres, October 17, 1993.
3   October 20, 1993 (Jerusalem).
4   Martin Indyk (b. 1951) served twice as the US Ambassador to Israel (1995–7 and 2000–1), Assistant Secretary of State for Near East Affairs during the Clinton administration, and US Special Envoy for Israeli-Palestinian Negotiations (2013–2014) during the Obama administration.
5   A phone call between Peres and Dennis Ross, November 1, 1993.
6   Conversation between Rabin and Peres, November 2, 1993.
7   Françoise Sagan, *David et Bethsabee*, Preface: Shimon Peres, Editions Armand et Georges Israel, Paris, 1990.
8   The division of British-mandated Palestine into Transjordan and Palestine in 1921 caused continuous disputes regarding the border's parameters in the Arava Valley. With the signing of the peace treaty between Israel and Jordan in 1994, Israel acknowledged that it had been occupying some Jordanian land in the Arava and agreed to cede it back to Jordan.
9   Peres was referring to Yitzhak Rabin's 1979 memoirs, *Service Book*, in which Rabin called Peres a "tireless schemer," a term that stuck to Peres from that point on, pained him greatly, and aggravated his hostility toward Rabin.
10 Jordan controls the body that administers the properties on the Temple Mount for religious and social purposes (*waqf*).
11 Conversation between Rabin and Peres, January 17, 1994.
12 Meeting with Secretary of State Warren Christopher, December 7, 1993.
13 Conversation between Rabin and Peres, January 17, 1994.
14 January 29, 1994 (Davos, Switzerland).
15 The three people Arafat mentioned led Palestinian factions that perpetrated serious terror attacks against Israel: George Habash, leader of the Popular Front for the Liberation of Palestine; Ahmed Jibril, leader of the Popular Front for the Liberation of Palestine—General Command; Nayef Hawatmeh, leader of the Democratic Front for the Liberation of Palestine. Jibril and Hawatmeh's organizations split off from George Habash's organization, who was also the founder of the Rejectionist Front, which opposed any compromise with Israel.
16 Conversation between Rabin and Peres, April 18, 1995.
17 April 24, 1995 (Amman).
18 Meeting between Peres and King Hussein, April 24, 1995.
19 Meeting between Peres and Clinton, April 30, 1995 (New York).
20 May 8, 1995.
21 May 22, 1995.
22 May 26, 1995.

Chapter 6

1 In Hebrew, the word for "rower" (chatran) is the same as for "schemer."
2 Baruch Goldstein (1956–94) was an extreme far-right religious fanatic who committed the 1994 Cave of the Patriarchs massacre in Hebron, murdering 29 and wounding 125 Palestinian Muslim worshippers. He was killed by survivors of the massacre.
3 Jewish families settled in Tel Rumeida in Hebron in 1983 and called their neighborhood "Admot Yishai"—Jesse's Lands.
4 November 18, 1994.
5 The soldier Nahshon Waxman was abducted by Hamas militants, who demanded in exchange for his release the release of 200 Hamas prisoners including the organization's leader, Sheikh Ahmed Yassin. Waxman was murdered by his kidnappers during an IDF rescue attempt (October 14, 1994).
6 April 28, 1994.
7 August 28, 1995.
8 October 12, 1994.
9 The rhymes refer to two of Rabin's closest advisors: Eitan Haber and Shimon Sheves.
10 November 27, 1995.
11 Until Israel began moving away from a socialist economy (starting in the 1980s), the Histadrut, Israel's national trade union, along with the government, controlled most of the economy. As such, Histadrut served as a backbone of support for Israel's Labor Party. With the increasing liberalization of the Israeli economy, Histadrut's prominence, along with its political power, declined. (Peres used to complain that Rabin disregarded the social and political values of Histadrut.)
12 March 10, 1995.
13 November 6, 1995.
14 December 4, 1995.
15 Peres believed that the return Israel received for its withdrawal from the Sinai (a cold peace with one Arab state) would not suffice this time, maintaining that Israel should receive normalization and peace with the entire Arab world.
16 December 15, 1995.
17 January 20, 1996.
18 Majdal Shams is a Druze village on the slopes of Mount Hermon in the Golan Heights. The village has been controlled by Israel since the 1967 Six-Day War and is located near the ceasefire line between Israel and Syria.
19 January 28, 1996.
20 February 5, 1996.
21 Yahya Ayyash (1966–96) was Hamas's main bomb maker. In that role, he earned the nickname "the Engineer." The bombings he planned caused the deaths of more than seventy Israelis. The Shin Bet (Israel's internal security service) killed him in 1996.
22 Israel gave Palestinian officials VIP cards to ease their movement.
23 Rafael "Raful" Eitan (1929–2004) was an IDF Chief of the General Staff (1978–83) who later became a right-wing politician.
24 Farouk Kaddoumi (b. 1931) served as Secretary-General of the Central Committee of Fatah and the head of PLO's political department in Tunisia.
25 August 8, 1995.
26 Uzi Dayan (b. 1948) was a major general in the Israel Defense Forces (IDF). In his capacity as the head of the IDF's Planning Branch (1993–6), he led the security committee of Israel's delegation to peace talks with the PLO, Jordan, and Syria.

27 Peres–Arafat meeting, April 18, 1996 (Erez Crossing).
28 Muhammad Dahlan (b. 1961) is the former leader of Fatah in Gaza. Following the signing of the Oslo Accords, Dahlan headed the Preventive Security Force in Gaza.
29 Naftali Bennett (b. 1972) is a right-wing Israeli politician who has served in various ministerial capacities, including interim defense minister (2019–20). In the IDF's Operation Grapes of Wrath (1996), Bennett served as a company commander of an elite commando unit in South Lebanon.

Chapter 7

1 In compliance with the Oslo Accords, Israel withdrew in December 1995 from Palestinian cities in the West Bank excluding Hebron. The negotiations regarding Hebron were tougher and took more time because of the Jewish civilian presence in the city and Hebron's holy sites (especially the Cave of the Patriarchs). The agreement was finalized in January 1997 under Prime Minister Netanyahu, who had defeated Peres in the 1996 elections.
2 October 27, 2000.
3 November 10, 1994.
4 November 1, 2000.
5 Muhammad Rashid (b. 1958) was a longtime economic and political adviser to Arafat.
6 *Yediot Aharonot,* November 3, 2000 [Hebrew].
7 *Yediot Aharonot,* November 17, 2000 [Hebrew].
8 *Yediot Aharonot,* January 19, 2001 [Hebrew].

Chapter 8

1 December 9, 1993.
2 A protectorate state during the Apartheid era in South Africa.
3 The Taba region at the north of the Gulf of Eilat was a point of contention between Israel and Egypt. International mediation in 1989 determined that the area was part of the Sinai Peninsula and that Israel was obligated to transfer it to Egypt.
4 February 28, 1995.
5 Peres liked to use the term "constructive borders" because it was deliberately vague and each side could interpret it as it wished, enabling Peres and Sharon to make political progress; Peres believed that over time, he would be able to push the cart onto his own preferred track.
6 August 7, 1994.
7 May 3, 2001 (the White House, Washington).
8 October 15, 2001 (Prague).
9 February 11, 1994.
10 September 1995.
11 October 1998.
12 March 27, 2001.
13 May 2, 2001.
14 This initiative presented a ceasefire proposal, confidence-building measures, a settlement freeze, a renewal of the security coordination, and a resumption of final-status negotiations.

15 The report was drawn up by a committee chaired by Senator George Mitchell, setting out a plan to resume the peace process after the Al-Aqsa Intifada, its main points being: the violence would end, the Palestinians would fight terrorism, Israel would freeze settlement construction, and negotiations would resume.

16 May 27, 2001 (Jerusalem).

17 June 29, 2001.

18 Peres was referring to Arafat's speech at Davos on January 28, 2001, in which he had said: "The current Government of Israel is waging, for the last four months, a savage and barbaric war, as well as, a blatant and fascist military aggression against our Palestinian people. In this aggression it is using internationally prohibited weapons and ammunitions that include in their construction depleted uranium."

19 November 2–3, 2001.

20 November 5, 2001.

21 George Tenet (b. 1953), the director of the CIA, devised a plan in 2001 to achieve a ceasefire between Israel and the Palestinian Authority.

22 September 10, 2001.

23 September 15, 2001.

24 This nickname refers to the period of time Ariel Sharon's parents found refuge in Georgia during the Second World War.

25 September 16, 2001.

26 Hannah Bavli (1901–1993) was considered the highest authority in Israel on manners and etiquette.

27 Kanafeh is a traditional Middle Eastern dessert made with thin noodle-like pastry (Kadayif) and sweet cheese soaked in a sugar-based syrup.

28 In a shooting attack near the Tekoa settlement (September 20, 2001), 26-year-old Sarit Amrani, mother of three children, was murdered. The Al-Aqsa Martyrs' Brigades, which identified itself as the military wing of Fatah, claimed responsibility for the attack.

29 September 26, 2001.

30 October 15, 2001.

31 Rehavam Ze'evi (1926–2001) was assassinated by members of the Popular Front for the Liberation of Palestine (PFLP), a Marxist–Leninist organization. At that time, the PFLP was PLO's second-largest faction (Fatah was the biggest).

32 October 17, 2001.

33 October 21, 2001.

34 December 3, 2001.

35 December 12, 2001.

36 January 2, 2002.

37 January 19, 2002.

38 February 24, 2002.

39 Ibid.

40 March 5, 2002.

41 Sharon refers to a suicide bombing in the Beit Yisrael neighborhood in the center of Jerusalem (March 2, 2002). Eleven civilians were killed, including two infants, three children, and two teenagers. Al-Aqsa Martyrs' Brigades, which identified themselves as the military wing of Fatah, claimed responsibility for the attack.

42 April 11, 2002.

43 "Kitchen cabinet" meeting, May 3, 2002.

44 May 27, 2002.

45 Uri Dan, "Where are you, Mr. Hollander?" *Makor Rishon*, October 26, 2001 [Hebrew].

46 Area A is under the civil and security control of the Palestinian Authority. Area B is under the civil control of the Palestinian Authority and the security control of Israel. Area C (comprising 60 percent of the West Bank) is under the exclusive control of Israel.

47 October 15, 2001 (Prague).

48 Peres added in his own hand: "In accordance with 242, 338."

49 The Ad Hoc Liaison Committee—the conference of donor states to the Palestinians.

50 November 11, 2001.

51 *Haaretz*, December 28, 2001 [Hebrew].

52 Cabinet decision, December 30, 2001.

53 December 31, 2001.

54 Following the Six-Day War, the UN Security Council passed Resolution 242 (November 22, 1967) which became a key foundation of the Middle East peace process in the subsequent years. The resolution called on all states in the region to respect each other's sovereignty, and required the "withdrawal of Israeli armed forces from territories occupied in the recent conflict." Israel claims that the resolution does not require it to withdraw from all territories.

55 February 1, 2002.

56 February 8, 2002.

57 February 10, 2002.

58 March 11, 2002 (Jerusalem).

59 April 19, 2002.

60 The proposed Saudi Initiative was endorsed by the Arab League Summit (Beirut 2002). It calls for the resolution of the Arab–Israeli conflicts, in exchange for full Israeli withdrawal, the establishment of a Palestinian state in the West Bank and Gaza Strip with East Jerusalem as its capital, and resolution of the Palestinian refugee issue.

61 The settlement of Kfar Darom, which was founded in 1946, was conquered and destroyed by the Egyptian army in the War of Independence, and was re-established after the Six-Day War.

62 Sharon revealed his plan to evacuate the seventeen Israeli settlements in the Gaza Strip in an interview with Yoel Marcus on February 2, 2004. My meeting with him took place in his Jerusalem office on December 30, 2003.

63 Speech in Jerusalem to the Conference of Presidents of Major American Jewish Organizations, February 18, 2009.

64 November 21, 2005.

65 Walla report on meeting at Blich High School in Ramat Gan, February 21, 2006.

Chapter 9

1 July 15, 2007.

2 July 29, 2000.

3 *Haaretz*, June 19, 2004 [Hebrew].

4 Full text of this paragraph in the Palestinian Declaration of Independence, proclaimed in Algiers on November 15, 1988: "Despite the historical injustice done

to the Palestinian Arab people in its displacement and in being deprived of the right to self-determination following the adoption of General Assembly resolution 181 (II) of 1947, which partitioned Palestine into an Arab and a Jewish State, that resolution nevertheless continues to attach conditions to international legitimacy that guarantee the Palestinian Arab people the right to sovereignty and national independence."

5   September 4, 2008.
6   May 5, 2009 (Washington).
7   May 5, 2009.
8   March 3, 2011.
9   March 24, 2011.
10   March 29, 2011.
11   April 5, 2011.
12   April 7, 2011.
13   September 20, 2010.
14   May 19, 2011.
15   *Yediot Aharonot,* May 20, 2011 [Hebrew].
16   May 27, 2011.
17   June 17, 2011.
18   The Quartet—whose members are the United States, the European Union, the United Nations, and Russia—is intended to facilitate a coordinated international policy for the purpose of advancing the Israeli–Palestinian peace process.
19   July 11, 2011.
20   July 16, 2011.
21   July 28, 2011.
22   *Maariv,* August 16, 2012 [Hebrew].
23   Ibid.
24   June 9, 2012.
25   Ibid.

Chapter 10

1   During a lunch in Jerusalem (June 3, 1996).
2   The French minister of defense during the Suez Campaign (1956).
3   The head of the Defence Ministry's delegation in Paris during the Suez Campaign.
4   The negotiations in Washington with the Jordanian–Palestinian delegation, headed by Elyakim Rubinstein (1991–3).
5   Terje Rød-Larsen, the Norwegian mediator in the Oslo negotiations.
6   The deputy defense minister in the War of Independence.
7   Yitzhak Rabin dubbed Peres an "indefatigable schemer" in his 1979 book *Service Book.*
8   George Mitchell (b. 1933) served as President Obama's envoy to the Middle East.

Index

Acknowledgments

Special thanks to the Commissioning Editor Rory Gormley, to the Bloomsbury Publishing team, to Eylon Levy (English translator), Shmuel Rosner (Hebrew editor) and to the people who assisted, commented and encouraged: Avi Ohayon, Avinoam Bar-Yosef, Barry Geltman, Boaz Eliash, Daniel Abraham, Eli Kind, Eliav (Babu) Gil, Gali Romano, Hananiya Herman, Ido Sharir, Naomi Gil, Neli Oren, Rachel and Zelig Shalgi, Rami Tal, Salah Elayan, Tamar Nevo-Gur, Yael Menuhin, Yosef Avi Yair Engel and Yotam Gil.